Art Nouveau

ART POCKET

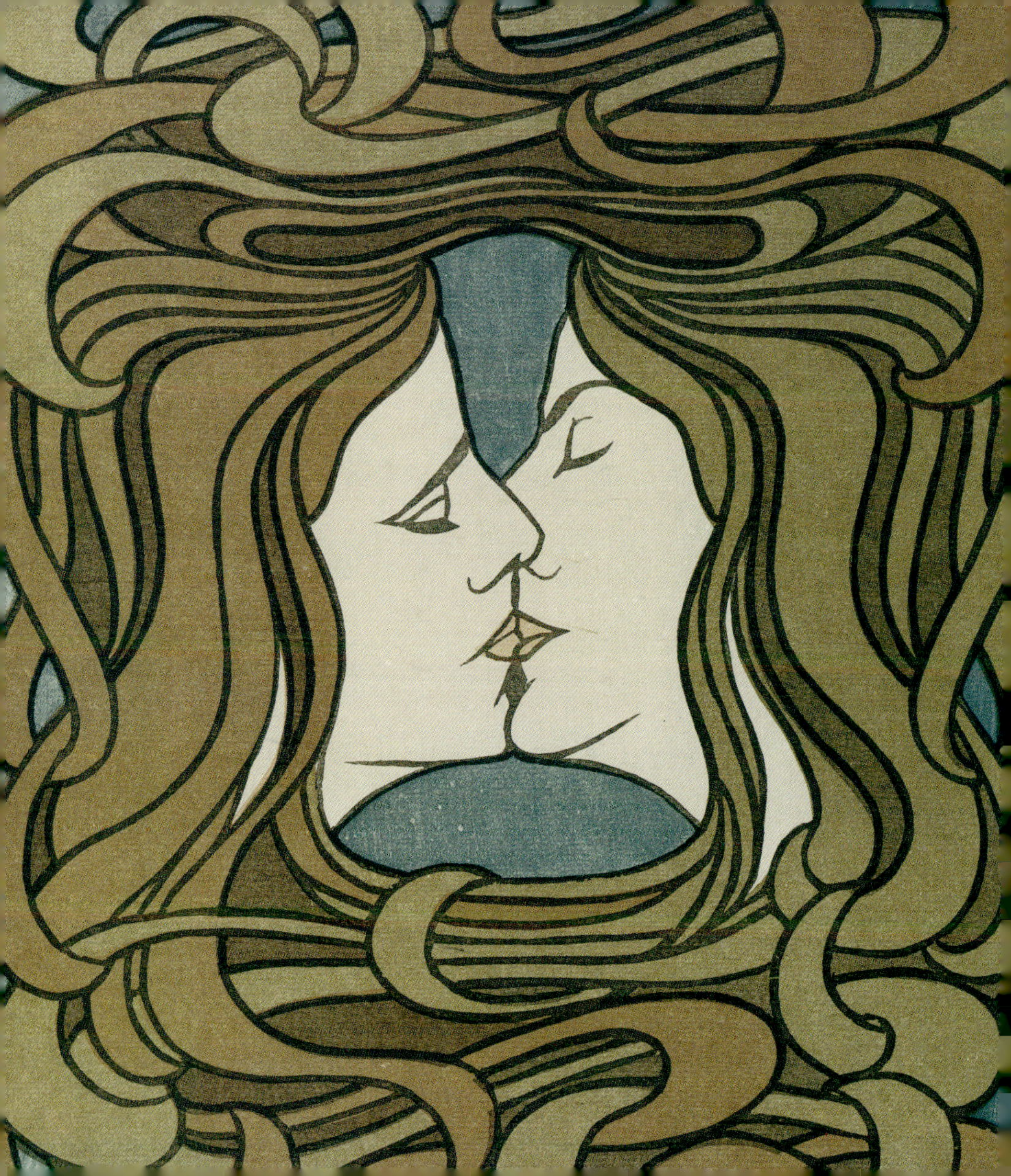

Anke von Heyl

Art Nouveau

ART POCKET

h.f.ullmann

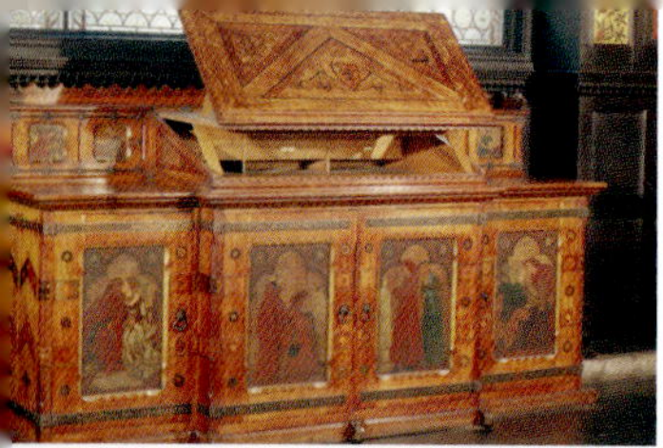
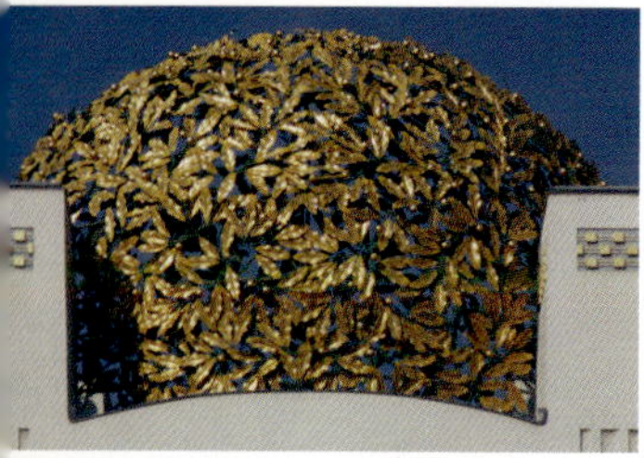
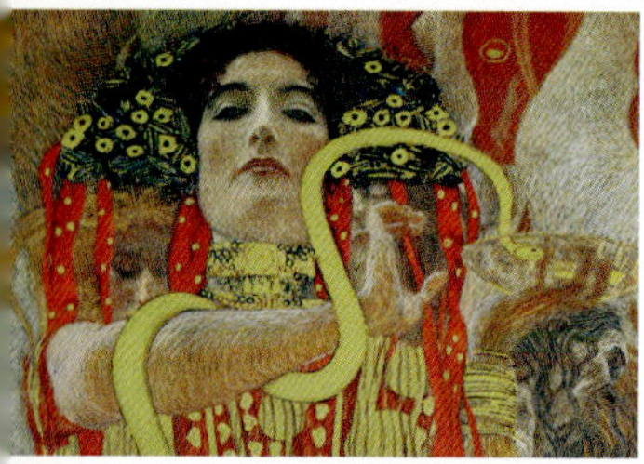
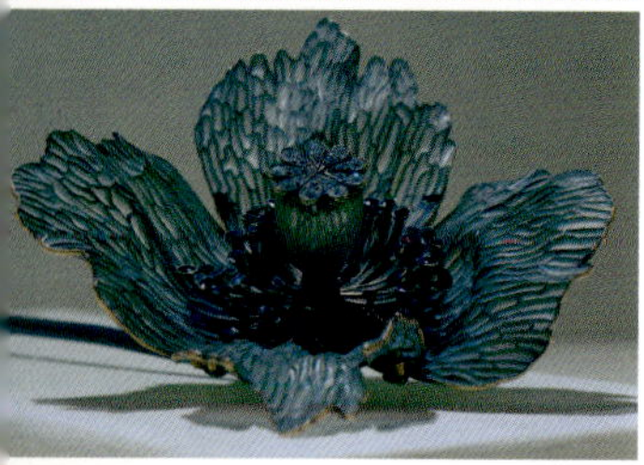
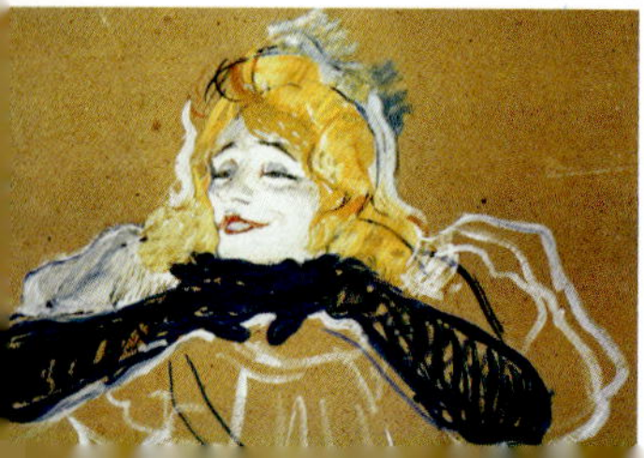

Contents

Illustration p. 2: Peter Behrens, *The Kiss,* woodcut, 1898

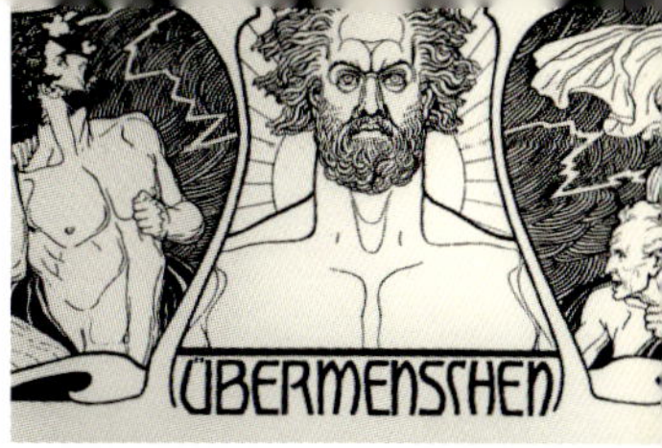

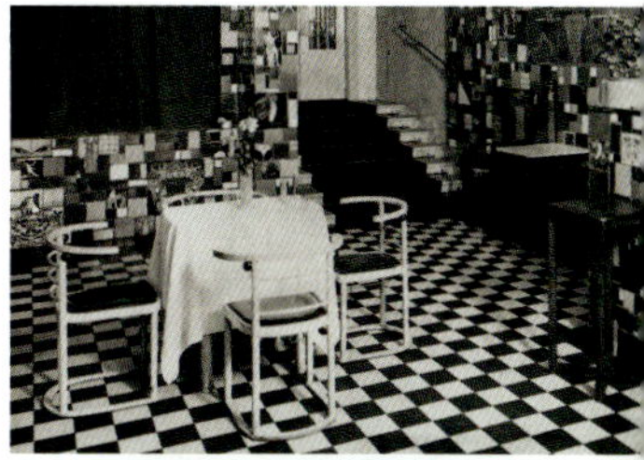

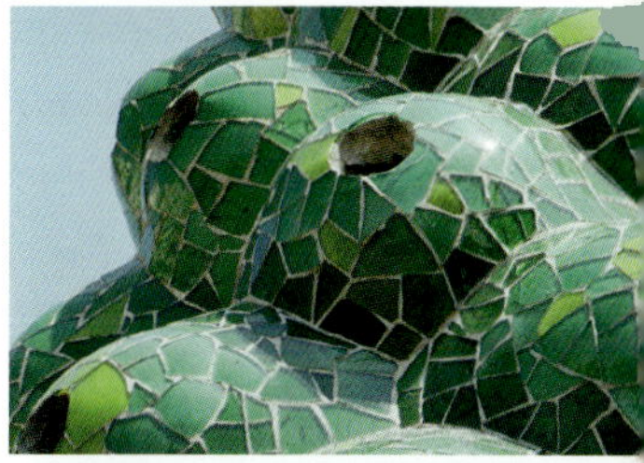

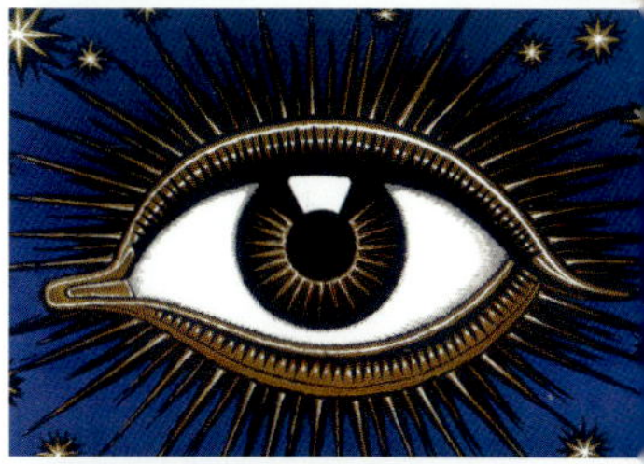

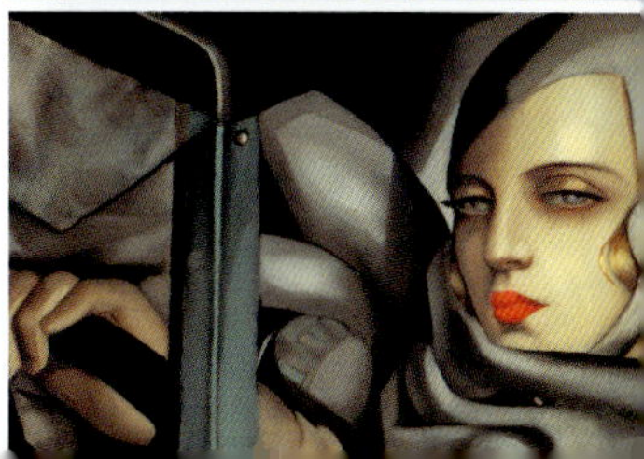

Art Nouveau: Many Paths, One Goal

Koloman Moser
Decoration on the façade of a house by Otto Wagner (detail)
1898/99
Vienna, 6th district, Linke Wienzeile 38

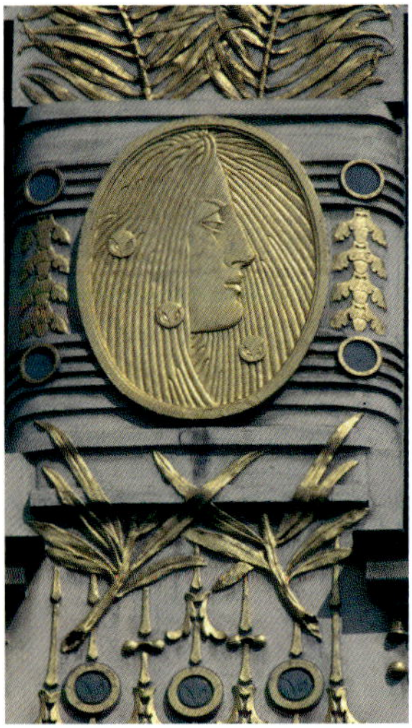

Louis-Théophile Hingre
Poster advertising Théophile Roederer's champagne
1897, color lithograph
121.7 × 55.2 cm
Private collection, Paris

When the art dealer Siegfried Bing opened a gallery under the name L'Art Nouveau in Paris in 1895, there was no commonly used term for the new international trend in fine and applied art. The French expression that was adopted by the English-speaking world has proved to be an evocative phrase for the style: "Art Nouveau" is a name that quickly stimulates a flood of images in the mind's eye. It is often associated with curvilinear forms, stylized details, flowing hair and elaborate decoration.

On closer examination, however, scarcely any other term in art history is so intangible, so difficult to define in terms of established facts as Art Nouveau. So what do we mean when we speak of Art Nouveau?

A Variety of Terms

Unsurprisingly, different countries and languages used different words to describe the style. *Jugendstil* (Youth Style) was the German name for a movement that strictly speaking was confined to Germany, while developments in Austria were referred to as the *Secession Style.* A look at other countries reveals a confusing plethora of terms that were associated with the movement. Expressions such as *Stile Floreale* in Italian (also known as Lily Style or Wave Style), the Belgian *Style Nouilles* (Noodle Style) and the French variation called *Style Coup de Fouet* (Whiplash Style) derive from purely formal aspects of this art. The name that was generally adopted in Italy was *Stile Liberty,* following the success of Sir Arthur Lasenby Liberty in exporting products of the English Arts and Crafts movement to Italy. It was later also often referred to as *Stile Inglese.*

In England developments in art were summarized around the year 1900 by the phrase *Modern Style.* This was the origin of the terms *Stile Modernista* and *Modernismo* that appeared in Spain. *Nieuwe Kunst* (New Art), as it was called in Holland, and the term *Style 1900* also express the mood of renewal at the beginning of a new century. The association of the movement with one of its most important centers, Vienna, produced the terms *Vienna Style* and *Secession Style.* There are also such interesting variations as *Style Metro,* which refers to a combination of applied arts and technical progress, and *Yachting Style,* a phrase occasionally used for Henry van de Velde's ideas on interior design. The less common term *Style Jules Verne* reflects the relationship that was seen to the Utopian schemes of Verne's science fiction, which appeared to anticipate modern times in the mid-19th century.

The German expression *Jugendstil* first appeared at an exhibition for the printing industry in Leipzig in 1897. To call the movement Youth Style was of course an act of mockery on the part of critics who did not appreciate the novel and flowing decorative details that the magazine *Jugend* used with

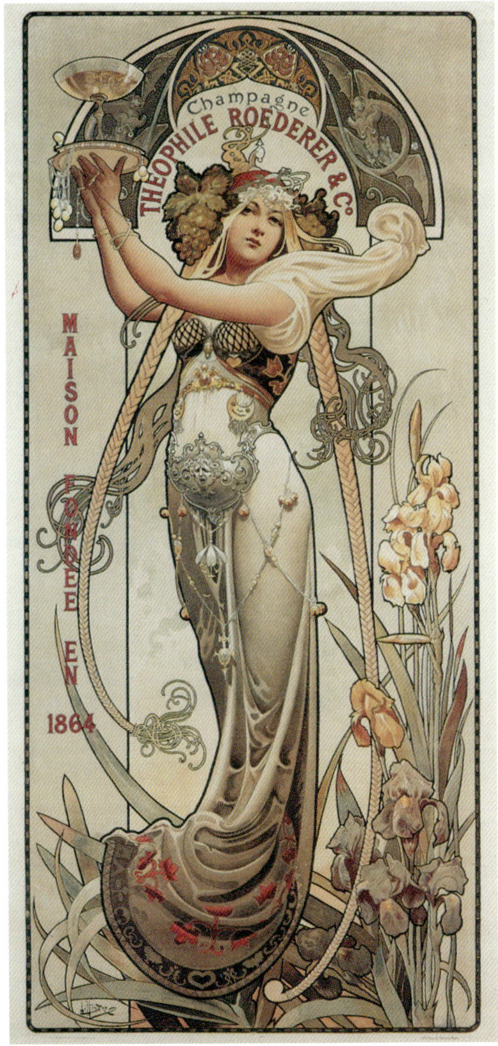

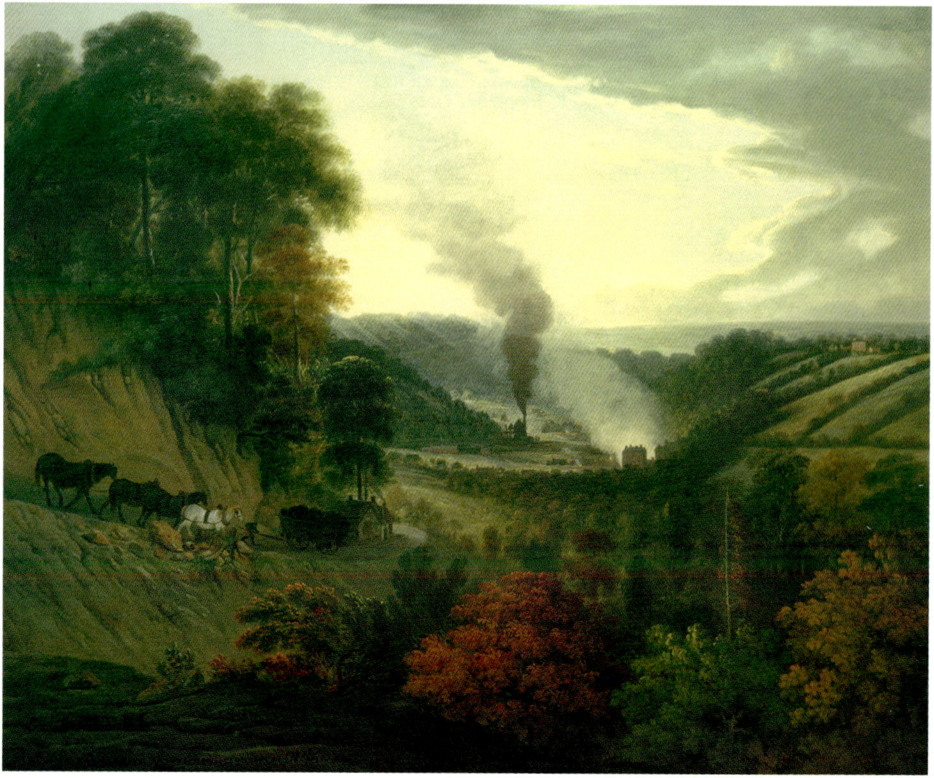

William Williams
A Morning View of Coalbrookdale and Parts of the Extensive Iron-works
1777, oil on canvas
120 × 126 cm
Shrewsbury Museum of Art

such success. However, by this date many of the characteristics that are today subsumed under the heading Art Nouveau were already well established.

Fin de Siècle

Faced with these and many other names, it is easy to become lost in an endless list of different facets of Art Nouveau. This phenomenon in the history of art is said by some to be the first truly modern art movement of modern times, and is described by others as escapism, a flight into a purely aesthetic realm that comes close to kitsch. *L'art pour l'art* was a movement initiated by Victor Hugo in the 1830s that claimed art should be autonomous. This was indeed to become one of the main themes of the following years and of the artistic currents connected with Art Nouveau. A contrasting expression, decadence, is used equally often to denote the atmosphere of the time, associating the era with a doomsday mood. The idea of decadence expresses both sensual refinement, on the one hand, and a degree of disgust in the face of decay on the other hand.

Rata Langa
Caricature of a capitalist
c. 1890, drawing

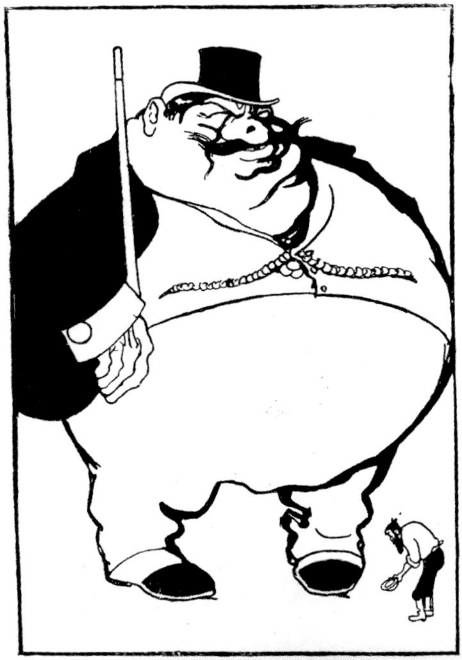

Fin de siècle is a phrase frequently applied to the whole range of different styles of the late 19th century. The term derived from a comedy that premiered in Paris in 1888, portraying in an ironic manner the mood of the bourgeoisie as the turn of the century approached. In connoting the contrast and tension between the impoverished proletariat and the decadence of an over-exquisite style of life, the term *fin de siècle* reflects many aspects of Art Nouveau that are significant in intellectual history. As the bourgeoisie attached particularly great importance to the beautiful things in life, this era has been termed the *belle époque.*

The concept of beauty or, to put it another way, aesthetics, provided an important impulse for discourse on the style of the period. Themes that occupied artists in the period around 1900 were not only the *Aesthetic Movement,* the term used to summarize trends in the English-speaking world, but more generally the issue of educating popular taste with the aim of making the world a beautiful place to live.

Mirror of the Times

If the Art Nouveau movement is to be defined as an era, a core period between 1880 and 1910 can be identified. There were of course initial trends and later offshoots before and after this period. In a relatively short space of time, more or less exactly the years at the turn of the century, an artistic language emerged that can be regarded as one of the most exciting phenomena in the recent history of ideas. The principle of renewal and the association of art and life are the parameters within which the Art Nouveau movement should be examined.

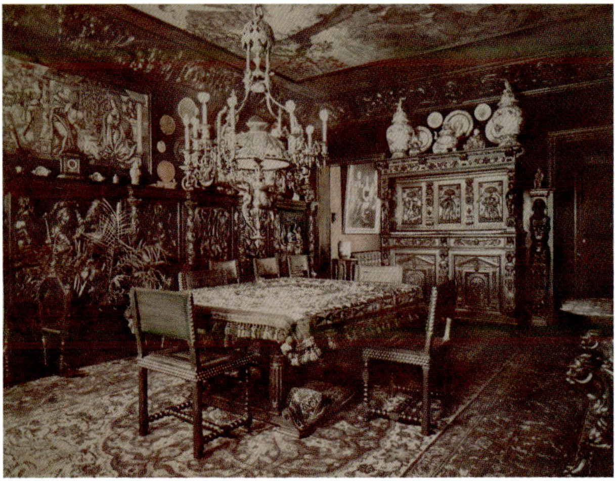

Émile Zolá's apartment in Paris
Dining room
c. 1895, photograph

It is essential to consider the state of society as a whole in those years. This society had experienced an unprecedented transformation of the circumstances of life around the turn of the century. The change in social structures resulted in new tasks for art, which was no longer harnessed for the old religious themes or the purposes of the ruling class. At the same time industrial development led to the rapid growth of cities; this new urban environment was the seedbed for technical discoveries.

When looking at the development of the arts shortly before the emergence of the new style, which started as early as 1870 with the first appearance of the Arts and Crafts movement, it is clear that the historicism of the second half of the 19th century had led to a prevailing mood of resignation in respect of new artistic ideas. In the wake of the Romantic movement and Realism, little more than an insipid eclecticism remained. However, the repetition of old forms, which for lack of stringent formal principles ended in overloaded pomposity, was no solution when the world was on the threshold of a new age. Here art was expected to provide a new and decisive impulse. Whether this represented a romantic and Utopian reaction to the dominance of machines or paved the way for modern design, whether it was a reaction against eclecticism or the wish of modern man for self-expression – the intellectual context puts Art Nouveau in focus and yields insights into the spirit of the times as it was manifested in this style.

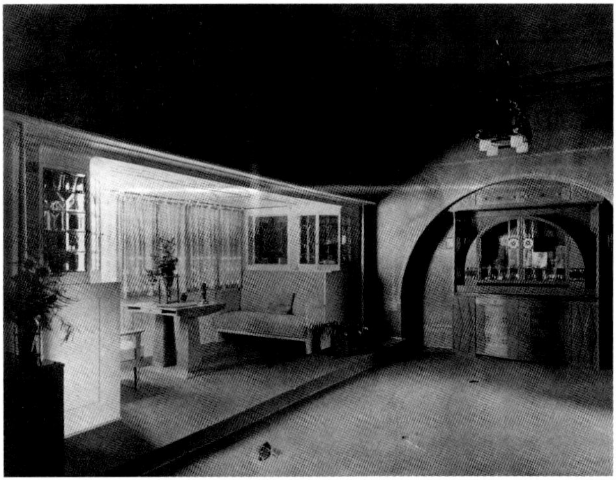

Joseph Maria Olbrich
Hessisches Zimmer
(Hessian Room)
designed for the exhibition
Modern Decorative Art
in Turin
1902, photograph

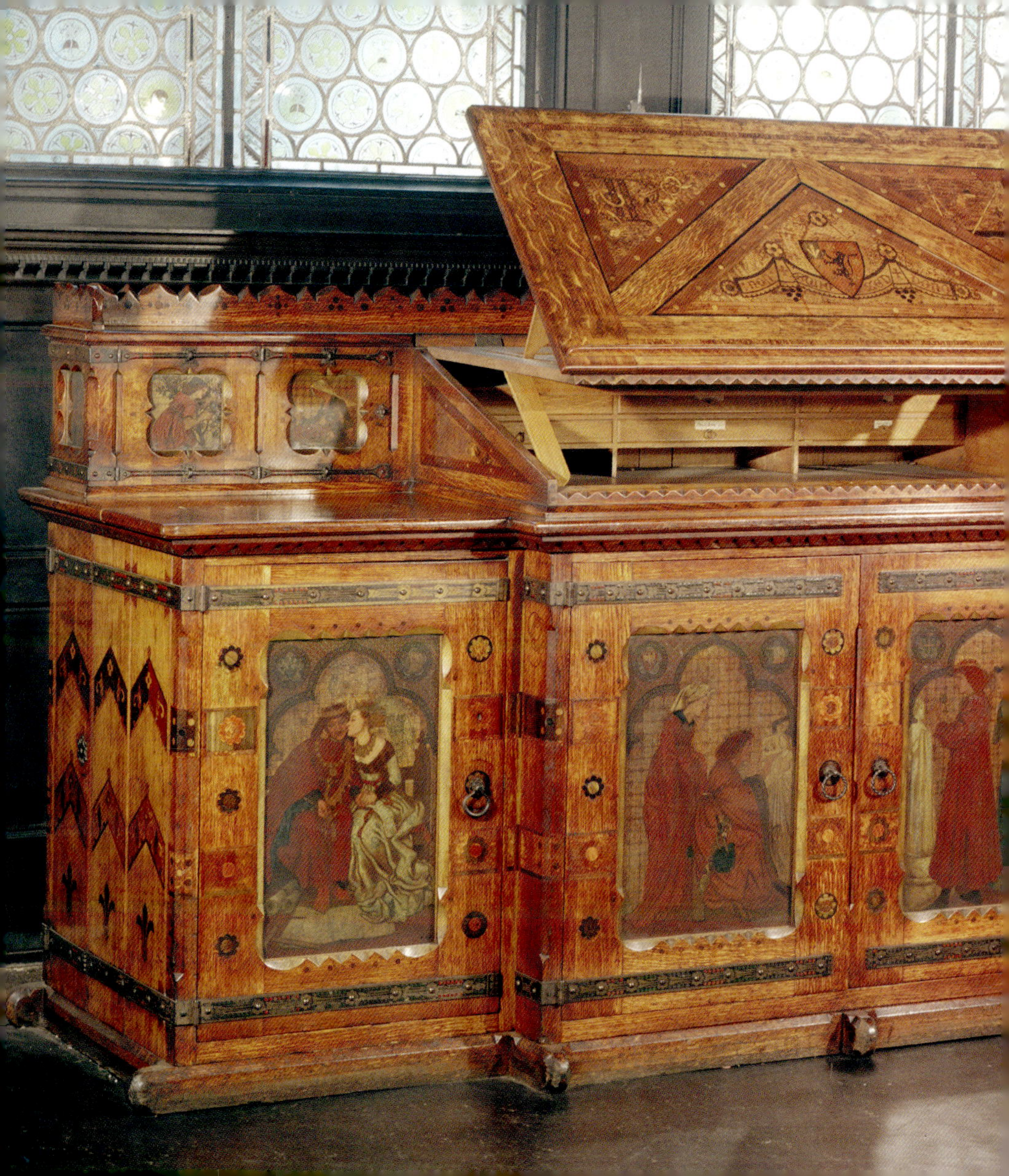

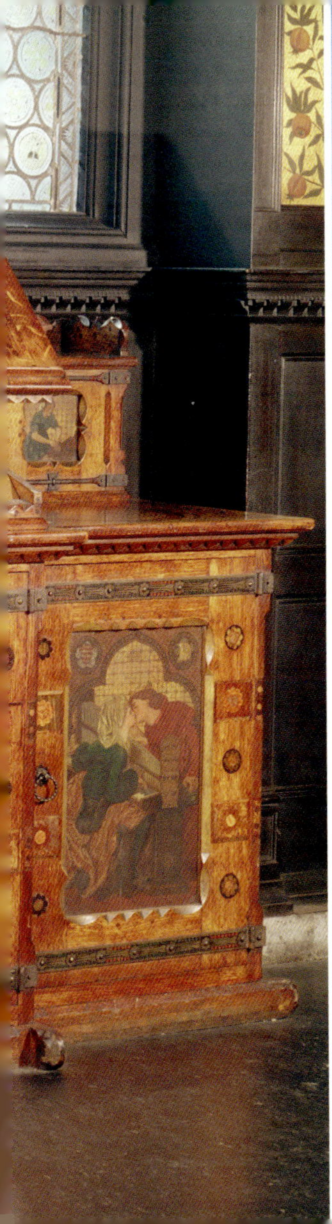

The Arts and Crafts Movement

Smoking factory chimneys and people working to the rhythm of machines: in the mid-19th century this was the face of the industrial revolution, which Friedrich Engels saw as the principal event in the history of the world. Mass production was the result of new technologies. It conquered Europe like a machine consuming everything in its path. Its victims were creativity and the quality of life. As so often, however, changes of this nature created countercurrents and stimulated a search for new models of life, work and, above all, art. The reaction to this crisis even developed to the point where some believed art offered the only answer to the question of how to live.

John Pollard Seddon
King René's Honeymoon
1862, oak cabinet with painted sides (William Morris)
Victoria and Albert Museum, London

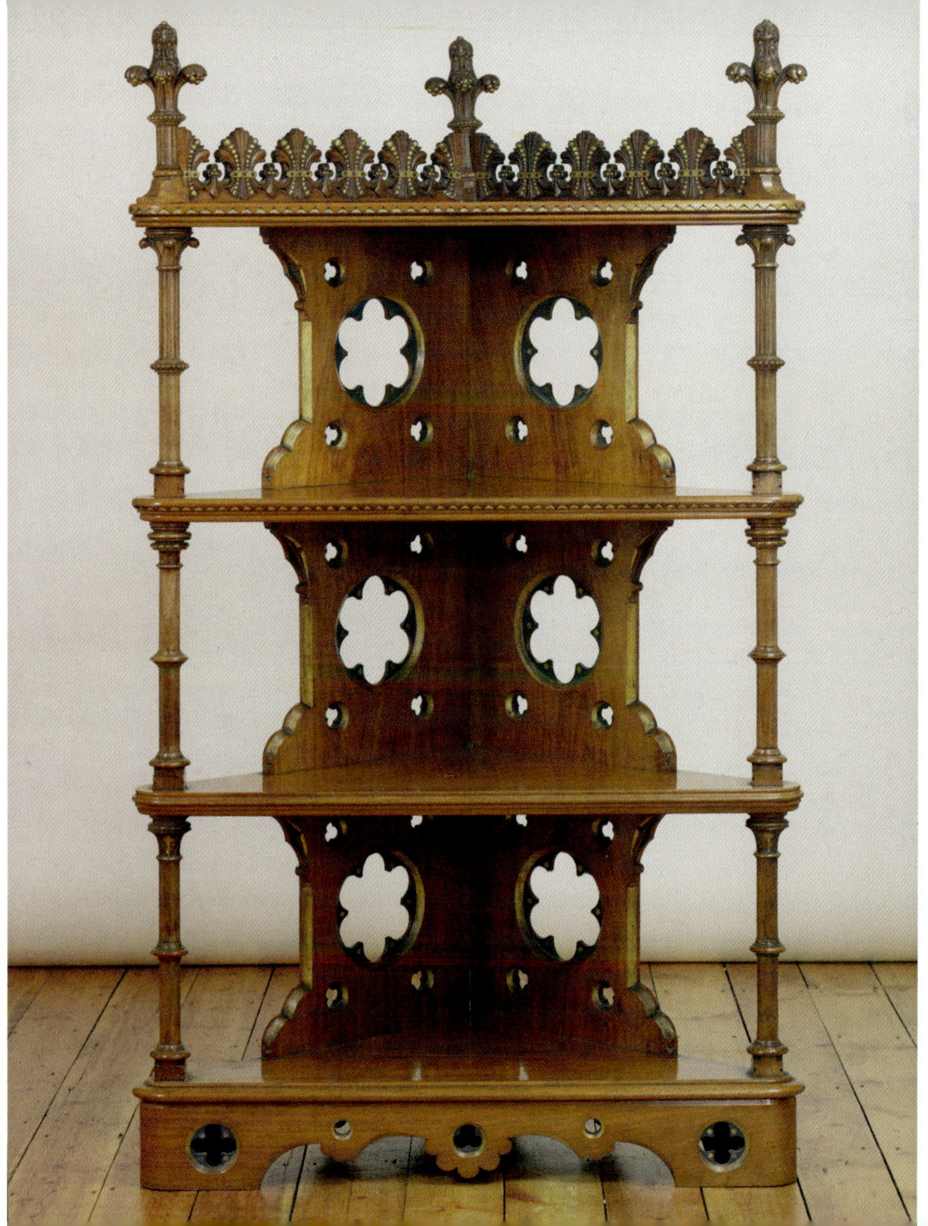

How It All Began

The impulse came from England. The demand that life and art should be in harmony, that the environment in which people lived should be deliberately designed, clearly originated there. The movement that came into being cast a completely new light on the subject, especially on the applied arts. The foundation of the Arts and Crafts Exhibition Society in 1888 gave the movement its name, and the ideas of the art critic and social reformer John Ruskin provided an important basis as early as the mid-19th century.

Today, when considering his main demand that the value of handicraft skills should be reappraised, his views seem simplistic. The alienation of humans from work and their enslavement to the speeding machine represented an urgent problem at this time. Ruskin's writings describe the ideal artistic conditions for work. For him the model of the medieval workshop gave craftsmen the opportunity to control their own work and above all permitted a freedom of thought that he regarded as essential for creative output. This point of view necessarily emerged in reaction to the devastating consequences of industrialization, which were more evident in England than in other parts of Europe. Critics saw the effects of this development on the applied arts and the production of everyday items as symptomatic. On all sides there were calls for simplicity, for honest manual work and a new appreciation of materials.

United in the Cause of New Design

Ruskin's words were balm for the troubled souls of dispirited artists, more and more of whom took up his ideas – especially writers and art critics. Ruskin's publication of *The Stones of Venice* in 1853 was the basis for a new attitude

John Pollard Seddon
What-Not, Gothic display shelves
c. 1860, walnut
Private collection

John Ruskin
Tracery windows of Giotto's Campanile, Florence
Published 1884 as an etching by James Charles Armytage
Private collection

to Gothic architecture and art that the Arts and Crafts movement gratefully adopted. As these views attached great importance to providing training specific to the task, in the last third of the 19th century an increasing number of schools were founded that were to take a similar approach and in particular teach the relevant craft skills. One of the most important of these was the Central School of Art and Crafts, which opened in London in 1896 under the direction of W. R. Lethaby. An experiment conceived by Henry Cole in 1847 shows how early these trends began in England and how significant they were in the evolution of new directions in art. In a project named Felix Summerly's Art Manufactures he aimed to unite the fine arts and the applied arts. To this purpose he asked many artists to design a specified number of everyday items: mustard pots, salt cellars, shaving bowls, etc. In this way the first steps were taken which in the following years led painters and other practitioners of the fine arts to feel called upon to act as the designers for a new age.

The Shakers, an American religious community, took up impulses of the Arts and Crafts movement and developed them into extremely purist furniture designs that had a strong influence on the modern movement.

One of the main characteristics of the Arts and Crafts movement was its advocacy of simple design on the one hand, and high-quality materials on the other. The materials were intended to speak for themselves and the design to be free of any superfluous ornamentation. In this respect the movement provided one of the decisive impulses for modern design. Although design was meant to be simple, the theoretical approaches and the variety of groups that were founded within the movement were all the more complex. In 1882 the architects Arthur Heygate Mackmurdo and Herbert P. Horne founded the Century Guild, an association that aimed to make a radical break with historicist attitudes to art. "Craft is the true root of art," asserted Walter Crane, who founded the Art Workers Guild in 1884 on the model of medieval guilds. Adherents of this philosophy moved to the country to lead the simple life of

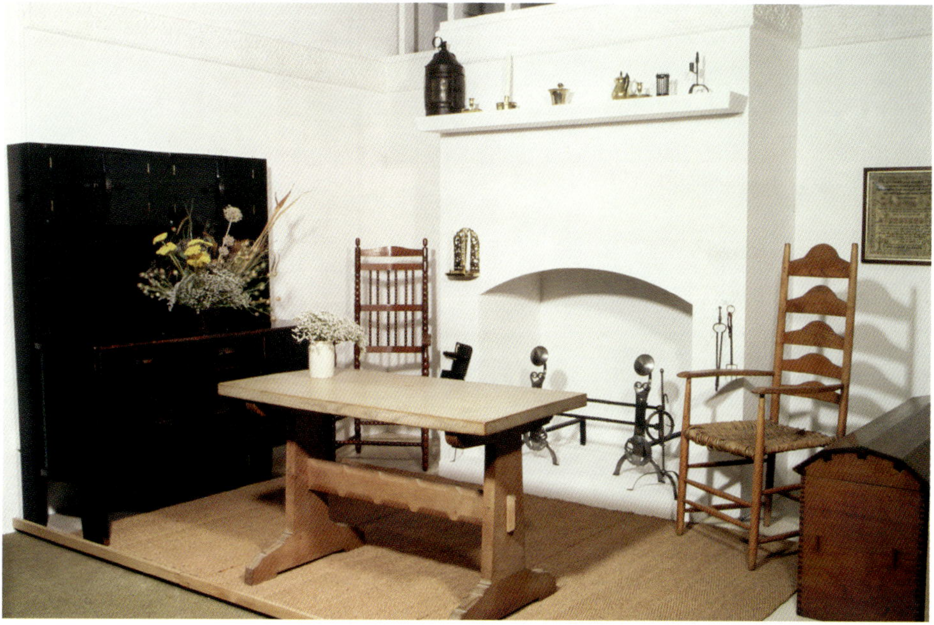

medieval craftsmen in communities of the like-minded, united in their wish to turn their backs on industrial society.

Ernest Gimson and Ernest Barnsley
Interior with Arts and Crafts furnishings, 1905–30
Cheltenham Art Gallery & Museum, Gloucestershire

The New Idea Spreads

The Studio magazine, founded in 1883, played a major role in spreading the philosophy of the Arts and Crafts movement, which developed its own particular terminology to accompany the new ideas. Concepts such as "unity of design," "being true to the material," "honesty of construction," "democratic design," "joy in labor" and "simplicity of life" gained currency and were transformed into generally used phrases around 1900. The establishment of numerous workshops on the English model all over Europe and as far

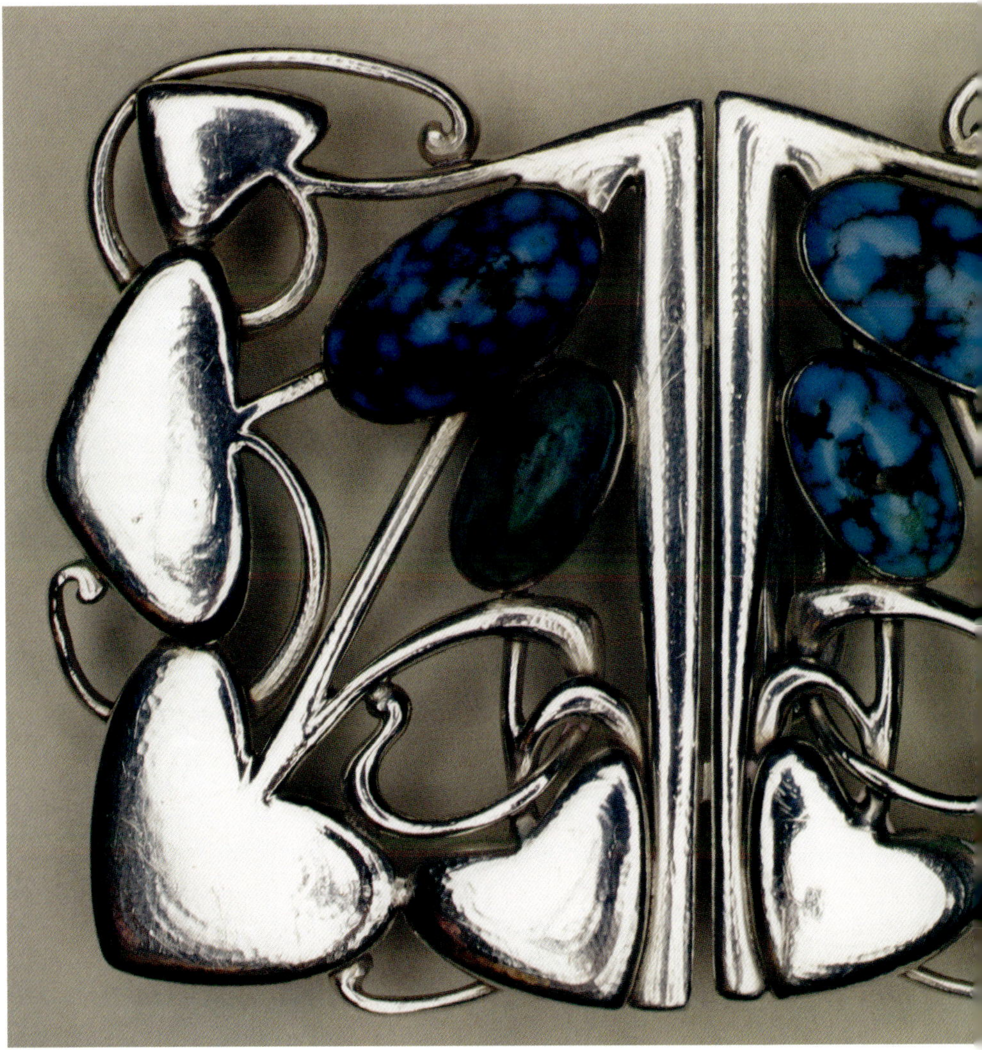

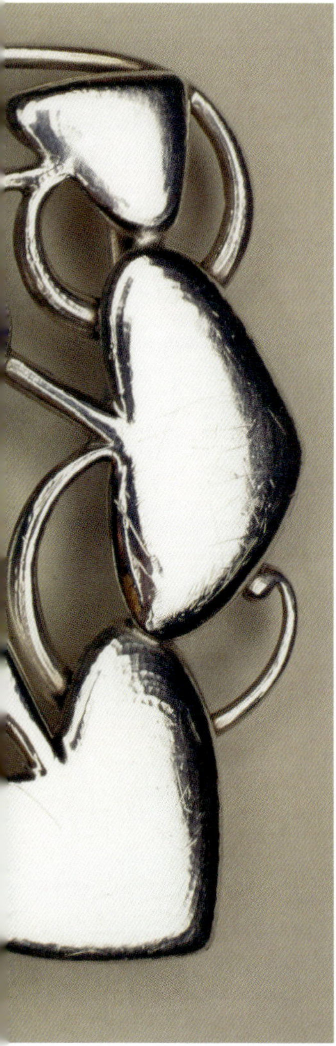

as North America shows the widespread reception of the movement. Immigrants to the New World took old craft traditions across the Atlantic with them, so that, in the very place where, on the one hand, the native population was being displaced, on the other hand a degree of enthusiasm for folk art and craft skills was retained. Far to the east, too, in Japan, the Arts and Crafts movement flourished in the so-called Mingei period, though this did not happen until the late 1920s, when the emphasis lay on the beauty of everyday objects and, above all, traditional ceramic crafts were celebrated. The further evolution of the Arts and Crafts philosophy that led to the founding of the Werkbund in Germany was a particularly important influence on modern design.

Archibald Knox
Belt buckle
1903, various materials
Cheltenham Art Gallery &
Museum, Gloucestershire

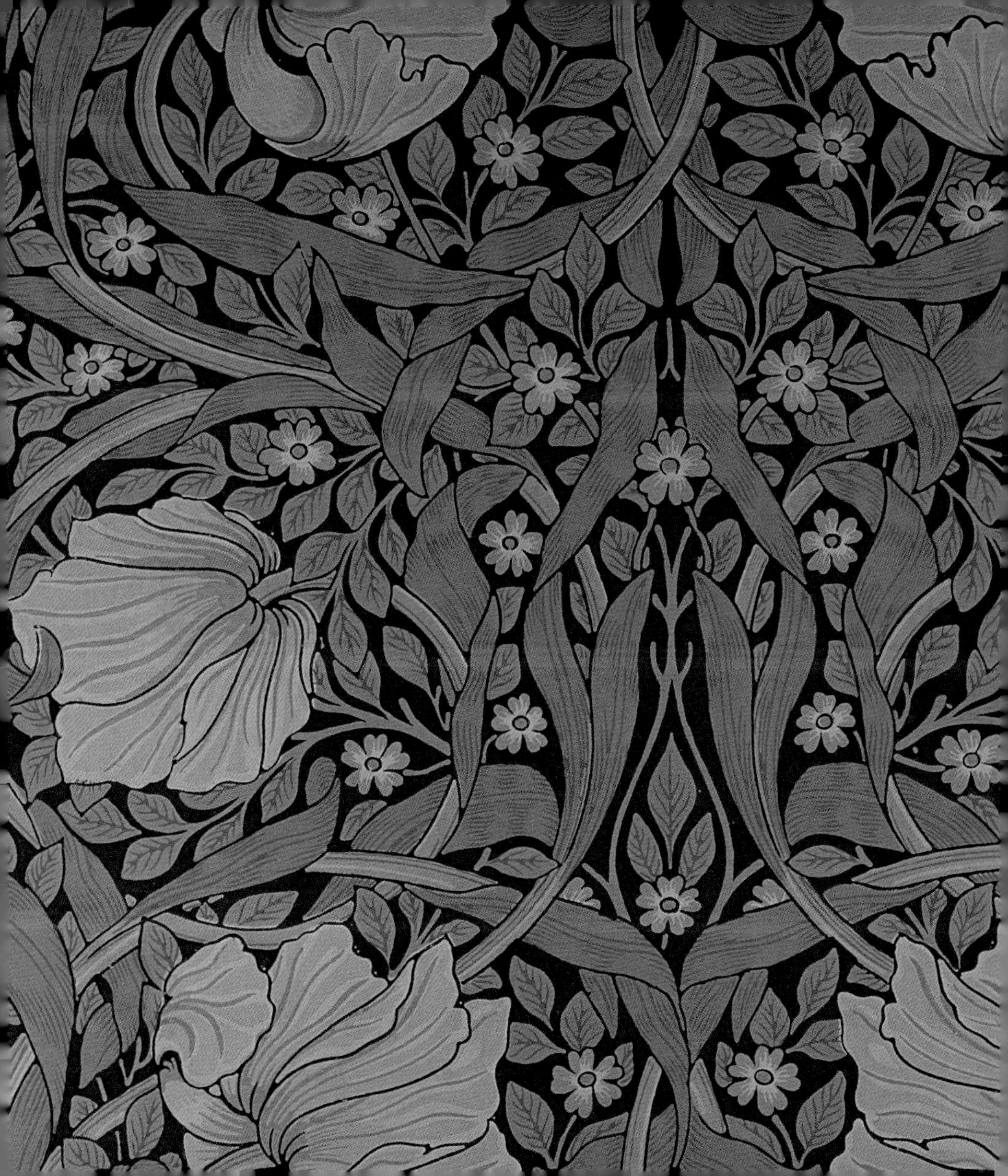

William Morris – The Great Reformer

Who would have thought that the little boy who delighted in riding through the woods near his home on the outskirts of London would one day become an avant-garde artist whose ideas were to have a lasting influence on the development of modern applied arts? Many phenomena that were later to be important in the era of Art Nouveau had already appeared in the work of William Morris as interesting initiatives for reform. The furnishing of his home is just one instance of this, an area in which artists such as Henry van de Velde and Franz von Stuck followed his example. The idea of founding a company to produce crafts also began with Morris and was later much imitated.

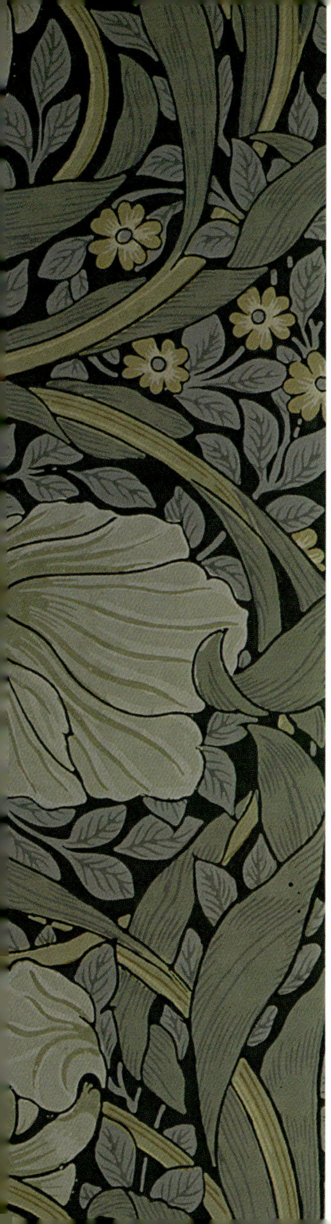

William Morris
Pimpernel wallpaper, 1876
Private collection

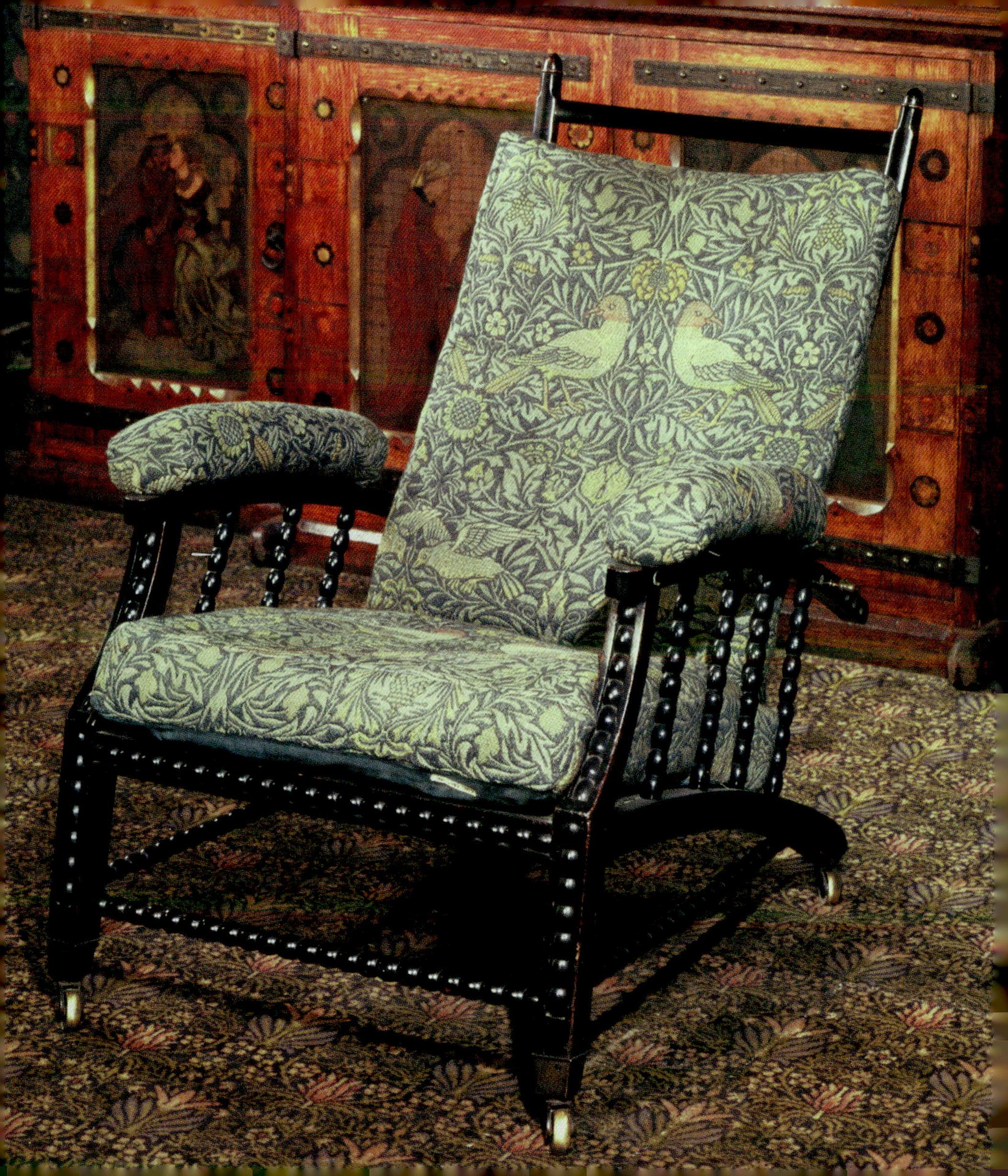

First Contacts

William Morris was born to a middle-class family. The success of his father, who became wealthy through dealings on the stock exchange, gave Morris the opportunity to attend Oxford University, where he made the acquaintance of Edward Burne-Jones.

This was to become a fertile lifelong friendship between two artists. They shared a passion for poetry and an admiration for John Ruskin, whose writings they discussed. Burne-Jones was one of the artists associated with the Pre-Raphaelite Brotherhood, and brought the painter Dante Gabriel Rossetti into Morris's circle of friends. After completing his university studies Morris began an apprenticeship with George Edmund Street, an extremely successful architect of the time who was best known for his neo-Gothic buildings.

William Morris
Chair
c. 1870, ebony, upholstered with the *Bird* tapestry, wool
Victoria & Albert Museum, London

Cooperative Work

A commission that the two friends Morris and Burne-Jones received by chance charted their future course. They were given the task of decorating the Debating Room of the Oxford Union, and began enthusiastically to select episodes from the Arthurian legends as the subjects of murals.

Although their limited expertise – in particular they did not adequately

William Morris and Philip Webb
Red House
1859/60
Bexleyheath, England

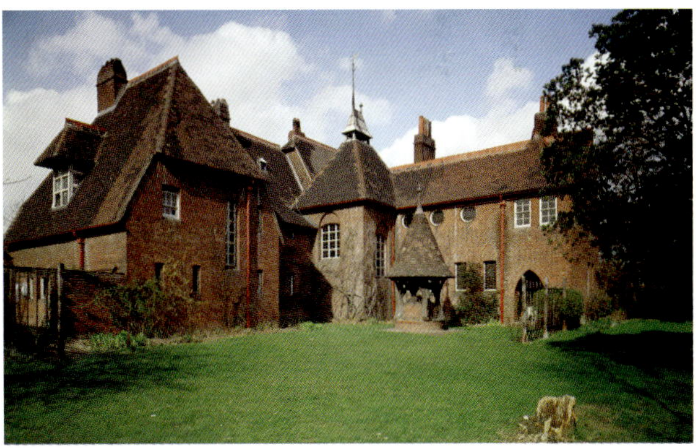

master the technique of fresco painting – meant that they never completed the commission, the experience that they gained in working as a team on a decorative project of this type was invaluable. They were resolved to continue such work. In the meantime Morris had married the beautiful Jane Burden, whom he met through Rossetti and Burne-Jones, and bought a house in the country which was to be the next project in this field: the Red House.

William Morris
Single Stem wallpaper
Private collection

Philip Webb, another friend from the early years, was given the task of designing the whole house in the style of an old English cottage – but with a modern touch. All guests, who were of course artists without exception, were called upon to take part in adorning the house, and so the Red House quickly became a center of creativity through the cooperative work of Morris's friends, their regular meetings and the lively atmosphere there.

Business Venture

This work was the basis for the foundation of Morris, Marshall, Falkner & Co. in a state of high euphoria in April 1861. The company combined the idea of common labor that derived from the medieval workshop with the aim of giving a commercial purpose to the participants' creative activities. Only a year later the new company was successful at the International Exhibition in London, which led to commissions for interior furnishing and decoration. Work of this kind was

Dante Gabriel Rossetti
Proserpina
c. 1873, oil on canvas
42 × 22 cm
Tate Gallery, London

the specialty of the group since the proven cooperation of all their talents at the Red House. They designed wallpaper and stained-glass windows, which were highly popular at that time, and went into production with their carpet patterns. However, widespread recognition of the artistic quality of the company's designs unfortunately did not lead to commercial success. The situation was exacerbated by personal conflicts resulting from the dominant role that Morris wished to play in the company. The liaison between Jane Morris and Rossetti, which was only half-heartedly kept secret and clearly developed from their painter-model relationship, was certainly no less a problem.

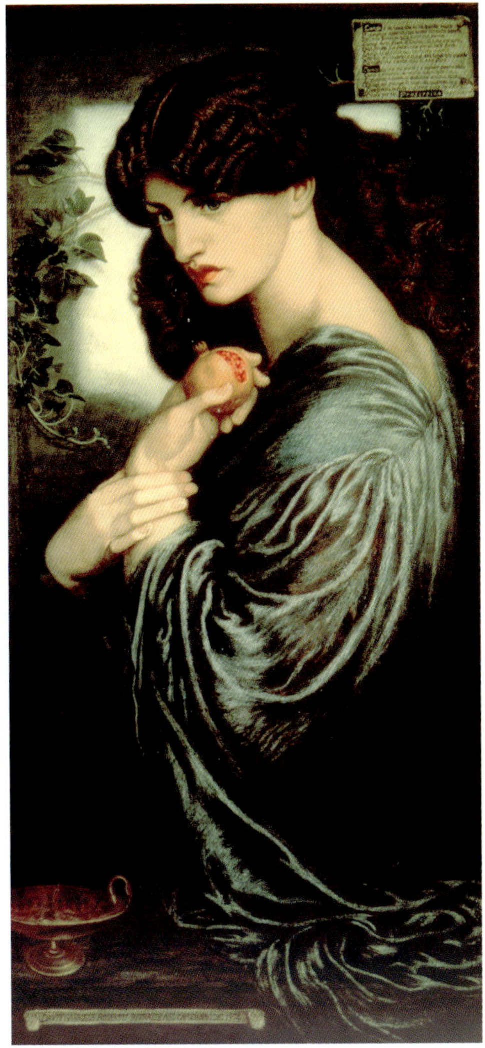

Poets and Philosophers

Morris increasingly withdrew from the business and devoted himself to his political contacts. As Utopian ideas of creating a better world had long been the driving force behind his work, he was strongly attracted to the theses of Marx and Engels. He never entirely grasped the communist way of thinking, laboring to understand *Das Kapital,* and Engels regarded him as a socialist more by emotion than conviction. Nevertheless Morris adopted some of the ideas of the two founders of communism and used them in his literary work, especially in the novel *News From Nowhere.* In

William Morris
Bedroom in Kelmscott Manor,
c. 1871
Kelmscott, Oxfordshire

Portrait of William Morris
c. 1890
Photograph

1875 he founded Morris & Company, where he achieved the goal of steering the firm towards efficient production. For the first time he was financially successful.

New Ideas for Paper and Fabrics

"The poet and wallpaper maker": this phrase coined by the author Henry James shows what made Morris known to the public. Wallpaper, which was in fashion, was ideally suited to the creative potential of the new design as Morris practiced it. He believed that the purpose of art was inextricably connected with the creation of a beautiful and comfortable home. The wallpapers, carpets, furniture and decorative items that he designed were all subordinate to this idea. In order to achieve the best possible results, he experimented with new techniques in order to achieve complex effects of color and form.

His work in the period after 1874 was characterized by an unbelievable abundance of ornament, which often had a three-dimensional effect. With designs such as the famous *Strawberry Thief*, in which he skillfully superimposed vegetable dyes, Morris had resounding successes that made him one of the leading designers of the new movement for many years.

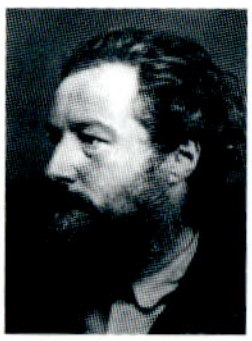

William Morris

1834–96

1847 Morris's father dies; he inherits a considerable fortune

1853 Matriculates at Exeter College, Oxford; friendship with Edward Burne-Jones

1854 Travels to Belgium and northern France with Burne-Jones; studies Flemish old masters

1856 Short-term apprenticeship in architectural practice of G. E. Street; friendship with Dante Gabriel Rossetti

1859 Marries Jane Burden, a model popular with the Pre-Raphaelites

1860 Moves into the Red House

1861 Foundation of Morris, Marshall, Falkner & Co.

1865 Moves to London

1871 Journey to Iceland

1883 Member of the Social Democratic Federation

1887 Publishes *The Aims of Art*

1888 Publishes *Signs of Change*

1889 *A Tale of the House of the Wolfings* published: a story in verse form that strongly influenced Tolkien's *Lord of the Rings*

1890 Publication of *News From Nowhere*

1891 Founds the Kelmscott Press

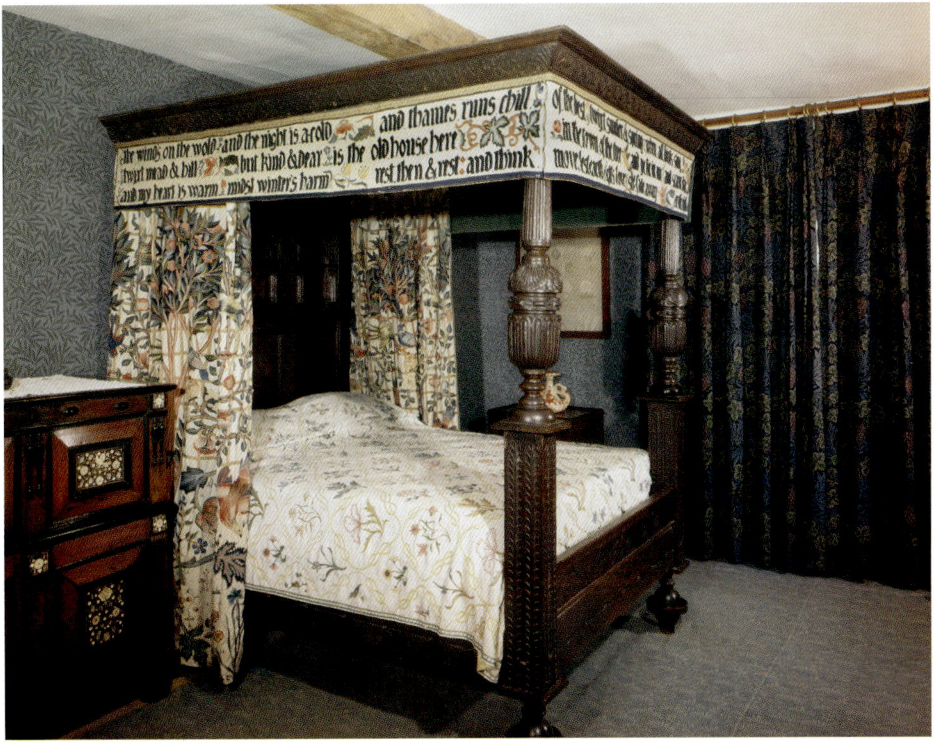

In 1881 Morris took over a textile factory at Merton Abbey, and his fabric designs were acclaimed all over Europe. The move to Kelmscott Manor enhanced his truly inexhaustible creativity even further. It was thus inevitable that Morris, still extremely active as a writer, should turn to the art of printing books. After founding the Kelmscott Press he was to produce models of far-reaching importance for the relationship between lettering and illustration. We will return to this subject later.

Next double page:
William Morris
Fabric pattern: *The Strawberry Thief*
After 1861, chintz
Victoria & Albert Museum, London

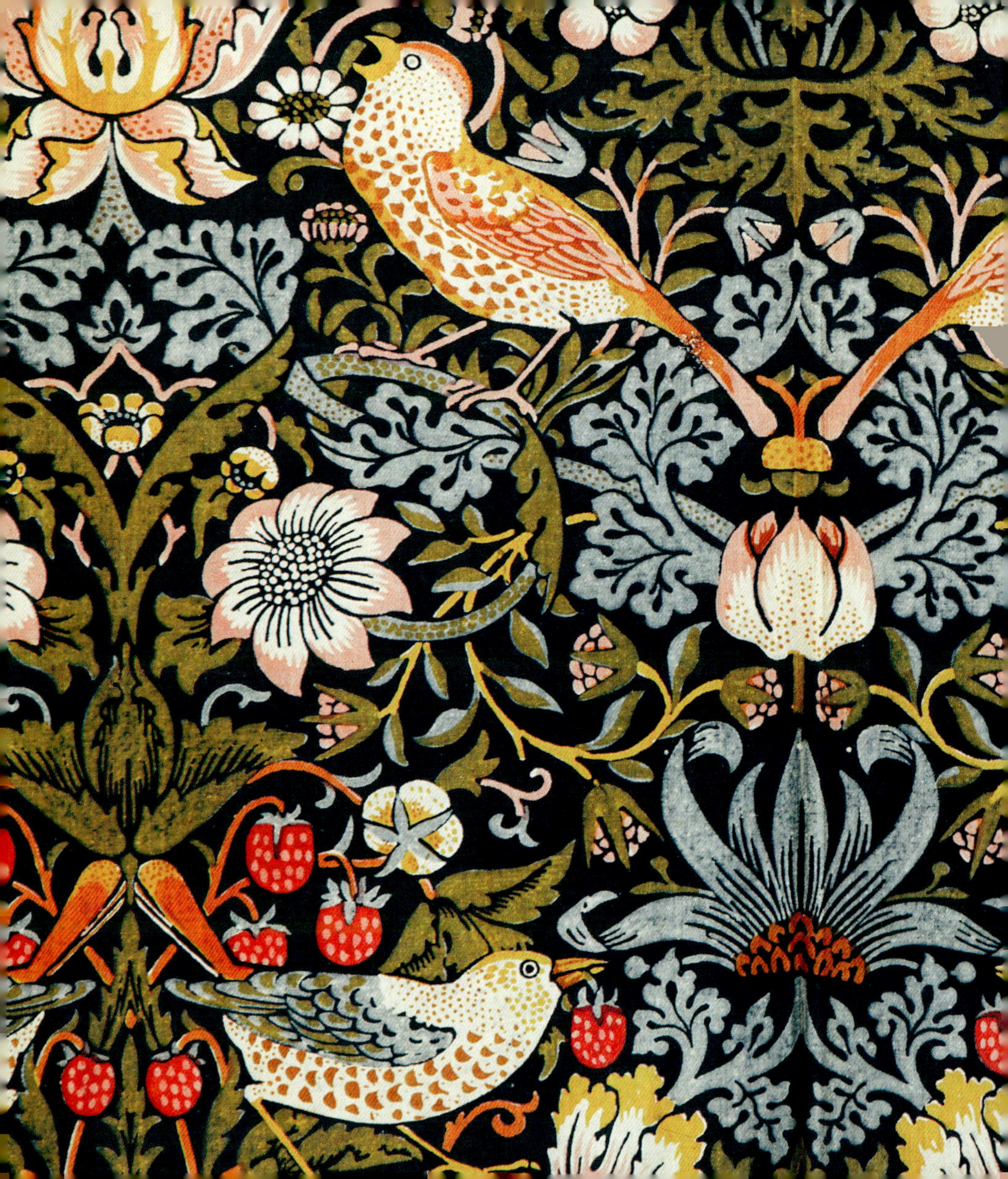

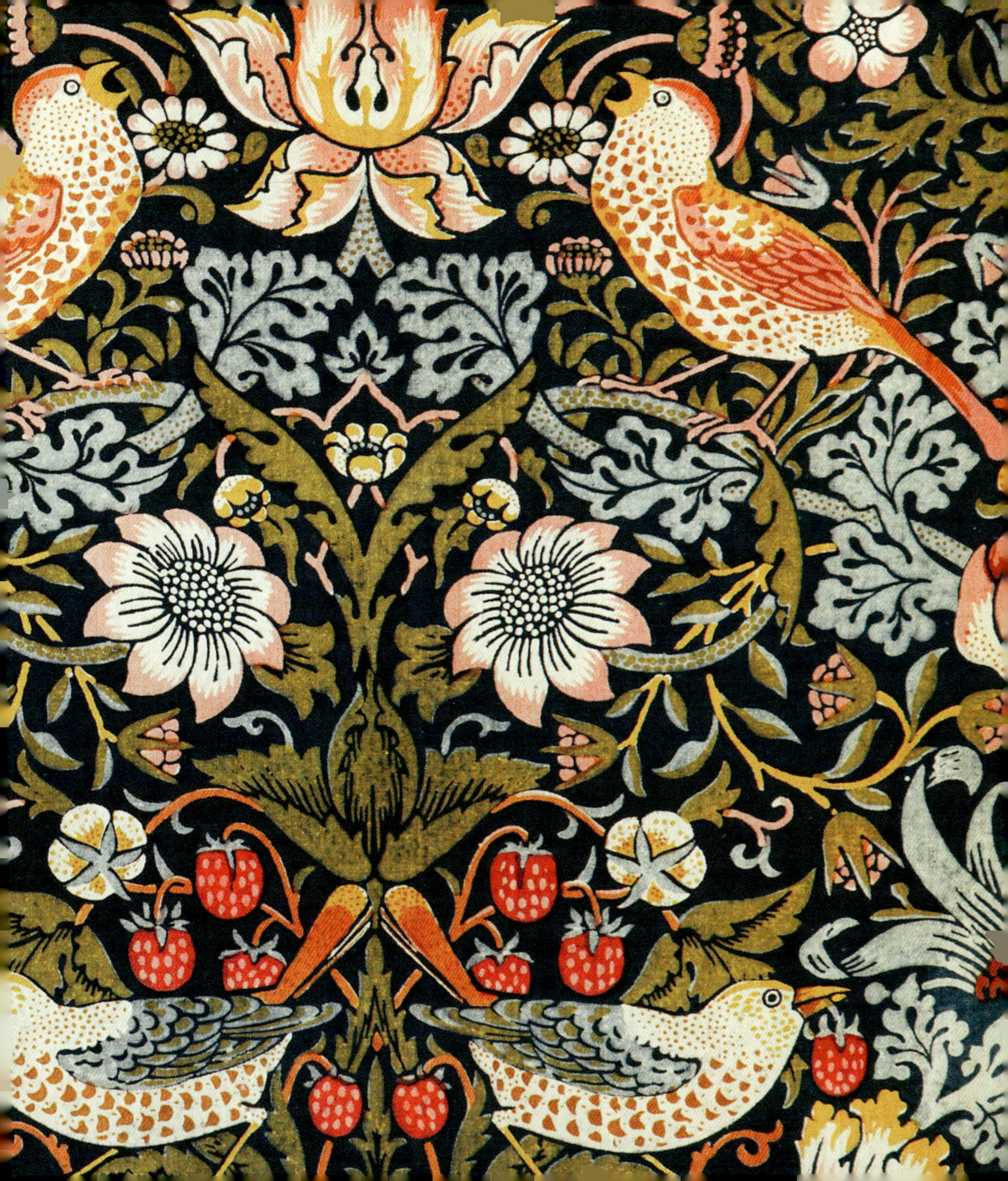

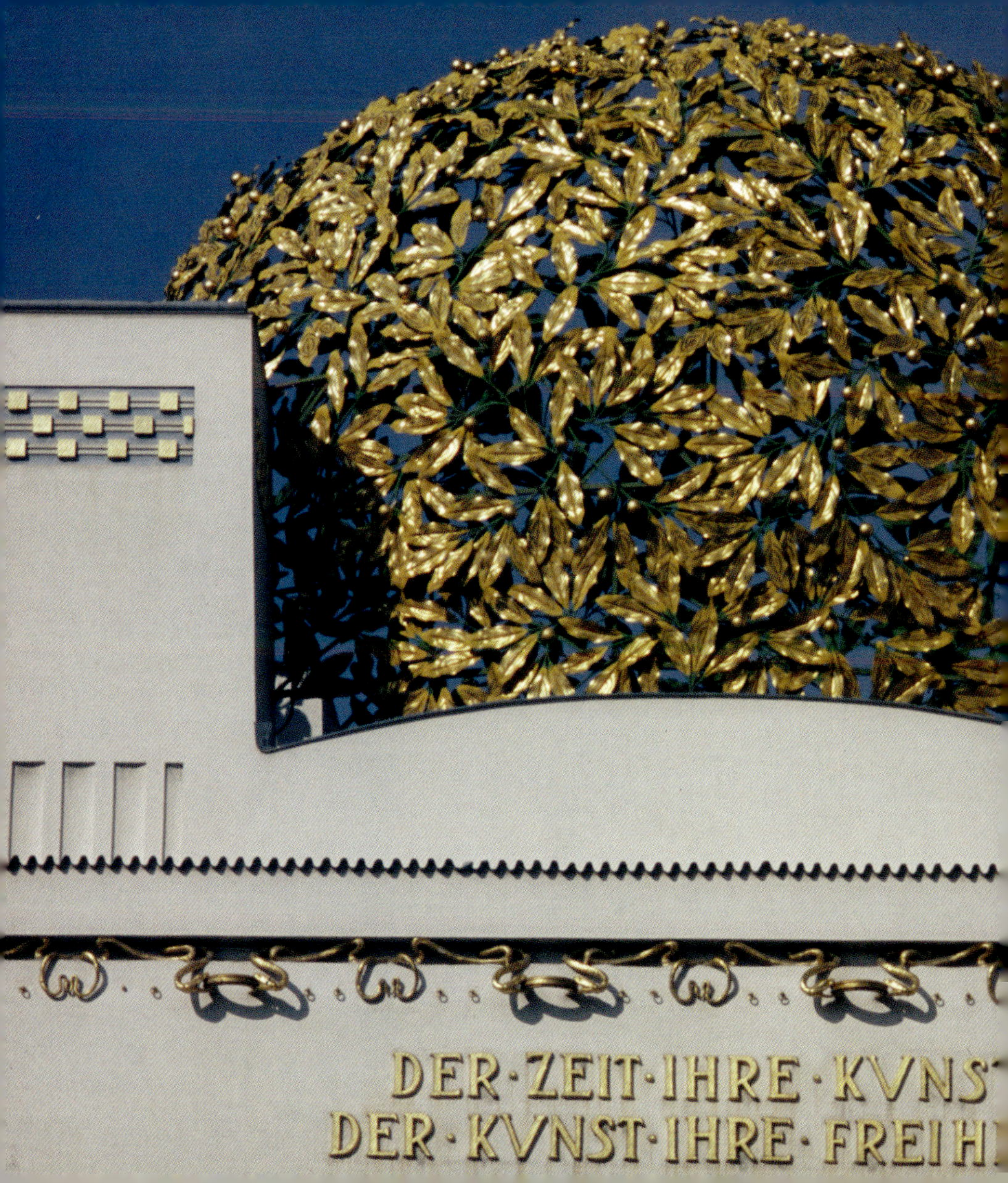
DER·ZEIT·IHRE·KVNST
DER·KVNST·IHRE·FREIH

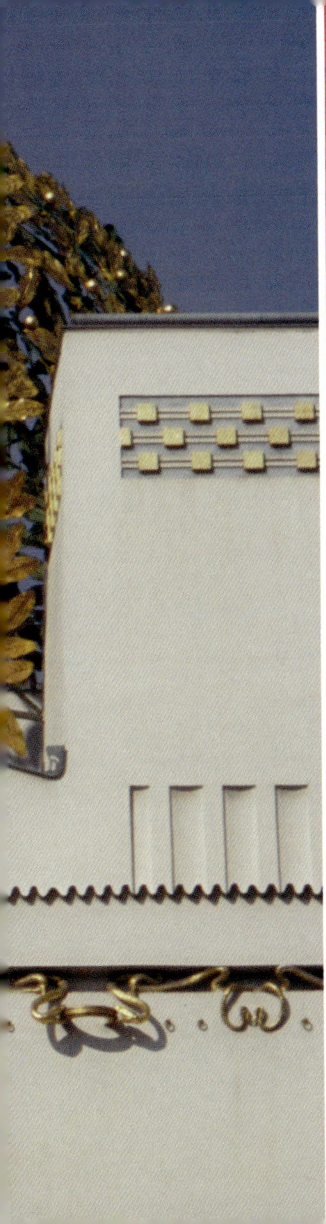

Secessions, Centers, Workshops

There can hardly have been a period when more associations of artists were formed than at the transition from the 19th to the 20th century. It was a time of ferment. New forces were trying to find their way, and in doing so they sometimes took an indirect course. The new movement often expressed itself outside the main cities: artists may not have loved what was provincial, but they loved the provinces. There was also an interesting phenomenon of networking between different centers, a conveying of ideas and approaches from one to another, but also the movement of individual artists within the art scene. Magazines provided new means of communication. In this way, Art Nouveau spread with unprecedented speed, and everyone could participate in the new trends.

Joseph Maria Olbrich
Secession Building, partial view: dome of gilded laurel leaves and inscription above the door, 1897/98, Vienna

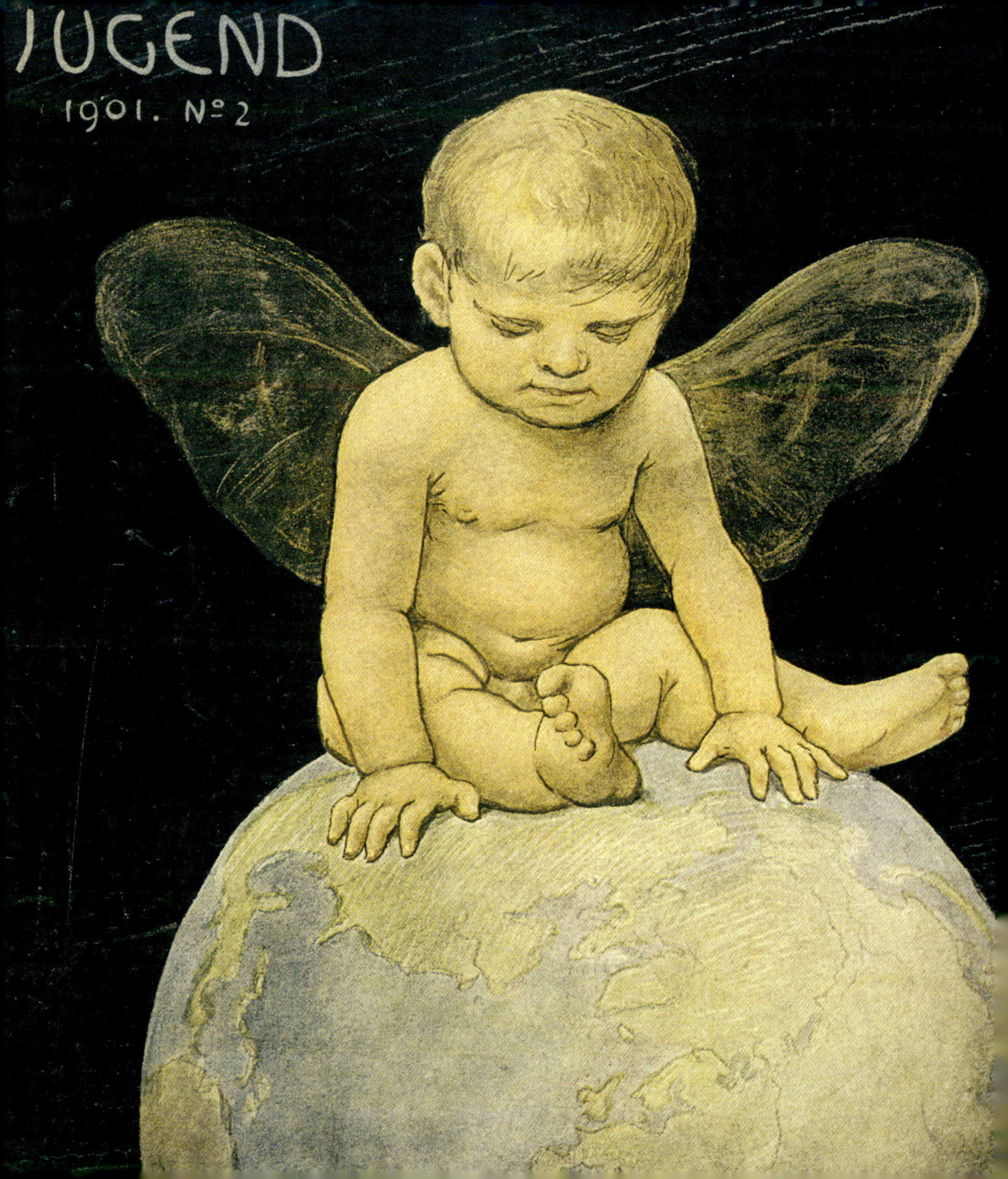
JUGEND
1901. No 2

An Important European Center: The Vienna Secession

In the Vienna of 1890, high society loved the sensual orgies painted by the establishment artist Hans Makart. Slick salon art loved to portray naked figures, though only in the guise of mythology. Despite this there were some lovers of art who sought renewal. Sissi, the Austrian empress, saw herself as being more up to date, and was well pleased with the airier and more modern ceiling paintings in the Hermesvilla in Lainz that Klimt completed after the death of Makart. However the establishment, with the support of the emperor, preferred the rigid conventions of history painting. A few years earlier, under the patronage of Emperor Franz Josef, Austrian artists had formed an association, the Wiener Künstlerhaus (Vienna House of Artists), to look after their interests, but the younger generation felt it did not represent them. And not only young artists felt this way: one of their most vehement spokesmen was the 85-year-old Rudolf von Alt, who told the emperor that, although he was very old, he was not too old to support some-

Hans Thoma
The Year's Festivals: New Year.
Front cover of the magazine *Jugend*, 21 December 1900 (detail)
1900, color print

August Endell
Wall design of *Elvira* studio
1896/97, plaster (destroyed)

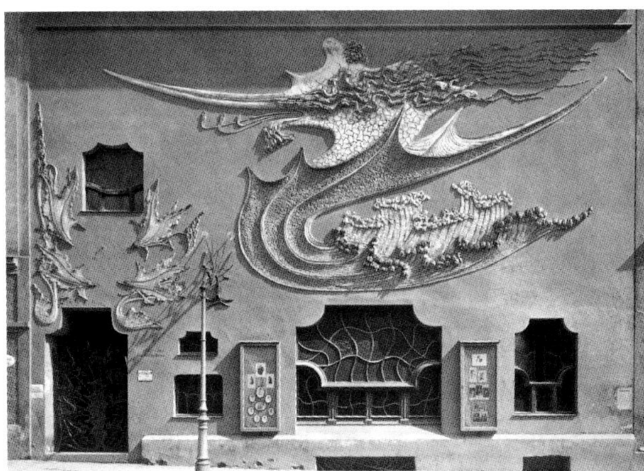

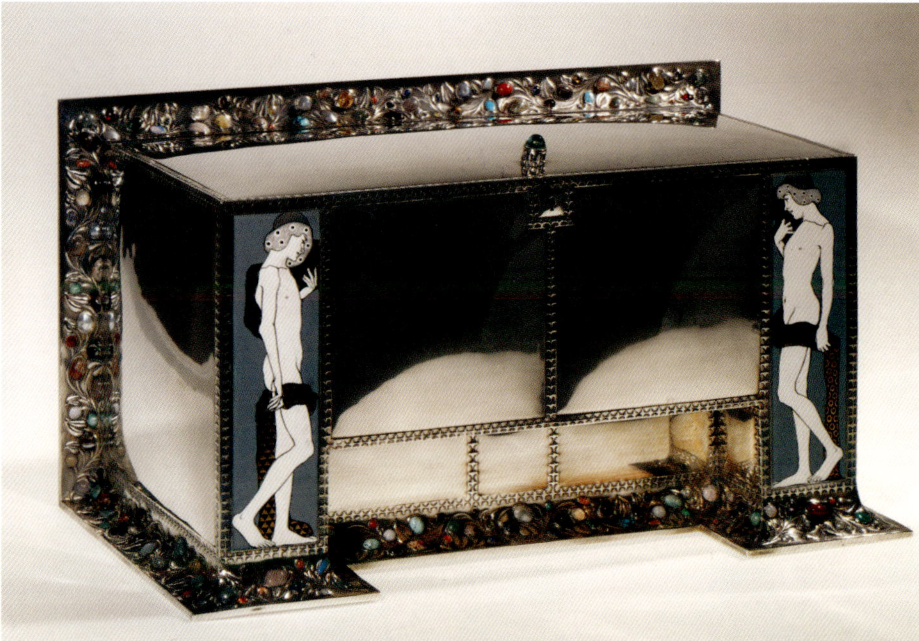

Koloman Moser
Jewelry box
1905/06, silver, enamel and semi-precious stones
Museum für Angewandte Kunst, Vienna

thing new. Artists and architects such as Gustav Klimt, Joseph Hoffmann and Koloman Moser joined forces and found an outlet for their energies by breaking away to form the Secession. They called for a "war" against "the old passive routine" and "Byzantine rigidity." A letter was sent to the chairman of the Künstlerhaus to inform him that the Vereinigung bildender Künstler Österreichs (Union of Austrian Artists) had been formed. It was signed by Gustav Klimt, who had been chosen as president. The young comrades-in-arms quickly agreed that they needed a place to exhibit, as one of their principal aims was to present their art to the public.

In 1897, almost simultaneously with the foundation of this union, Olbrich had submitted first designs for a new building to the Vienna city authorities. The structure that was approved provisionally for two years was eventually to become one of the most important architectural works in of the modern era, and today still stands on its original site. "To every age its art and to art its freedom" was the motto over the entrance to the Secession Building, which was inaugurated in 1898 and was the venue for several spectacular exhibitions in the following years.

The establishment of the Wiener Werkstätte (a "Production Cooperative of Craftsmen in Vienna") initiated a new phase in Art Nouveau that is regarded to this day as one of the most productive of that period. Here two professors at the Vienna Kunstgewerbeschule (School of Applied Arts), Josef Hoffmann and Koloman Moser, joined forces with the businessman Fritz Waerndorfer in 1903. Waerndorfer was not only extremely enthusiastic about art, but was especially interested in the question of how to express artistic genius in items of everyday use. The combination of artistic élan and an entrepreneurial attitude was so unbeatable that the Wiener Werkstätte had branches in New York and Zurich at one stage.

Koloman Moser, whom Hermann Bahr once described as "an artist in a thousand," developed the elegant and precious style of the Wiener Werkstätte, which he left, however, in 1907 to devote himself entirely to painting.

The Belgian Contribution

Between 1890 and the end of the century Brussels became a leading center of modern art. In the two lawyers Octave Maus and Edmond Picard, the young art scene in Belgium had two highly committed patrons, who afforded a spiritual home to artists such as Theo van Rysselberghe, James Ensor, Fernand Khnopff and Henry van de Velde with their magazine *L'Art Moderne* and a gallery called Maison d'Art in Picard's house.

This cultural climate is the background to the emergence of some extraordinary architecture and a true master

Paul Hankar
Chemiserie Niguet store,
now a flower shop
1896, Brussels

in Victor Horta. From 1892 Horta used exposed iron for structural and decorative purposes in the construction of a number of private homes and public buildings. In 1893 he built Hôtel Tassel, which surpassed all previously known architecture with its structure of exposed cast-iron and glass, its organic forms and soft, curving lines. Horta's teacher Alphonse Balat is said to have burst into tears at the sight of Hôtel Tassel.

Paul Hankar differed significantly from Horta, partly because his clients were less wealthy. As economical use of resources was important for them, Hankar's work owed a great deal to the Arts and Crafts movement, which believed that to honor the materials was one of the first principles of design. Hankar's buildings also betray the influence of Japonisme, which helped his style to develop beyond his early neo-Gothic approach. His own house was the first of a series that he built in Brussels. They astonished observers with their unusual "art on architecture," which involved his friend Adolphe Crespin painting the houses or making richly ornamented wall paneling. The interiors, too, were sumptuously decorated, and Hankar designed a whole series of furniture. The autonomous Hankar style that was created in this way came to an abrupt end with the sudden death of the architect.

Paul Hankar

1859 – 1901

1876 Hankar, the son of a stonemason, studies sculpture at the Academie des Beaux-Arts in Brussels, where he meets Victor Horta

1879 Learns to work with iron from Henri Beyeart

1896 Hankar designs an artists' colony with studios and homes, planned to be built in Westende but never realized

1897/98 Builds a house in Rue Defacqz in Brussels for the rich widow of an aristocrat, and has a free hand in the interior, for which he designs the furniture himself; the unusual and bold designs for the house gained Europe-wide recognition

1889 Designs Palacio de Chávarri in Bilbao

1897 Works with other artists on the contribution of Belgian Congo to the Ethnographic Exhibition in Brussels

1898 In cooperation with Adolphe Crespin remodels the Chemiserie Niguet

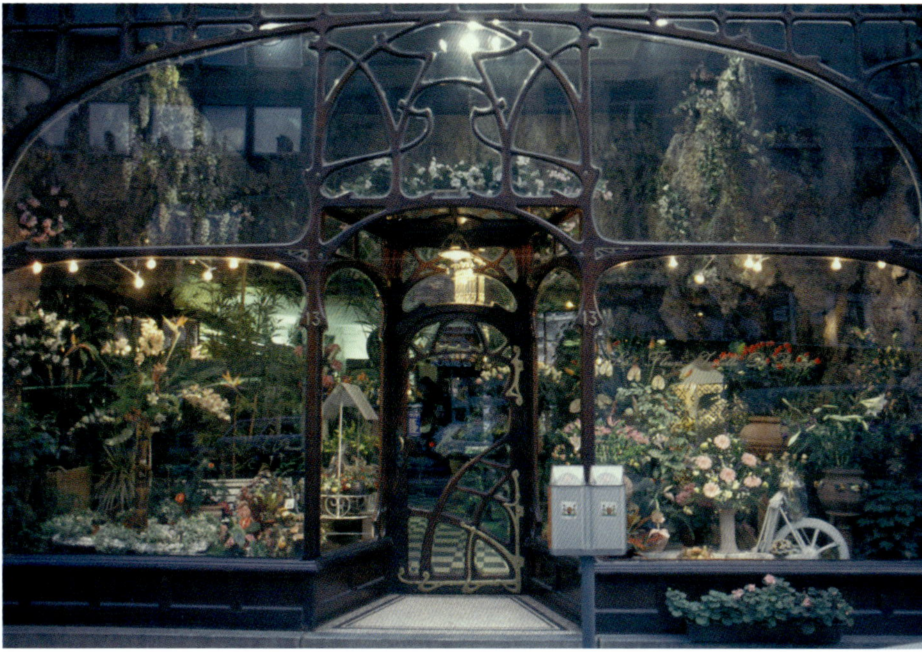

A Focal Point for New Trends: The Munich Secession

The welcoming district of Schwabing and the liberal attitude of the Wittelsbach royal house seemed to be an unbeatable combination when it came to providing fertile ground for artists. In spring 1892 the Verein bildender Künstler München – Sezession (Munich Association of Fine Artists – Secession) started a new era in the Bavarian capital.

The founders of the association were Franz von Stuck, Wilhelm Trübner and Fritz von Uhde. Change was the order of the day, which made the Secession the focal point for all artists from Munich and the surrounding area who

Following double page:
Heinrich Vogeler
Summer Evening (left to right: Paula Becker, Agnes Wulff, Otto Modersohn, Clara Westhoff, Martha Vogeler, her brother Martin Schröder, Franz Vogeler and Heinrich Vogeler in front of the Barkenhoff in Worpswede)
1905, oil on canvas
175 × 306 cm
Grosse Kunstschau, Worpswede

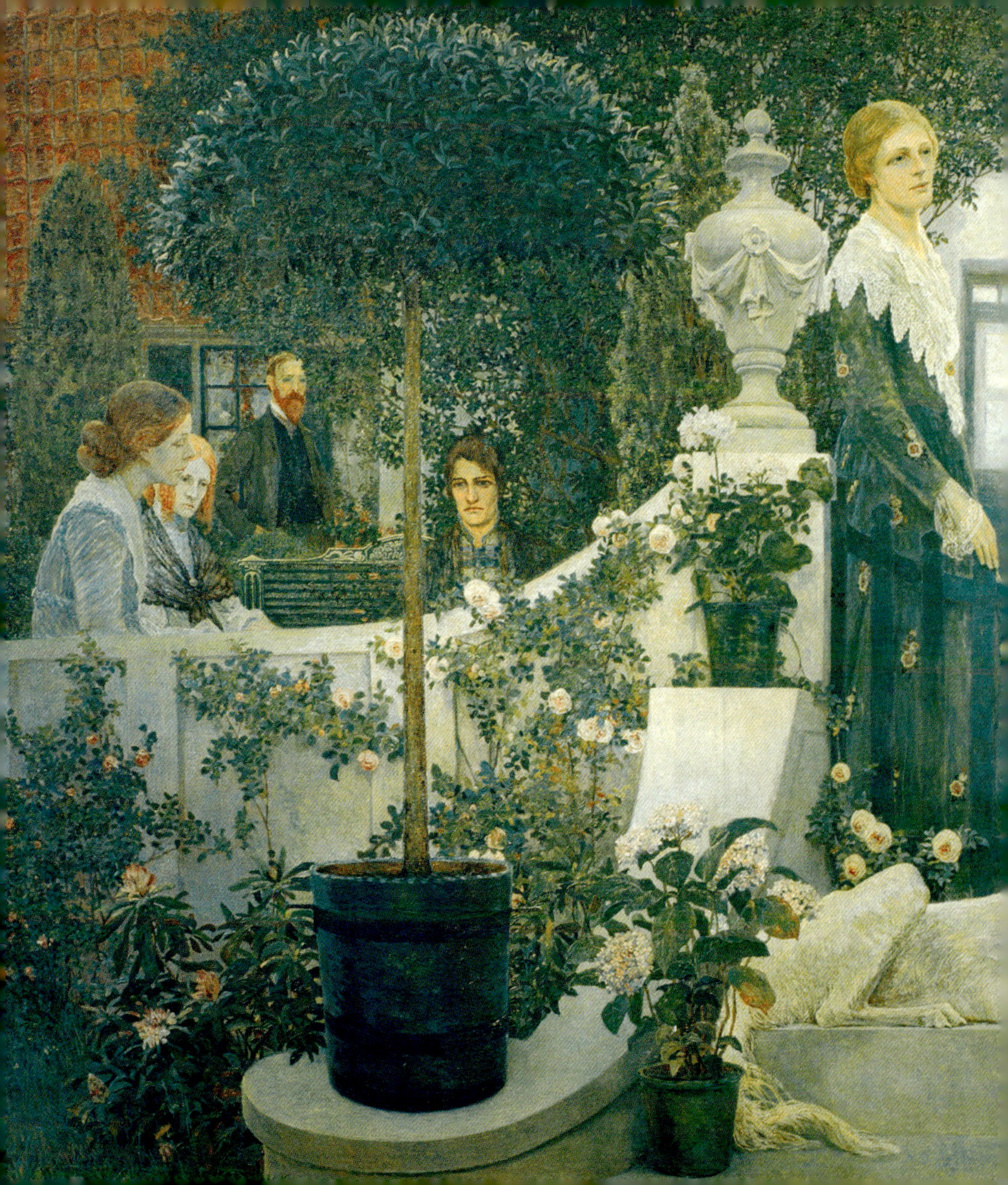

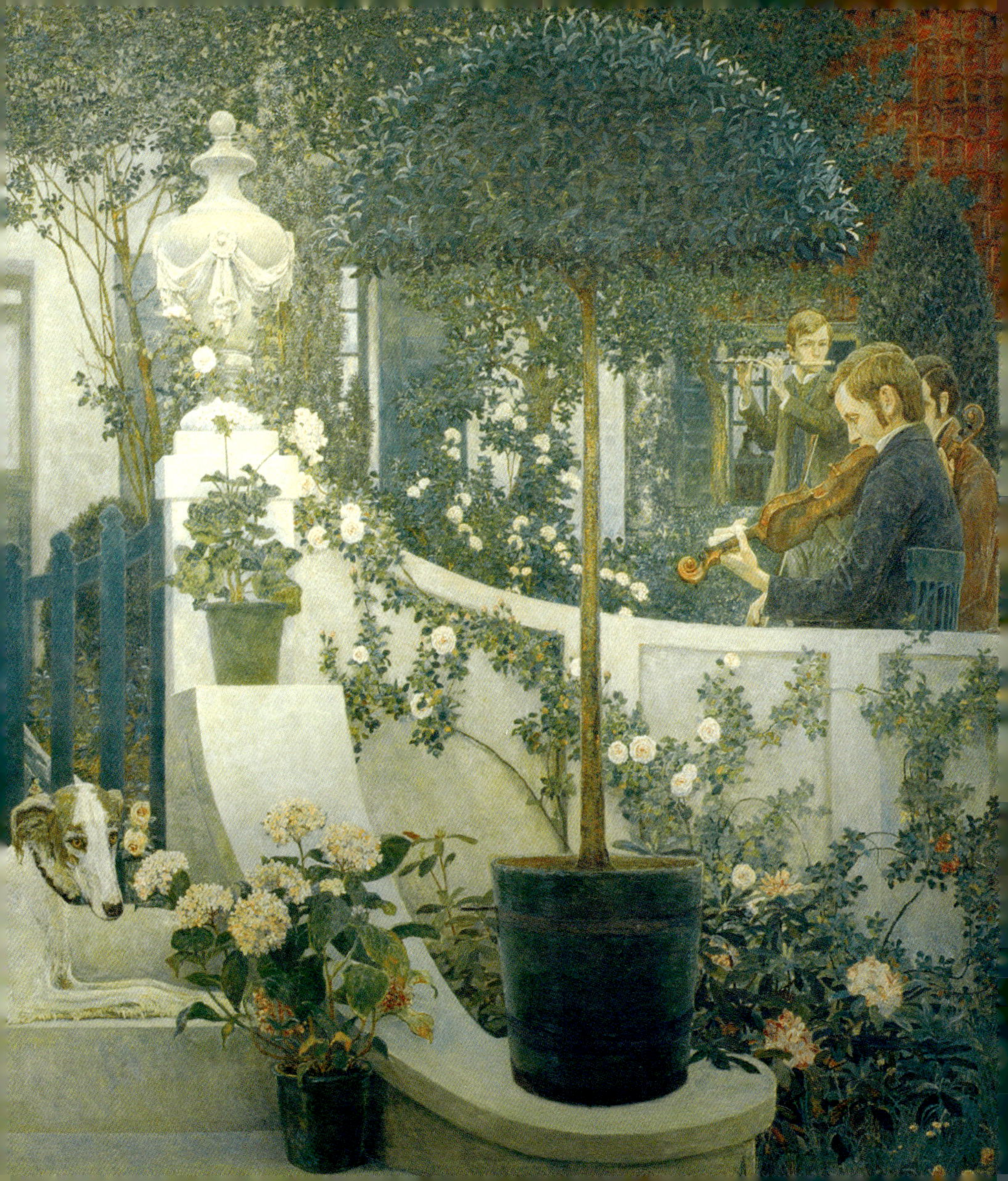

felt that the existing artists' associations cramped their individuality. The Deutsche Kunstgenossenschaft (German Art Cooperative) launched by Franz von Lenbach worked on old principles which the new artists wished to scatter with a breath of fresh air. They soon demanded an international exchange of ideas and regular annual exhibitions. Franz von Lenbach felt only contempt for these "mischievous upstarts," who nevertheless achieved considerable success with their first exhibition in 1893. Later, several of them joined together on the English model to form the Vereinigte Werkstätten für Kunst im Handwerk (United Workshops for Art in Crafts) in 1898.

They found important stimuli in folk art, in which they saw an honest approach to artistic work. They followed the lead of William Morris in pursuing this idea, which was propagated by Richard Riemerschmid in particular; his disciples were Hermann Obrist, August Endell and Bernhard Pankok, among others. The leading light of the Munich Secession was the charismatic Franz von Stuck, who turned his residence into a total work of art, a composition that unified living and work. Stuck was the "prince" with the potential to usurp Lenbach's dominant position. It was not long before high society was captivated by his ostentatious style, which was intended to provoke and fascinate.

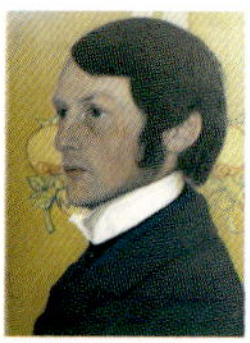

Oskar Zwintscher
Heinrich Vogeler
1902, oil on board
45 × 40 cm
Private collection

Heinrich Vogeler

1872 – 1942

After the death of his father in **1894**, Heinrich Vogeler, son of a very wealthy merchant family from Bremen, had the means to lead a relatively carefree existence as an artist. His experiences in the First World War, for which he – like many other artists – volunteered, made him a radical pacifist. In **1918** he addressed a passionate appeal to the German emperor in verse form. His conversion to Communism and placing his cottage Barkenhoff at the disposal of a commune were undoubtedly products of his experiences in the turbulent postwar years. In **1931** Vogeler traveled to Moscow for a long stay, which turned into a journey of no return when the National Socialists took power in Germany. As an immigrant he was forcibly resettled to Kazakhstan from **1936**. He died there in **1942** and was buried in an unmarked grave.

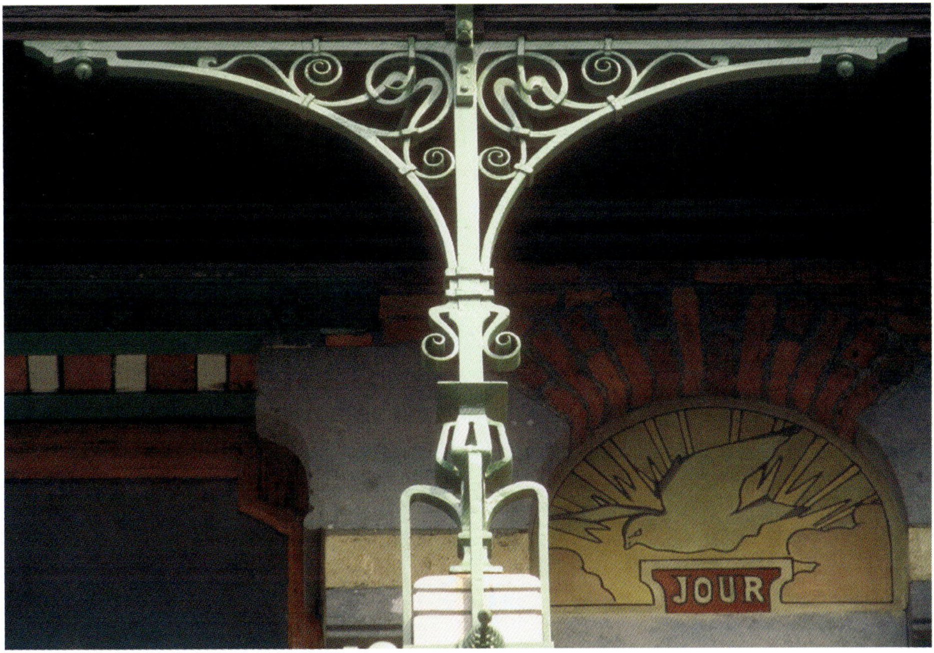

Retreat to the Provinces: The Worpswede Artists' Colony

In Düsseldorf Mimi Stilte, the daughter of a north German businessman, sang the praises of her home village of Worpswede to a boarder in her aunt's house. It was not long before the penniless art student Fritz Mackensen invited himself to spend the summer months at her family home and enjoyed carefree days in the entrancing landscape of the Teufelsmoor (Devil's Moor). In 1884 he persuaded his fellow students Otto Modersohn and Hans am Ende to pay a visit. This was the beginning not just of a long friendship but also of an artists' colony, founded in 1889, which provided an important impulse for art around the year 1900.

Paul Hankar
Maison Hankar, detail of a balcony support
1893
Brussels, Rue Defacqz 71

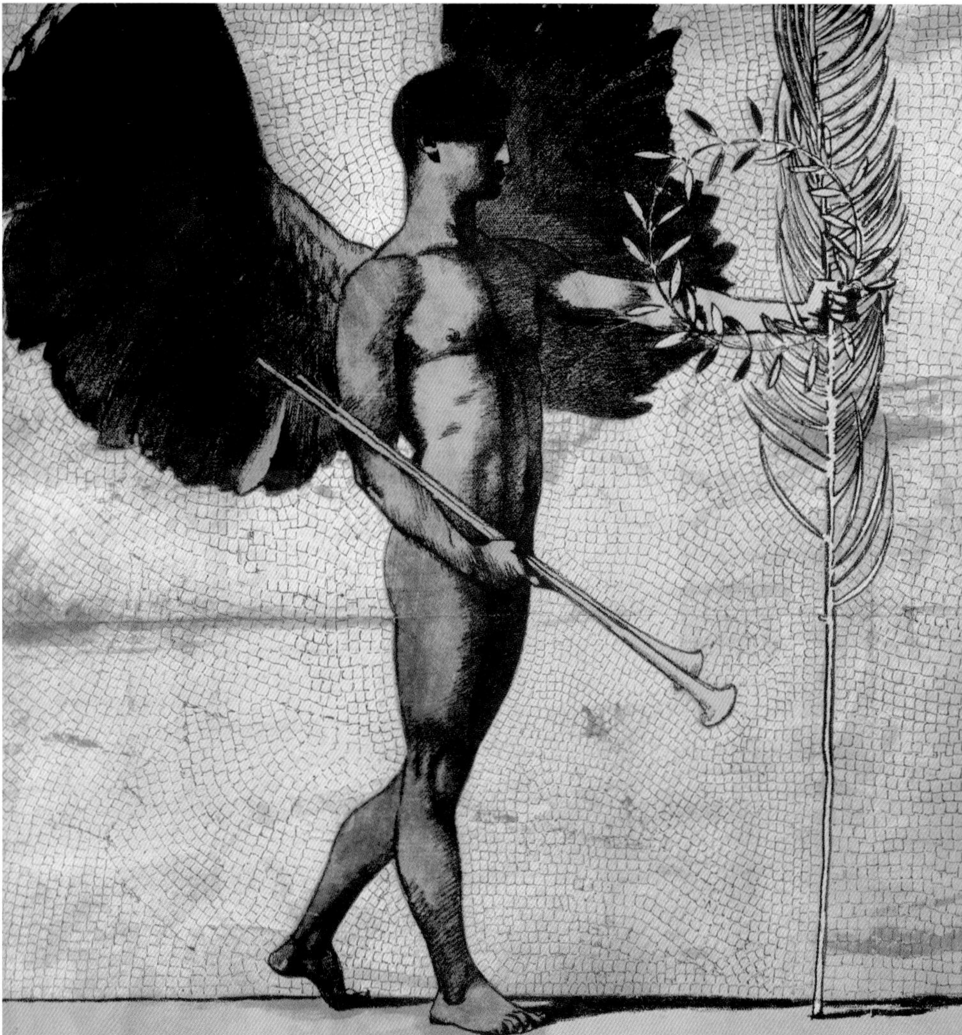

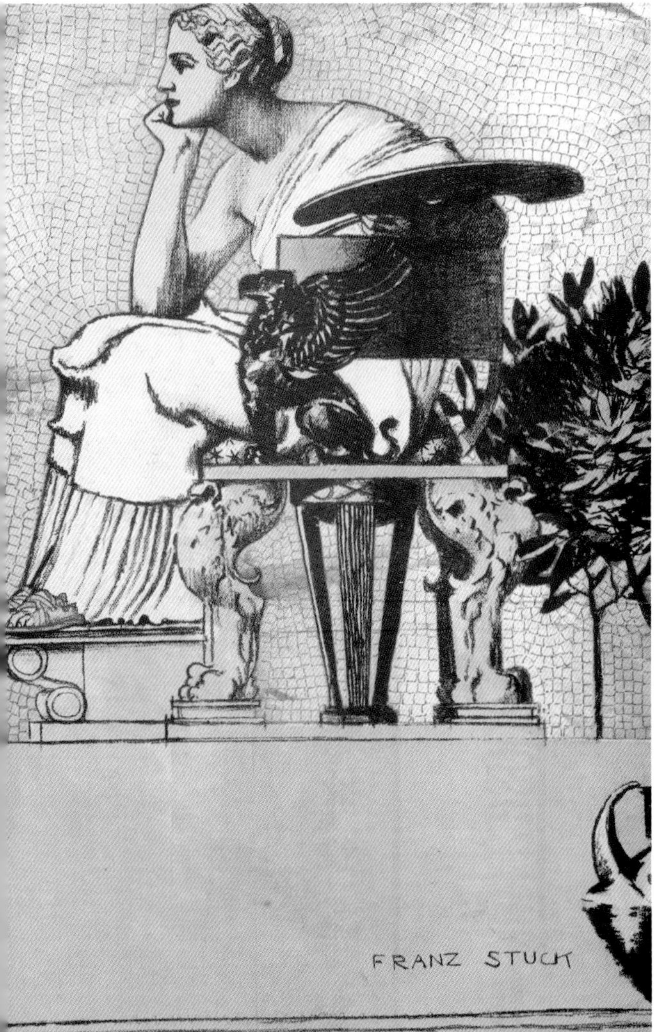

As in the decoration of his artist's residence, Franz von Stuck had recourse to classical models for this design. In the background of this sketch in oil he hints at the golden mosaic stones with which he aimed to enhance the effect and achieve greater opulence in the finished work.

Franz von Stuck
Allegory of Painting with the Spirit of Fame (design for wall decoration), detail
1905, oil on paper
66.5 × 81 cm
Sammlung Georg Schäfer, Schweinfurt

Koloman Moser
Brass vase,
Wiener Werkstätte, 1903
Museum für Angewandte Kunst,
Vienna

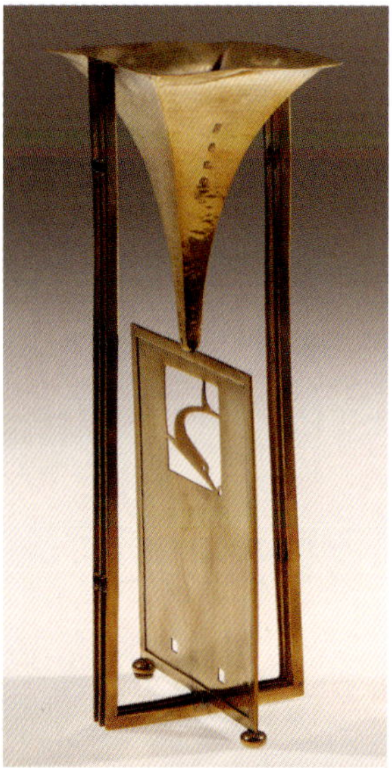

Franz von Stuck
Poster for the International Art Exhibition of the Munich Association of Fine Artists (Secession) in Prinzregentenstrasse
1898, color lithograph

Taking their example from the French Barbizon and Nabis painters, the Worpswede artists looked to find happiness in nature.

In 1894, after Heinrich Vogeler had joined the group, Mackensen founded the Künstlerverein Worpswede (Worpswede Artists' Association), which had great success with exhibitions in Bremen and Munich in 1895. When Vogeler bought a rustic cottage named Barkenhoff and made it into a work of art, the little village in the Teufelsmoor became a rendezvous for artists and writers from all over Germany. Vogeler had a gift for forming attachments to others and arousing their enthusiasm by organizing riotous festivities, which he designed down to the last detail. The poet Rainer Maria Rilke was one of the greatest admirers of the colony. Vogeler went so far in pursuit of his idea of reshaping everyday life that, in order to put his own designs into serial production, he founded the Worpsweder Werkstätten in 1908 with his brother. However, by then the community of artists in Worpswede had already broken up. The years when it flourished around 1900, culminating in three marriages – Otto Modersohn and Paula Becker, Clara Westhoff and Rainer Maria Rilke, Heinrich Vogeler and Martha Schröder – had already passed.

Bearer of the New Message: The Art Magazine

When the new century was in its infancy, the number of artists' associations increased almost daily. In the period when Art Nouveau was developing, the continual search for companions and opportunities to exchange ideas was an important aspect of the movement which was to have an effect on its specific artistic results. One phenomenon in the context of modern communications had only recently emerged, and was closely connected with the tendency to form associations: the magazine. It seemed as if the one was not viable without the other.

Ver Sacrum (Sacred Spring) was consciously developed as a program for the new movement in Vienna. The new creative impulses of the arts were presented as a mythological spring sacrifice. The texts and illustrations of the new magazine were intended to educate readers, win them over to artistic innovations and also to have a didactic influence on their taste. Artists regularly produced their design proposals for the magazine, which was planned to appear every two months, and writers such as Hermann Bahr composed sagacious texts. Although some items of local color from Vienna were deliberately included in the periodical, it nevertheless became known beyond the city in the other centers of the arts. The use of magazines as a medium of communication is an astonishing phenomenon, which began with magazines of the Arts and Crafts movement such as *The Studio* and, with the publication of *Jugend* (Youth), can be regarded as characteristic for Art Nouveau. Firstly, it was possible by this means for new forms, ornamentation and stylistic details to be passed on, copied and absorbed with lightning speed in a manner unknown in previous centuries. Secondly, the articles underpinned the style in theoretical terms and encouraged reflection on its results. Original supplements with graphic work, which attracted great attention, stimulated this genre in a completely novel way. The first

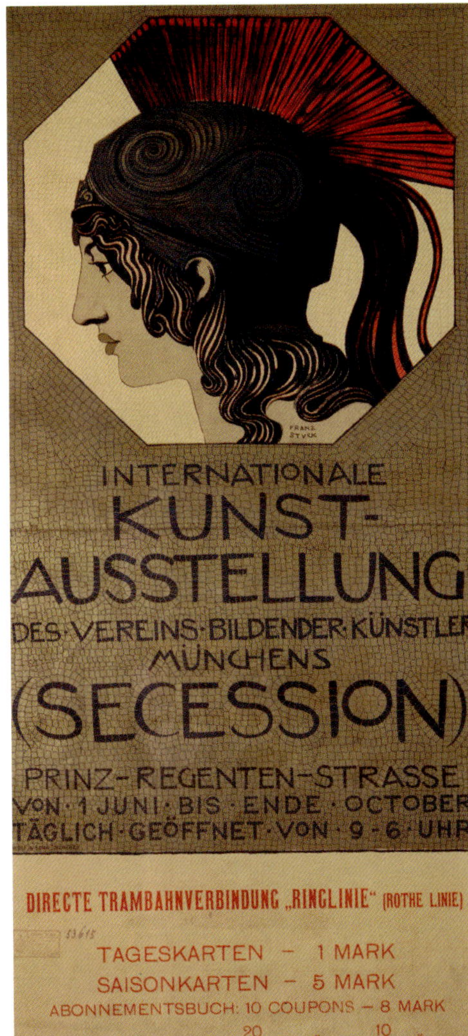

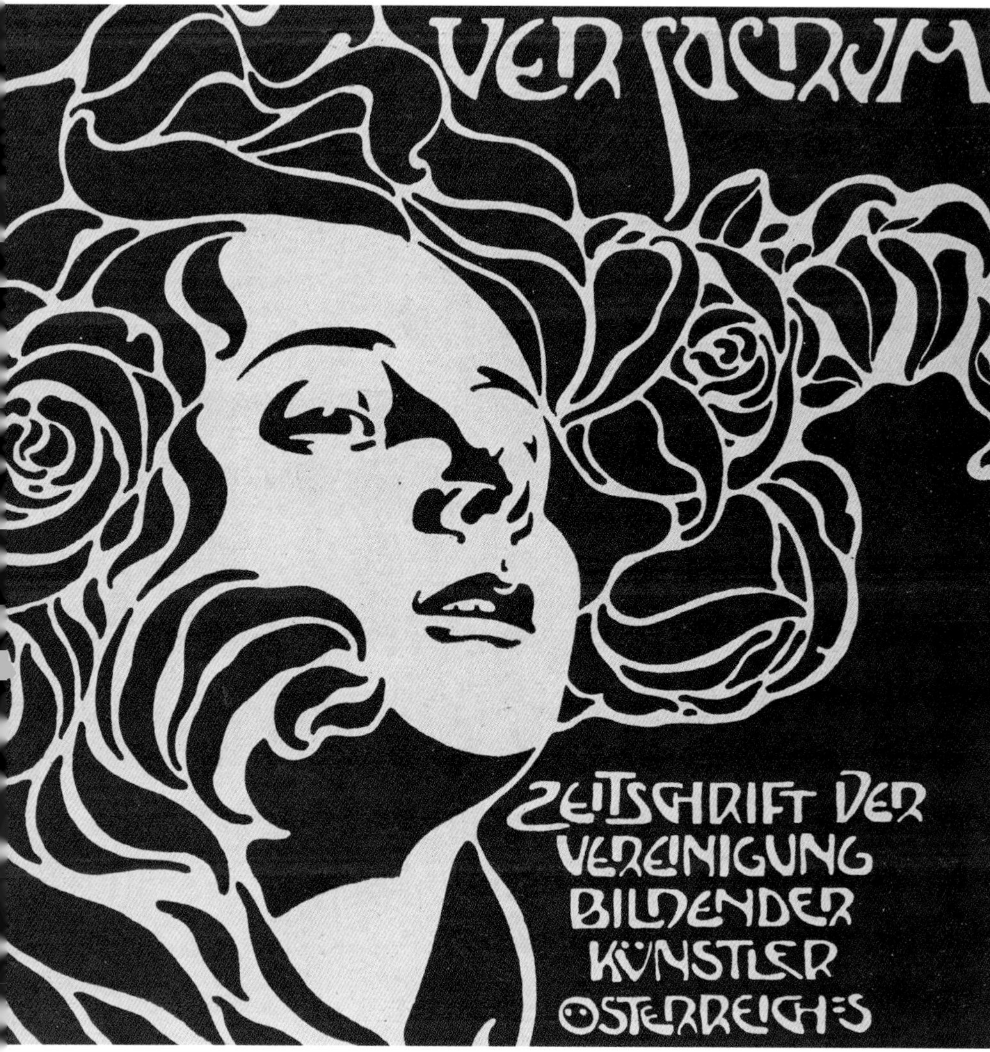
VER SACRUM
ZEITSCHRIFT DER
VEREINIGUNG
BILDENDER
KÜNSTLER
OSTERREICHES

publications were *Revue Blanche* (1891) in France, *The Yellow Book* (1894) in England, *Pan* (1895), *Jugend* (1896), *Simplicissimus* (1896) and *Die Insel* (1898) in Germany, and *Ver Sacrum* (1898) in Austria. The expensive style of production meant that most of these periodicals had a short lifespan, which makes two exceptions, *Die Jugend* and *Simplicissimus,* all the more conspicuous. For decades these magazines supplied the art scene with important information, discussions of exhibitions and new publications. In contrast to most magazines, *Jugend* was the project of a single individual, who provided the idea and the finance. For Georg Hirth the name *Jugend* (Youth) was programmatic, and he was personally committed to making it successful. He not only sacrificed his valuable collection of porcelain to pay for it, but also had the brilliant idea of ensuring the continued existence of *Jugend* with the proceeds of sales of original graphic work from the magazine. He quickly gained a following that extended beyond the city of Munich, and the graphic art from *Jugend* became a sought-after collectors' item.

Koloman Moser
Cover of *Ver Sacrum*, issue 4 (detail)
1899, lithograph
29 × 29 cm
Private collection, Vienna

Monsieur Bing's Gallery – The Invention of Art Nouveau

Sir Frank Brangwyn
Dance, design for the entrance to Samuel Bing's Maison d'Art Nouveau in Paris
1895, oil on canvas
255 × 155 cm
Private collection

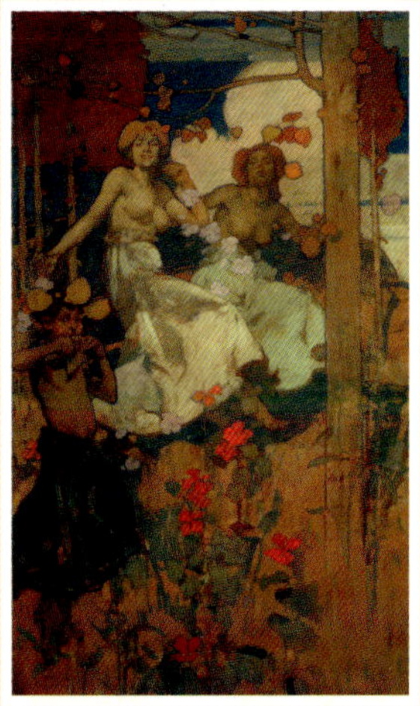

Samuel Bing came from Hamburg. His brother-in-law was the German consul in Japan and his brother managed one of the most important trading stations in Yokohama. In 1880/81 Bing himself undertook an extensive buying trip to Japan, China and India, and from the 1880s his gallery in Rue Chauchat in Paris was the address of choice for lovers of Japonisme.

At that time Japanese art was applauded by many artists and art critics as an impulse for the avant-garde in the renewal of European art. Painters such as Monet and Toulouse-Lautrec wore kimonos, and van Gogh admired Japanese colored woodcuts. Japanese crafts were shown at the world exhibition of 1878, and Bing, whose family had long traded in luxury goods and who had founded a porcelain factory in 1863 with Jean-Baptiste Leullier, became an expert in the field. His excellent commercial contacts in Japan enabled him to take a leading position in this fashionable business. He reinforced his status by publishing the magazine *Le japon artistique: documents d'art et d'industrie.*

Establishment of a European Network

When it seemed that the mode for Japanese art was being forgotten in the wake of modern artistic developments, the gallery owner and businessman Bing, who was nothing if not resourceful, looked for new fields of activity and proved to have an excellent nose for sniffing out new trends. On a visit to Brussels he discovered the Maison d'Art that the lawyers Picard and Maus had founded, and from that time pursued a scheme to open a similar business in Paris. He remodeled his gallery and opened it on 26 December 1895 under the programmatic name Art Nouveau, presenting works in a completely new way. Bing had

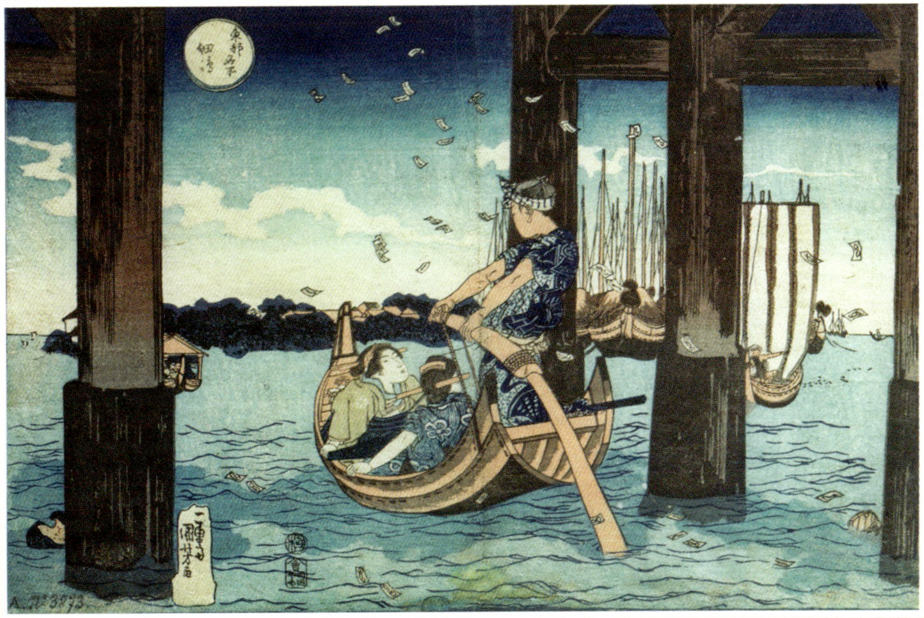

long argued that crafts and furniture should be displayed together in homely surroundings. In Brussels he entertained hopes that Horta, then already famous, would support his cause in the role of chief designer.

It may have been a stroke of luck that Horta declined, as Henry van de Velde, then unknown, started his career as a designer when Bing hired him to produce work for the Galerie Art Nouveau.

"L'Art Nouveau will throw down the gauntlet to everything that is ugly and pretentious in the things that surround us and imbue them with perfect taste, charm and simple beauty, down to the most trivial items of everyday use."
L'Art Moderne, 5 January 1896

Utagawa Kuniyoshi
Tsukudajima from the series *Famous Views of Tokyo* acquired by Samuel Bing, 15.11.1887
1835, colored woodcut
24.7 × 35.8 cm
Musée des Arts Décoratifs, Paris

Place of Pilgrimage for the New Art

The style of presentation in the new gallery aroused enormous expectations and an almost inconceivable level of curiosity on the part of the Parisians. The Galerie Art Nouveau was not a shop in the established sense of the word, but welcomed interested visitors as a salon where the most beautiful arts of the time were gathered.

Siegfried "Samuel" Bing

1838 – 1905

1823 Moses Michael Bing establishes and import and export business in Hamburg, which soon trades in French luxury goods

1834 Birth of Samuel Siegfried Bing in Hamburg

1863 Bing is the leading dealer in Paris for "curiosités" and through the foundation of the Leullier porcelain factory enjoys wide recognition as a producer of crafts

1880 and **1881** Bing travels to Japan to import suitable products; several essays on Japanese ceramics cement his reputation as an expert in this field

1895 Samuel Bing ceases trading in Japanese crafts and in December opens his Galerie d'Art Nouveau, which soon acquires the name Maison Bing

1898 Edward Colonna joins Bing's workshops

1900 The Pavillon d'Art Nouveau is a triumph for Bing at the world exhibition in Paris

1904 Bing retires from the business

Bing commissioned Frank Brangwyn, who was born in Belgium and trained by William Morris, to paint the rooms. The architect who remodeled the gallery, Louis Bonnier, was also recruited in Belgium. Bing carried out his scheme for what became known as Maison Bing according to precise ideas of how a culture of modern domestic life should develop. He gave several renowned artists and designers the task of furnishing and decorating different rooms. Maurice Denis designed a bedroom, Éduard Vuillard an antechamber, Paul-Albert Besnard a salon with wall decorations, the Australian Charles Conder a boudoir, and Henry van de Velde and Georges Lemmen one gentleman's room each. Van de Velde also designed a living room and a dining room. The Nabis artists Paul-Élie Ranson and Maurice Denis were commissioned to paint the rooms.

The results conveyed Samuel Bing's idea of "new living" just as he had imagined it. Not only items of furniture, but all the fixtures, fittings and contents of the rooms – lamps, wallpaper, carpets and dinner service – were subordinated to the new principle of unified design. This manner of designing rooms was pioneering work, and by presenting five of his rooms at an art exhibition in Dresden in 1897, Bing showed that he firmly intended to spread his ideas. He realized fairly quickly that workshops of his own were indispensable for developing new models and manufacturing the designs. However, in addition to this Bing gave licenses to other producers to make craftwork on the basis of the designs that he initiated. As a businessman it was clear to him that the way forward was to put his philosophy into practice by going into mass production so that the idea could reach the market.

Samuel Bing's pavilion with an exhibition of work by Lalique during the world exhibition of 1900
Photograph
Bibliotheque des Arts Décoratifs, Paris

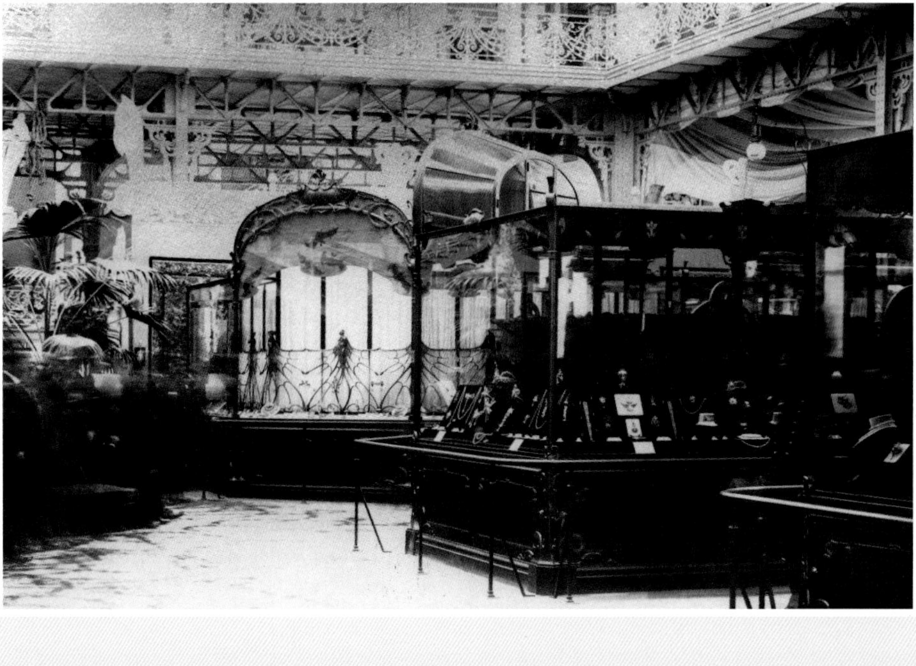

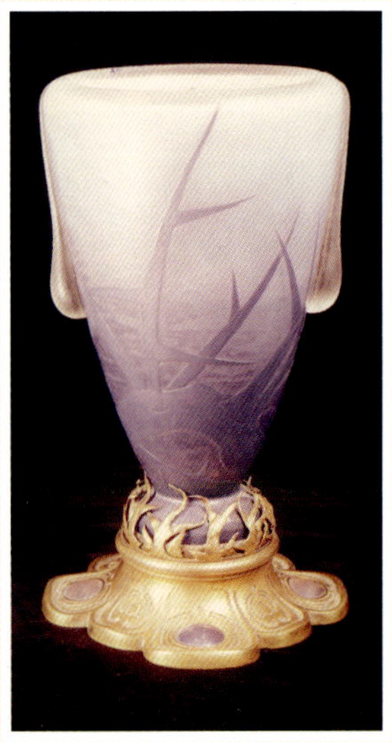

Louis Comfort Tiffany
Favrile vase with ormolu base
Victoria & Albert Museum, London

Sales Representative for Crafts

Even before Bing set out for the USA in 1894 in search of new ideas, he had heard about developments in glass design, which Louis Comfort Tiffany had taken to a completely new level. The world exhibition in Chicago in 1893 had made Tiffany's work famous, and Bing returned from America with the idea of having designs by European artists executed by Tiffany.

On arriving back in Europe Bing commissioned the Nabis artists to produce drawings for window glass, which he then intended to send to America for production. He proudly presented this successful collaboration to the Société Nationale des Beaux-Arts. This brilliant scheme resulted in one of the first transatlantic business partnerships, and Bing enjoyed success at the world exhibition of 1900 as the representative of the sought-after Tiffany glass. Tiffany, who had operated his own glass factory on Long Island since 1893, had invented opalescent Favrile glass and used the technique to produce fascinating items. Tiffany achieved renown not only for his production of jewelry and furniture, but above all for his flower-shaped lampshades, which had pieces of colored glass arranged in the style of a mosaic between lead strips. Tiffany furnished the White House in this style, and Samuel Bing paved the way for his conquest of the living rooms of wealthy citizens in Europe. From 1900 Bing expanded his role as representative of American crafts by selling the popular Rockwood porcelain from Cincinnati, which was made according to the philosophy of the Arts and Crafts movement.

The Great Triumph

The world exhibition of 1900 was the pinnacle of Bing's achievement as intermediary for the new style. Bing had teamed up with the young designer Edward Colonna in 1898, and they were later joined by Georges de Feure and Eugène Gaillard. With these three Bing had the right team for furnishing a pavilion at the exhibition. His plan was to communicate modern design in the form of a total work of art. At the entrance Gaillard placed a sofa in the middle of an eye-catching floor mosaic. Bing took up once again the idea of unusual wall painting, and recruited the young artist José Maria Sert for the task. Colonna's mastery of elegant, flowing lines produced an impressive salon.

The Pavillon d'Art Nouveau was one of the highlights of the 1900 world exhibition. Never before had such a thorough, detailed plan been executed to such high standards. It was a clear demonstration of the triumph of the modern style of living, and it surpassed by far the other pavilions, some of which were still decorated in the weighty historicist style.

Louis Comfort Tiffany
Magnolias and Iris window,
Tiffany Studios, New York

c. 1908, Favrile leaded glass
153 × 106.7 cm
Metropolitan Museum of Art, New York

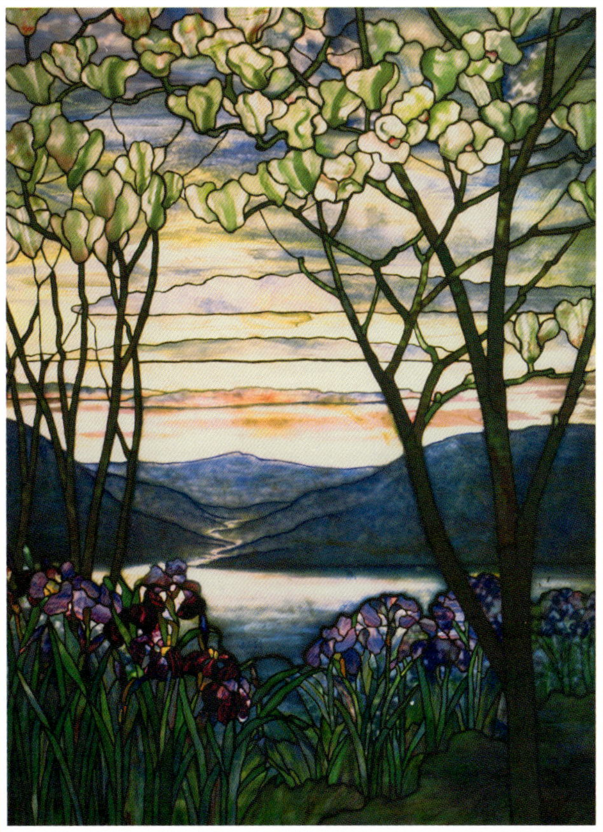

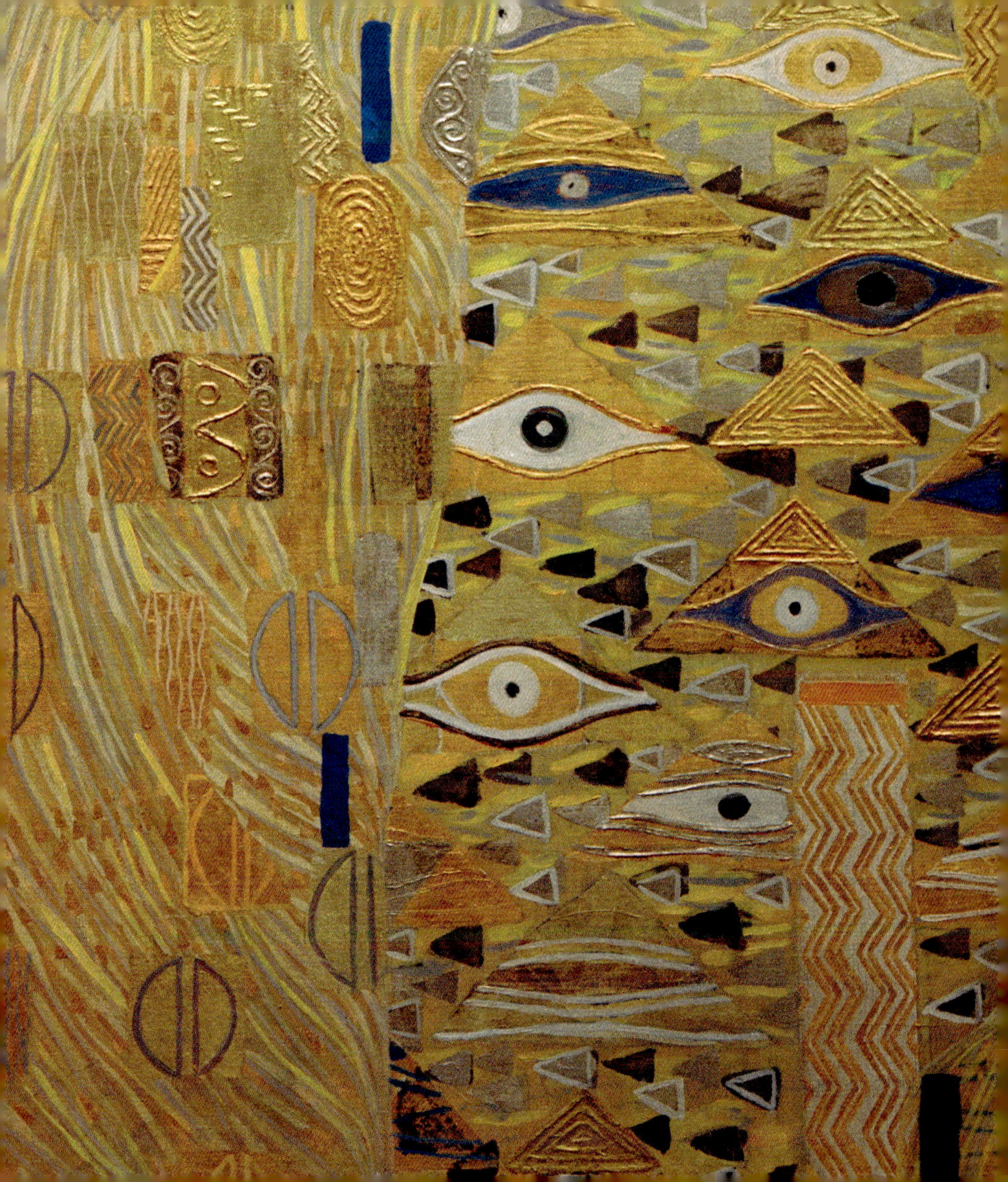

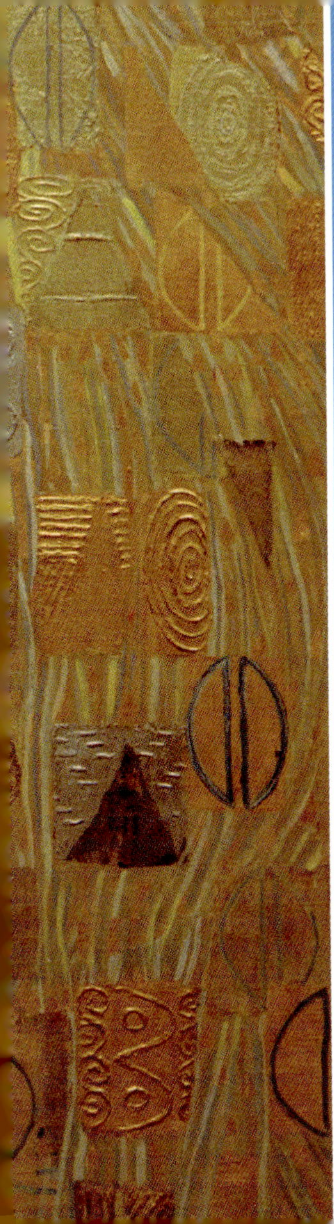

Nature and Ornament

Back to the origins of being
Seven billion years before my birth
I was an iris
Beneath my shimmering roots
Another star revolved
On its dark water
My giant blue flower floated

Arno Holz published this poem in the magazine *Ver Sacrum*, and Koloman Moser painted an illustration for it that naturally showed an iris – one of the most common plant motifs of Art Nouveau. The poem conveys the idea of the cycle of nature as a primeval force which the reader should try to perceive. This represents an all-embracing aim characteristic of many works of Art Nouveau.

Gustav Klimt
Adele Bloch-Bauer I
1907, oil, silver and gold
on canvas
138 × 138 cm
Neue Galerie, New York

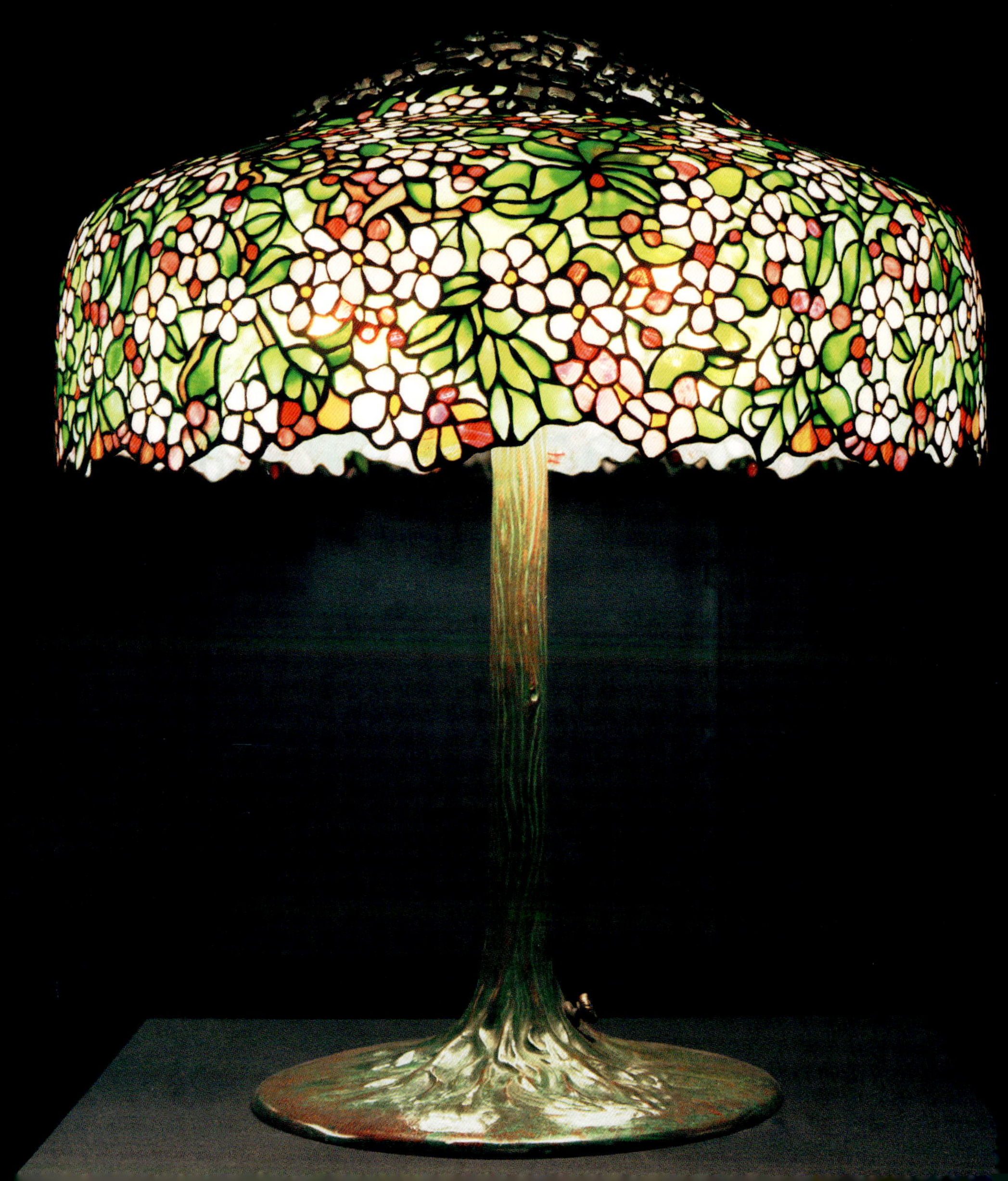

A Breath of Fresh Air: New Forms

Nature supplied the fresh stimuli that many creative artists urgently sought, feeling as they did wearied and worn down by an old repertoire of forms that seemed to repeat itself endlessly. In the early phase of Art Nouveau, in particular, floral ornament sprouted on all sides. This type of nature-based representation dominated the new style – two-dimensional and in silhouette.

This approach was supported by literary quotes such as Oscar Wilde's "Form is the secret of life." At the very beginning of the Arts and Crafts movement the first theoretical discussions on this subject were held: in 1856 Owen Jones published a treatise entitled *Grammar of Ornament.* Van de Velde also wrote about the earliest experiences of humans with elementary, repeated lines drawn on empty surfaces. He emphasized the psychological perception of "ornament" and "line," which he thought should be able to generate "feelings."

In his work *Kunstformen der Natur* (Artistic Forms of Nature), begun in 1899, the biologist Erich Haeckel provided a decisive impulse for renewing the formal language of art. Until 1903 he worked on 100 plates with drawings of animals and plants that he intended to serve as inspiration for craftsmen. At the same time he pursued with missionary zeal the idea of introducing the beauty and richness of nature to as many people as possible. Numerous artists embraced the message of his drawings. "What could arouse our sentiments of life more strongly than the graceful lines of the long tentacles of a jellyfish swaying in the water"? (J. M. Olbrich)

Louis Comfort Tiffany
Apple Blossom table lamp, also called *Cherry Tree*
c. 1902–06, Favrile glass, copper-leaded, height 78 cm
Private collection

Émile Gallé
Fire screen, 1900, marqueterie using various types of wood
Victoria & Albert Museum, London

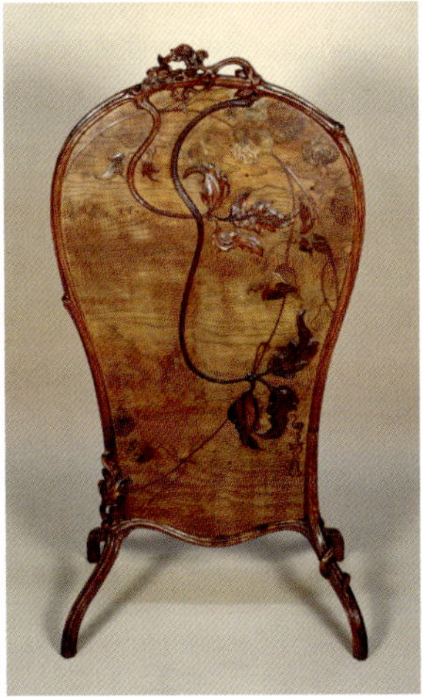

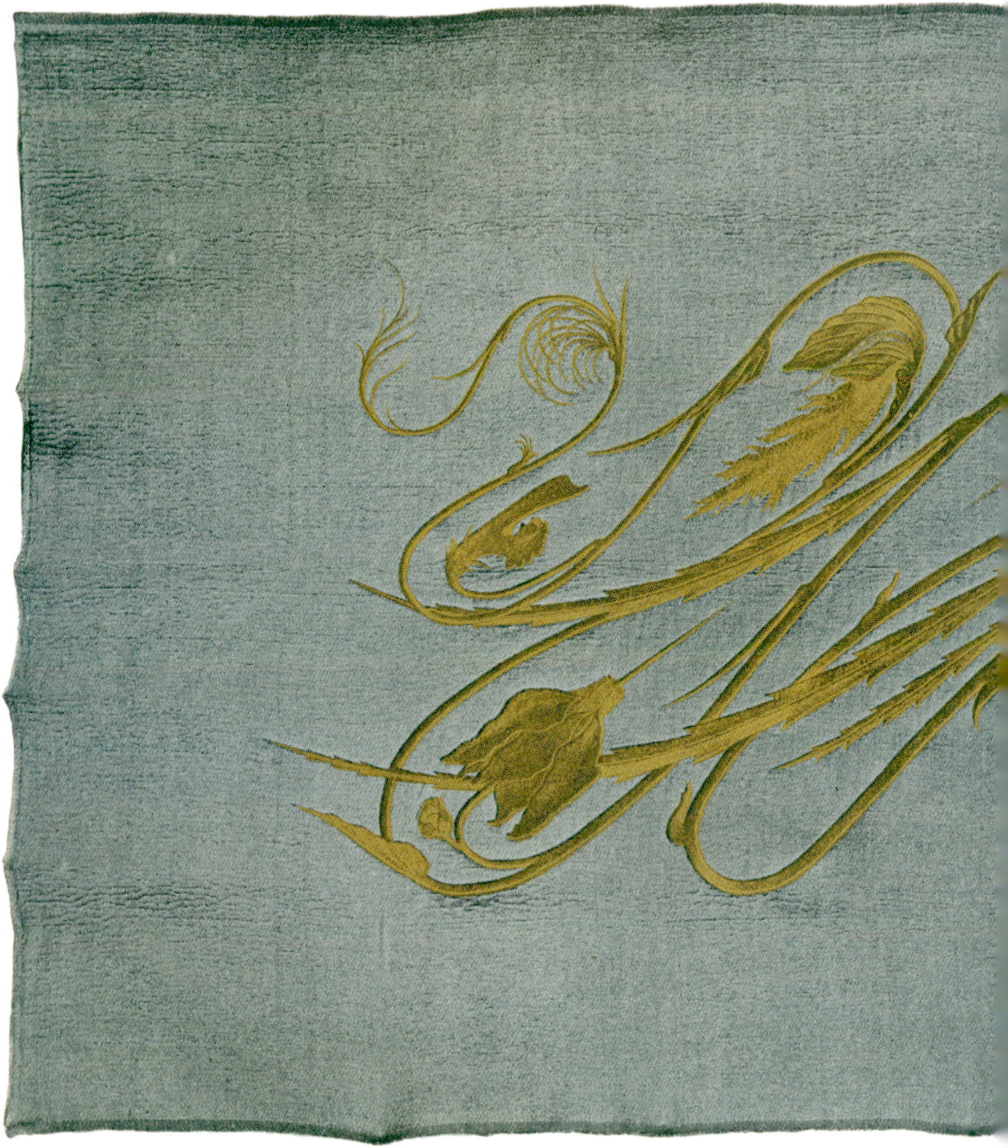

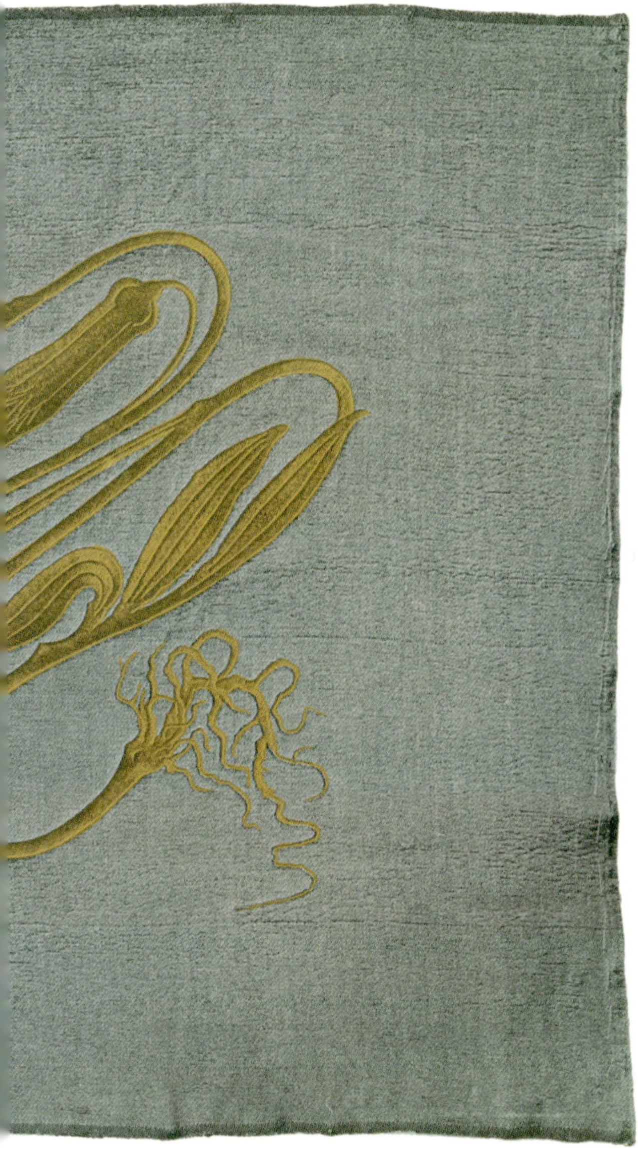

Hermann Obrist
Whiplash, wall-hanging, 1895
Reproduction by textile workshop of Elisabethenstift Darmstadt
Original: Stadtmuseum München

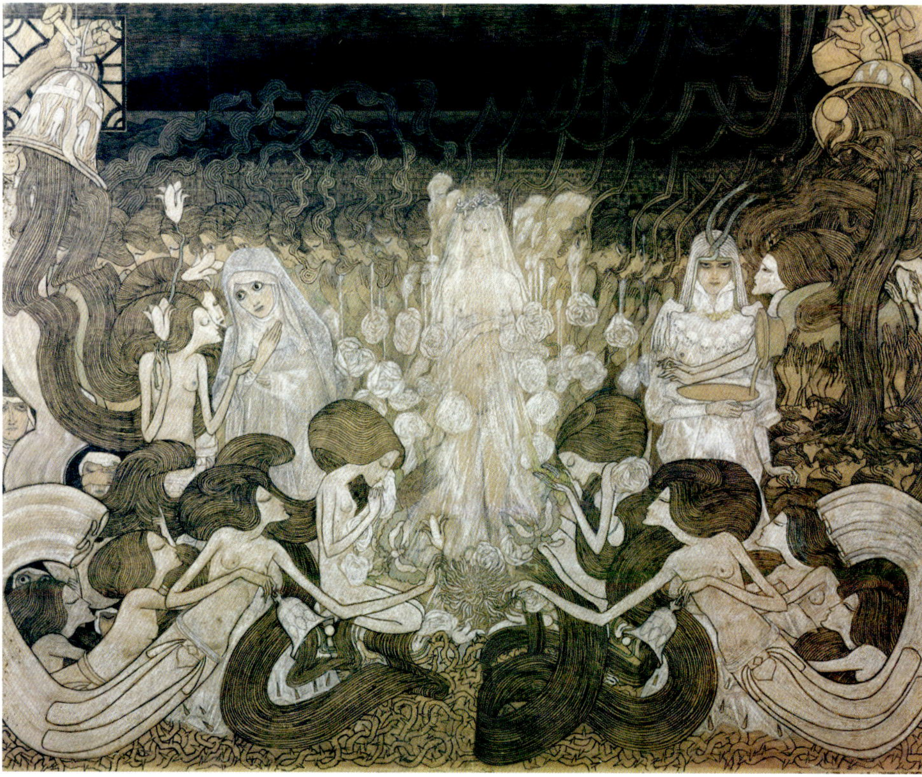

Jan Theodore Toorop
The Three Brides
1893, chalk on paper
78 × 98 cm
Rijksmuseum Kröller-Müller, Otterlo

Art Nouveau – Floral and Stylized

One particular object, which could not have had a more lasting effect, is often cited as the starting point in the emergence of a style of Art Nouveau that is known as "floral." This was the famous "whiplash," a wall-hanging designed in 1895 by the Munich artist Hermann Obrist that was embroidered with a depiction of a cyclamen. Obrist used detailed botanical studies to support his view that the creative process essentially consists of only three parts: "Here am I, there is nature, and here is the object that I am to decorate." With his "whiplash" Obrist produced an ornament that can be regarded as a model for the whole formal language of Art Nouveau. The unique curving motion that he imparted to the plant recurred later in the stair banisters and fabric patterns of the age.

Artists such as Otto Eckmann and Hans Christiansen made the organic line of plants into ornamental standards. The best example of this is Christiansen's rose. However, this trend outlived its time. Increasingly, new currents appeared that saw ornament in a less naturalistic way. Henry van de Velde was one of those who developed strict basic formal concepts, especially for perceiving space. Others, for example the Viennese artist Josef Hoffmann, went one step further by means of starkly simplifying ornamentation, although it could still originate in the observation of nature. On a journey to Capri Hoffmann was inspired by the sight of square white houses with the landscape as a backdrop and used this to develop his black-and-white contrasts, which he valued so highly because they had never before appeared in craftwork.

Jules Aimé Lavirotte
Door in Avenue Rapp
in Paris, 1902

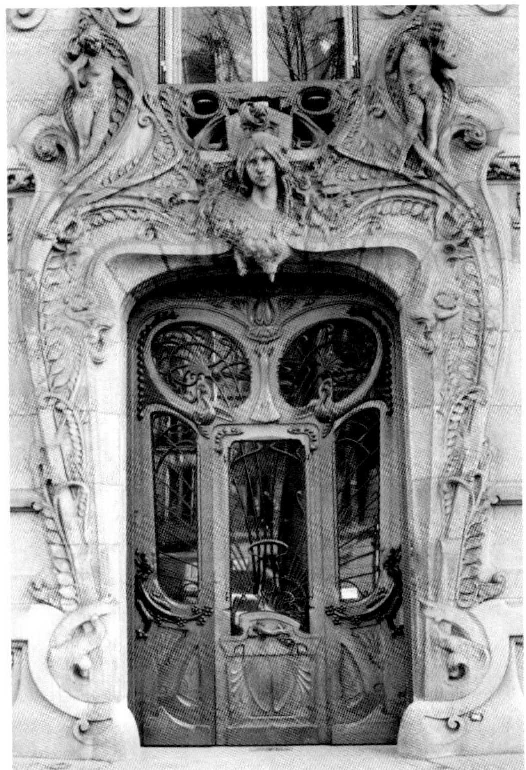

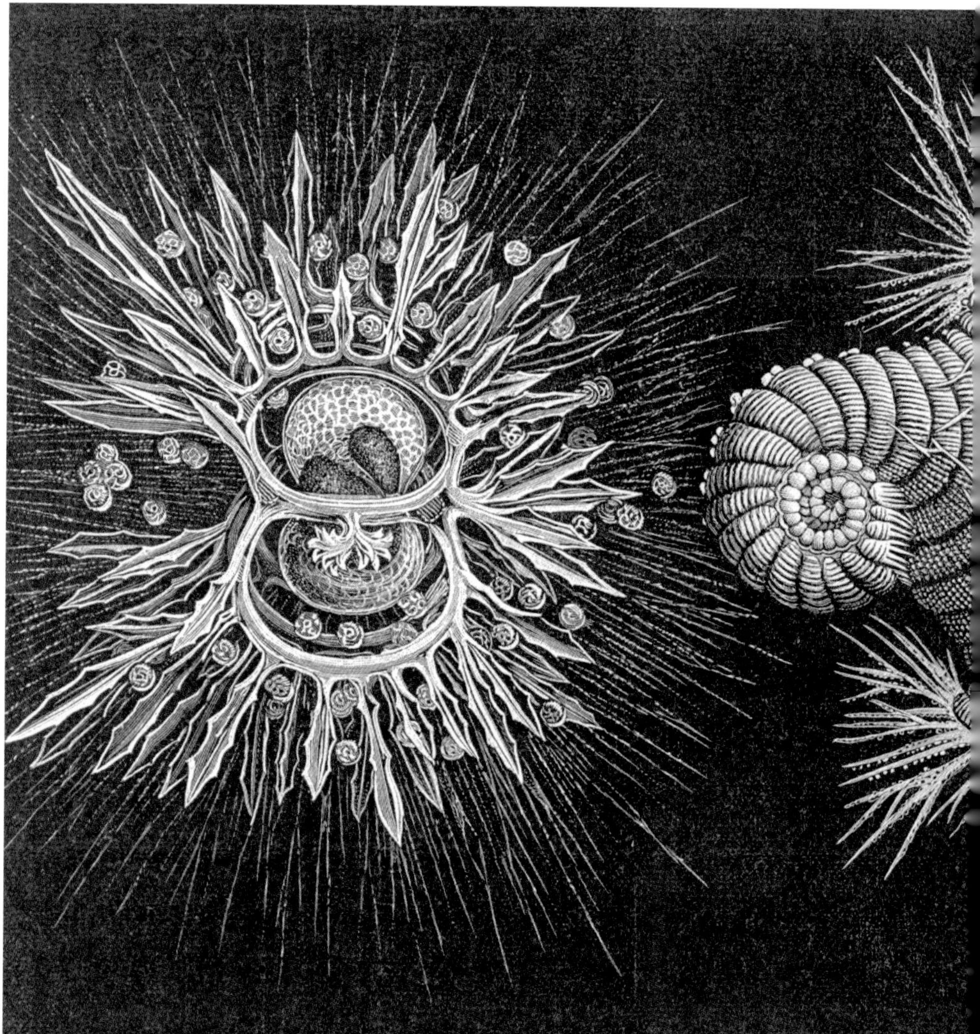

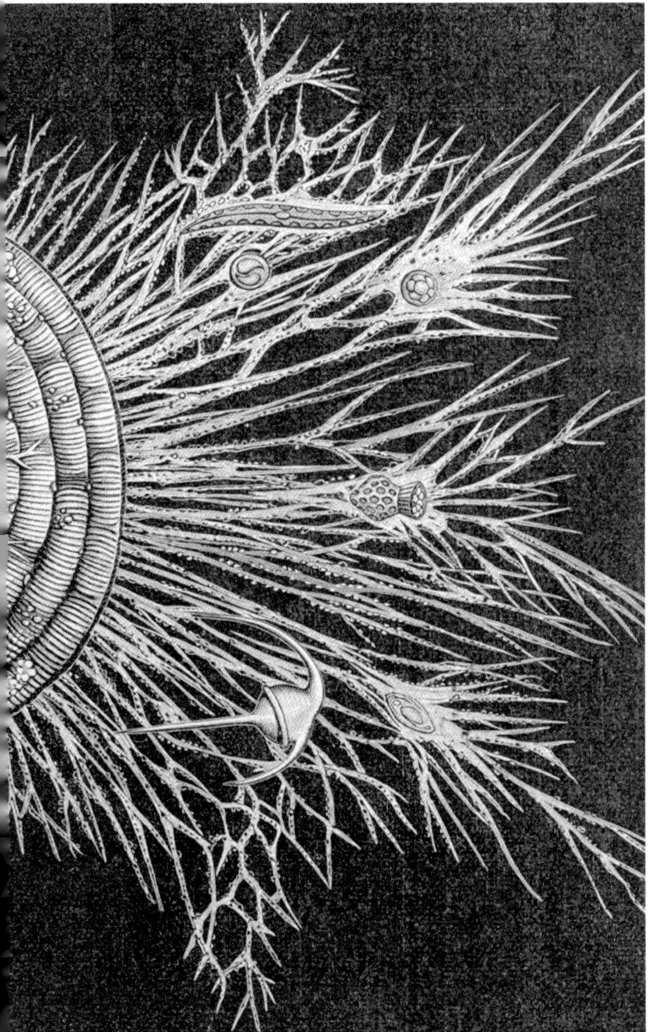

"From the soul's depths it
pushes to the light, /
and lies before us like
a garden, /
where magic blossoms
of imagination /
bloom thousandfold
in beauty and in
splendor – /
'tis wonderful to wander
in their glory! /
... as blow the winds of
spring and new life /
sprouts afresh and surges
to the light! /
Our age, too, desires a
language /
to give its longing a new
form – / ...
It storms and thrusts
ahead on every side! /
Clear the way! ..."
J. Avaris: "To the Old and
the Young!"

Rhizopod forms
Erich Haeckel
1906
Woodcut from *Der Mensch und die Erde* (Man and the Earth), ed. H. Kraemer

Loïe Fuller – Art Nouveau Dancer

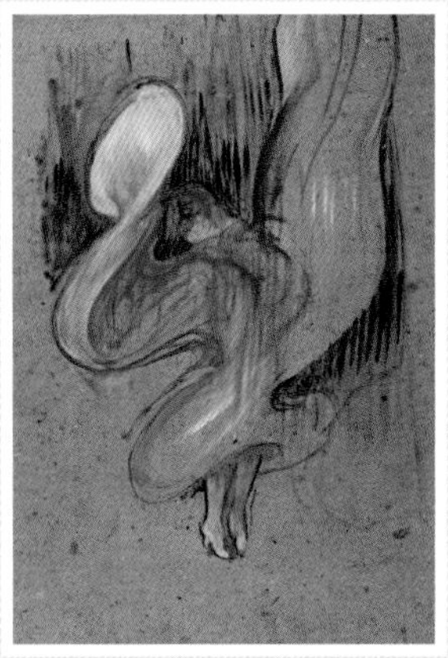

Henri Toulouse-Lautrec
Loïe Fuller aux Folies Bergère
1891/92, black chalk and oil on board
(study for a color lithograph)
63.2 × 45.3 cm
Musée Toulouse-Lautrec, Albi

"It's a butterfly – a butterfly" was the reported reaction of spectators to one of the first performances by the American dancer Loïe Fuller. This spontaneous outburst of enthusiasm shows how skillfully she stage-managed her performances in order to cast a spell on her audience.

The remarkably large number of works of art that took Loïe Fuller and her dancing as their motif demonstrates what a great inspiration she was for Art Nouveau. In 1893, using the complex process known as iris printing, a fascinating series of lithographs was published in which Henri Toulouse-Lautrec attempted to capture the Loïe Fuller's characteristic appearance. By introducing delicate gradations of color to the prints, he achieved a congenial interpretation of her performances. Here, as so often, he seems to have been an attentive observer behind the scenes. However, he never gained an official commission to produce a poster for Fuller. A poster by Jules Chéret, with a certain lively sweetness but artistically less interesting than those of Toulouse-Lautrec, announced Loïe Fuller's appearance at the Folies Bergère in the fashionable contemporary style.

She Came, She Danced, She Conquered

Loïe Fuller, whose real name was Marie Louise Fuller, came to Europe in 1892 and showed the Parisians a dance that she had invented a few years earlier: the "serpentine dance." She adopted the idea of moving fabrics from other dances such as the "skirt dance," a precursor of the cancan, and developed it. Fuller devised a number of tricks to accentuate the eccentric movements of her performance: the stage was hung with black curtains and black velvet laid on the floor to provide a perfect backdrop for her dance, which she illuminated with cold-light spots and – the latest fashion – electric lamps.

"La Loïe" or the "electric fairy," as she was also called, was a most remarkable person, whose stage performances and dance should be regarded as more than a contribution to modern choreography: they were an aspect of the artistic avant-garde of the time. The poet Mallarmé gives a close-up view of "La Loïe" in a poetic description that lives up to her style of dance: "Radiant and cold, the dancer disappears in a formidable bath of fabric, throws light on many a swirling theme, from which she makes a wide-spun web bloom: a petal and a butterfly, both gigantic, raging surf, but clearly and perceptibly ordered throughout. Her rapid, melting transitions set free phantasmagorical explosive gases from twilight and the grotto – like a swift change of

Paul Rieth
Isadora Duncan's Dance School in Berlin
1904, drawing for *Jugend* no. 48
Archiv für Kunst und Geschichte, Berlin

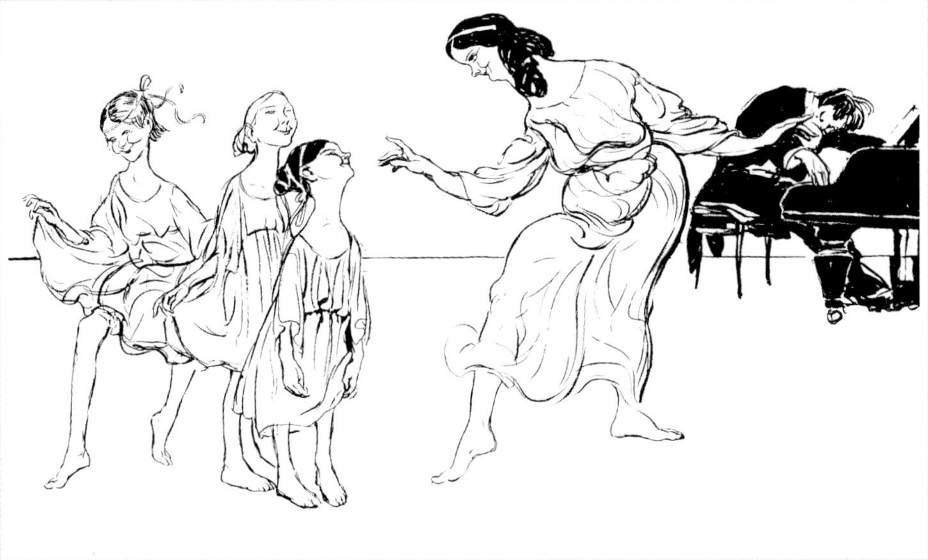

Raoul Larche
The Dancer Loïe Fuller, sculpture (table lamp), 1900, bronze, fire gilt, height 45 cm
Staatliche Kunstsammlungen, Kassel

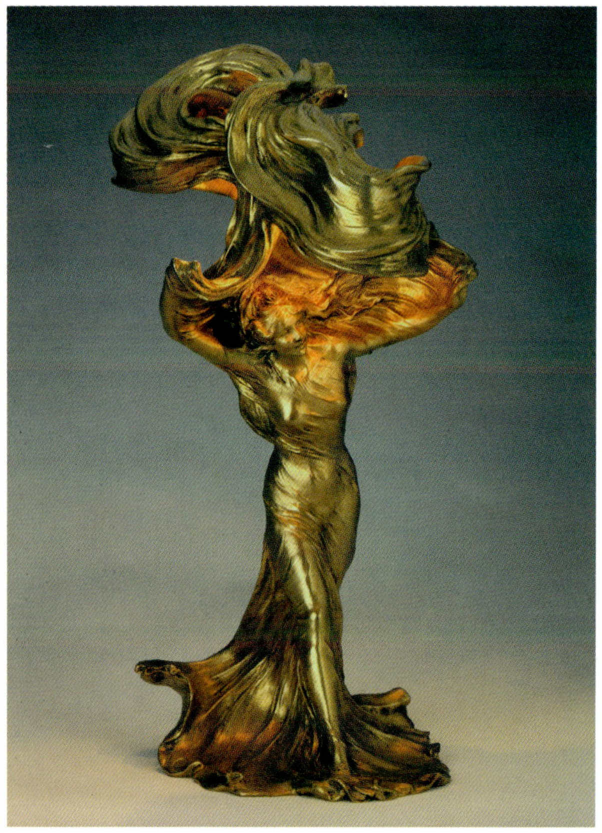

passions, joy – grief – anger: to transport them, violent or faded, into a play of prisms requires the turbulence of a soul brought into the open as if by sleight of hand."

New Departures in Choreography

Loïe Fuller developed her choreography from a variety of dances: the serpentine, the violet and the butterfly dance, the white dance, the fire dance, the lily. The names alone of these dances conveyed a clear message and matched perfectly the formal canon of the time.

The fire dance, in which by means of lighting she appeared to be standing in an all-consuming flame, is said to have been especially impressive. Her robes of thin silk were unbelievably delicate, and in places more diaphanous than opaque. Nevertheless the erotic flirtation of other varieté performers was not Fuller´s métier.

She concentrated on the artistic expressiveness of lengths of fabric which she twirled high into the air by means of long batons that were attached to the ends of her sleeves. By elaborately painting the fabrics with snake motifs and abstract decoration she later integrated them even more closely into her performances.

American woman dancers had a decisive influence on the evolution of modern dance in the period around 1900. The outstanding figure was Isadora Duncan, the pioneer of expressive dance, which she began to develop in deliberate contrast to the strictly controlled movements of classical ballet. Duncan modeled her dance on that of ancient times, wore appropriate costume and danced barefoot, which was then seen as something of a sensation. After this it was Mary Wigman who adopted the new free style and made it into expressionist dance. Thanks to Wigman's friendships with artists of her era, in her case too there was a fascinating interaction between dance and the fine arts.

Success at the World Exhibition

To return to Loïe Fuller: whereas Duncan's performances were based on dances of ancient times and Wigman developed a combination of free gymnastics and bodily movement, Fuller's style of dance was characterized by lyrical lightness. She also set new standards in technical matters. The experiments that she performed with different kinds of template, etched plates of glass and other materials, in order to impart a structure to light, deserve great admiration. Her theme was living, colored and manipulated light, and here she was at the forefront in an age that marveled at the wonder of electricity. For all the courage that she demonstrated in this work, if she had known how dangerous it was to use radium and that the bright, gaudy light would later cause permanent damage to her eyes, she would surely not have achieved such remarkable results. Her theatre, which served simultaneously as a sort of "Loïe Fuller Museum," was a triumph at the world exhibition of 1900. The pavilion was decorated with a plaster relief that seemed to freeze one of her dancing fabrics. It was a masterly presentation of her dance and her technical stage effects. Interestingly, this did not satisfy her. She enhanced her program with performances by dancers from Japanese Nô theatre, thus supplying further proof of her avant-garde atti-

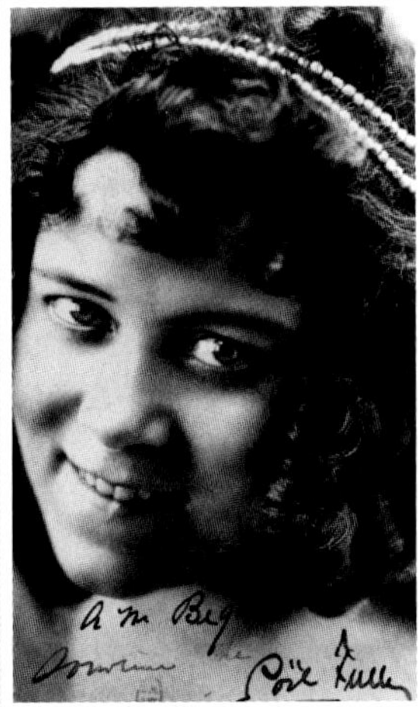

Loïe Fuller
Photo with signed dedication
Probably 1900
Bibliothèque Nationale, Paris

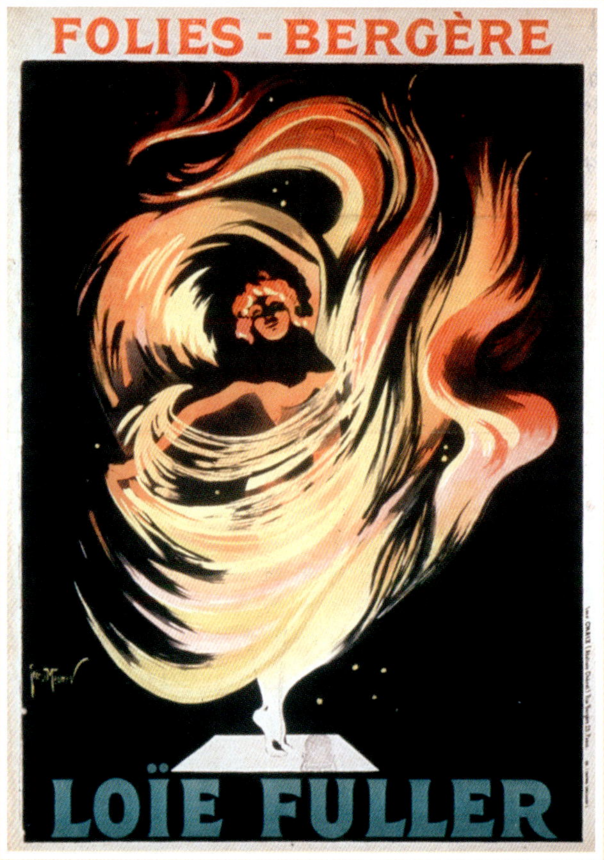

Georges Meunier
Folies Bergère – Loïe Fuller
c. 1900, color lithograph
for a poster
Musée de la Publicité, Paris

tude: the influence of Japonisme extended to the field of dance.

Loïe Fuller and the Avant-Garde

Loïe Fuller had close friendships with many leading intellectual figures of her day. Rodin was among them, and his pupil Raoul Larche made the legendary "Loïe Fuller lamp": it caused a sensation by illuminating three different sculptures to create a living interpretation of a dance. The lamps, of which only a few were produced, quickly became highly sought-after items of modern interior design and represent a highlight of the new artistic style.

"La Loïe" was first and foremost a dancer, but she was innovative not only in this field and that of stage effects. She is also seen as an extremely interesting pioneer of the new medium of film. The close friendship that Fuller maintained to the queen of Romania resulted in two films based on fairy tales written by the queen under the pseudonym Carmen Sylva. In

1919, in collaboration with her long-time companion Gab, Fuller realized a film project under the title *Le Lys de la vie,* for which she was primarily responsible for the sets and requisites.

Two things show how modern this goddess of the dance was in planning and furthering her career. Firstly, she created her own myth by writing *Fifteen Years of a Dancer's Life.* She shrouded her own biography, and especially the details of her costumes, in mystery, which of course enormously enhanced the aura that she projected of being an extraordinary person. Secondly, she proved to be an astute businesswoman who at an early stage had the idea of patenting her stage equipment and also her choreographic ideas. This was by no means an exaggerated course of action, as many imitators appeared shortly after her first performance in Paris. None of them, however, lived up to the original.

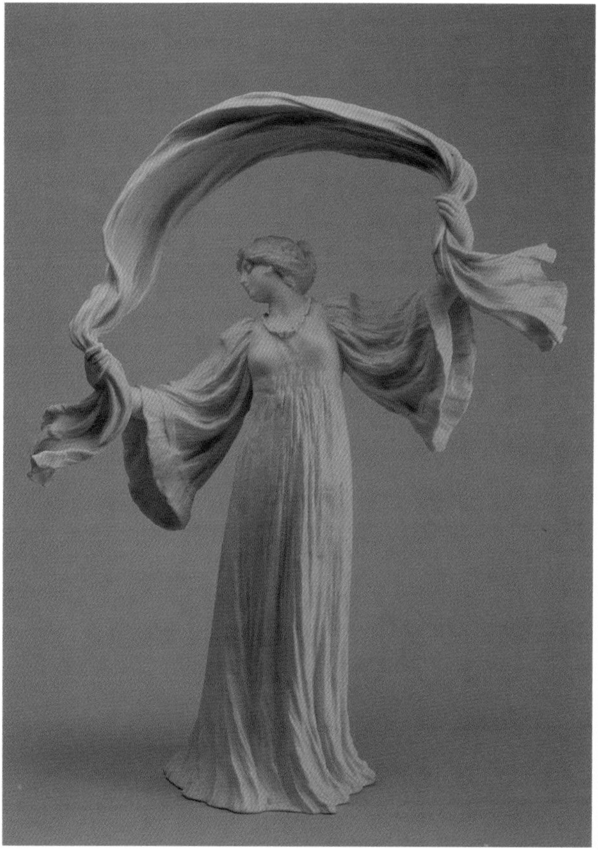

Agathon Leonard
Dancer, part of a service from Sevres
1900, biscuit porcelain
Eremitage, St Petersburg

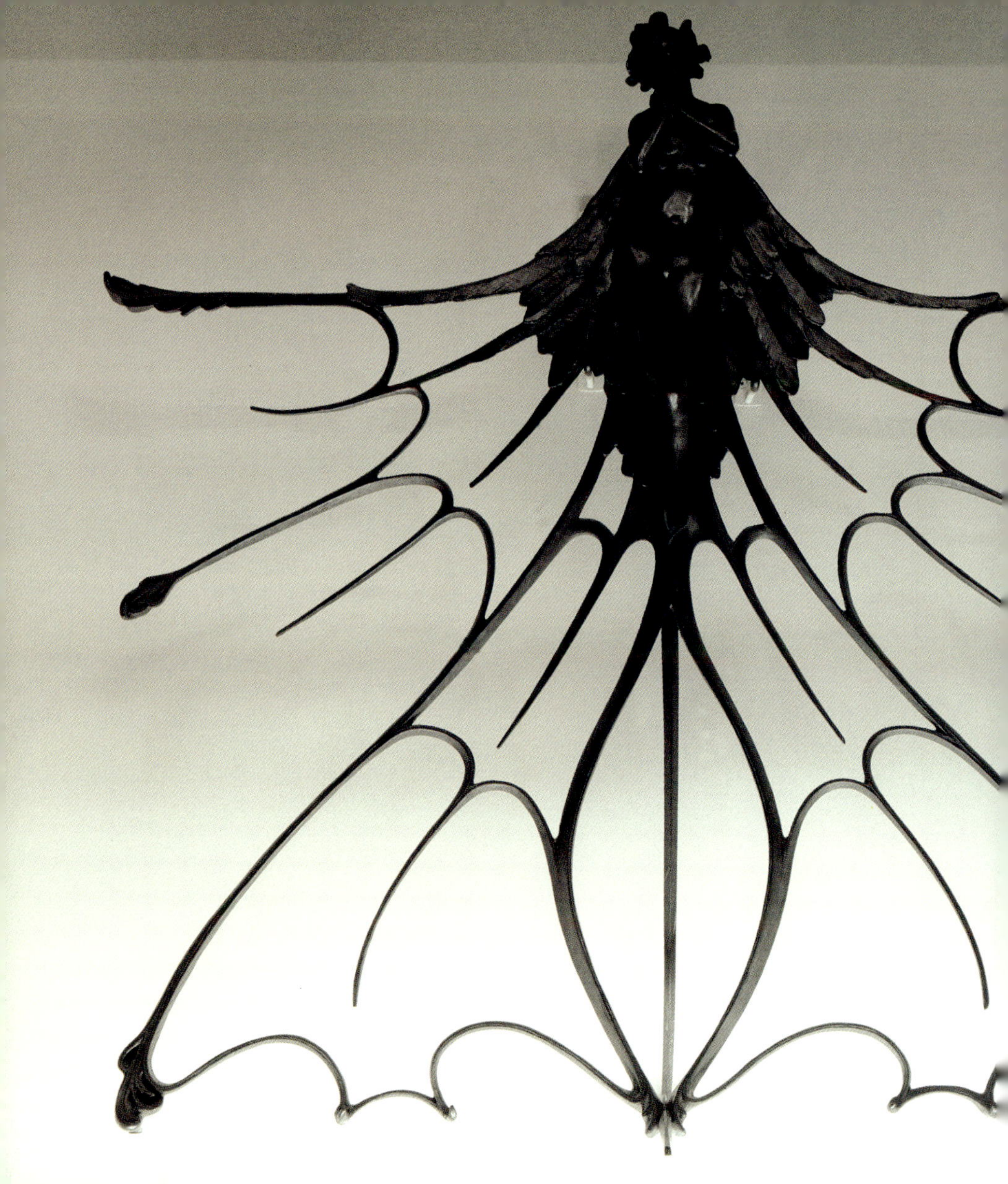

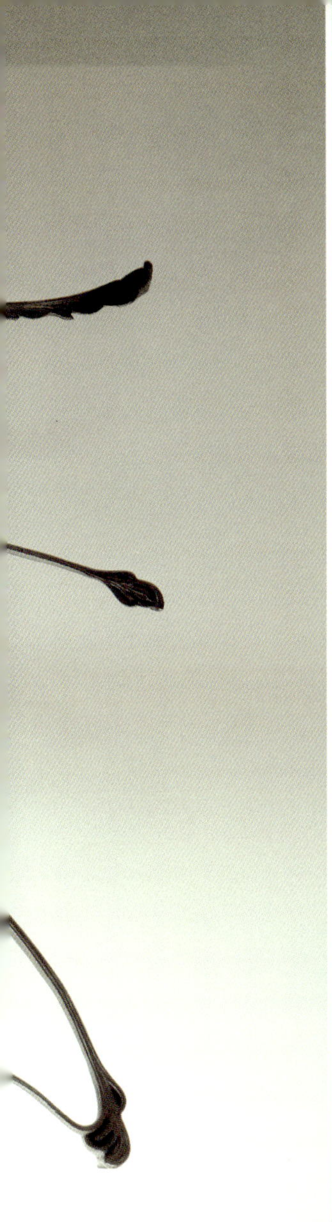

Kiss of the Dragonfly Woman

René Lalique and the Art of Modern Jewelry

“Tout Paris” was in raptures – over jewelry that did not even include expensive diamonds and the most precious metals. Instead these pieces used surprising, unusual materials or displayed ivory and semi-precious stones. At the turn of the century René Lalique broadened artistic horizons with regard to materials for the jeweler’s art by employing such exotic items as tortoiseshell and horn or technical subtleties such as enamel work. This is why the great master Émile Gallé described him as the inventor of modern jewelry. In further developing the art of glasswork, Lalique followed Gallé’s success as a pioneering glass designer and reinforced the reputation of France as a nation of glassmakers by introducing new processes.

René Jules Lalique
Bronze lattice with a female figure
1900, chased bronze with patina,
height 99 cm
SMPK, Kunstgewerbemuseum, Berlin

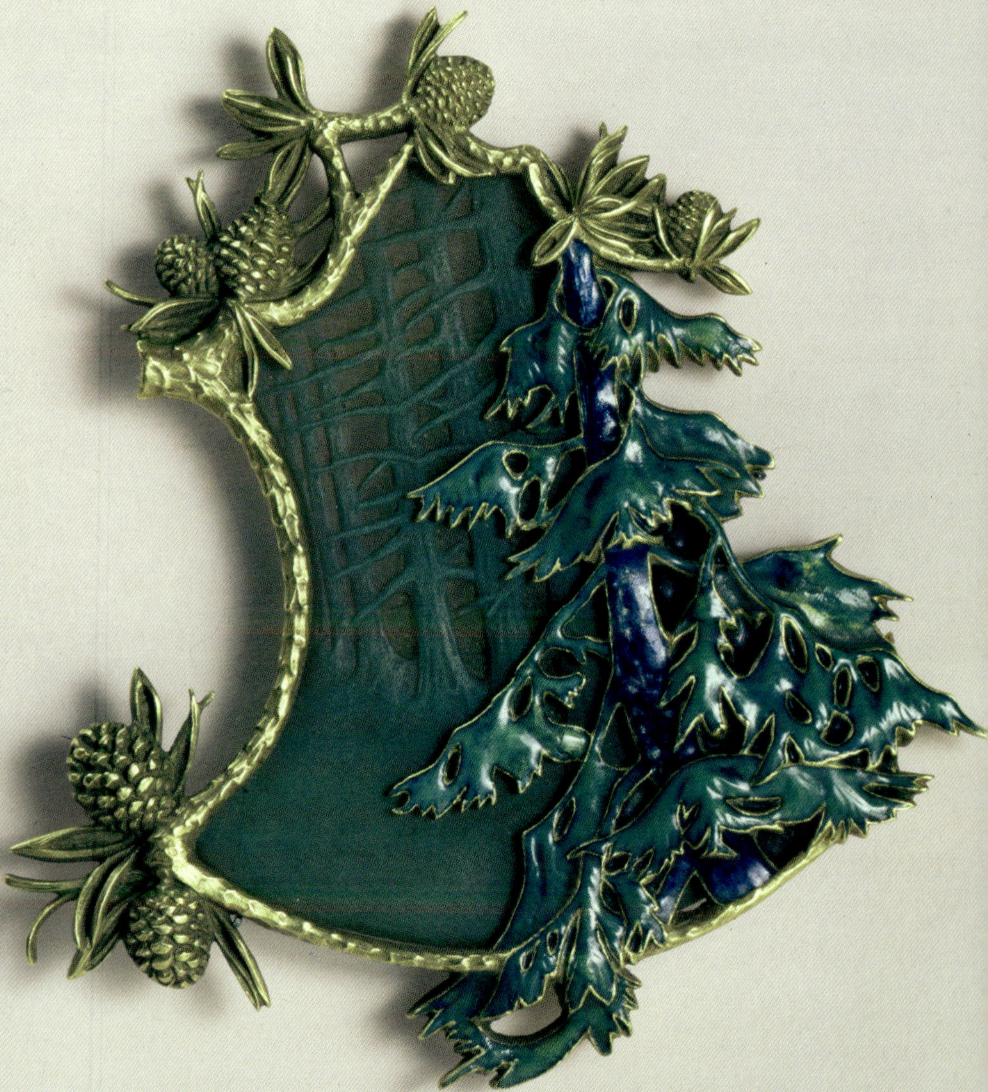

Humans, Animals, Sensations

What a triumph for the new art! Acclamation of the applied arts was founded on the craving for ever new sensations, which were theatrically presented at the great exhibitions as the public had come to expect. An iron lattice of hybrid creatures, half dragonfly and half human, framed the precious exhibits; fabric draped above it depicted a heaven of twinkling stars to which scarily beautiful bats had been added. At a time when the public taste demanded decadence, this was right on target, and drew crowds of people to the showcase at the world exhibition of 1900. However, the true fascination lay in the exhibits themselves, items of jewelry like little sculptures that took the viewer into another world of mystic hybrid creatures and imaginary plants.

The creator of these fairy tales in jewelry was René Lalique from the Champagne region. His extraordinary talent for drawing was noticed at an early age. Despite the early death of his father, Lalique took plenty of time over his apprenticeship. He spent two years training in London alone, where the products of Arts and Crafts designers impressed him. The drawings that he made in his early years for Parisian jewelers such as Cartier exhibit the close-

René Jules Lalique
Brooch with winter landscape
1900/01, gold, glass and enamel
Eremitage, St Petersburg

René Jules Lalique
Comb
Museum Calouste Gulbenkian, Lisbon

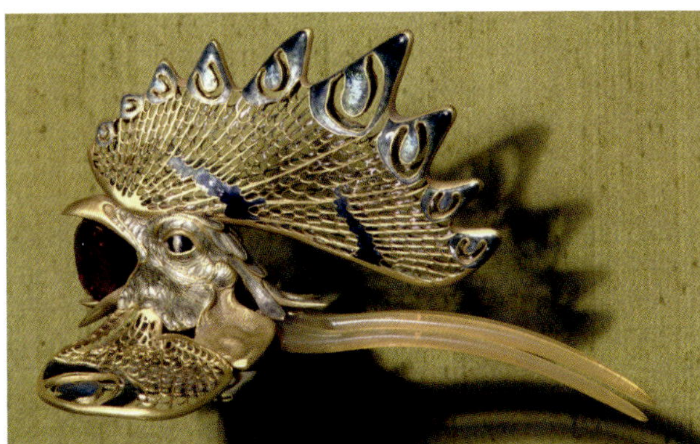

ness to nature of his English models. Lalique's attitude to design was heavily influenced by his studies at the École Bernard Palissy in Paris: many of his later designs are reminiscent of the lifelike animals and plants on 17th-century festive platters. In 1884 Lalique went into partnership with the jeweler Varenne, but was not truly content until his takeover of a jeweler's atelier enabled him to produce his own jewelry.

In 1895 he opened his own shop, and in the same year made an impression with a piece that was decorated with a naked woman. This was something completely new, and from then on mythological interpretations of the female figure became his trademark. René Lalique specialized in "petites choses charmantes," which became genuine masterpieces in his hands.

René Jules Lalique

1860 – 1945

1860 Birth of René Lalique, son of a sales representative

1872 Apprenticeship; first as a draughtsman, later as a goldsmith at the École des Arts Décoratifs in Paris

1876 Lalique's father dies

1878 Lives in London (until 1880)

1884 Foundation of Lalique et Varenne

1885 Acquires the workshop of a Parisian jeweler

1894 Bing sells work by Lalique; commissions from Sarah Bernhardt

1905 Opening of a shop on Place Vendôme

1907 Takes over a glassworks in Combs-la-Ville near Paris

1909 First designs for perfume bottles

1914 Production of glass vessels for hospitals and pharmaceutical applications (until 1918)

1918 Glass factory: Verrerie d'Alsace René Lalique & Cie. in Wingen-sur-Moder; serial production of pressed glass objects

1928 Commission to design the dining car of the Orient Express

1945 René Lalique dies on 5 May

The Charm of Nature

One of Lalique's special inventions was the "femme fleure," a combination of a flower and a female figure whose delicate limbs and translucent body were the perfect inspiration for the jeweler's new creative ideas. A certain morbid touch that resulted from a hybrid spider or dragonfly creature fitted the era perfectly, of course. Indeed the idea of illusion provided by a true-to-life replica of an insect that crawled through a lady's decolleté and was

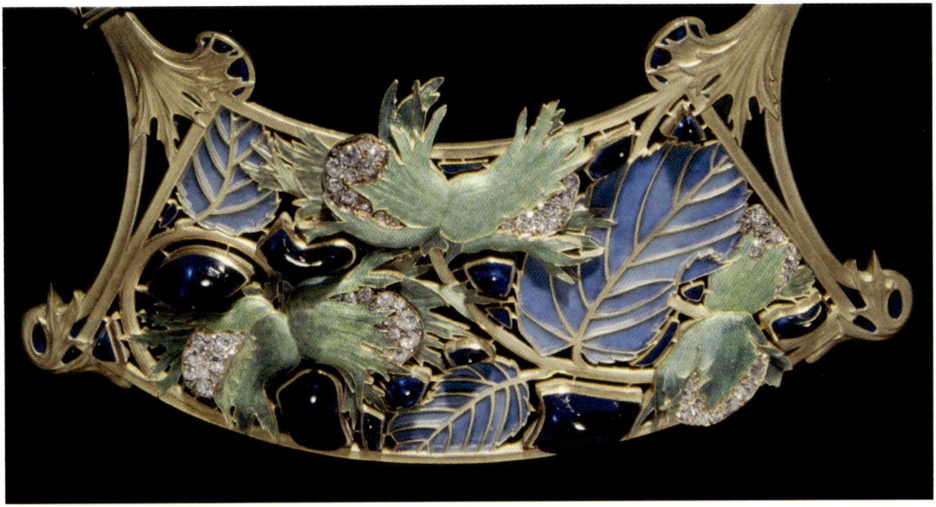

crowned by extravagant diadems was the *dernier cri* in the age of decadence. And it was René Lalique who, quite literally, made the diadem blossom once more. Originally serving as insignia to show the sovereignty of the few, it now conquered everything in its path, becoming an essential constituent of fashionable evening dress. A mermaid diadem incorporating an enormous opal was probably the most extravagant item that Lalique ever made.

A winter landscape of glistening snow; the last rays of the sun on the branches of a fir tree: these were the impressions that Lalique put into material form in the best of his jewelry. In doing so he demonstrated that he was a true master of his craft, who could combine not only gold and diamonds but also glass and semi-precious stones into a single piece that compelled admiration. He was fascinated by the Japanese view of nature, which stylized the beauty and chance effects of landscape to form magnificent images.

René Jules Lalique
Noisette necklace (detail)
1900, gold, translucent enamel, diamond
Musée des Arts Décoratifs, Paris

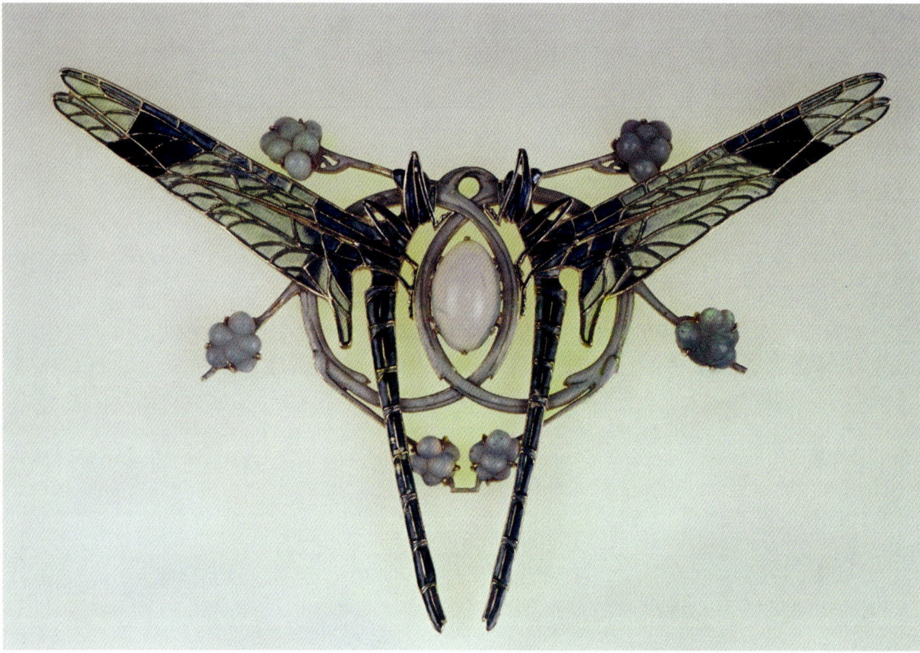

René Jules Lalique
Hairpin
Private collection

Lalique pursued this idea by creating jewelry that depicted miniature landscape scenes. His models for this were undoubtedly works in the style of the Japanese woodcut artist Utamaro, whose prints hung in his atelier.

Collectors and Admirers

After impressing Paris at the world exhibition of 1900, Lalique set out in 1904 to conquer the New World. The world exhibition in St Louis brought him a resounding success and the custom of numerous wealthy American collectors. On his stand he not only presented jewelry in glass cases, but also demonstrated its production in a kind of show. Here it is clear how his fascination with craftsmanship impacted on his work.

His most passionate admirers included the divine Sarah Bernhardt, the dandy par excellence Count Robert de Montesquiou and, above all, the oil millionaire Calouste Gulbenkian. Gulbenkian not only bought Lalique's exquisite pieces and placed them in showcases in his home; his precise instructions also played an instrumental part in many extravagant inventions. He was of Indian descent, and it is easy to imagine that Lalique's masterpieces reminded him of the treasure chambers of Indian maharajas. The most spectacular result of this association between collector and artist was probably the brooch of a dragonfly woman whose delicate, elf-like body seems to be caught in the claws of a dragon.

Lalique met his patron through Sarah Bernhardt, one of the greatest stars of the *belle époque*. She liked to underpin her image as a woman with an extravagant nature by means of eye-catching activities. She would, for example, take a fully grown panther for a walk along the street, and showed herself to the public in other ostentatious poses. She was a true *"princesse des gestes"*! Who could be surprised to learn that she was one of the best friends of René Lalique, who ardently admired her and profited from stage jewelry that assisted Bernhardt in her dramatic performances. Subsequently society ladies were pleased to be photographed wearing items by Lalique, some of which were extremely lavish.

Decadent luxury for fashionable ladies! Opulence and ostentation were the order of the day, and ladies adorned themselves like princesses with the delicate creations of Lalique, the king of jewelry. The diaphanous enamel dragonfly wings with which Lalique added naturalistic decoration to many items are particularly dainty.

Old and New Techniques

In producing to his own designs from 1895, René Lalique had always endeavored to introduce new techniques to the creation of jewelry. His own workshop, which was adorned with fresh flowers at all times, served as a kind of laboratory in which he could experiment with new materials. He tried

Next double page:
René Jules Lalique
Dragonfly diadem (detail)
1900, gold, diamonds, emeralds, aquamarine
Width 13 cm
Private collection

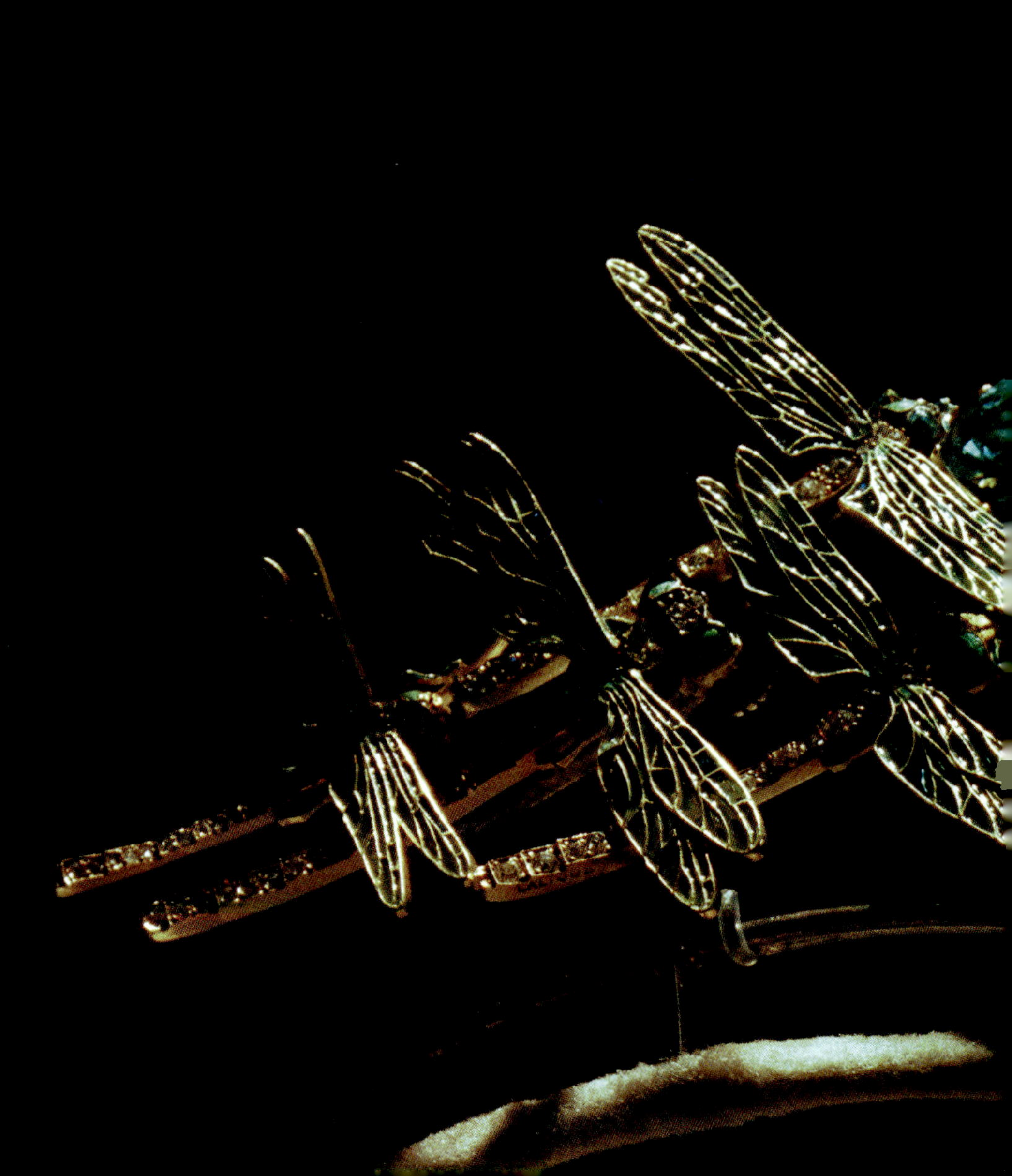

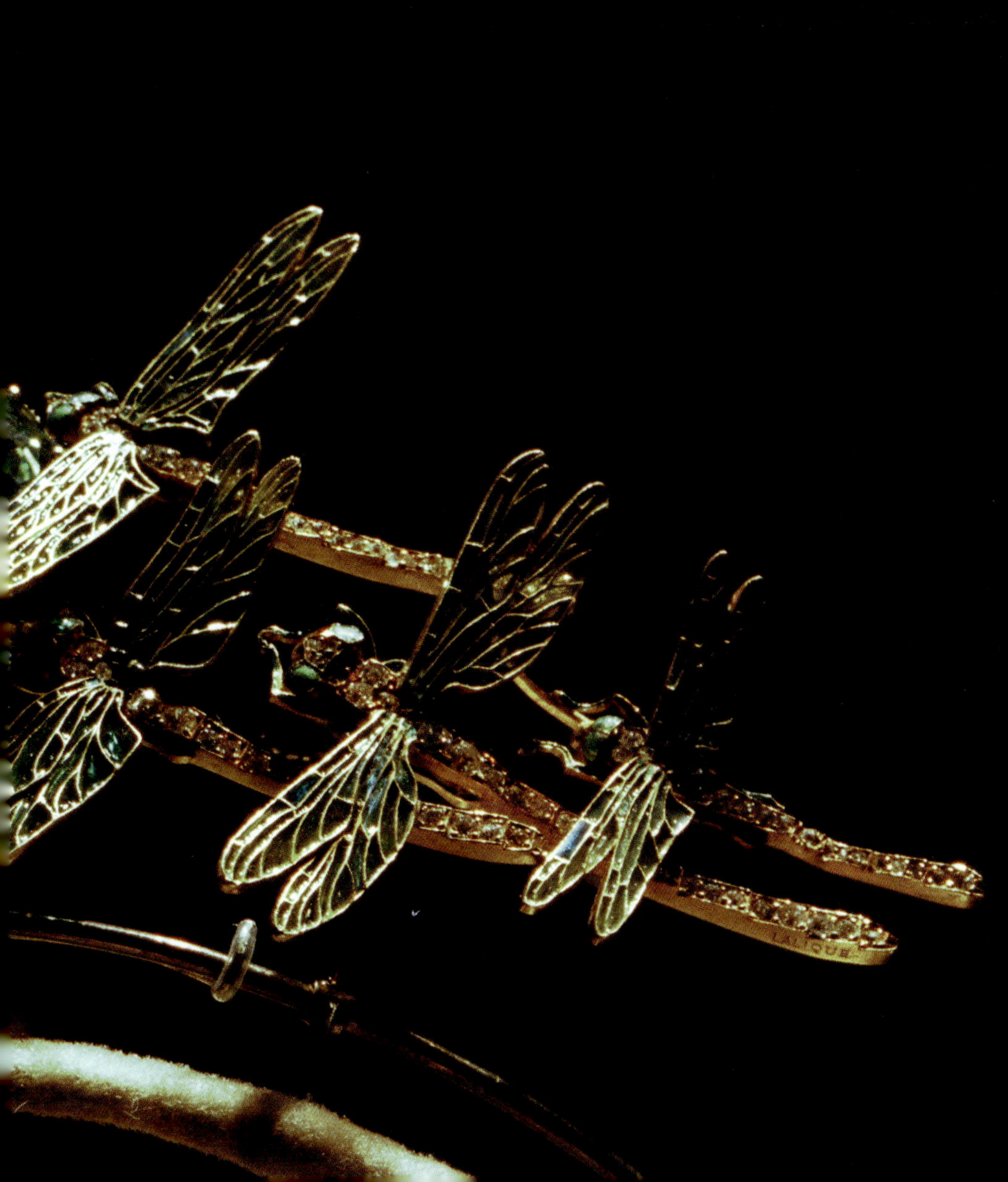
LALIQUE

to file horn and cover it with an iridescent skin in order to lend it an even more mysterious aura. He tried out different versions of the technique of enameling, which had fallen into neglect. The so-called plique-a-jour enamel with which he decorated the gossamer wings of his numerous dragonfly figures was incredibly delicate. In the hands of Lalique molten gold, too, became living matter that flowed over his pieces. From his father-in-law and brother-in-law, who were sculptors, he had learned the technique of "tour à réduire," by means of which he could scale down large models into extremely small miniatures. In this way he set new standards for the jeweler's art.

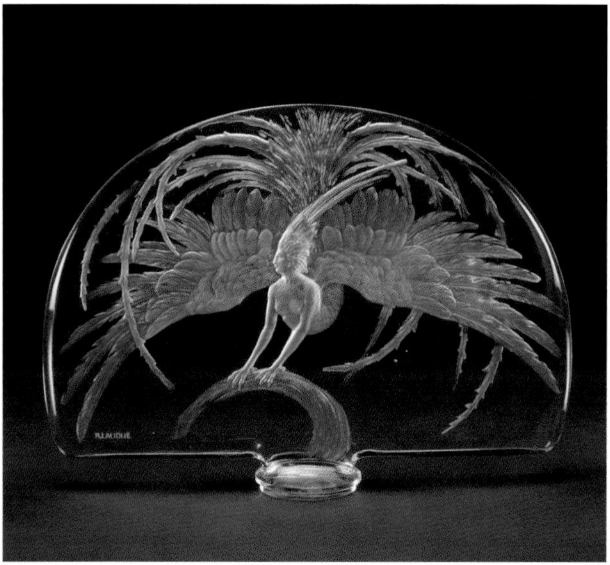

René Jules Lalique
Firebird centerpiece
1923, cut glass
Height 32 cm
Private collection

It is understandable that Lalique's works, which were made by such elaborate means, were usually unique items. The insistent demand that resulted from a veritable cult for Lalique was satisfied by numerous imitators, a fact that probably induced Lalique himself to turn his attention to working with glass. At the age of almost 50 he started a new career and devoted all his energy to gaining experience with the new material. The death of his wife, whom he loved above all else, in 1909 may have been a reason why he took the radical step of turning his back on the production of appealing jewelry. With remarkable zeal, Lalique dedicated himself to trying out processes such as lost-wax casting. In the goldsmiths' guilds of previous centuries this technique was taken for granted, but it had become a forgotten skill: to make a mould by placing a second layer, made of wax, around a core, covering it and hardening both the core and the outer covering in a kiln, while the wax melted and flowed out through narrow channels. In this way finely worked glass objects could be produced on which every detail was formed in relief.

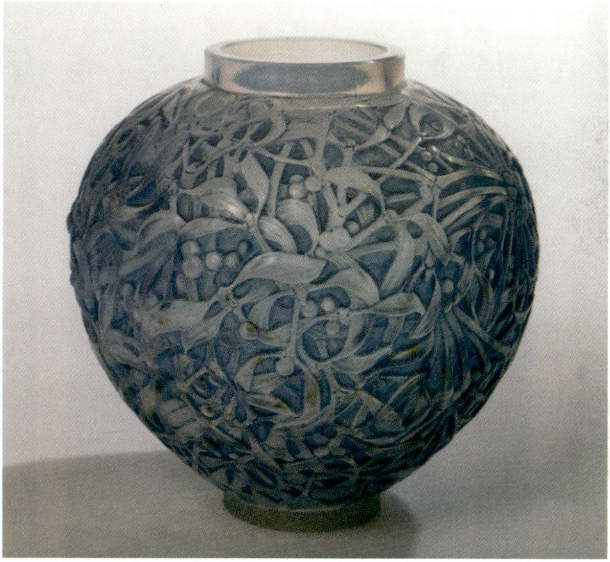

René Jules Lalique
Mistletoe vase
1920, blue patina on opal glass
Private collection

Success with Glass

Lalique displayed glass objects for the first time in 1905, when he opened his shop on Place Vendôme. Lalique's involvement with this fragile material received a new impulse when he opened a small factory near Paris in 1907. Here he could carry out chemical experiments, and he indeed succeeded in inventing a special kind of glass which was bright, crystalline and transparent. The chemical composition of his glass was the critical factor, and later he was the first artist in glass to develop a product that was truly black. In 1912, when he exhibited his wonderful glass items for the first time, he attracted the attention of the perfumer François Coty. Until then Coty had sold his exclusive perfumes in crystal bottles that cost a fortune and were extremely laborious to manufacture. He now gave a commission to design a perfume bottle to Lalique, who was delighted to comply. The external details of the bottle referred to the nature of what was inside – an artistic freedom that was not possible before the new techniques of glass production were developed. In an age when society liked to express itself by means of luxury, René Lalique's items suited the purpose, like the magnificent objects of the late Renaissance. Those who could afford to do so took pleasure in showing the wonderful artistic items that they possessed, and to own a work by Lalique was the ultimate luxury. Again and again he found new ideas for designs in glass, and his crowning achievement was to represent architectural concepts in glass. Colored glass played an increasingly important role in his late works. Lalique produced astounding designs with abstract plant patterns cut into a frosted surface. To this day collectors of his work have no peace of mind until they own one of these gems. He also designed the dining car of the Orient Express and, with what had meanwhile become a sizeable team including his son Marc, supplied 27 hood ornaments for automobile manufacturers such as Citroën.

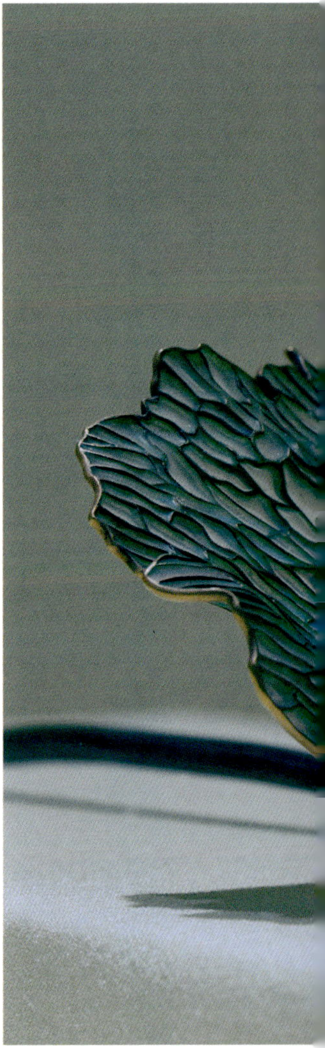

René Jules Lalique
Hairpin
1897, gold, silver, diamonds,
cloisonné and plique-a-jour enamel
Height 7.5 cm, width 10.5 cm,
length 23.5 cm
Musée d'Orsay, Paris

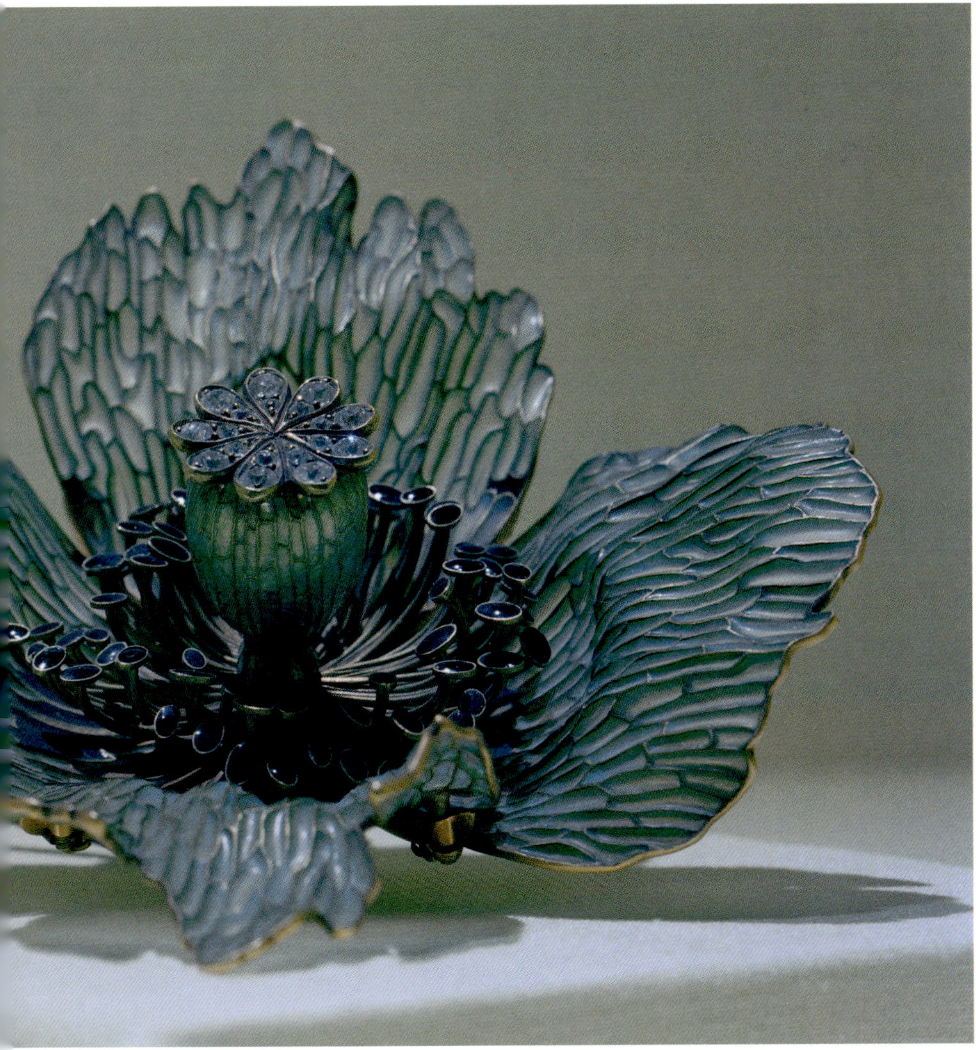

Femme Fatale – Erotic Art Nouveau

Gustav Klimt
Salome or *Judith II*
1909, oil on canvas
178 × 46 cm
Galleria Internazionale d'Arte Moderna, Venice

Dark eyes cast a melancholy look at the viewer, the classical profile is finely drawn, and a cascade of curly locks frames a pale face: "woman" par excellence, the projection of an ideal image. The contrast to this is the dangerous woman, an interpretation of the female image which owed much to the spirit of the times and became nothing less than a cult: an outbreak of "*femme fatale*" fever! Demonic women gazed at the viewer on all sides.

It cannot be a coincidence that the decadent image of the

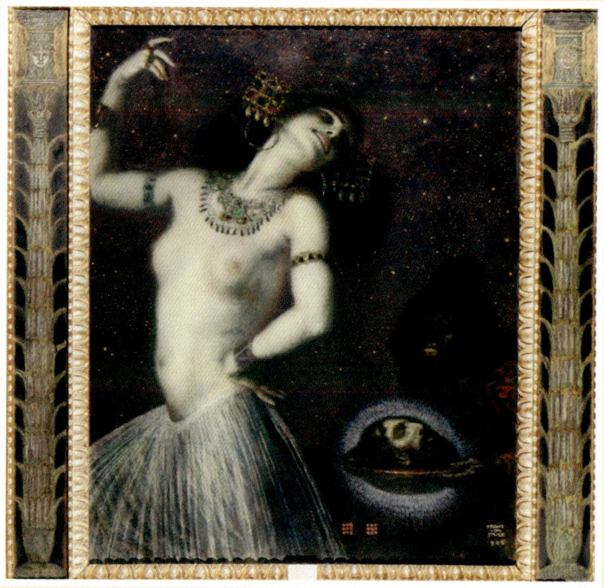

Franz von Stuck
Salome
1906, oil on canvas
115.5 × 62.5 cm
Städtische Galerie im Lenbachhaus, Munich

femme fatale reached its apogee in the art and literature of the late 19th century. With her counterpart, the *femme fragile,* the *femme fatale* filled the paintings and pages of the turn of the century, and seemed to feel thoroughly at home in the atmosphere of the *fin de siècle* with its luxurious salons and *belle époque* jewelry. This era has an aura of the mystic and magical, which in combination with an air of decay seemed to generate a strangely black and heavy mood. At the same time it is an age characterized by a shift in values, as far as the family and attitudes to roles are concerned, and by the emergence of female emancipation. The spirit of psychoanalysis, which attempted to reduce every aspect of life to one single factor, the libido, was in the air. The relationship between men and women had been disturbed, producing strange and exotic fantasies.

Strong Women

Not only the fine arts, but real life, too, witnesses the emergence of women who can be regarded as the epitome of the *femme fatale:* Lou Andreas-Salomé, for example. The name alone of this writer, psychoanalyst and feminist evokes the idea of a man-eating intellectual, whose life story was spiced by her close relationships to such great thinkers as Nietzsche, Freud and Rilke. An interpretation of the *Mona Lisa* that now appears almost grotesque shows how edgy the mood between the sexes must have been at the *fin de siècle* and how deeply it influenced attitudes to art in that era: the poet Théophile Gautier described the Mona Lisa's smile as an expression of uncomfortable lust combined with the knowledge of its disastrous consequences.

Salome and Sphinx

There is a noticeably frequent occurrence of motifs like Salome and the Sphinx, female figures that leave the observer torn between fascination and horror. In the prudish atmosphere of the Victorian period these lascivious portrayals of women had a special power to excite and stimulate. Salome, the biblical figure whose arts of

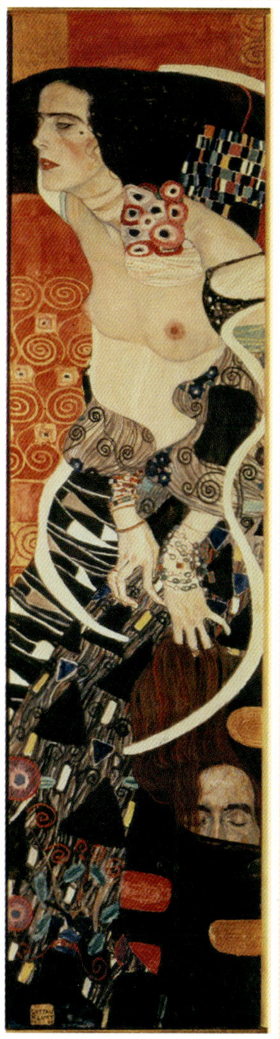

seduction brought about the death of John the Baptist, was depicted by artists such as Klimt and Stuck as the archetypal "malevolent woman." The pure sensuality of the female bodies that were depicted, often enhanced with gold and jewels, was justified as being a rendering of a morally edifying story from the Bible. The fact that a painting could both be erotic and depict death made it a perfect subject for the appreciation of art in a decadent era.

LULU – The Literary *Femme Fatale*

LULU, in a morning dress of green silk, stands motionless in front of the mirror, furrows her brow, strokes it with her hand, feels her cheeks, parts from the mirror with a discontented, half-angry look, moves to the right, turning round several times, opens a casket on the desk, lights a cigarette, (…), lies down on the chaise longue, opposite the mirror, (…).

SCHWARZ: (…) Every day I feel as if I am seeing you for the very first time.

LULU: You are dreadful.

SCHWARZ sinks to his knees in front of the chaise longue: (…) It is your fault.

LULU, stroking his hair: You are wasting me.

SCHWARZ: But you are mine. (…) Now that I have you, I have nothing else – I have lost myself altogether …

LULU: Try to be calmer.

Excerpt from: F. Wedekind, *Earth Spirit*, 1895 – Act I – Scene I

The effect of Franz von Stuck's painting is heightened by his portrayal of a dance, which is a symbol for a state of intoxication. Stuck was interested in the battle of the sexes as part of the human condition, and illustrated the theme in a variety of motifs.

For artists and poets, the mythological Sphinx figure represented a new facet of the theme of the sexes. No-one brought this creature to life more strikingly than the Belgian Fernand Khnopff, who was known for his leanings towards the occult. He also loved the androgynous type of woman, a trait that derived from his sister Marguerite. He drew attention to the cat-like nature of the Sphinx, here mingled with the exotic sensuality of a leopard. The Sphinx nestles up close, shows tenderness by closing her eyes, and is about to give the boy a passionate kiss. However, this kiss, this seduction will not lead to consummation, as the Sphinx is not human below her neck and normal sexual love is impossible. The man who falls in love

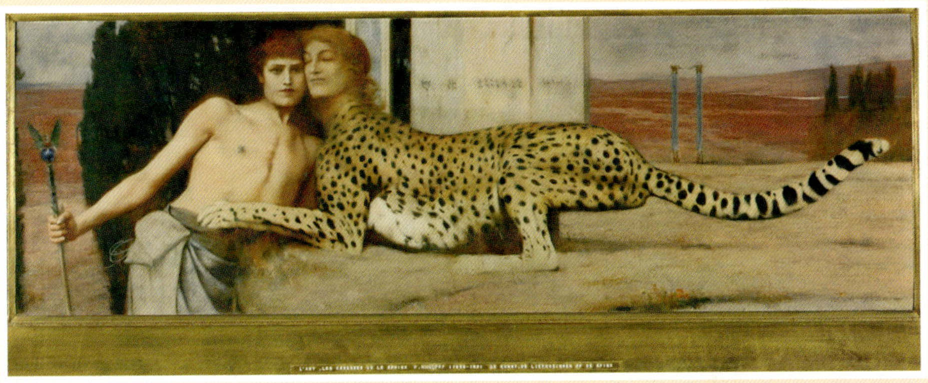

with such a woman is lost: she cannot return his love. Oscar Wilde took up this theme in his short story *The Sphinx without a Secret*. Franz von Stuck even succeeded in conveying this characteristic of the Sphinx in psychological terms solely through the posture of the naked woman, without needing to portray her hybrid nature.

Franz von Stuck and Women

The role of woman as *femme fatale* is, however, most obvious in the works that Franz von Stuck painted from 1893. Again and again he returned to the subject of "sin". His *femme fatale* presents her white body in suggestive contrast to the dark background and intensifies the mood of animal desire by wearing a fur stole. The evil eyes of the dangerous serpent flash out of the darkness. Franz von Stuck's extremely daring combination of woman and snake, which could hardly be depicted as a phallic symbol more explicitly than in the version he painted in 1895, presents the erotic and provocative nature of this biblical theme of seduction. Heeding the voyeuristic tendencies of the public, he staged his *Sin* in an altar-like setting in his villa, an ensemble designed as the residence of a prince of the arts. Stuck was clearly fascinated by the erotic appeal of this subject, and in

Fernand Khnopff
The Sphinx or *Caresses*
1896, oil on canvas
50.5 × 150 cm
Musées Royaux des Beaux-Arts, Brussels

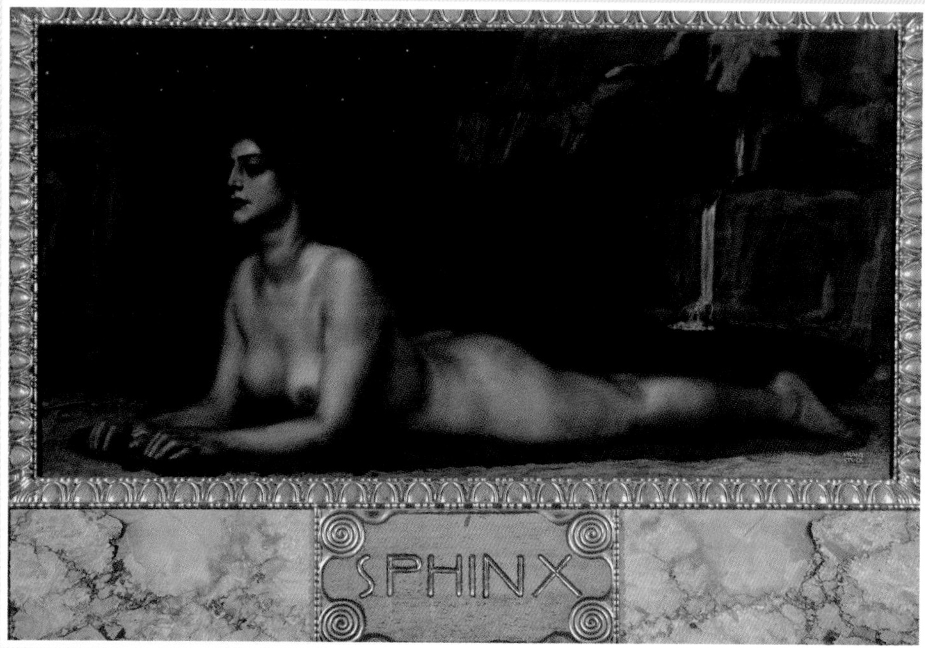

Franz von Stuck
Sphinx
1904, oil on canvas
83 × 156.5 cm
Hessisches Landesmuseum, Darmstadt

later portrayals he dispensed with its justification as being a biblical scene, now depicting pure sensuality.

The Taste of the Era

In a period when the dominant moral values meant a restrictive attitude towards erotic themes and the subject of lust, fantasy appeared to take flight. The senses were positively "humidified," as Stefan Zweig fittingly put it. In his description of the *femme fatale,* Charles Baudelaire had recourse to drastic language: "Woman is hungry, and she wants to eat." In these words he showed how the myth of the all-consuming woman manifested itself at the *fin de siècle,* above all in literary sources. While in the real world female workers toiled in the factories and the suffragettes demonstrated for women's right to vote, the parallel world of the arts brought forth the *femme fatale*. Later visual imaginings resulted in the figure of the "vamp," whose kisses were like the embrace of a blood-sucking monster. The black romanticism of the turn of the century reveled delightedly in this theme.

Compared with the explicit depictions of masturbating models that got Klimt into a great deal of trouble, or the way in which Egon Schiele expressed sexuality, the erotic associations of paintings with the *femme fatale* motif are restrained. Like Salome's veil, they do not reveal everything, but precisely because of this they stimulate boundless fantasies.

Franz von Stuck
The Snake Woman (Sin)
1895
Piccadilly Gallery, London

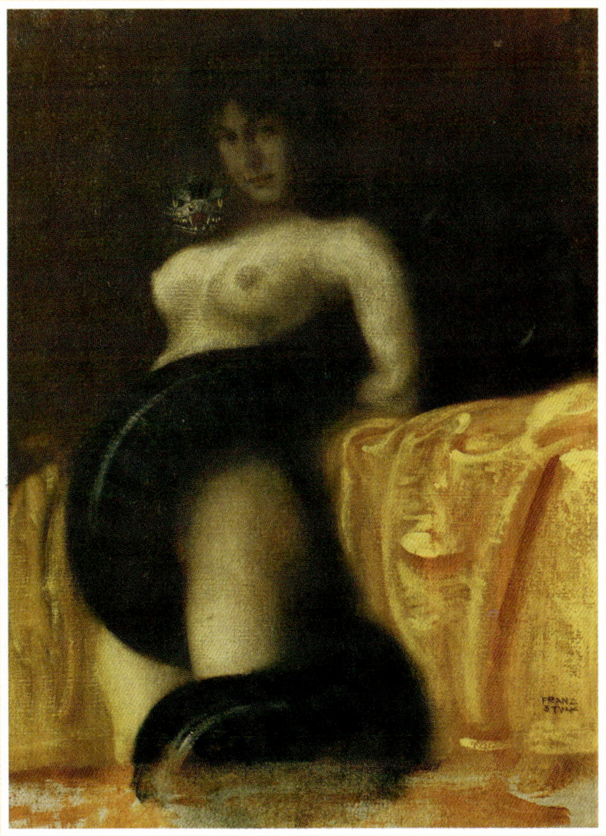

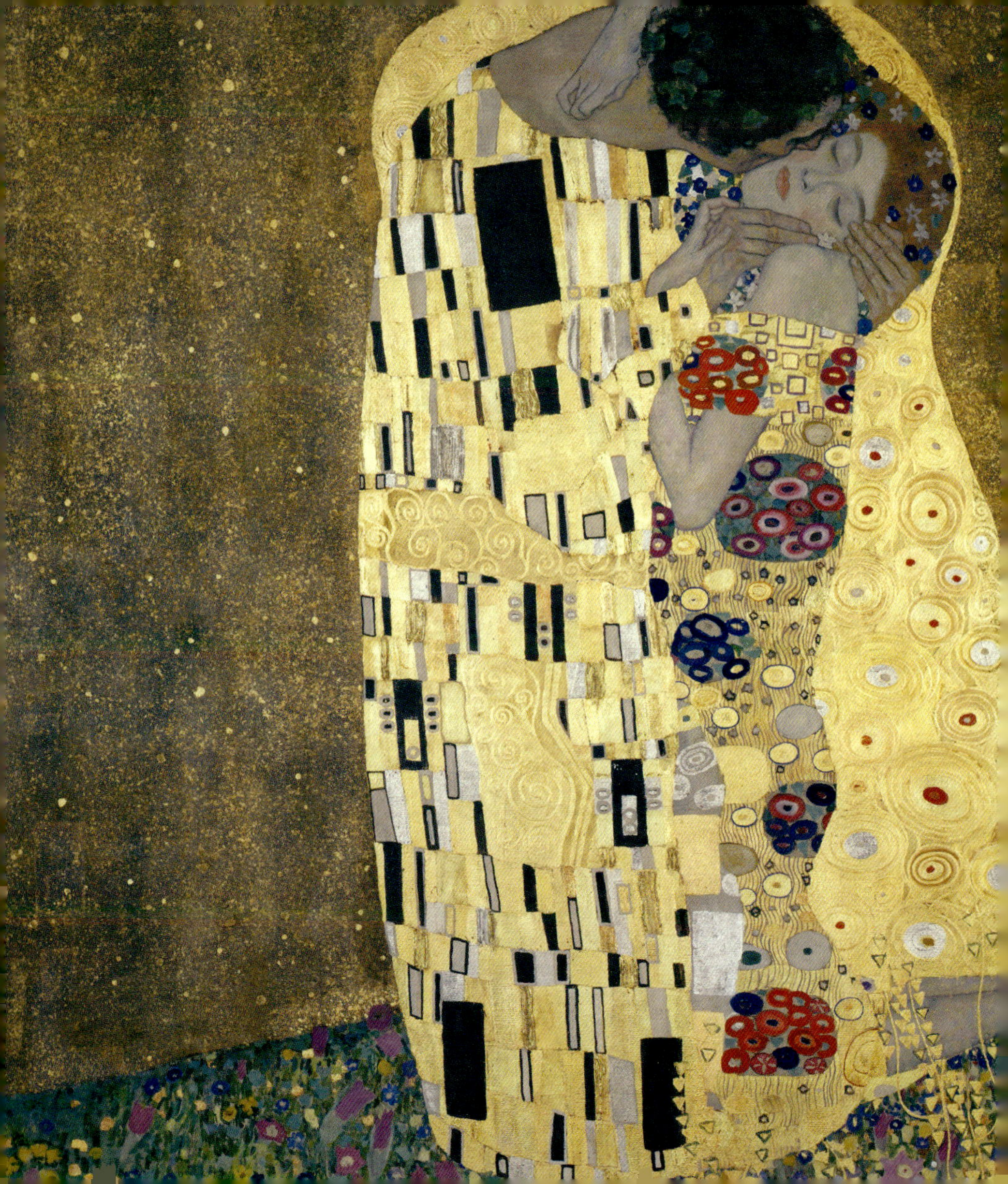

The Myth of Gustav Klimt

Why did he believe that he was not "especially interesting"? Scarcely any other artist of the time, the threshold of a new era that fascinates us today, arouses such curiosity: on the one hand for his sensational art, on the other because so many mysteries surround him. Gustav Klimt was an exceptional figure in painting around 1900 and one of the immediate precursors of modern art. His role in a leading center of Art Nouveau provides insights into the paradigm shift of this period, and to this day the aura of genius surrounds his art. The exorbitant prices paid for his work on the international art market are one reason for this. Interestingly, a look at the period before his great triumphs reveals an earlier career, a "Klimt before Klimt."

Gustav Klimt
The Kiss
1908, oil on canvas
180 × 180 cm
Österreichische Galerie
in the Belvedere, Vienna

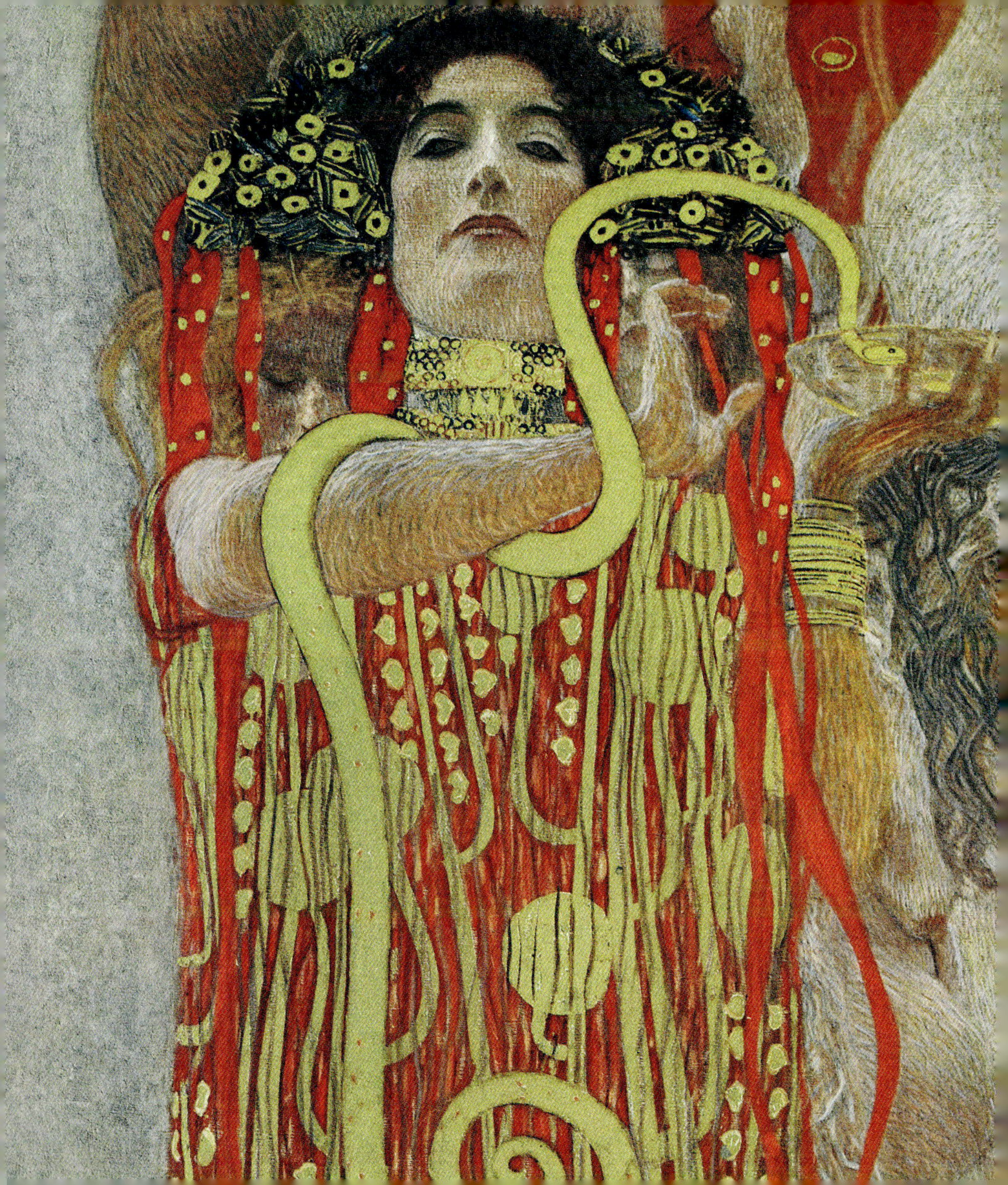

A Gifted Boy

Gustav Klimt
Hygieia, detail of *Medicine*,
1907, oil on canvas,
430 × 300 cm (total size of
ceiling panel for the Great Hall
of Vienna University)
Burnt in 1945 after evacuation
to Schloss Immendorf

Gustav Klimt was born in 1862 in the Vienna suburb of Baumgarten. His father, a gold engraver from Bohemia, had a large family. Two years later his brother Ernst was born; in 1867 came a further son, Georg. Gustav Klimt was close to his two brothers, a relationship that later led to fruitful cooperation. Gustav's remarkable talent was discovered early, and at the age of just 14 he was permitted to attend the Vienna Kunstgewerbeschule (School of Applied Arts), where Ferdinand Julius Laufberger was among his teachers and where he met his later ally Franz Matsch.

In 1881, not yet 20 years old, the Klimt brothers and Matsch founded a communal workshop in which they actively looked for commissions under the commercial name "Künstler-Compagnie" (Company of Artists). Through the good offices of Klimt's teacher Laufberger, who recognized the young men's talent, they quickly found opportunities to show what they were capable of. These projects, which met with acclaim in the society of imperial Austria, included work at the Kunsthistorisches Museum in Vienna, the so-called Hermesvilla and the staircases of many theatres. Although he seemed to belong to the tradition of Hans Makart, it was soon realized that Klimt had the talent for higher achieve-

Gustav Klimt
Brooch with replica of *The Kiss*,
1908, gold and diamonds,
5.5 × 5.5 cm
Private collection

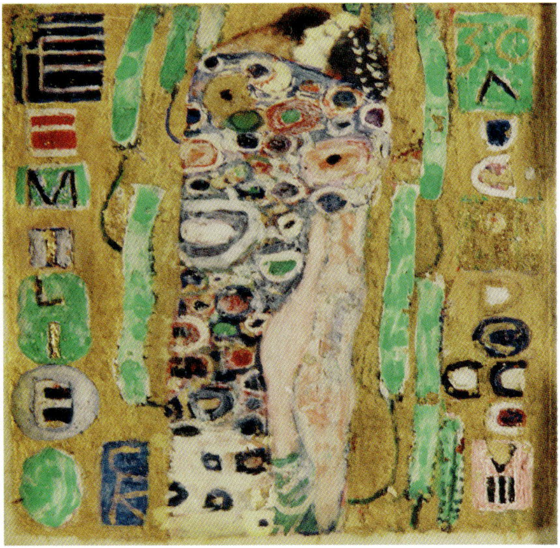

Gustav Klimt
Fräulein Emilie Flöge
1902, oil on canvas
181 × 84 cm
Wien Museum, Vienna

Gustav Klimt
Photo *c.* 1910

ments. In 1891 the members of the Künstler-Compagnie joined the Künstlerhaus, the association of Austrian artists, and participated profitably in the fashionable salon art of the time.

Everything in Gustav Klimt's life had gone swimmingly, but fate dealt him heavy blows in 1892. The sudden death of his father made him the head of a family with growing children for whom he was now the breadwinner. When his beloved brother Ernst died in the same year, Klimt's world seemed to be collapsing around him. Here, too, he felt he was under an obligation – to his brother's young widow Helene, who was the sister of his friend Emilie Flöge, and to her new-born daughter. It seems likely that, if he had been able to stay on the course that the Künstler-Compagnie had set, Gustav Klimt would one day have been Makart's successor. If this had happened, however, he would never have turned into the exceptional artist that he in fact became after these events.

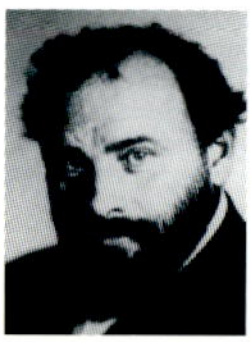

Gustav Klimt

1862 – 1918

1862 Birth of Gustav Klimt, son of a gold engraver

1876 Klimt and his brother Ernst attend the school of the Austrian Museum for Art and Industry

1883 Foundation of the Künstler-Compagnie with Ernst and Franz Matsch

1891 Klimt joins the association of Viennese artists (Künstlerhaus)

1892 Death of father and brother

1894 Commission for the faculty paintings at the university

1897 President of the newly founded Secession (until 1899)

1902 Paints *Beethoven Frieze*

1905 Leaves the Secession, abandons commission for faculty paintings

1907 *Adele Bloch-Bauer I*

1907/08 *The Kiss*

1909–11 Works on *Stoclet Frieze*

1912 President of the Austrian League of Artists (founded 1906)

1916 Exhibits with Schiele and Kokoschka at the Berlin Secession

1918 Gustav Klimt dies from the effects of a stroke

Scandal!

In 1892, while Matsch was still his partner, Klimt received a commission that was to affect his development decisively. The artistic commission of the University of Vienna called for proposals for ceiling paintings in the Great Hall. Matsch entered his own designs, probably intending to steal a march on Klimt, but they were rejected. He had to produce new designs, and finally brought in Klimt for support. The new scheme consisted of a painting at the center symbolizing the light of reason, around which representations of the four faculties of Medicine, Philosophy, Law and Theology were arranged. This proposal was accepted, and Klimt set to work on Medicine, Philosophy and Law.

What followed was one of the momentous artistic scandals of modern times. It showed how Klimt, in rejecting the traditional path of historicist allegory, had departed from the mainstream. Klimt worked on the faculty paintings for more than ten years. Offence was caused above all by the emphasis on nudity, which he incorporated into the paintings as an element beyond time. At first the intention was to instruct him to adapt his designs to the conservative style of Franz Matsch. Then anti-Semitism and nationalist hysteria entered the furor about the faculty paintings: phrases such as "Jewish impudence" were used, and it was allegedly "an orgy of mendaciousness" to describe such work as Austrian art. Klimt tried as far as possible to concentrate on his work and remain aloof from the debate. However, eventually he gave in. Although he had to borrow the money from a patron, he repaid the fee that he had

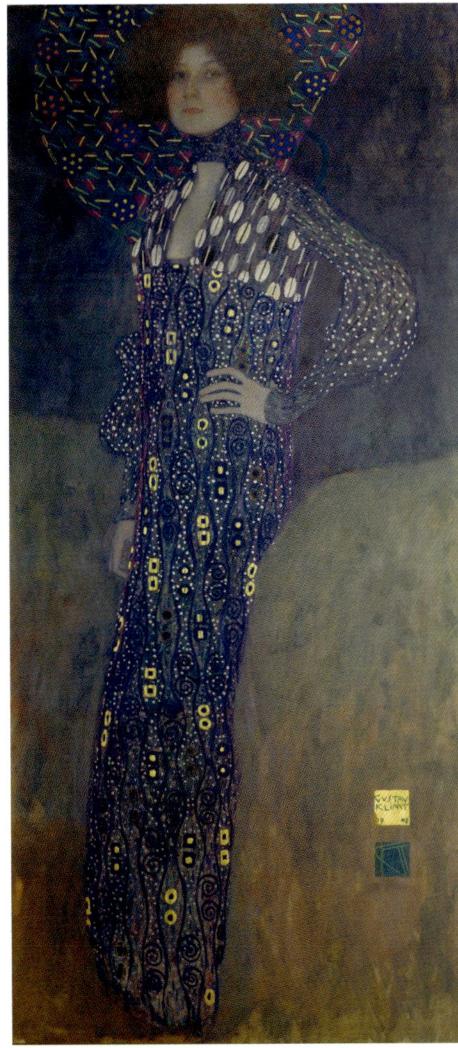

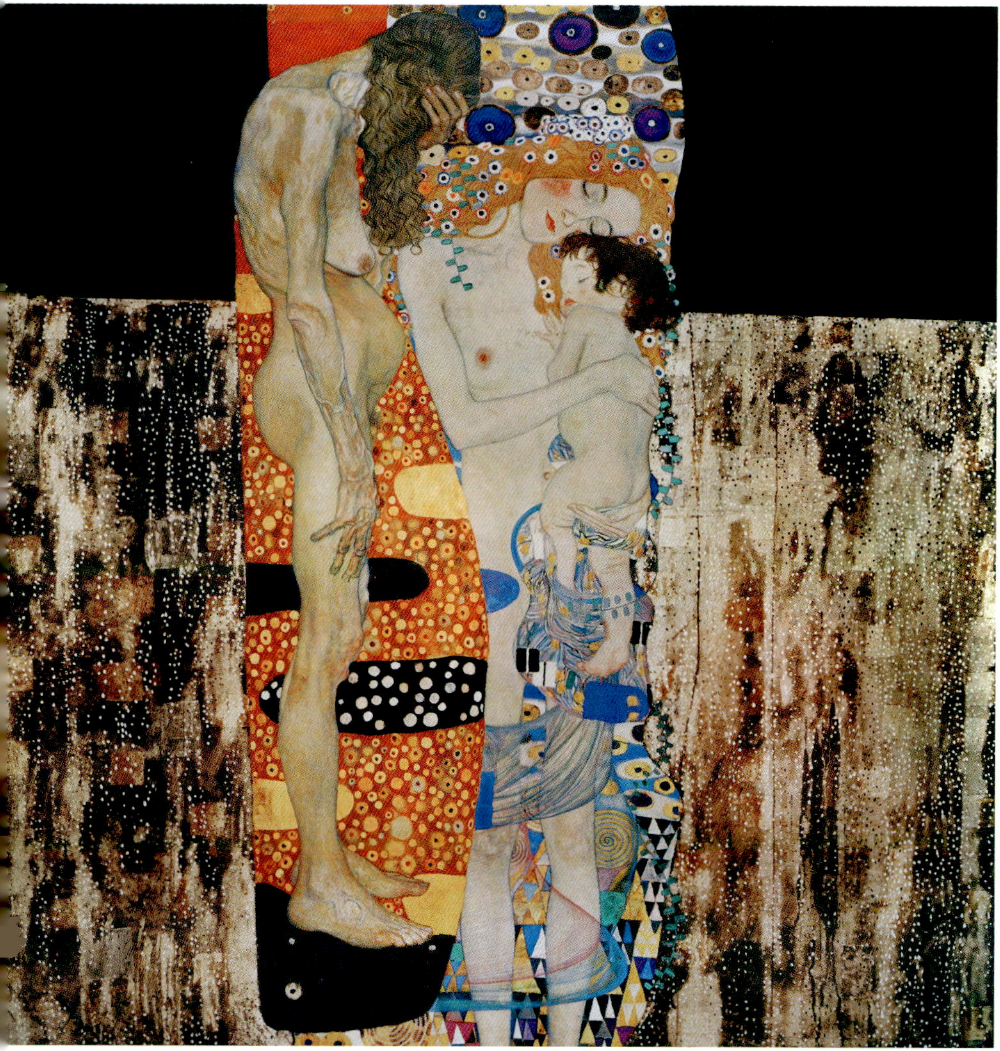

received for the commission and took back his three paintings, which he nevertheless planned to put on public display. Back in 1902, in his painting *Goldfish,* he had appended the subtitle "to my critics" to the provocatively outstretched posterior of a female figure, and *Nuda Veritas* of 1899 had made the artist's attitude as clear as could be. The painting was inscribed with a quote adapted from Schiller: "It is bad to please everyone." In spite of the problems that faced Klimt following the artistic and political stir about his work, it can be concluded that the controversies undoubtedly contributed to his development. The subject of nakedness, which he again and again depicted in a provocatively open manner, continued to be one of Klimt's central themes.

Klimt portrayed old age unsparingly in the form of a haggard woman who holds a hand to her face at the approach of death. In front of her, harmoniously united, are a young mother and her child to symbolize the fresh start of the cycle of life.

Golden Klimt

In a Secession exhibition of 1903 Klimt presented himself to the Vienna public and showed his new style in 48 paintings and a number of drawings. A conspicuous feature, which certainly appealed to public taste, was his "golden phase". Here he demonstrated the enthusiasm for Byzantine mosaics that he had acquired on a journey to Italy. The influence of the all-pervading Japonisme was also evident. Klimt hung many roll-paintings in his studio and loved the patterns on the fabric of kimonos. The paintings in an extremely tall format of the phase after 1900 seem to derive from Japanese artistic models.

A closer examination of the precedents that inspired Klimt's art shows how important the Secession exhibitions were for him. As the aim of these exhibitions was to spread ideas, they included paintings by artists from other countries such as Fernand Khnopff and Jan Toroop, both of whom made their mark on the work of Gustav Klimt. A solo exhibition of 1903 also finally revealed the murals of the *Beethoven Frieze,* which had been covered up. Here, in

Gustav Klimt
The Three Ages
1905, oil on canvas
173 × 171 cm
Galleria Nazionale d'Arte
Moderna, Rome

a Secession exhibition of the previous year that was conceived on the lines of a gesamtkunstwerk (a total work of art combining different disciplines), Klimt surpassed himself. It was a great stroke of fortune that no-one felt able to remove Klimt's paintings after the end of the exhibition.

The *Beethoven Frieze* is unique in the radical way the art is reduced to essentials and in his personal approach, which employed allegories of Beethoven's Ninth Symphony. On a surface 34 meters long and two meters high, Klimt presented three groups of themes that he had evolved as an analogy to music: firstly genius, suffering mankind and knights; secondly hostile forces: gorgons, a giant, sinful passions, misery; thirdly genius and poetry, the arts, choir and the embrace. The giant was especially impressive. Klimt depicted it as an ape and joined it to the goddesses of destiny to create a hostile force. In opposition to this he first used his motif of the kiss, which represented the *Ode to Humanity* and was intended to reveal far-reaching symbolic meaning. In 1907, with *The Kiss,* Klimt painted a seminal work of Secession art, a painting that presented the union of man and woman in a mystical and lyrical manner. This motif recurs on a brooch bordered with diamonds that Gustav Klimt gave to Emilie Flöge on her 34th birthday – proof that their relationship was more than just platonic.

Visitors to the Beethoven Exhibition entered the room on the left, where Gustav Klimt's frieze took them by the hand in thematic terms from the very start. *Gnawing Grief* was followed by *Human Longings,* which flew up above. Everything culminated in the conciliatory *Kiss* for the whole world.

A Kiss for All the World

The sensational Beethoven Frieze impressed Adolphe Stoclet, a wealthy banker from Brussels who stayed in Vienna with his wife in 1902. Back in Brussels he commissioned Josef Hoffmann to build a fine town house for him and asked Gustav Klimt to produce a similarly impressive frieze in the form of a mosaic for the dining room. Through his close cooperation with the designer Hoffmann, Klimt succeeded in developing an abstract formal language that was closer to craftwork than to painting. The frieze on the

Gustav Klimt
Beethoven Frieze, detail with the figure of *Gnawing Grief*
1902, casein paint on plaster
Height: 220 cm
Österreichische Galerie in the Belvedere, Vienna

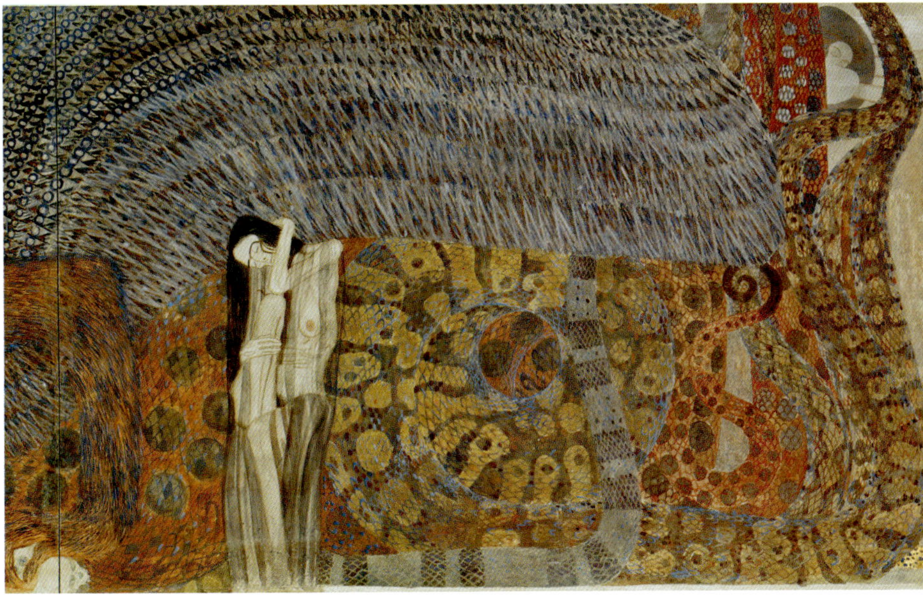

end wall is adorned by an amorphous composition: images such as the Tree of Life and a further kiss motif are based on the dominant geometrical forms, which seem to be tangible when executed as a mosaic. The frieze for Stoclet is a further example of a fruitful alliance with a wealthy patron. This was also a characteristic of Klimt's later career, when he was above all a portrait artist for the *"haute juiverie,"* the rich Jewish citizens of Vienna.

One reason why Klimt turned to portraiture was his withdrawal from public commissions after the disappointing results of his work for the university. On the other hand, portrait painting also clearly shows the individuality that repeatedly emerges in Klimt's work. In addition to his many affairs with his models, which are reflected in his paintings,

Following double page:
Gustav Klimt
Beethoven Frieze, detail, *A Kiss for All the World*
1902, casein paint, gold leaf, semi-precious stones, mother-of-pearl on plaster,
height 220 cm
Österreichische Galerie in the Belvedere, Vienna

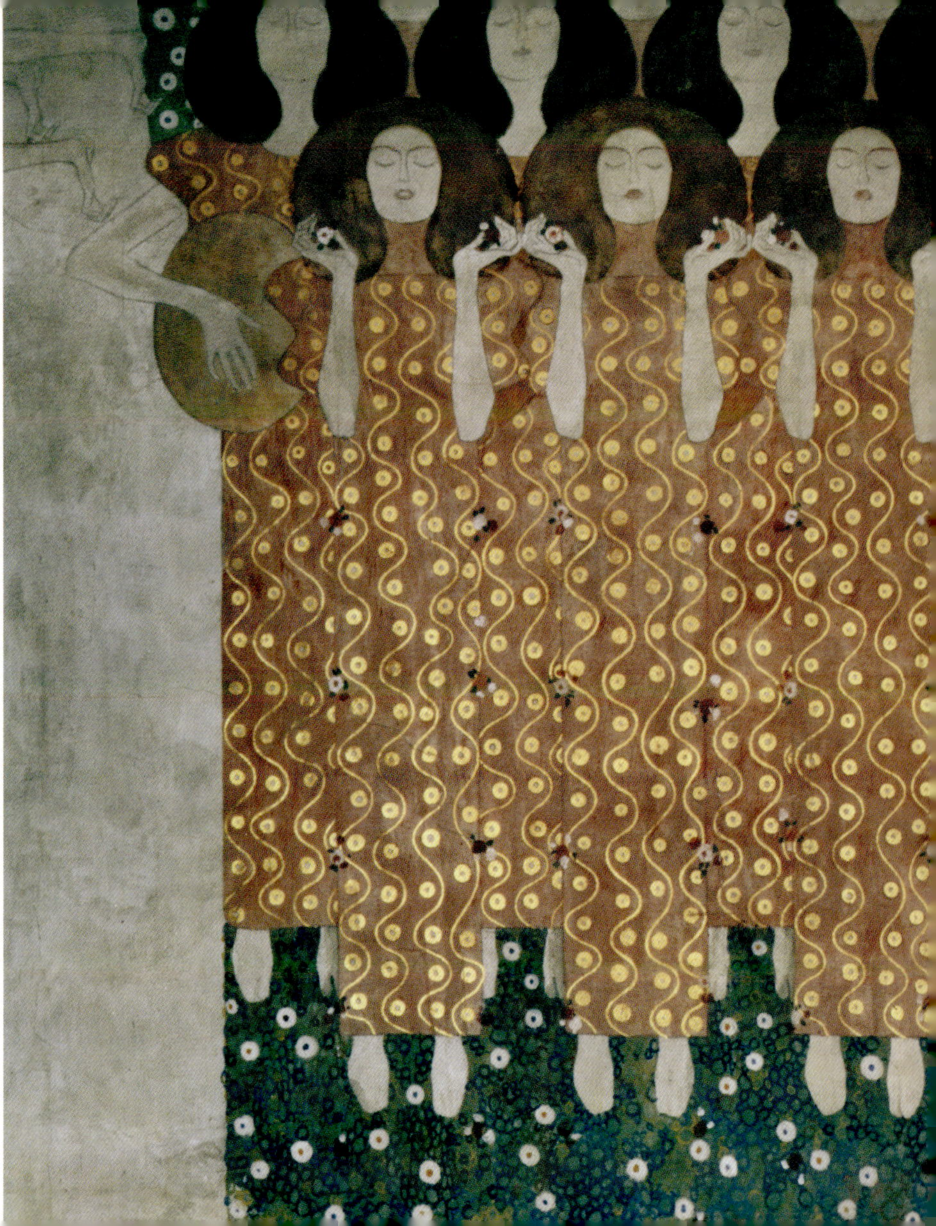

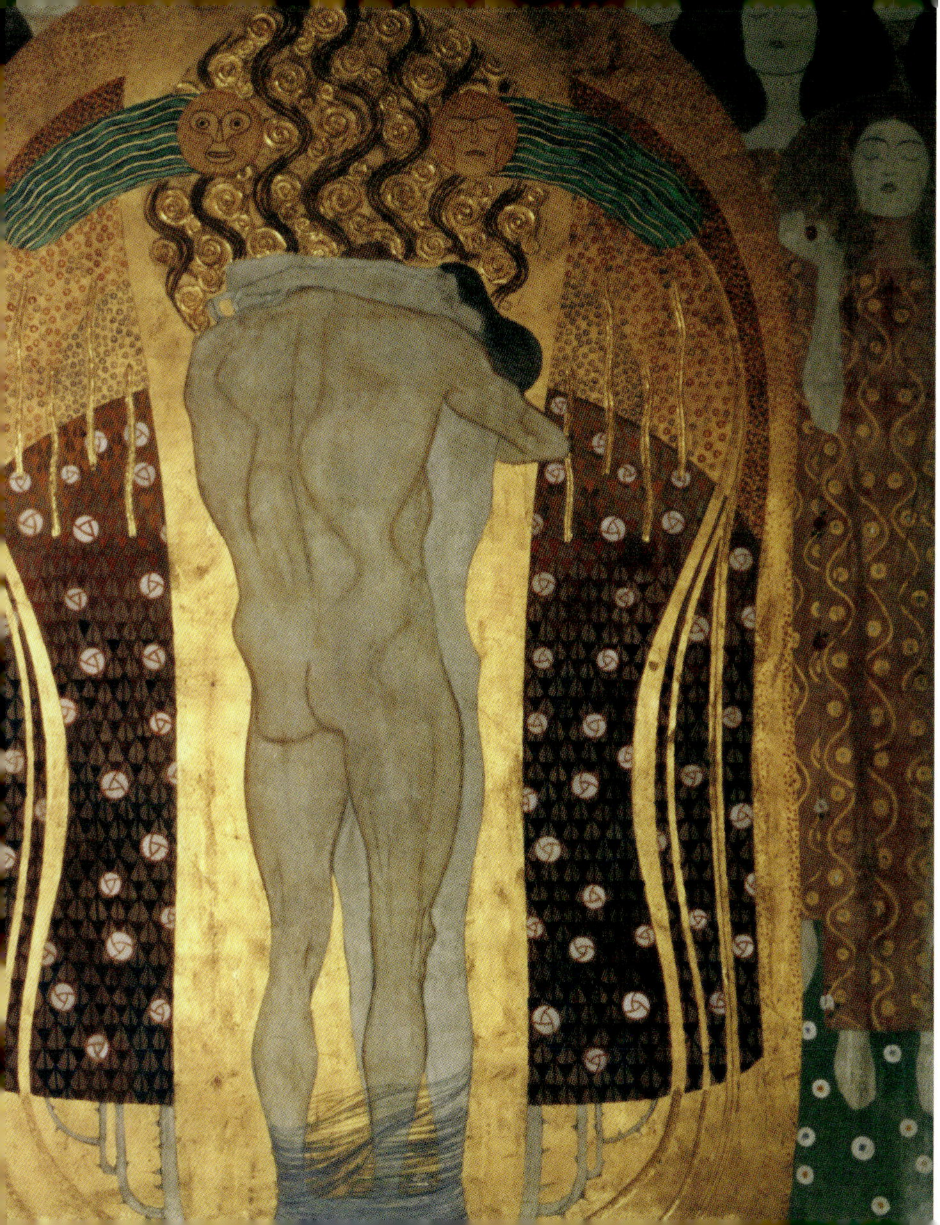

Gustav Klimt
Beethoven Frieze, middle of end wall, *The Hostile Forces*, detail: *The Giant Thyphoeus, Unchastity and Immoderation*, 1902, casein paint on plaster, 220 × 636 cm, Österreichische Galerie in the Belvedere, Vienna

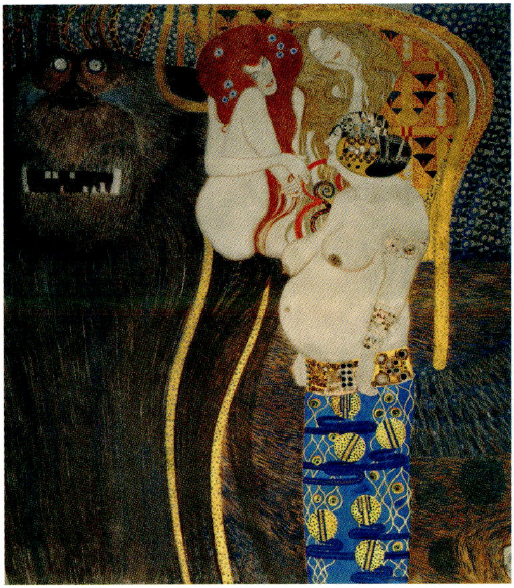

including depictions of the children who resulted from these relationships, Klimt seems to have been attracted to the new class of modern open-minded society women. Adele Bloch-Bauer was one such woman. She was married to a much older man, childless after a series of miscarriages, ailing and at the same time intellectual, elegant and perpetually in search of spiritual inspiration. Her friendship with Klimt was close, and she first appeared in his work as Judith in the painting of that name in 1901. So powerful is her presence as a *femme fatale* that it is tempting to interpret this woman, with her arrogant gaze and coquettish charms, as Salome.

Painting of the Century

In the picture that Klimt painted of Adele in the role of Judith eight years later, he revealed a completely new approach to portraiture. Here he does not regard the woman as the subject, but embeds a portrayal of her into an ornamental motif. In 1912 the series of portraits ended in a depiction of this confident woman in decorative surroundings that are obviously influenced by Japanese art. However, the crowning achievement was to be a portrait known as *Golden Adele,* which was instrumental in the celebration of Klimt as an epoch-making artist. Ferdinand Bloch commissioned Klimt to paint a portrait of his wife in 1903, and the artist began work on its composition. He quickly decided on the basic structure, which was an enthralling conception with its daringly cropped motif of the central figure. However, about 100 further sketches were needed before the finished portrait could be presented in 1907. Inspired by the ideas of the Wiener Werkstätte, which had provided the contact for his cooperation with Hoffmann in Brussels, Gustav Klimt concentrated on the interaction of the portrait with abstract ornamentation. He emphasized the wide cape that enfolded Adele. This gave her a static appearance reminiscent of the formulaic nature of religious art.

The large number of female portraits that followed *Golden Adele* shows how Klimt was passed on in Viennese society from one client to another. Often the impatient patrons grabbed the pictures from him in a condition that he would not necessarily have regarded as finished. Klimt was no smooth talker at society events; he found making conversation hard work. He spoke in a broad Vienna dialect, conversed reluctantly and was regarded as shy and withdrawn.

He loved to flee with Emilie Flöge to the summer idyll of Lake Attersee, where he painted wonderful landscapes, work in an important genre that enriched his late oeuvre. Although they appear somewhat unspectacular in comparison with the intoxicating invention of golden paintings and the daring hints of abstraction in the friezes, Gustav Klimt's late landscapes are also experimental images that presented unexpected perspectives in the square format that he liked. Whether he was using a telescope or a template, Klimt looked for views that were out of the ordinary. He would never have thought of painting a panorama in the classic way. Instead he produced views of nature from above and below, giving it a structure by applying small patches of

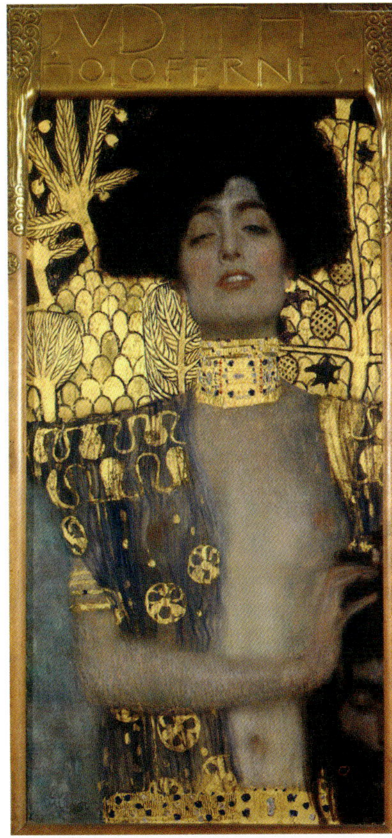

Gustav Klimt
Judith with the Head of Holofernes, 1901
Oil on canvas, 84 × 42 cm
Österreichische Galerie in the Belvedere, Vienna

paint – as if he wanted to be swallowed up by it. After all the excitement of the Vienna scene, he seems to have felt a great longing for relaxation and retreat. The end of the war makes Klimt's tragic death in 1918 after a stroke seem all the more the end of an era: the era of Klimt.

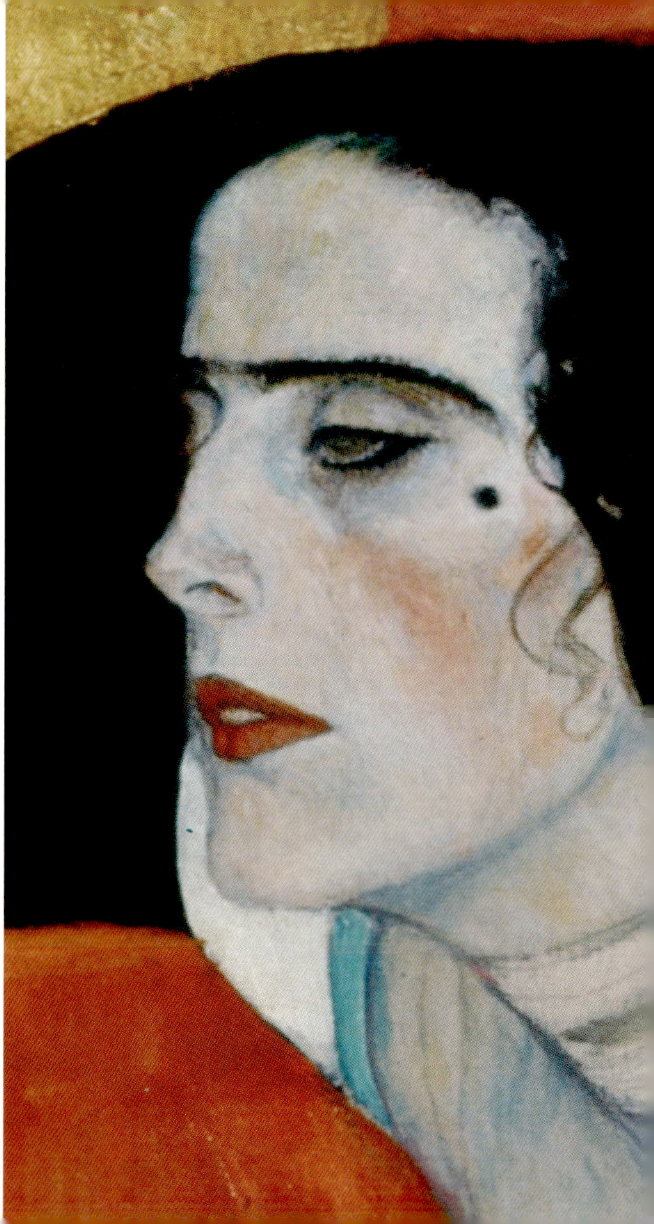

Gustav Klimt
Salome or *Judith II* (detail)
1909, oil on canvas
178 × 46 cm
Galleria Internazionale d'Arte Moderna, Venice

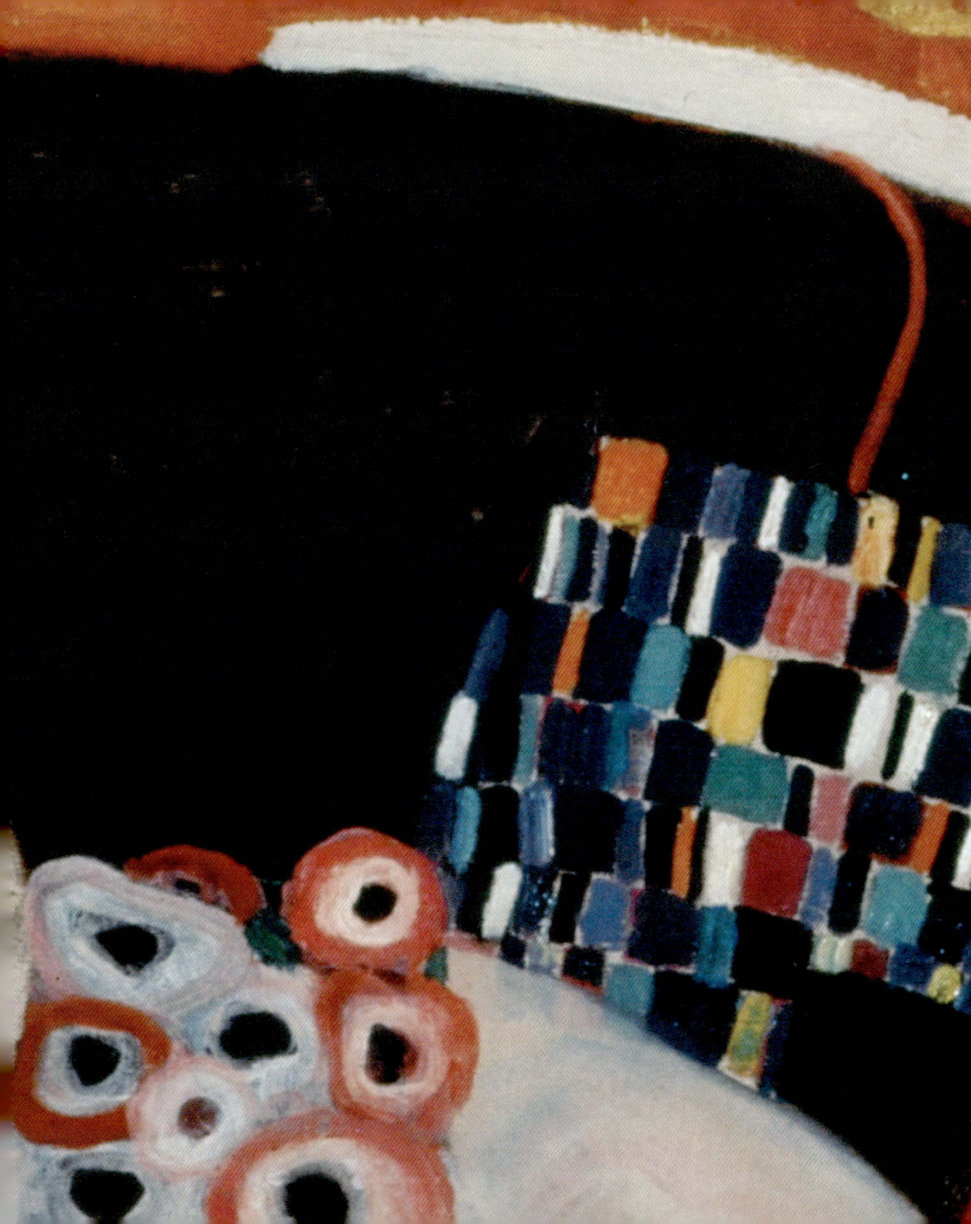

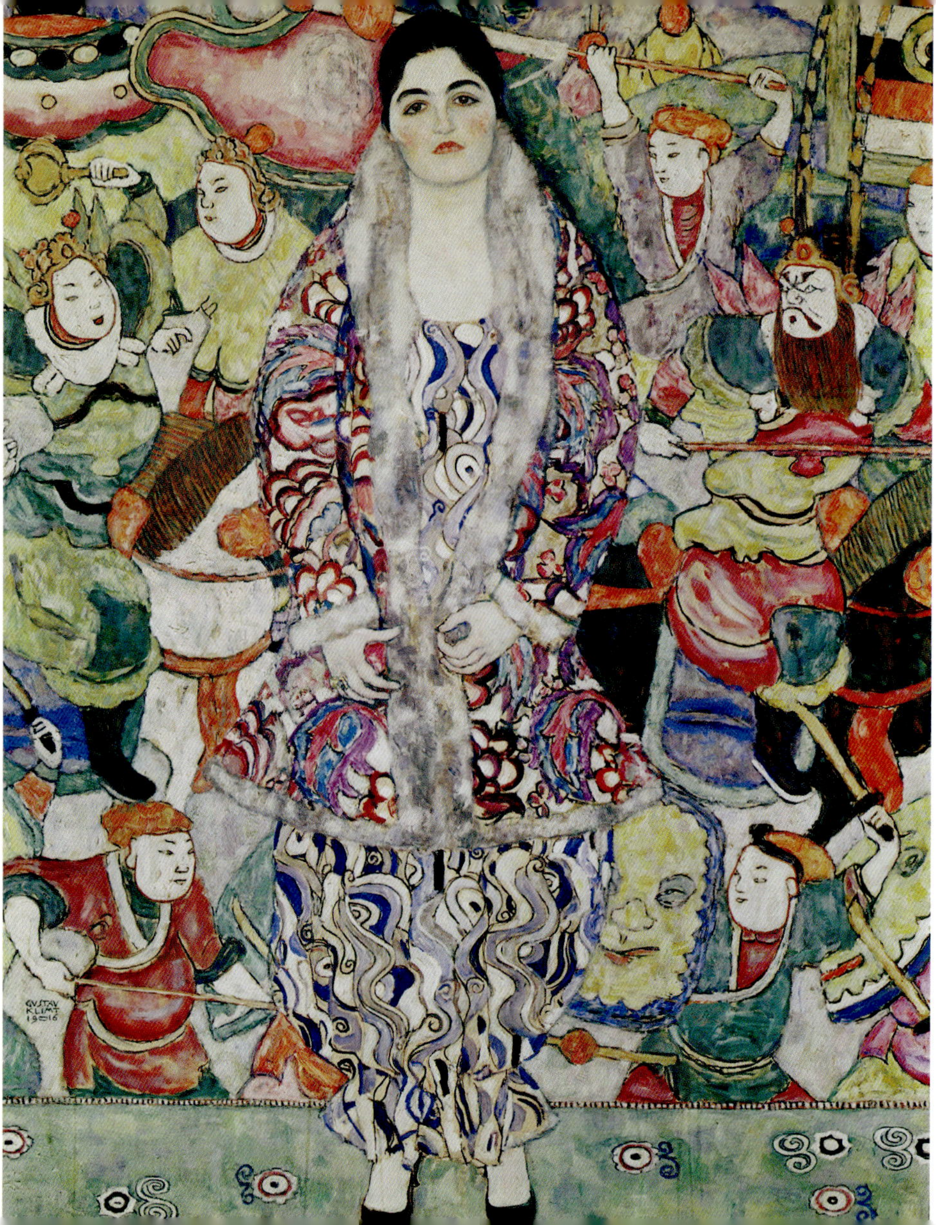
GVSTAV
KLIMT
19=16

Gustav Klimt
Adele Bloch-Bauer II
1912, oil on canvas
190 × 120 cm
Österreichische Galerie in the Belvedere, Vienna

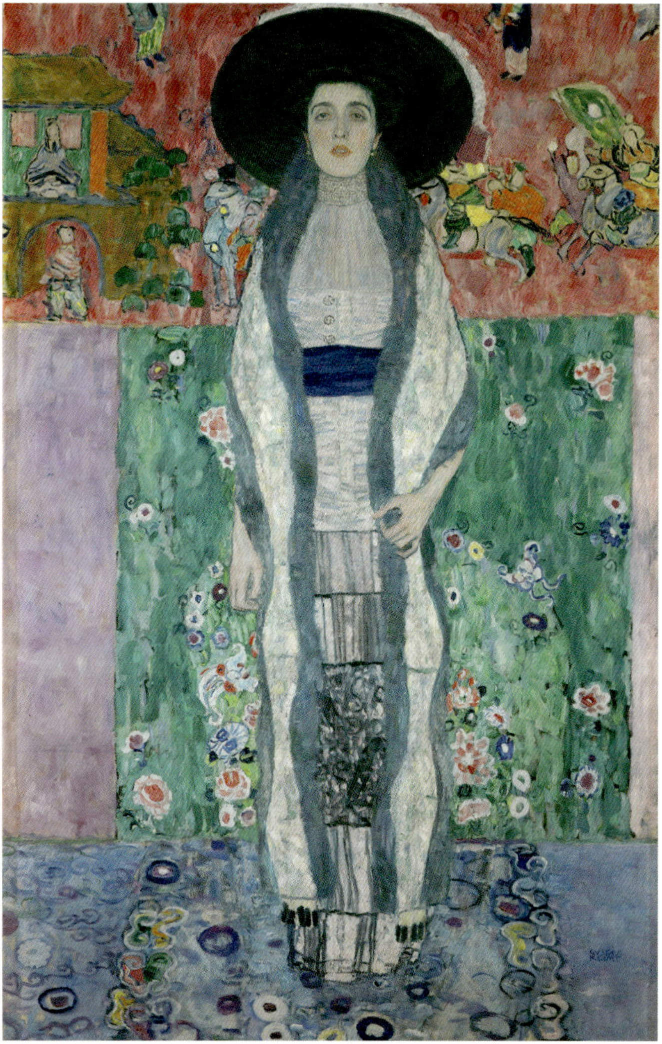

Gustav Klimt
Portrait of Friedericke Maria Beer
1916, oil on canvas
168 × 130 cm
Mizne-Blumenthal Collection, Tel Aviv Museum of Art

Following double page:
Gustav Klimt
Water Snakes II (The Girl Friends)
1904, oil on canvas
80 × 145 cm
Private collection

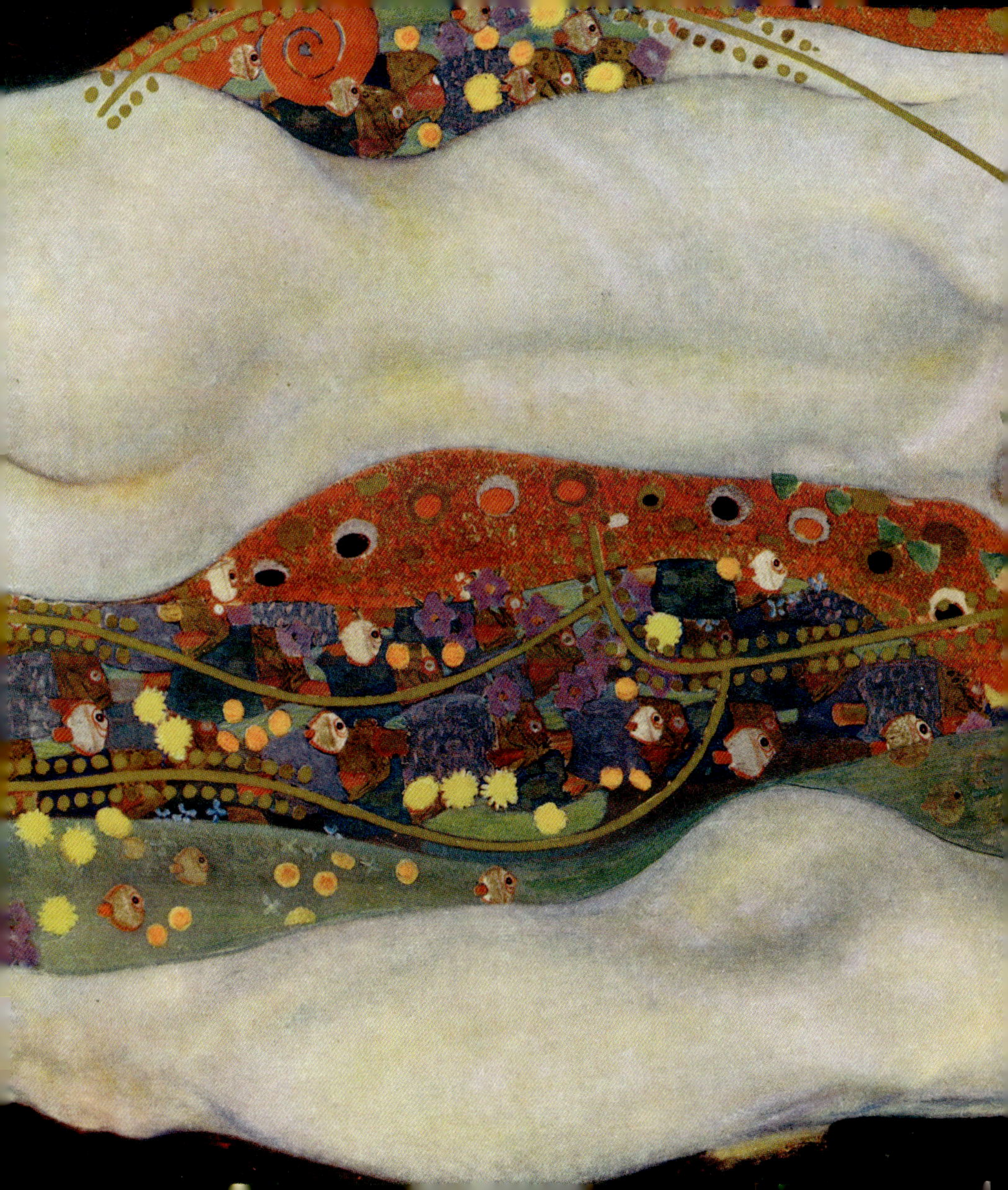

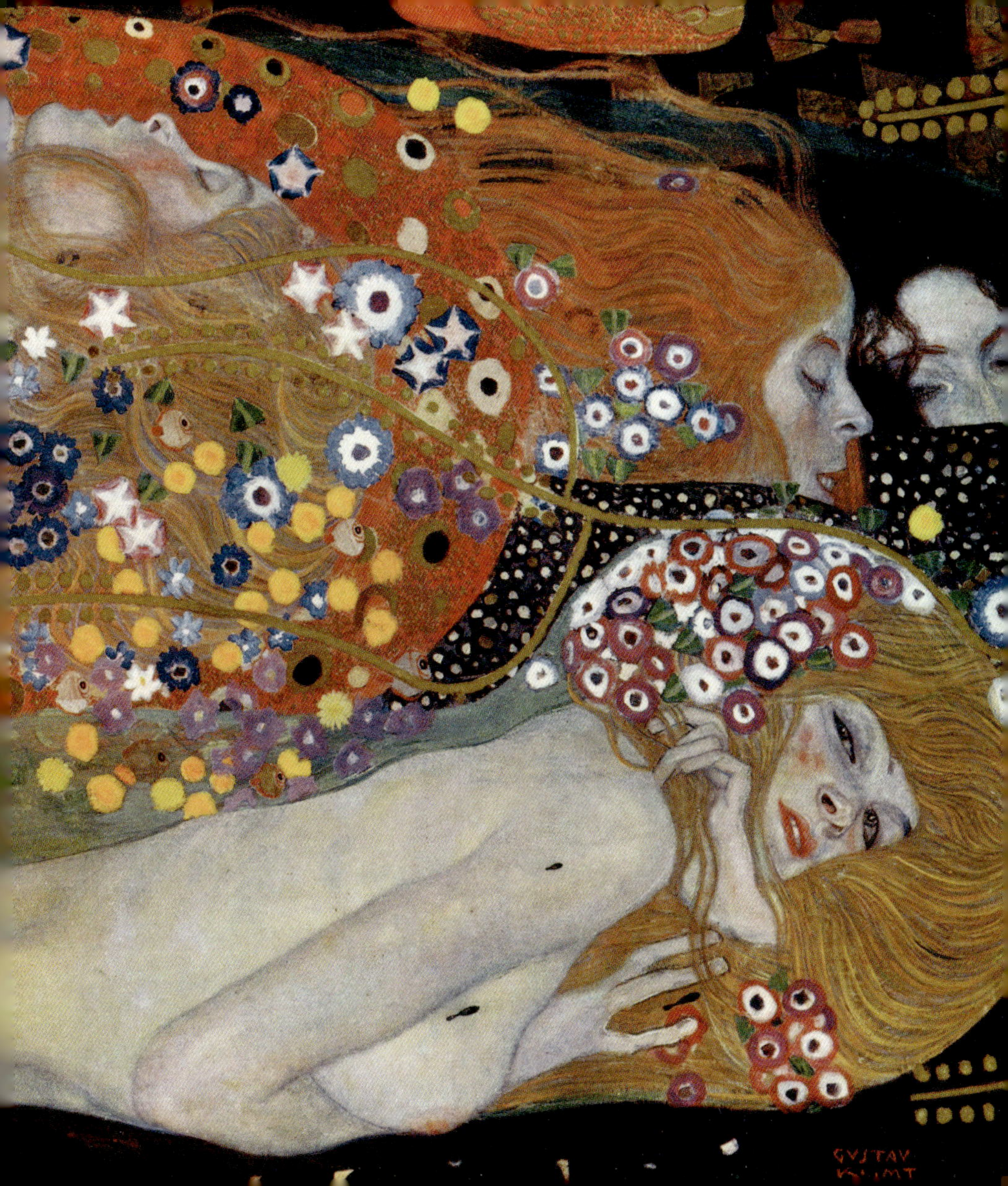
GVSTAV

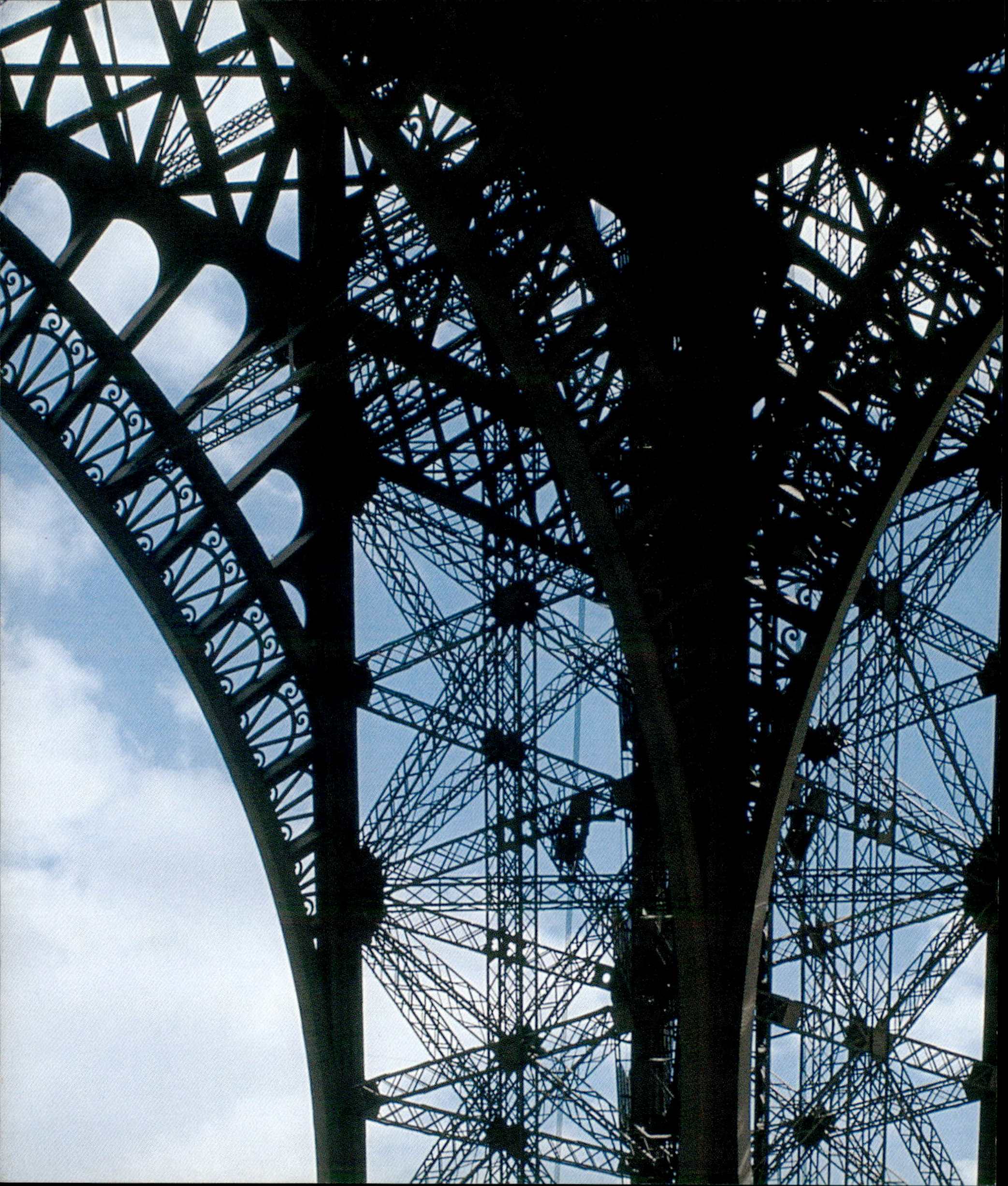

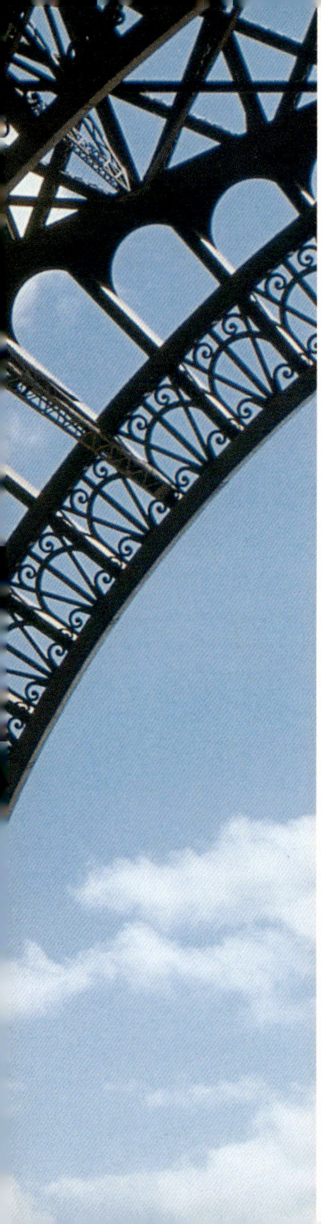

Modern Times – New Technology

Motor cars drove through the streets and airships crossed the sky. Pictures learned to move. New uses of materials such as iron and tin provided impulses for architecture and crafts. These technical innovations gave a more dynamic feeling to life in the years around the turn of the century. It is no coincidence that the repertoire of forms found in Art Nouveau contains so many bold, sweeping curves: they are the expression of these developments. The transformation of the modern city through inventions from underground railways to advertising hoardings and new palaces of entertainment opened up a whole range of opportunities for modern people to fulfill their potential.

Eiffel Tower
Pillar of the first platform
Photograph, undated

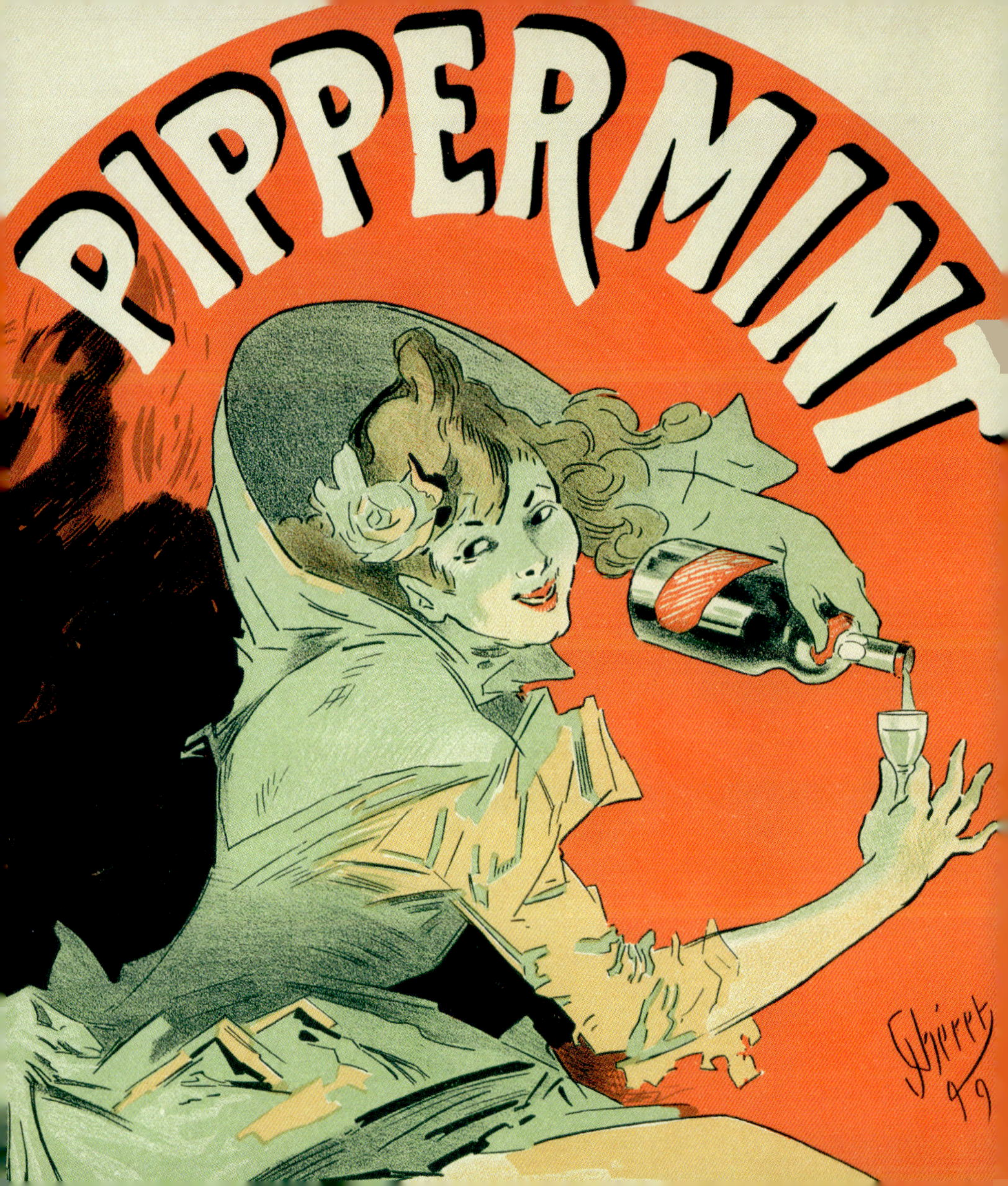
PIPPERMINT
Chéret
99

The Sky's the Limit

In 1889 Gustav Eiffel implemented an idea of a member of his staff, Maurice Koechlin, taking a trend that had begun with the iron structures of the mid-19th century to its triumphant conclusion by building the "tower of bare facts." Eiffel, who also took part in the planning of the Statue of Liberty, which was inaugurated in 1886, by designing the framework, successfully fought off all proposals for covering the metal structure and held to his course in the face of insults such as "the laughable commercial idea of a mechanical engineer" and "Paris's shame". "The future belongs to iron architecture – this much is certain" wrote Heinrich Pudor in 1902. "Today our primary requirements for interiors are air, light and spaciousness; iron construction is the most appropriate way of meetings these demands." Eiffel saved his tower from demolition by using it to conduct experiments in radio transmission, thus giving the tower a practical purpose.

Jules Chéret
Pippermint advertising poster
1899, color lithograph
Private collection

Advertisement for Odol
mouthwash in *Jugend,* no. 7
1903, photomontage
Archiv für Kunst und Geschichte,
Berlin

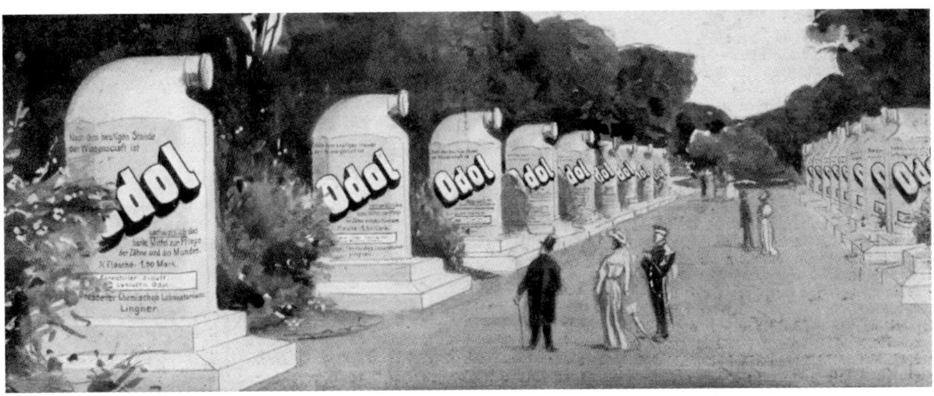

Brave New Consumer World

The turn of the century was marked by yet more developments that were to permanently change human perceptions. The invention of lithographic printing encouraged the emergence of poster art, which now began to take over the public arena.

Jules Chéret, who ran his own printworks and had an enormous influence on the development of advertising by producing a total of 1200 posters, is regarded as the outstanding exponent of this phenomenon. Chéret's simplification of forms and use of bold colors set the benchmark in the new field of advertising. His "cherettes," the nimble beauties on his posters, were the ideal presenters for an advertising message. The creation of brands took its course, and products such as Odol mouthwash became the symbols of a new age. The subject of hygiene was then highly topical, but in connection with the product Odol it is much more interesting to note that, for the first time, a carefully planned advertising campaign was carried out with deliberate use of artistic means. The advertisements published in the magazine *Jugend,* in particular, consciously lived up to artistic standards. The design of a curved bottle, for example, owed much to the characteristic taste of Art Nouveau in regard to form.

Chronology of Progress

1854 The German printer Ernst Litfass is given permission to erect "advertising columns"

1863 London Underground inaugurated

1872 Eadweard Muybridge make photographic series showing a horse galloping

1886 Carl Benz invents the precursor of the modern automobile

1889 Eiffel Tower inaugurated

1893 The businessman Karl August Lingner launches the mouthwash Odol in Dresden

1895 First public screening of a film by the Skladanowsky brothers in the Wintergarten music hall in Berlin
The Lumière brothers present their cinématograph in Paris

1900 The first airship flies
Paris Métro goes into operation

1901 Underground railway in Berlin opened

1903 Foundation of the Association of Brand Products in Berlin

1904 Opening of New York City Subway

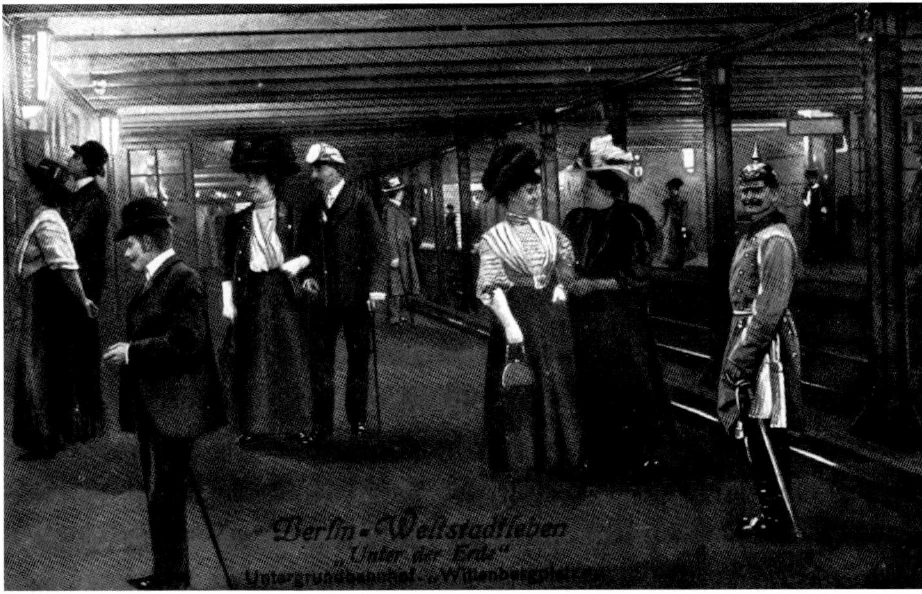

The Joy of Speed

The turn of the century was a time of decisive change, new ideas and new technologies. The development of moving pictures is often seen as a phenomenon that influenced the aesthetics of Art Nouveau through concepts such as speed and dynamism.

The invention of the automobile also had a significant impact. However, while few people could afford a motor car, the railways were the principal sign of how ways of life had changed at the threshold of a new era. The railway and its urban sister, the underground, symbolized the social, economic and cultural transformations of the time. The care taken over the design of metro stations in cities such as Paris and Berlin testifies to this.

Scene on railway platform, Wittenbergplatz, Berlin 1911, photomontage

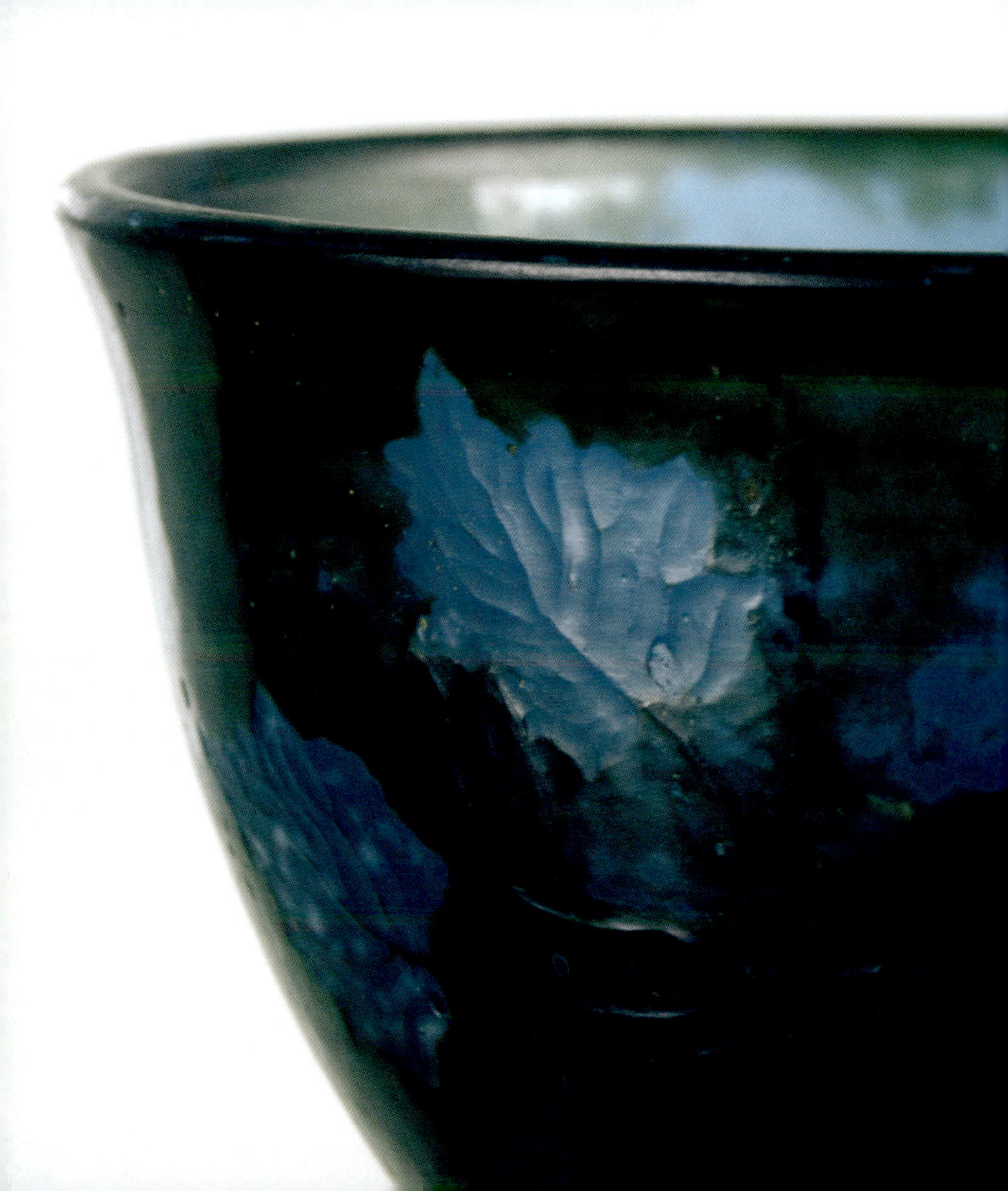

Magician in Glass:

The Art of Émile Gallé

Melancholy clouded the brow of the *fin de siècle* artist Émile Gallé and was responsible for many of his sensational inventions in glass-working. He was shaped by his upbringing in a Protestant family, where the Bible was read every evening. Gallé became an intellectual, who appreciated the decadent literature of the time and recorded for posterity in his own writings the things that moved him. When he died of leukemia at the age of just 58, he was regarded as one of the leading artists of his age in glass. Known for his passionate patriotism, but also smiled upon as a hopeless romantic, he put his emotions into wonderful objects, often performing pioneering technical feats to produce them.

Émile Gallé
Crystal glass bowl
Par un Telle Nuit
(For a Special Night)
(detail), 1894
Musée d'Orsay Paris

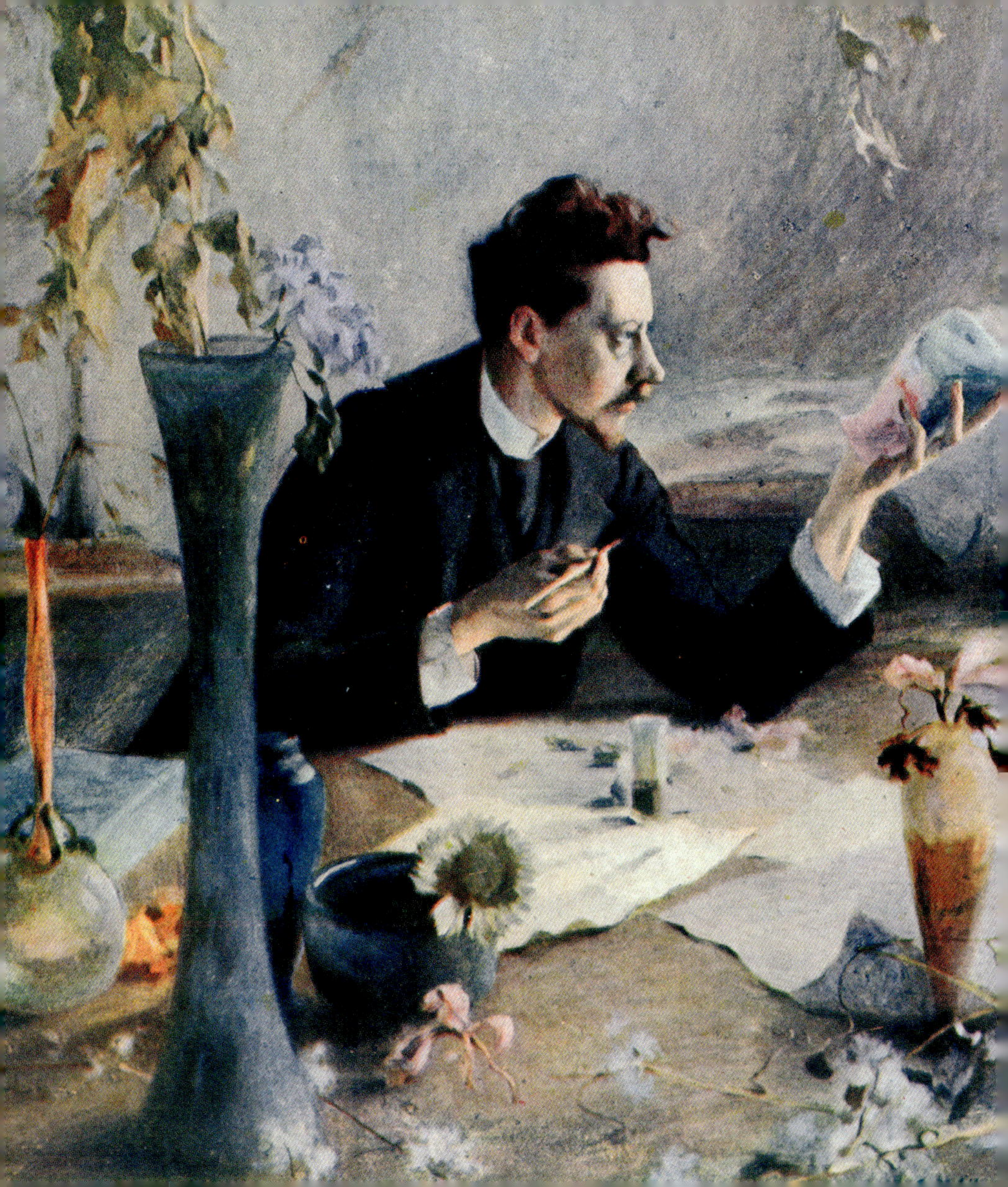

The Career of a Great Artist in Glass

When Émile Gallé was born to the Gallé-Reinemer family in 1846, he seemed predestined for a career as a craftsman. His father Charles Gallé, a porcelain painter from Paris, had married into a family that owned a small porcelain shop in Nancy. He quickly made it into a great success. It was a small but high-quality and profitable workshop for decorating and finishing glass tableware and porcelain which even had the honor of supplying the household of Napoleon III. One of Charles Gallé's employees brought his extremely gifted son into the business: Victor Prouvé, who drew superb designs. This was the beginning of a lifelong friendship between Victor and Émile, who was twelve years older. Émile Gallé and Victor Prouvé collaborated on the first designs for the famous *service de ferme*. However, before Émile became artistic director of his father's company, he first devoted a number of years to study and travel. In 1862 he went to Weimar to learn not only glassblowing but also to study philosophy, botany, mineralogy and zoology. This was the origin of his later passion for flora and fauna. His interest in mineralogy familiarized him with the process of making

Victor Émile Prouvé
Portrait of Émile Gallé
1909, color lithograph
Bibliothèque des Arts Décoratifs

Émile Gallé
Bowl with marqueterie intercalaire
Private collection

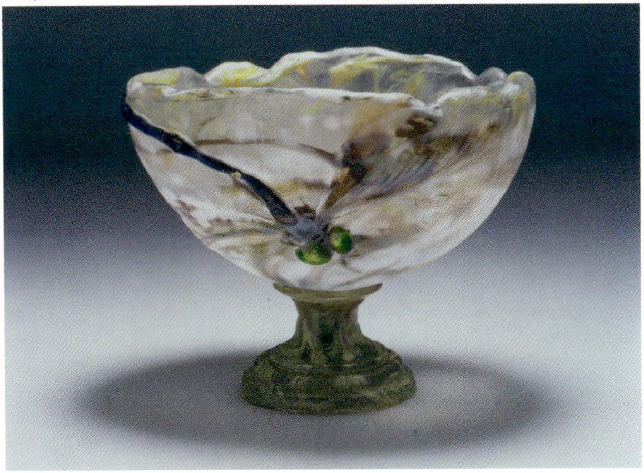

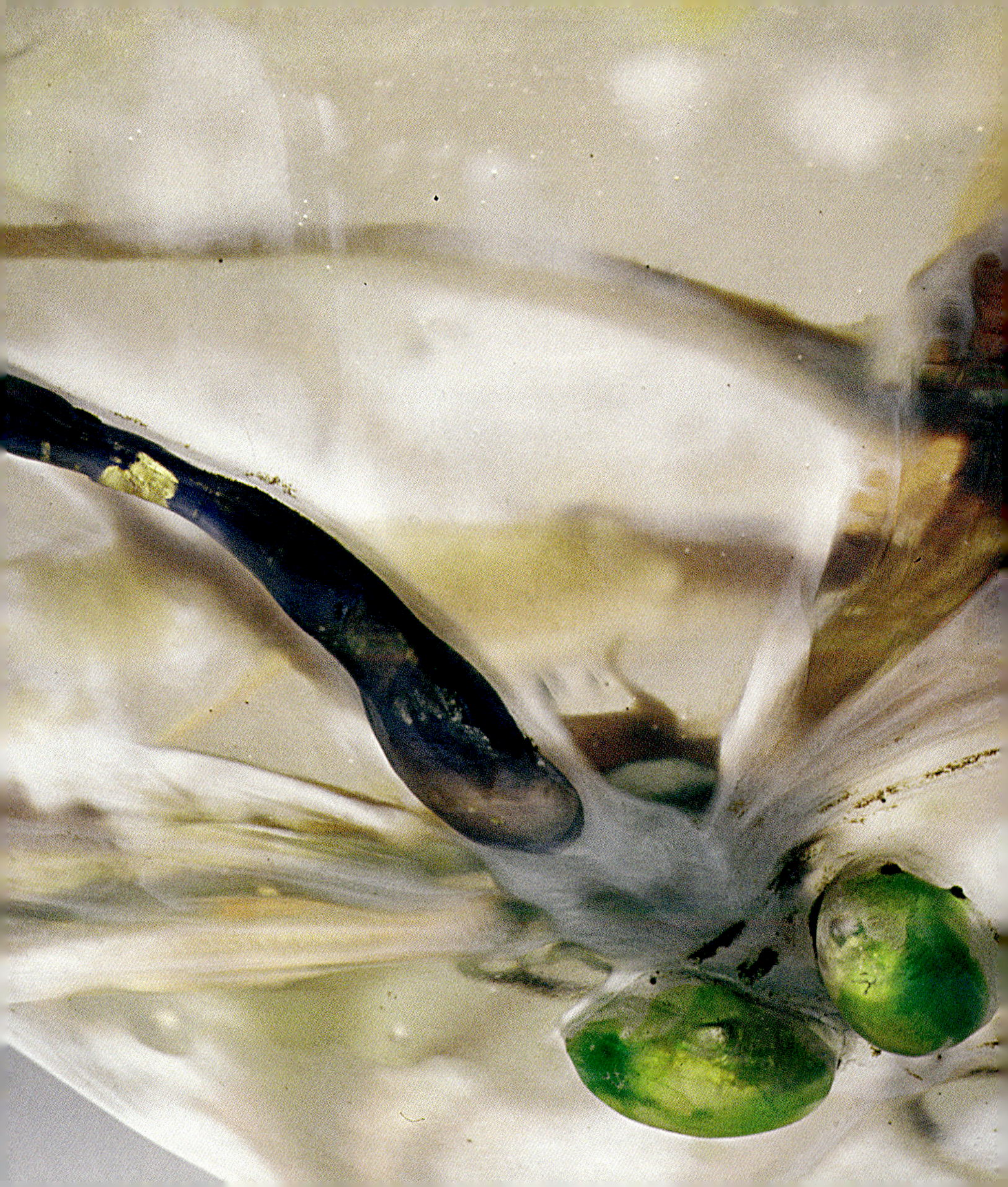

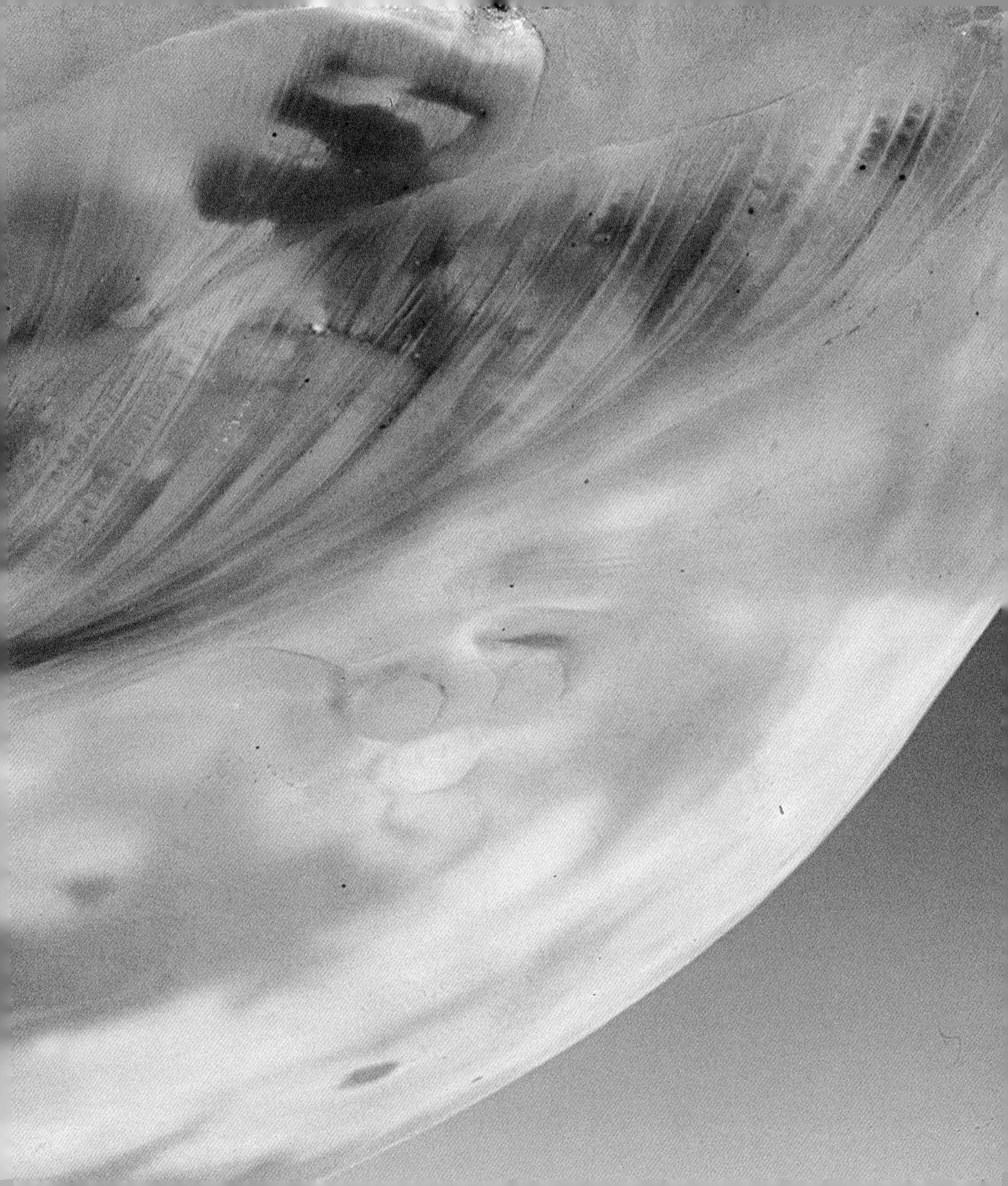

Previous double page:
Émile Gallé
Bowl with marqueterie intercalaire
(detail from p. 119)
Private collection

glass and paved the way for his numerous later inventions in this field. The young Gallé enjoyed the cultural climate of Weimar, a city of poets, and learned to love the music of Franz Liszt and Richard Wagner there. In 1866 he moved to Meisenthal, a center of glass manufacture in Lorraine, and completed an apprenticeship with a long-standing partner of his father. In the glassworks of Burgun, Schverer & Co. he thoroughly learned the trade of glassblowing. In these early years Gallé also studied painting and produced drawings that he was able to put to practical use in his father's company.

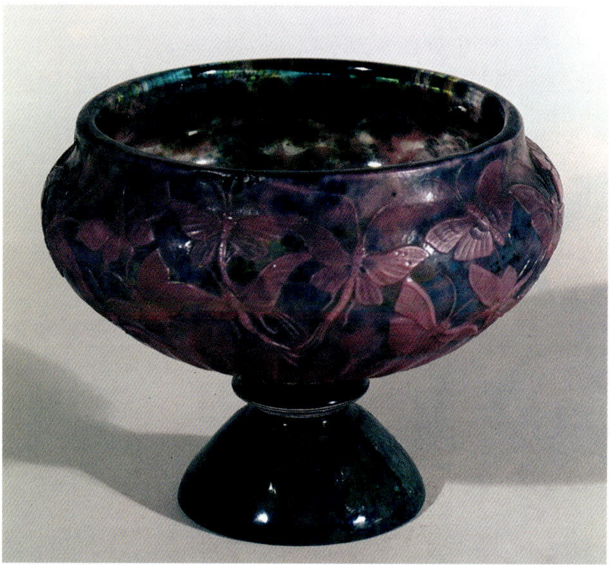

Émile Gallé
Bowl with butterflies and winged insects, 1889
Musées d'Arts Décoratifs

Stimulating Encounters

In 1871 he had the opportunity to represent the family company at an exhibition in London. Here he could make the acquaintance of the Arts and Crafts movement on its home territory, and he spent much time in the crafts museum, where he was first exposed to Japanese art. He was later to intensify this knowledge greatly through his close friendship with the nature researcher Tokuso Takasima, who was in Nancy in the early 1880s in order to study at the school of forestry. Gallé had intense discussions with Takasima about methods of planting and garden design. As an acknowledged expert in the field, Gallé was called to join the department of plants at the Paris world exhibition of 1878. The depth of his interest in botany is also evident from the fact that in later life he engaged in a lively exchange of ideas with the botanist employed by the city of Nancy and took on a gardener at his estate La Garenne for this purpose.

The decisive moment in the development of Émile Gallé as a glass artist can be dated to 1874, the year when his father passed the artistic direction of the company to him. Only four years later he triumphed at the world exhibition with a much-admired glass named "clair de lune," which indicated the path that Gallé would take. This milky-blue glass scored a bull's-eye with the taste of the times, and the enthusiasm that it aroused led to a flood of moonlight glass products by other manufacturers.

Émile Gallé
Vase with dragonfly above water lilies
c. 1900, flashed glass
Height: 37 cm
Private collection

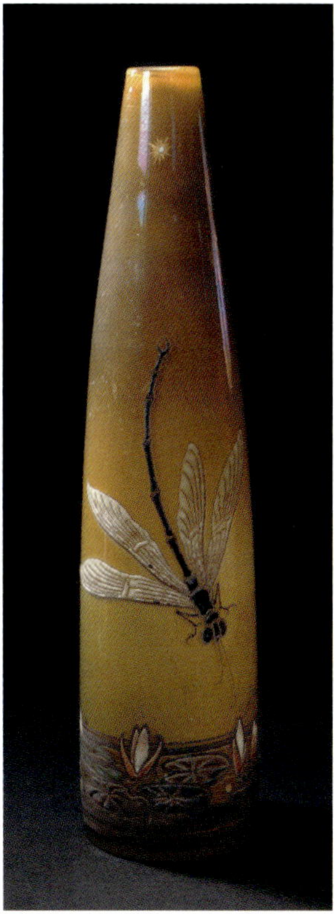

Inspiration from Nature

Even though the observation – indeed, the almost pantheistic veneration – of nature represents one of the essential foundations of Émile Gallé's art, he would never have considered simply imitating it. As he put it himself to the jury at the annual exhibition on the Champ de Mars in Paris: "The jury will surely note that, although nature is always my starting point, I try to liberate myself from it in good time in order to achieve my own character and manner of expression."

Gallé was always extremely well prepared when he attended the jury presentations for craft competitions and took detailed written explanations with him. This was the basis for *Ecrits pour l'Art,* which his widow Henriette published in 1908. These writings also contain the beginnings of his Symbolist view of nature, which endowed plants with a soul. He sang the praises of "Queen Rose" and expressed his fascination at the aura of the orchid, which provides food for all the senses and seems to encapsulate within itself all the mysteries of the world with its extraordinary form and its alluring scent. This plant appeared to be the very symbol of the era of decadence. Not only the orchid can be seen on many of Gallé's vases; intoxicating and deadly plants, too, such as hemlock give an emotional charge to his glass objects.

Gallé also experimented by including many insects on his works – as in Art Nouveau as a whole, the scarily beautiful dragonfly is the dominant creature – and created ostentatious showpieces similar to those of Mannerist art. His combinations of insects and a variety of techniques to create inclusions, which are reminiscent of age-old amber, are especially sophisticated.

In the field of ceramics, too, Émile Gallé handled the material in an equally creative and inventive manner. Here it was very easy to achieve sculptural effects by applying material to the surface, and the final glazing provided a wide scope for experiments.

Talking Glasses

If nature was his starting point, it was above all relationships to contemporary literature that brought his art to a new plane. In many works Gallé included literary quotes which reveal his known leanings to Symbolism. His so-called *verres parlants* (talking glasses) were probably the most important reinterpretation of the art of glass that followed from this practice. Gallé himself pointed out that in the field of decoration what matters more than anything is to generate an idea through an image. He created his *décor symbolique* as his own medium for this purpose.

In this approach Émile Gallé is a true representative of Art Nouveau, whose intention was not only decoration but also a Symbolist exaltation of the decorative theme. Gallé brought the use of inscriptions on glasses to a new level of refinement. With carefully chosen quotations he created a particular mood, which was intended to open up an abundance of further associations. With this in mind, quotes from Charles Baudelaire seemed most appropriate, especially, in view of Baudelaire's main work *Les Fleurs du Mal,* if they elevated his flower glasses to the status of a cipher for decadence. Baudelaire's floral mysticism contained influ-

Émile Gallé
Orchid Stalk vase
1884, faience, Barbotine painting, gold dust and applications
29 × 28 × 31.5 cm
Musée d'Art et d'Histoire, Geneva

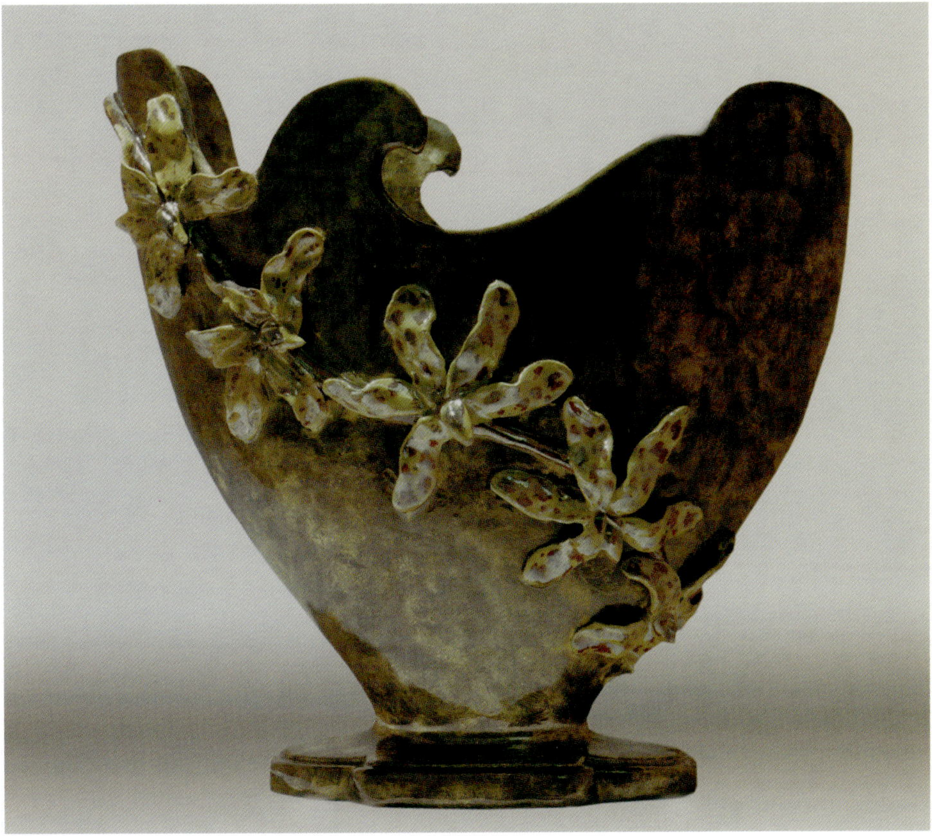

ential impulses for Émile Gallé's art. However, he also employed quotes from Victor Hugo, a writer with whom Gallé had much in common in terms of patriotic sentiment. Occasionally he made use of short poems by his wife and profound epigrams of his own to round off the series of "talking glasses."

Émile Gallé
Table lamp with rhododendron decoration, *c.* 1900, glass of various colors, cast in relief
Height: 47.5 cm
Private collection

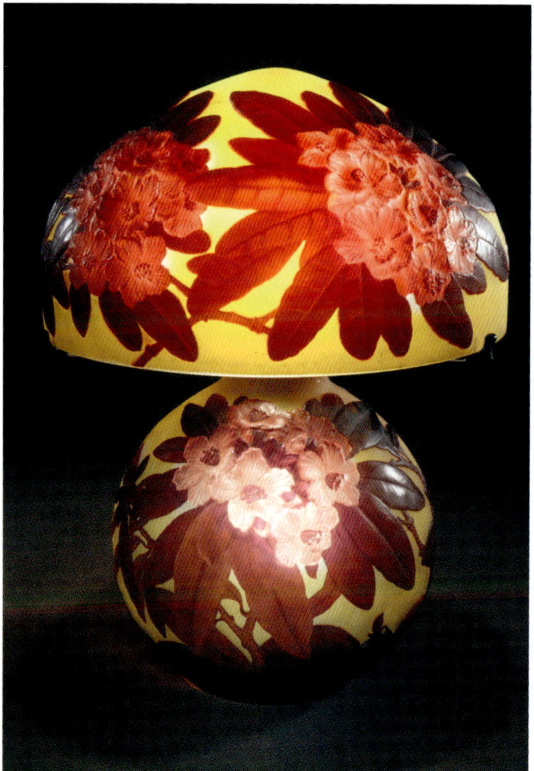

Expressive Materials

Gallé caused a sensation in 1889 at the world exhibition in Paris with his *vases de tristesse* (vases of sadness). On the one hand they were undoubtedly the result of successful experiments with so-called hyalith glass: a dark, almost black glass that nobody before him had been able to make. On the other hand, these objets d'art were truly in the spirit of the *fin de siècle* in that they embodied all the melancholy and heaviness of a decadent society. Gallé dedicated some of the *vases de tristesse* to the "forêts qui ne sont plus," the forests that once were, and others to good friends who had recently died.

The Paris world exhibition was a triumph for Gallé, the "magician in glass." He was admired for the more than 100 different shades of color in his glass, and his exciting techniques of production and decoration were celebrated. On 26 April 1889 Gallé had registered a patent for a complex technique of glassmaking that produced a highly impressive effect: marqueterie. The term was known from wood crafts, and with glass it functioned in a similar way: individual pieces of glass with specific shapes were inserted into the molten glass and rolled flat into the surface. This was in effect a simple principle, which must have been known to glass artists in ancient times, but the difficulty involved in this technique was the necessity to heat the glass vessel several times, in the process of which the various structures in the glass could react in different ways and cause the whole product to shatter. Here Gallé carried out numerous experiments that eventually showed him which temperatures and mixtures of glass would work best.

Gallé registered a patent for a second technique at the same time as that for *marqueterie:* patination. Interestingly, in this process he took advantage of an effect that troubled most glass-makers: the inclusion of particles of soot, which unavoidably float through the air in a glassblower's studio as a result of the open fire. A perfectionist, Gallé concluded that if he could not avoid this contamination of the glass, then he would at least bring it under control. He therefore deliberately used the effect to impart a structure to his glasses and vases that gave them the feel of other materials such as fabrics or a delicate layer of hoar frost. The popularity of this kind of glass as a mood-conveying material began with his invention of the patination technique.

Other experiments were conducted in Émile Gallé's laboratory. They all seem to have served the primary aim of conveying the master's feelings, dreams and ideas. With tin oxide, bone ash and the addition of lime Gallé developed an opaque glass. Where previous man-

Émile Gallé
Table lamp with hop decoration
c. 1900, grey glass with red cameo decoration
Height: 56.5 cm
Private collection

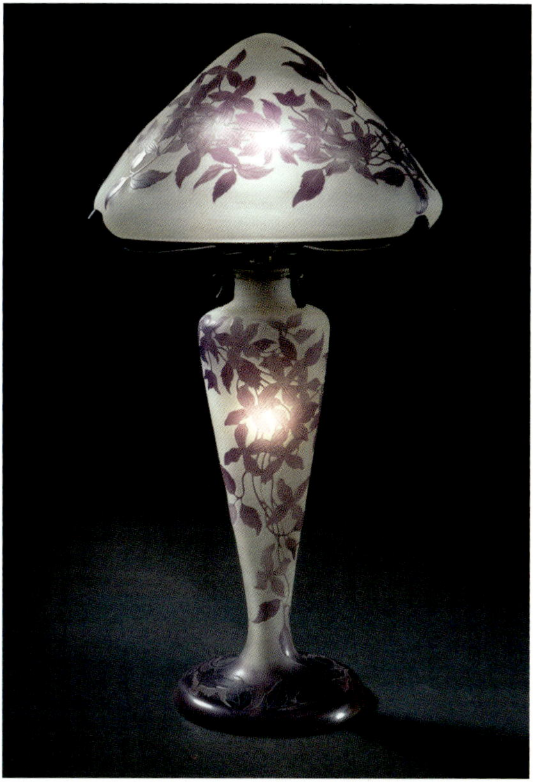

ufacturers had made efforts to impart the greatest possible transparency to their glass, Gallé achieved unprecedented virtuoso effects. The opaque glass, which resulted from a mixture of the molten mass with fluorides, had a mysterious shimmer. In developing black or red opaque glass, also known as hyalith glass, Gallé consciously used the aesthetics of the material to give his objects a mood. The technique that came into play here, flashed glass, had been used by Gallé since 1882, and he had brought it to absolute perfection. In this process the basic glass vessel is covered with a second layer of glass, usually in a different color. When staying in London Gallé had seen the famous Portland Vase in the British Museum, and the ancient cameo technique has a lasting influence on him. Now he used it to cut his landscapes and depictions of nature into different layers of glass.

Gallè adopted painting in enamel from the tradition of Baroque glass. The painting imparts a joyous rustic character to the green vases, and its range of colors forms a charming contrast to the intense green of the colored glass.

Success as a Manufacturer

Gallé was proud of his many inventions and never tired of praising their uniqueness: "After a huge number of experiments, I have developed no less than 100 different types of preparation and composition for manufacturing my polychrome items. The permutations of these allow me to achieve an unlimited variety of chances and nuances that have never before been realized in the art of glass." Apart from pride in his own work, however, Gallé also showed his admiration for the inventions of other great artists in glass. For example he had great respect for and produced imitations of the famous lava glass of Tiffany, whose factory had been a customer of Gallé-Reimener for a long period.

Gallé's most remarkable glass objects were never manufactured in large quantities. There were never more than five versions in one series. However, business considerations led Gallé's factory to develop mass production in parallel with this. The technique of etching made it possible to decorate a large number of glass items quickly. The undecorated vessels came from Meisenthal in Lorraine, which by this time was under German occupation. However, Gallé did not have a high opinion of etching, as much could be destroyed in this process and the artist's creativity took second place to the course taken by the etching fluid, which was sometimes random.

Items that he made, exceptionally, as unique pieces, are of special interest. Most of them were commissioned works such as the vase that he made for the 70th birthday of Louis Pasteur or one for the Belgian chemist Ernest Solvay, which Gallé mounted on a base of soda crystals in 1902. Gallé is also known to have made one-off items for the family of the Russian tsars, often in combination with holders produced by the famous jeweler Fabergé.

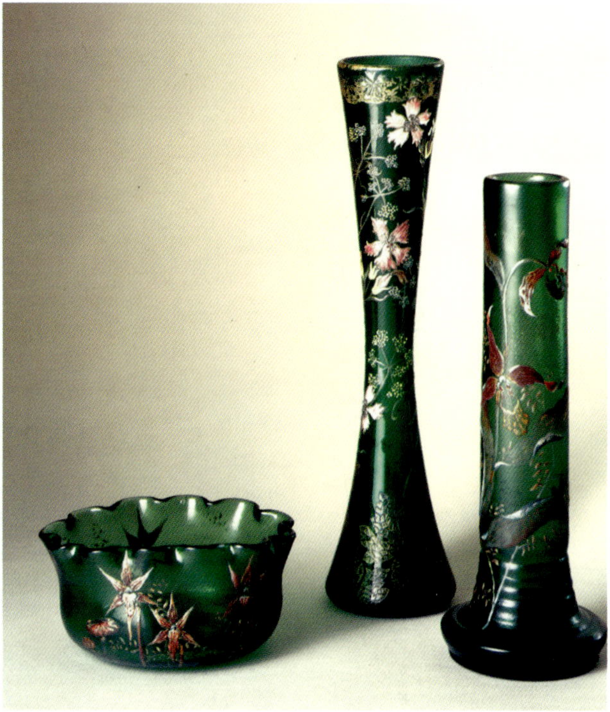

Émile Gallé
Ensemble with three vases
1892–94, glass with enamel painting
Augustiner-Museum, Freiburg

Gallé as a Furniture Designer

At the world exhibition of 1889 the master designer demonstrated that he was active in another field, and he did this with an incomparable fanfare. "Ma racine est au fond des bois," he had once announced theatrically: "My

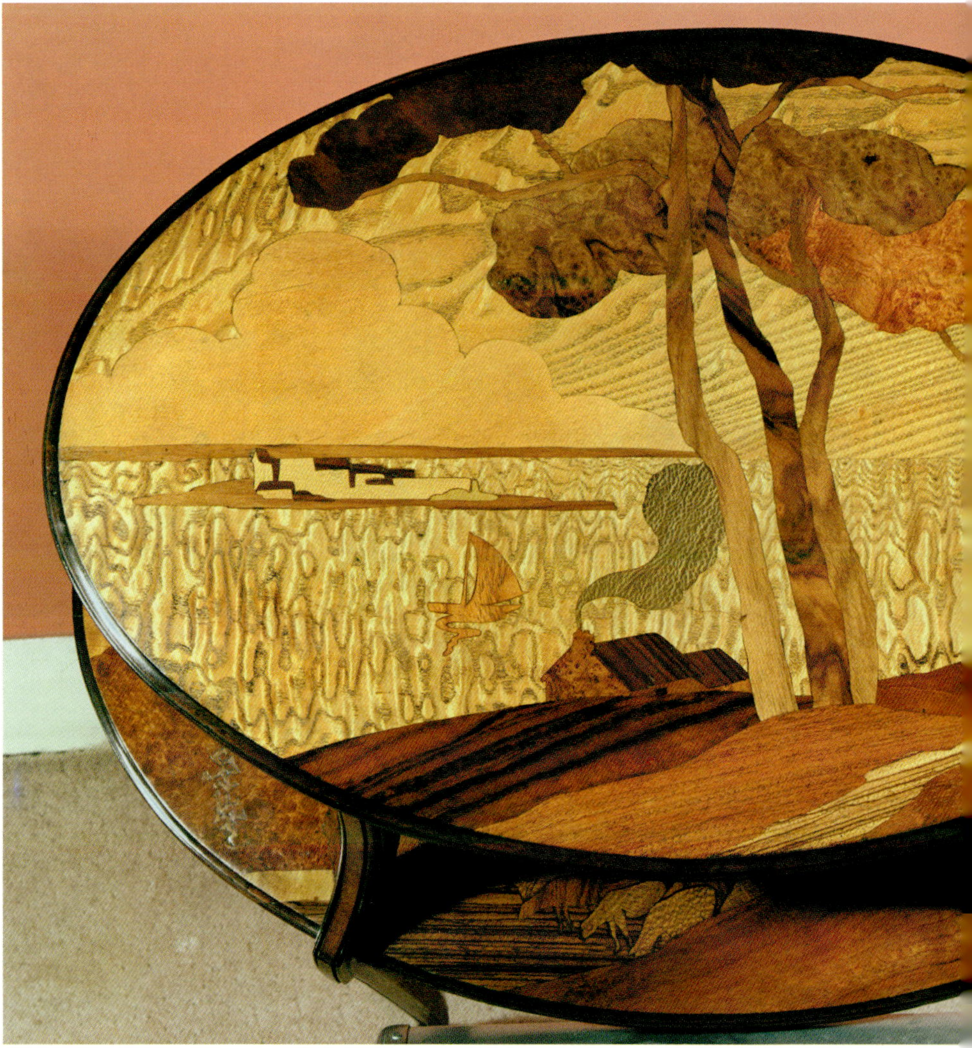

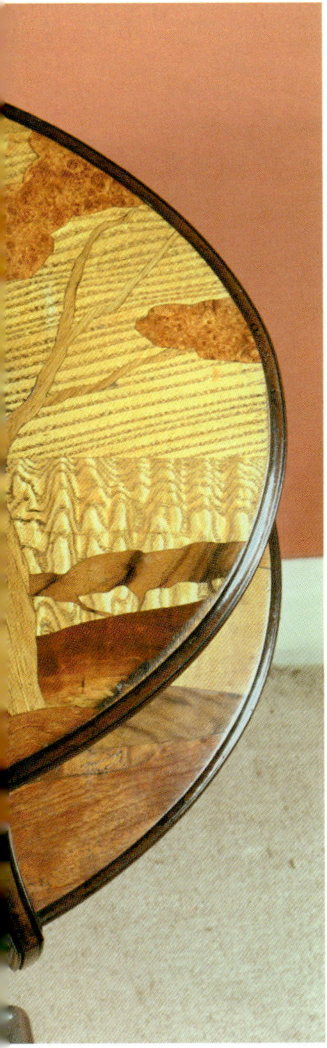

roots lie deep in the woods." He now presented his work as a furniture designer on the central Grande Galerie d'Honneur of the world exhibition in a pavilion that impressed visitors with its imposing height of 15 meters. A cedarwood showcase with an inner veneer of pale blue ash was decorated with apricot-colored veils. The crowning glory was a bower decorated with columns and fabrics flowing down from its roof. Here Gallé exhibited furniture on which he had been working for about five years. Two stories recount how a man who was specialized in ceramics and glass came to take up the work of a cabinet maker. One of them, probably an anecdote intended to create his own myth, was told by Gallè himself. Here he made a connection between his work in wood, which he described as having taken hold of him like nature's roots, with visions that appeared to him at the fascinating sight of the grain in wood. The other story begins with an invitation to Gallè to take part in the exhibition *La pierre, le bois, la terre et le verre* (Stone, Wood, Earth and Glass) in 1884, on the condition that he would produce something for each of these fields, i.e. not only ceramics and glass but also wood. The result of this was that Emil Gallé presented himself at the world exhibition of 1889 not only as a celebrated artist in glass, with glasses and vases shown in a kiosk of similar pomp to the furniture pavilion, but also as a *maître ebéniste,* a master cabinet

Émile Gallé
Table top
After 1890
Private collection

In their private sphere collectors could present the perfection of Gallé's objects as items of ostentation that were in no way inferior to the show furniture of previous centuries. Artistic appreciation and the tangible preciousness of the materials combined to a unified whole.

maker. Public enthusiasm for design in the private sphere, an enthusiasm aroused by the efforts of men such as Samuel Bing, undoubtedly played an important part. Customers were positively clamoring for furniture with the popular Gallé curve, and from the very beginning Gallé took care to give items for the mass market the same status as designs for special prestige objects. This reveals his social conscience: Gallé was an artist who not only intervened in political issues but also believed that good taste should be available to the less well-off classes. It was natural that Gallé should use the technique of *marqueterie,* which he had successfully applied to glassmaking, in his furniture designs too, by producing enchanting combinations of the delicate color shades of wood from different kinds of native fruit trees. As with his glass, he attempted to give a soul to the items of furniture by means of thematic programs. He made a "Rhine table," a dressing table with the title "The Scent of the Past" and a bed with an over-life-size moth carved into one end. In technical terms Gallé's furniture designs remained conventional, however, and resemble those of French ébénistes of the 18th century.

Final Triumphs

Gallé's true virtuosity, his delicate Mannerism, is revealed in his glass art. His late designs confirm this impressively. When their appearance and their meaning merged to form a harmonious whole, his works took on epoch-making significance. Artifacts such as these, which expanded the horizons of traditional art in glass, are the real legacy of Émile Gallé, whose development to a Modernist style abruptly ended with his early death. At the world exhibition of 1900 he once again surprised his admirers in the theatrical presentation of his stand. Its centerpiece was a miniature kiln; shards of glass and scattered equipment provided an unexpectedly intimate view into the artist's creative crucible.

Dining room, commissioned from Émile Gallé in 1902
Consists of: *panetière* (bread bin), with matching thematic plant ornamentation in intarsia work (grain, wheat); chair and table (unique items); vases, made between 1890 and 1919
Musée d'Arts Décoratifs, Paris

The following words were written above the opening to his little kiln: "But when men turn evil and distort truth and justice, come to me, you demons of fire! Shatter the vases and make the kiln collapse, so that all men may learn to be just"!

By this time Gallé had also taken a liking to the theatrical effects of modern electric lamps. He thought they suited a *fin de siècle* society that lusted after luxury and sensation. Gallé's work after the turn of the century was dominated by ostentatious lighting, including models with wilting petals and above all the legendary "hand of algae." His wife managed the company after Gallé's death. When the company once again took part in a world exhibition in 1925, it was obvious once and for all how much Gallé's work embodied the spirit of the *fin de siècle:* when seen alongside Art Deco glasses, they seemed to have come from a different world. However, their charm lies in just that: they seem to be from another world, a magical realm. And poetry is the key that opens the gate to this world.

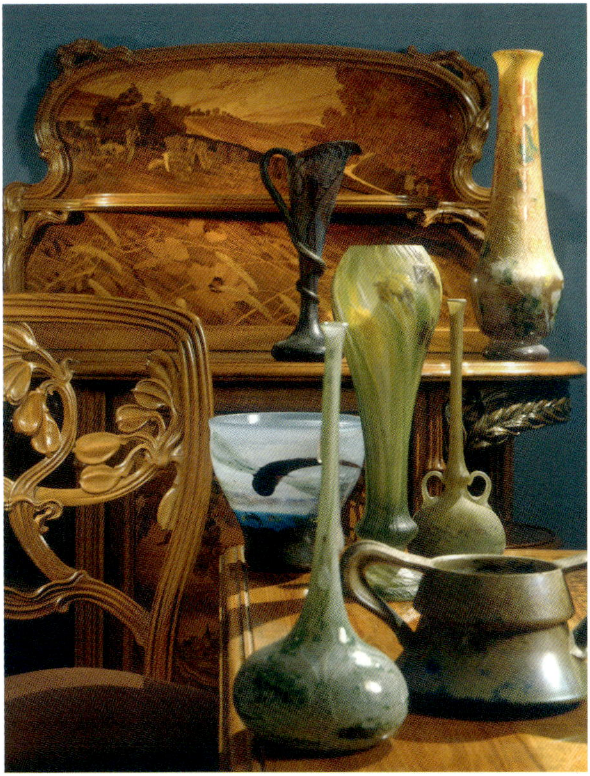

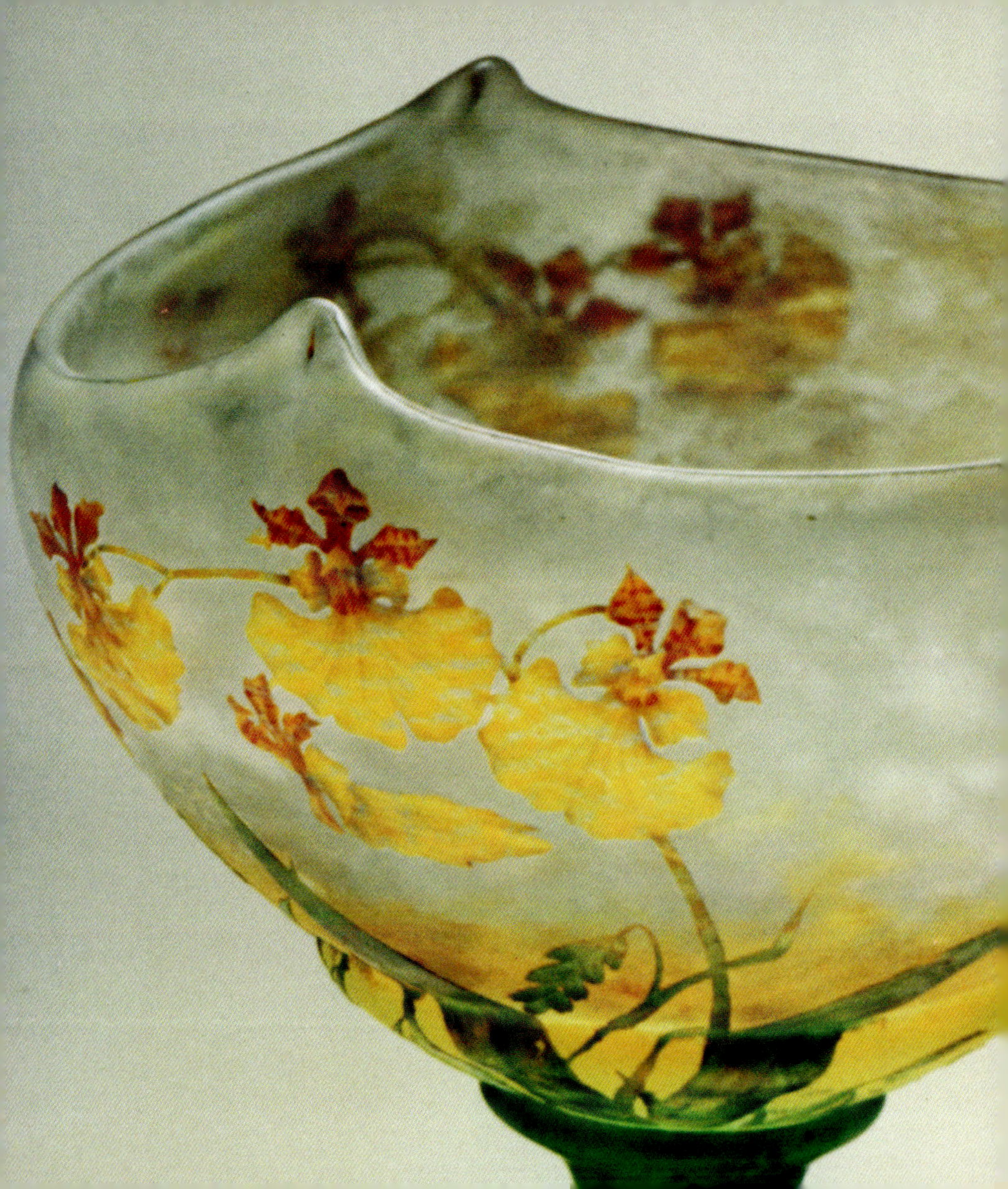

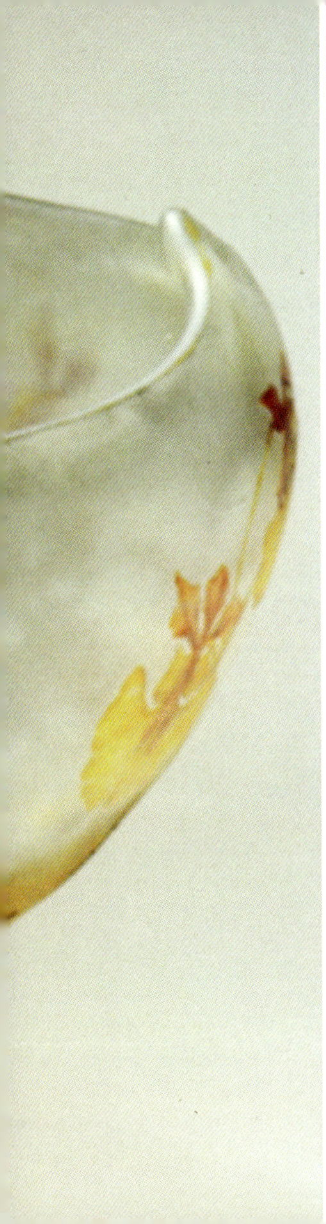

The School of Nancy

The Alliance Provinciale des Industries d'Art, founded in 1901, is a good example of how craftsmen at the turn of the century attended to the business aspects of their profession. After the success of craftsmen from Lorraine at the 1900 world exhibition in Paris, the founding of an association was a matter of course. The priorities of the School of Nancy were to promote crafts and especially to educate popular taste. With its close connection between art and industrial production, the capital of Lorraine even supplanted Paris as the leading center of arts décoratifs.

Auguste Daum
Table lamp (detail)
Glass, etched and cut

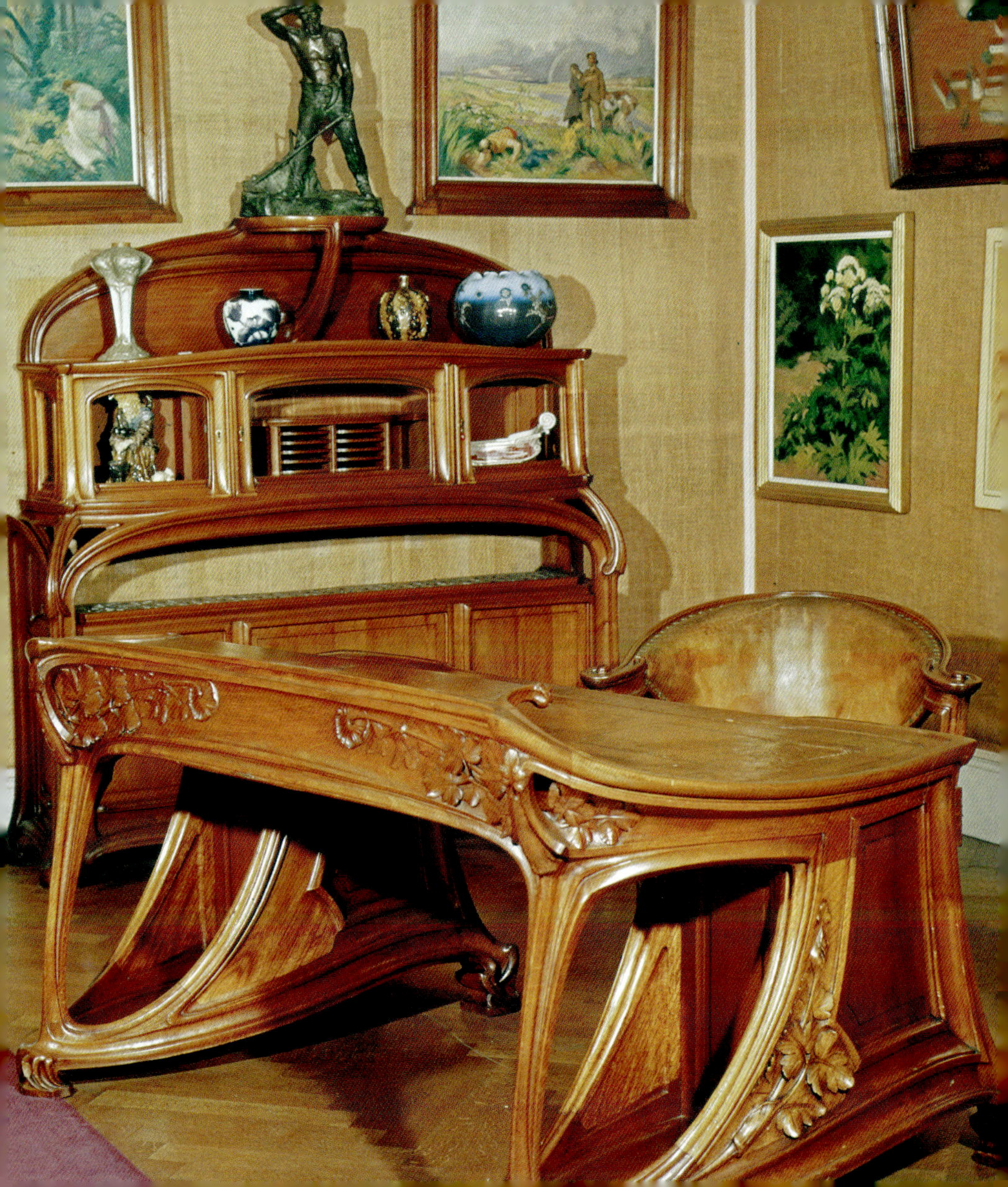

The School of Nancy

The Daum brothers operated a glass factory which could hold its own alongside Émile Gallé, the outstanding glass artist, and even surpass him in some ways. The founder of the factory, Jean Daum, came to glass production largely by chance. As a notary he had lent money to a glass factory, which he eventually had to take over himself, as it continued to make losses. His sons Jean-Antonin and Jean-Louis Auguste made the ailing business into a successful company which exists to this day and set new standards in series production.

Collaboration with extremely talented designers such as Henri Bergé, and at times also Louis Majorelle and Almaric Walter, the master of glass paste, lent the objects made by the Daum brothers considerable elegance, even in mass production. They staked their success on subtle variations in the glass surface, which they treated by means of monochrome etching and inclusions of glass powder. Designs for electric lamps were their great specialty: the new technology of electric lighting seemed ideally suited for creative ideas in glass and thus for the craft business. Like Gallé's designs, the glasses produced by the Daum brothers were characterized by a simply inexhaustible variety of natural motifs. In this regard all craftsmen from Lorraine, following a centuries-old tradition of designs based on nature, were of one mind. The School of Nancy had the goal of passing on this tradition to up-and-coming artists. Émile Gallé emphasized the need to establish a museum especially to support this aim.

"The School of Nancy is only waiting for the necessary resources in order to establish its own museum in Nancy, which will testify to its work and serve to educate

Eugène Vallin
Writing desk
1902
Musée de l'Ecole de Nancy,
Nancy

Louis Majorelle
Lamp from the Nenuphar series
c. 1902,
gilded bronze, glass
Musée d'Orsay, Paris

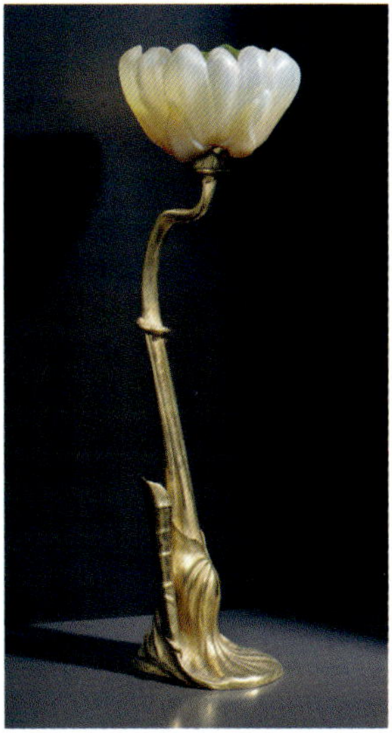

Daum Brothers
Two vases, with anemone decoration on the left, trailing flower decoration on the right
c. 1900, glass in differently colored layers
Height: 29.25 and 29.75 cm
Private collection

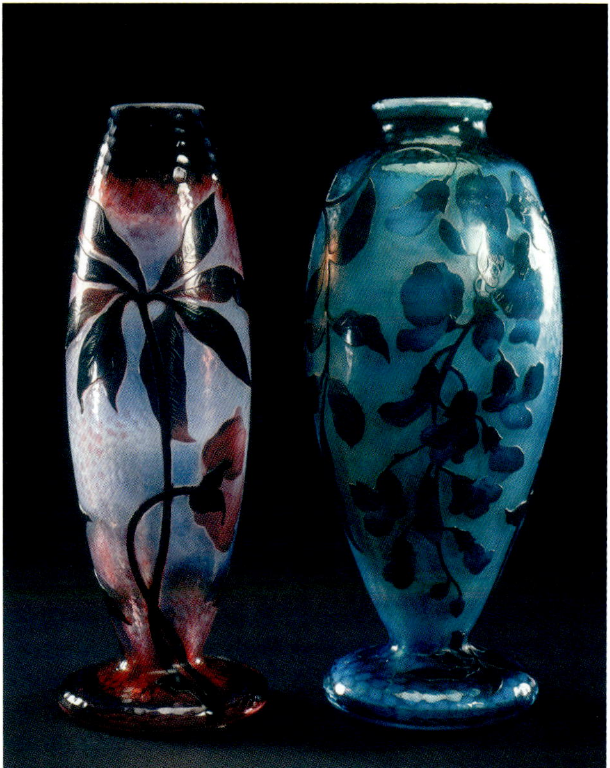

craftsmen and the public – a collection to preserve their masterpieces and models, to maintain their tradition."

The motto of the School of Nancy was "art dans tout" and "art pour tout," i.e. art that would pervade all areas of life and be accessible to everyone. One example for this was the success of the self-taught craftsman Eugène Vallin, who evolved confidently from his beginnings in the workshop of his uncle, which made church furnishings, and gained astonishing popularity with his concept of curves and counter-curves. He made the gate for the new Gallé factory. Established artists, too, developed their skills in the creative atmosphere that mergers of workshops and designers generated: Louis Majorelle, for example, who took over his father's long-established production at an early age. Majorelle increasingly distanced himself from the *style Majorelle* of his father and became a great master of the art of combining pieces of furniture with artistically worked metal fittings. In this way he made craft items that simultaneously marked his move to interesting and original metalwork.

Such a flowering of arts and crafts in consequence

of the collaboration of artists would, however, not have been possible without healthy economic growth. The basis for this was a young, wealthy society which settled in Nancy after the Franco-Prussian War of 1870/71. The demand emanating from this class resulted in unprecedented prosperity and made it possible to produce arts and crafts in large quantities, so that for some years Nancy was the leading center of crafts in France.

Daum Brothers
Vase with violet and cicada decoration
c. 1900, colored glass, polished and gilded
Height: 55.75 cm
Private collection

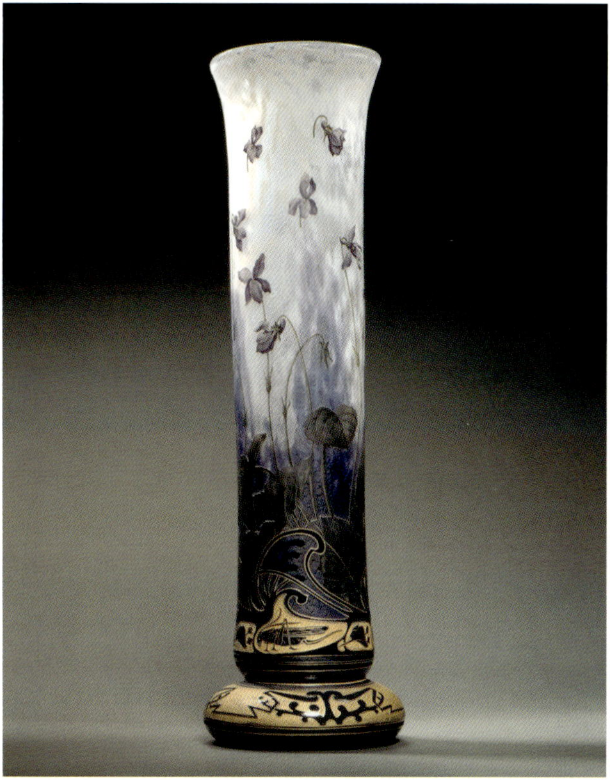

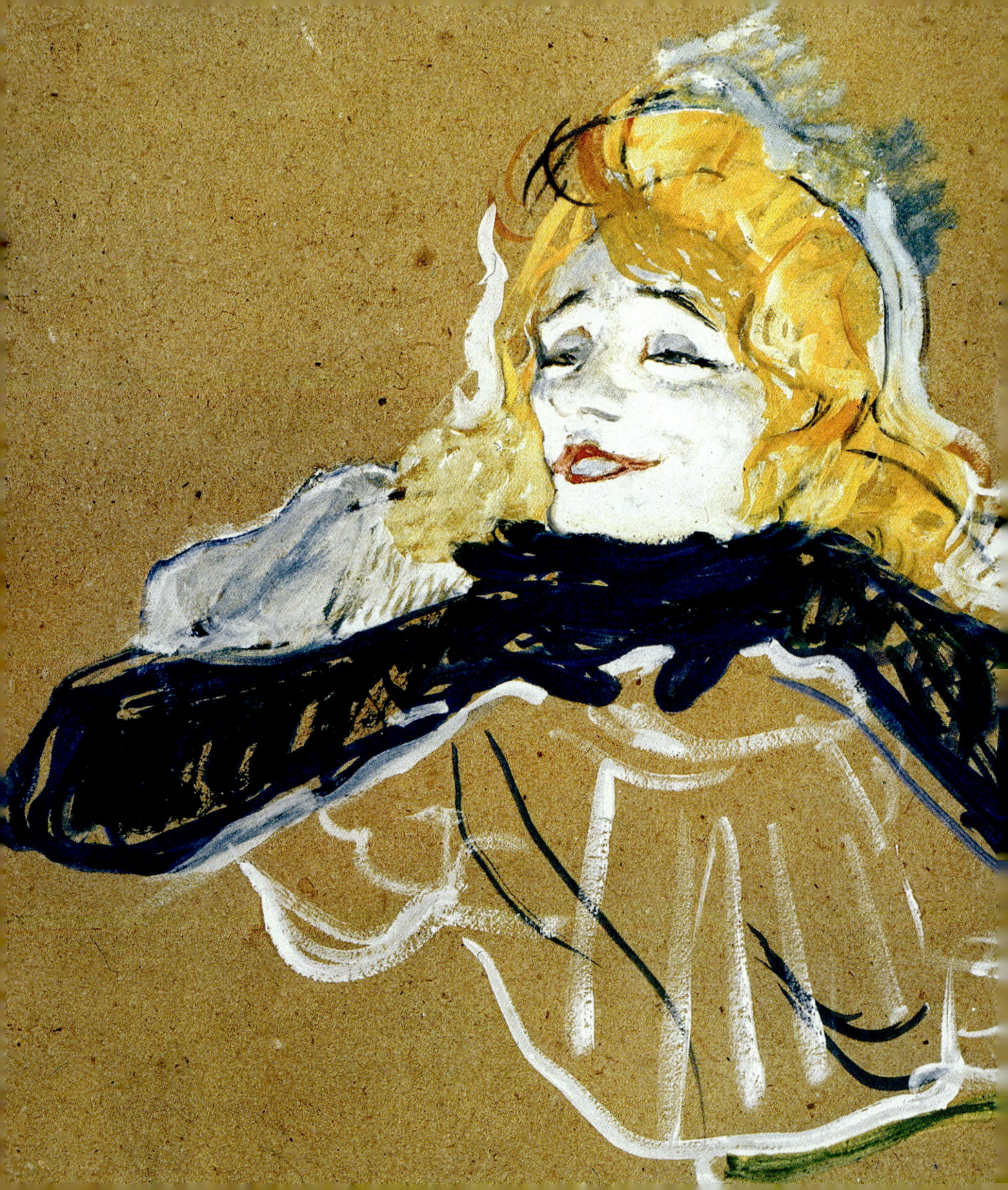

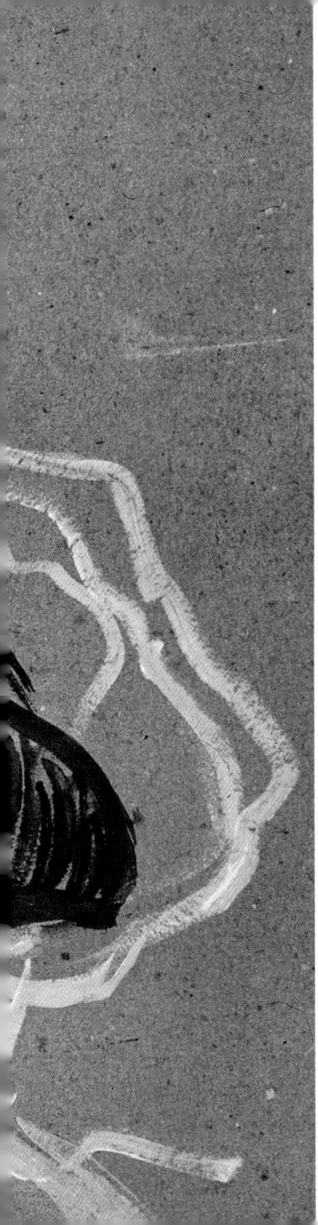

Theatrical *Belle Époque*

Black gloves were her trademark. They emphasized her image as a flamboyant diseuse, and Toulouse-Lautrec even made them the central motif of his paintings. Yvette Guilbert performed on the stages of the *belle époque,* a boom era for the entertainment business, and was the star of Parisian nightlife with her red wig and gaudy facial make-up. It was a period when stage performances flourished. Variety theatres and cabarets sprang up on every side. To be an actress was a fashionable profession, and no longer disreputable. There were personalities with their own unmistakable image: the goddess of the stage and the cult of the star made their entrance.

Henri de Toulouse-Lautrec
Yvette Guilbert sings Linger-Longer-Loo (detail)
1894, gouache on board
58 × 44 cm
Pushkin State Museum for the Arts, Moscow

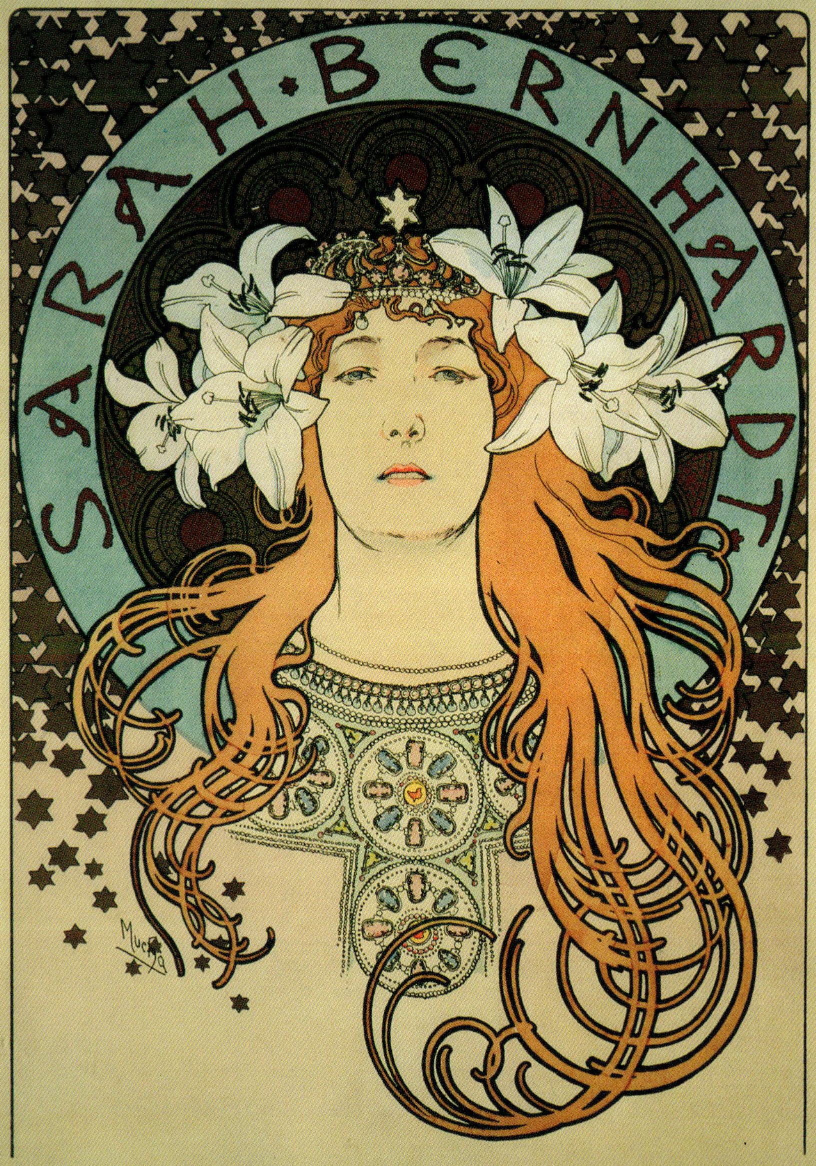
SARAH·BERNHARDT
Mucha

Goddesses of the Stage and Diseuses

A poster of her hung in Sigmund Freud's practice, and Oscar Wilde dedicated *Salome* to her: Sarah Bernhardt, one of the most famous actresses of the 19th and 20th centuries. She was born Henriette-Racine Bernardt in Paris in 1844 and from the age of 14, thanks to the influence of her mother's aristocratic lover, was trained at the famous Comédie-Française, where her first role was Iphigenie in 1862. After a tour of America in 1880 she played *La Dame aux Camélias* in London. This romantic and tragic role, perfectly suited to the taste of the *fin de siècle,* was to be her most famous. In 1882 she married Jacques Damala, a Greek diplomat, whose addiction to gambling and morphine almost ruined her financially and emotionally.

In 1899 Sarah Bernhardt played the title role in Shakespeare's *Hamlet* – a classic male role. For contemporaries she was identified with her star role as the *Dame aux Camélias.* This theme of the consumptive courtesan in an unhappy relationship was a great favorite of *fin de siècle* theatergoers.

The Diva and the Artist: The Rise of Alphons Mucha

In 1894 Bernhardt performed at her own theatre, the Théâtre de la Renaissance, playing the role of Gismonda, which she wished to advertise with a poster. The commission went to Alfons Maria Mucha, a Czech artist who had worked as a scene painter in theatres in the previous years. The manner in which Mucha portrayed her as a kind of saint within a sea of ornament is unusual: the poster, in extreme portrait format, is almost two meters high. At the time the printer doubted whether he could print it at all. However, Sarah Bernhardt was delighted – so enthusiastic that she decided to conclude an exclusive six-year contract with the young artist. This was the start of the exceptional career of the Art Nouveau artist Alfons Mucha. In the following years he not only caused a stir with more posters for

Alphonse Mucha
Sarah Bernhardt "La Plume"
(detail)
1896, color lithograph
75 × 55.5 cm
Mucha Trust

the divine Bernhardt (the outstanding examples were for her roles as *La Dame aux Camélias* and *Hamlet*), but also designed all her stage sets and costumes. When Sarah Bernhardt met Mucha she was already a celebrated actress. The projection of her image as a goddess of the stage, which the particular aesthetic of the posters achieved, made her into an icon beyond the borders of France. For Mucha, this collaboration with the actress meant his breakthrough as an artist. His individual style spread with lightning speed and became a fashion of the *belle époque.* His fame reached America. The prospect of enjoying his success to the full must have appealed to him, and in 1904 he set off to conquer the New World. However, his reception there was mixed. The fact that graphic art did not have the same status in America as in Europe was the main obstacle to his success, and so in 1910 he returned home to Prague.

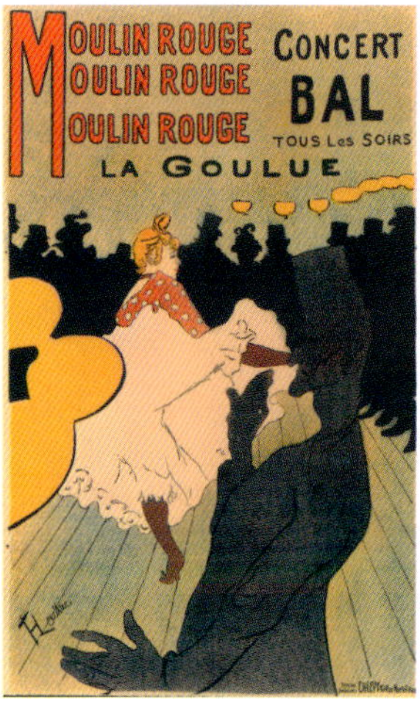

Henri de Toulouse-Lautrec
Moulin Rouge – La Goulue
1891, four-color lithograph
84 × 122 cm
Private collection

Eleonora Duse and Tilla Durieux

Sarah Bernhardt often undertook tours, during which she basked in and reinforced her extraordinary fame as an eccentric actress with a scandalous private life. During one of Bernhardt's performances in Turin she was seen by the then unknown Eleonora Duse, who resolved to attain equal renown. Duse even dared take on the role of *La Dame aux Camélias,* and showed that with her own, more reserved way of acting she could stand comparison to Bernhardt, whose style was ostentatious. She created the *femme fragile* of the stage, an alternative image to the *femme fatale* embodied by Bernhardt. While Eleonora Duse and Sarah Bernhardt captivated audiences in countries where Romance languages were spoken, in Austria and Germany there were other actresses who enjoyed similar admiration. It was well known that Franz von Stuck liked to portray dancers and actresses in their roles. One of his most powerful paintings is a portrait of Tilla Durieux as Circe. This actress was born in Austria as Ottilie Godeffroy, triumphed in Munich as Lulu and was adored by fashionable society with her intense style of acting. In 1903 Tilla Durieux – she had changed her name under pressure from her family – had her first great successes under the director and actor Max Reinhardt in Berlin. She played Salome, and from that time was seen as the prototype of the exotic, cat-like creature. In 1913 she played Circe in the drama of that name by Pedro Calderón, and a year later took on the star role of Lulu at the Künstlertheater in Munich. Durieux, who immersed herself in intellectual avant-garde circles, was married to the art dealer Paul Cassirer from 1910 until 1926. When she signed the divorce papers, he killed himself in an adjoining room. This tragic relationship with one of the most prominent art dealers of the time did at least result in countless portraits of the willful Durieux. Auguste Renoir, Lovis Corinth and Franz von Stuck all took an active part in shaping her myth.

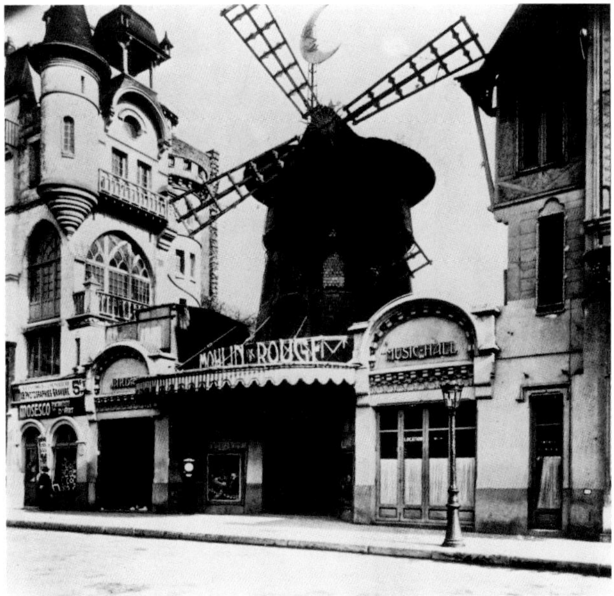

Eugene Atget
Moulin Rouge,
Boulevard de Clichy
c. 1890, photograph

Yvette Guilbert

In the years around 1900, alongside the stages for great dramatic art, there was also the dazzling world of variety theatre. The name refers to the many-faceted, changing

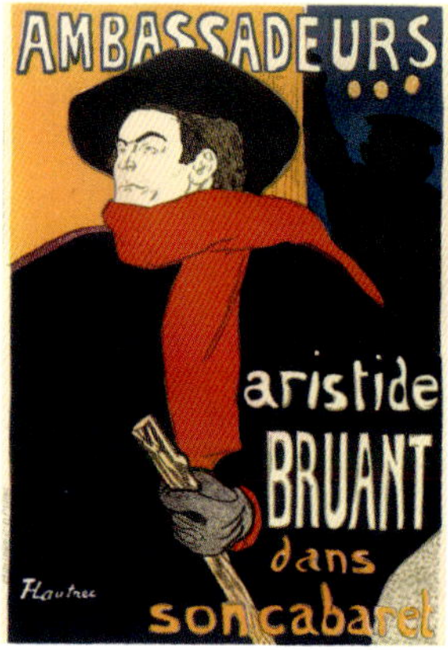

Henri de Toulouse-Lautrec
Poster for the chanson singer Aristide Bruant
1892, six-color lithograph
Private collection

entertainment that was offered, ranging from hippodromes with trick riders to lascivious dances and earthy proletarian cabaret. Yvette Guilbert was a celebrated star of the Bohemian scene who gained double fame through the works of Montmartre artists. She recited provocatively honed texts and made a mockery of the censors by simply omitting the prohibited words. She was one of the main attractions when the renowned Moulin Rouge opened in 1889. However, she would also perform at different venues in Paris on a single evening. She was an unmistakable figure in the nightlife of Paris, whose most famous chanson was about Madame Arthur, a lady who is kept by a rich beau.

The Stars of Henri de Toulouse-Lautrec

The legendary Moulin Rouge, which was opened by a former hippodrome owner named Zidler, put on a carnival-style potpourri of the most diverse attractions, from acrobats to salacious dancers and animal shows. One man felt most at home backstage among the artists: Henri de Toulouse-Lautrec, the frail scion of an old French aristocratic family. Sitting still in a position from which he could observe the performers, he drew them all. One of his favorites, apart from Guilbert, was the dancer La Goulue, who performed incredible feats of agility on stage and danced an erotic and lascivious version of the cancan known as the *chahut.* He also drew the tragic figure of Jane Avril, who was forced to spend her childhood in a lunatic asylum and now enchanted the *belle époque* with her expressive stage act.

Toulouse-Lautrec had come to Paris from Albi, his home in the south of France, and as a self-taught artist took a particular interest in the new technique of lithography. His job on the staff of the *Revue Blanche* gave him access to the *Caf' Conc',* concerts in bars and coffee houses, and to the stages at the Moulin Rouge and Chat Noir. In 1885 he met Aristide Bruant, who was then opening his Club Le

Mirliton. Bruant came from a markedly proletarian background, which he now brought to the stage as a singer.

For the artists of Montmartre he cultivated his image as a son of the working class. In accordance with this program, visitors to Le Mirliton were subject to a barrage of abuse as they walked through the door. Henri de Toulouse-Lautrec painted Bruant as the rebellious singer in the pose of a Bohemian, wearing his characteristic red scarf. Before he opened his own club, Bruant had a contract with one of the oldest and most popular cabaret venues of the city, the Chat Noir.

Chat Noir

Originally, when Montmartre was still a suburb with a rural character, it had a single inn for trippers from the city, the Moulin de la Galette, which had already been made known by the Impressionists. So-called citizens' balls, the only

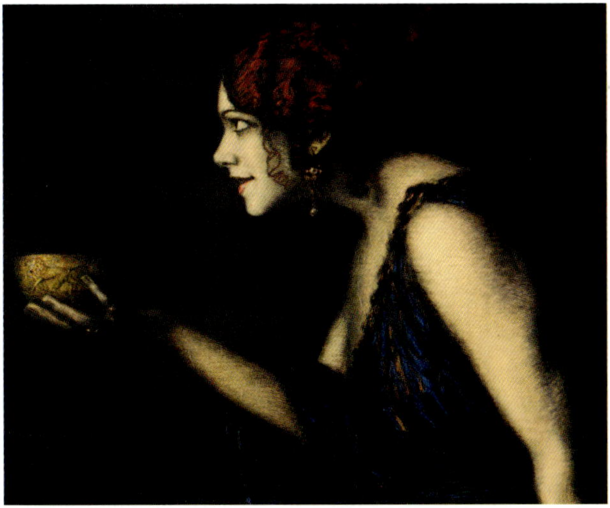

Franz von Stuck
Tilla Durieux as Circe
c. 1912/13, oil on wood
60 × 68 cm
SMPK, Nationalgalerie, Berlin

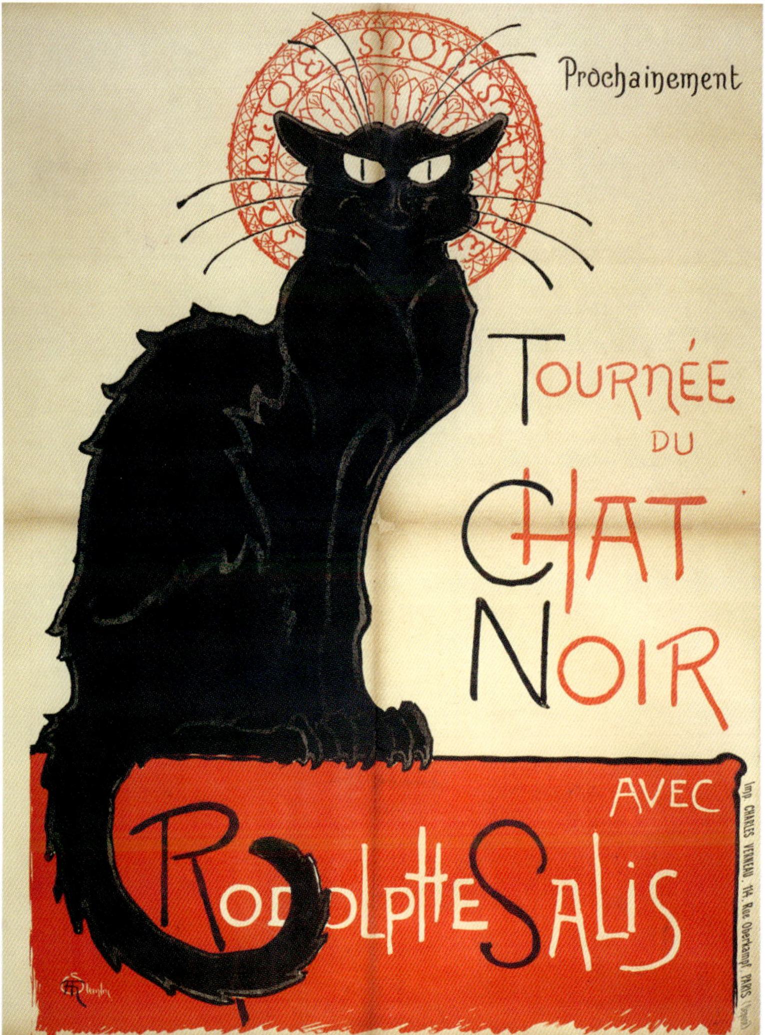
Prochainement
Tournée du
Chat Noir
avec
Rodolphe Salis
Imp. CHARLES VERNEAU, 114, Rue Oberkampf, PARIS

attraction far and wide, were held here once weekly. In 1878 the poet Émile Goudeau hit upon the idea of opening the first cabaret in Montmartre, Le Sherry-Cobbler. The great success of this establishment, which was a rendezvous for artists, attracted the son of a liqueur manufacturer, Rodolphe Salis. Salis had earned a modest living as a caricaturist in the Quartier Latin until his father put pressure on him to find a way of combining his passion for the life of an artist with the paternal profession of distilling. This was the beginning of the first true cabaret. Salis gave this art form its big breakthrough and created the place where the avant-garde intellectuals of Paris could encounter the gaiety of the demimonde: the Chat Noir. It was conspicuous because not only song and dance were on the bill: a prominent position was also given to the spoken word. This and the fact that Salis liberally covered the walls of Paris with attractive posters advertising the Chat Noir was responsible for the success of his establishment, which reflected the mood of the *belle époque* as no other. Steinlen's poster portrays the motionless cat as a mystic creature reminiscent of the stories of Edgar Allan Poe. It symbolized the free and unbridled pleasures that the nights of Montmartre held in store. Before his death in 1897 Salis chose the following epitaph for his grave: "God created the world, Napoleon created the Légion d'Honneur, and I created Montmartre."

The Chat Noir brought many cabaret ensembles from other countries to Paris and had a reputation far beyond the French capital. The cabaret closed in 1887, and many visitors to the world exhibition of 1900 vainly searched for it – including Pablo Picasso.

Théophile Alexandre Steinlen
Poster for a tour of the Chat Noir cabaret
1896, color lithograph
Musée Carnavalet, Paris

THE RAPE OF LUCREC

FROM T
SIEGE
DEA A
POST
BORN
THE T
LESSE
WINC
FALSE
SIRE,
LUST-BREATHED TAR
LEAVES THE ROMAN H
AND TO COLATIUM BE
THE LIGHTLESSE FIRE
WHICH IN PALE EMBE

Printed Graphics and the Art of the Book

Art Nouveau books were showpieces for proud collectors, greatly prized items thanks to the skills of artists. This was the golden age of exclusive editions that delighted their owners with new inventions in the field of typography. In Germany at the start of the new century a large number of committed bibliophiles upheld the tradition of printing. Many magazines contributed solutions to the question how to reform the relationship between type and pictures. Innovative design was an essential part of the program of these publications. Modern production methods, too, encouraged the spread of artistic graphics, and a new genre developed in the field of special and exclusive editions.

William Morris
(Kelmscott Press)
The Rape of Lucrece from *The Poems of William Shakespeare*
(detail from p. 153)
1893, woodcut
Biblioteca de Catalunya, Barcelona

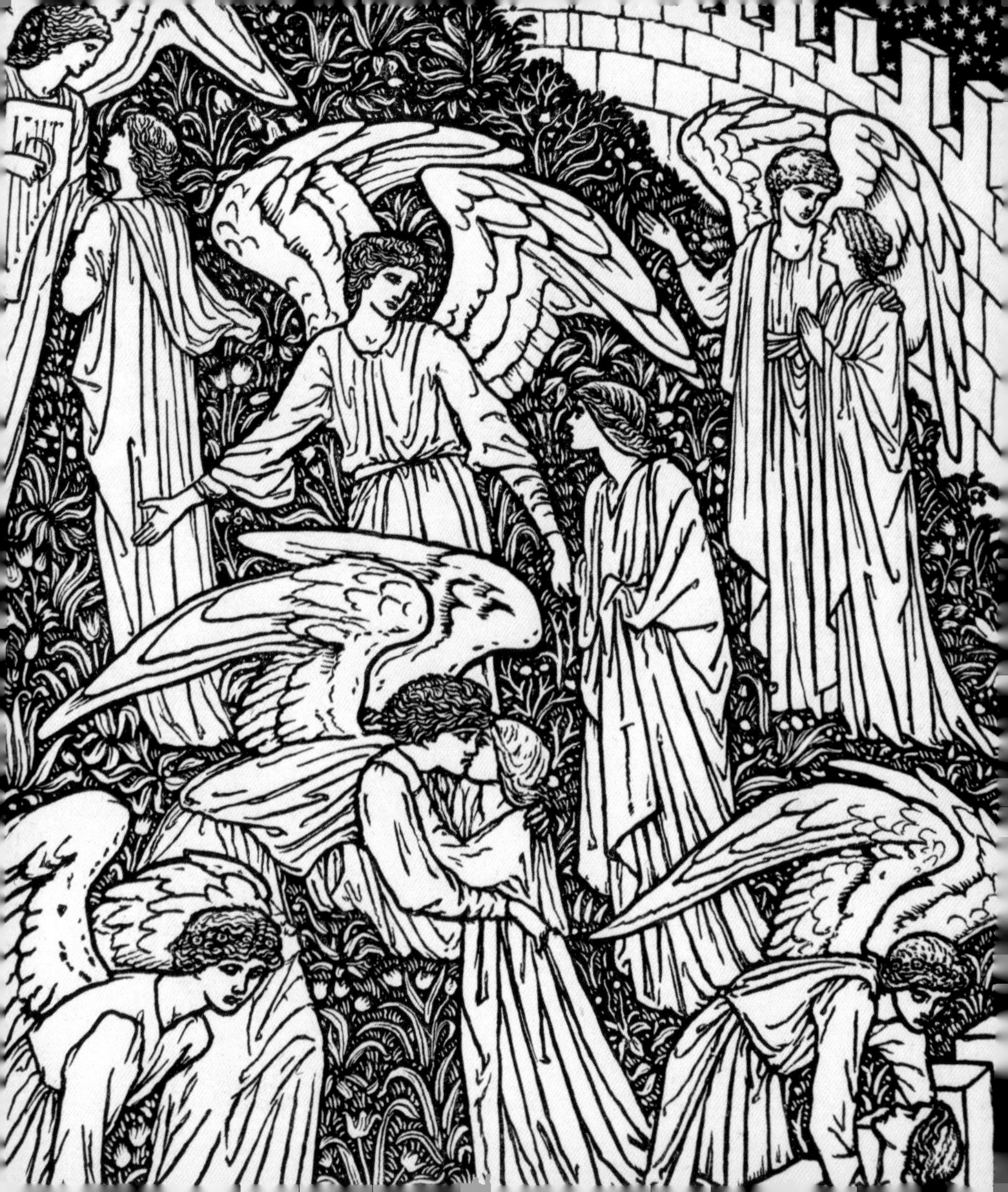

Private Presses and New Typefaces

In 1888 Emery Walker was invited by the Arts and Crafts Exhibition Society to deliver a lecture about the history of printing. Walker, an employee of the Typographic Etching Company, was a friend of William Morris, who after the lecture enthusiastically took up the idea of developing a new type in collaboration with Walker. "Here is a new craft to be mastered and perfected," was Morris's conviction. "First of all the pages must be clear and easy to read, which can hardly be the case unless, secondly, the type is well formed." It was inevitable that these thoughts would lead Morris to founding his own printing press, which started work under the name Kelmscott Press at Kelmscott House in Hammersmith. Initially Morris wanted Walker to be a partner in the enterprise, but Walker preferred to fulfill the role of independent consultant, and Morris set out on his new adventure in the art of the book as the sole proprietor. This subject fitted his concept of an ideal work of art: the type and the illustrations, the bindings and the paper were to form an aesthetic unity. It goes without saying that industrial printing presses were not used: only hand printing was considered. In its eight years of existence Morris's Kelmscott Press produced a total of 53 books,

William Morris
(Kelmscott Press)
Angels behind the Inner Sanctuary from *The Kelmscott Chaucer,* (detail), 1896, woodcut
Private collection

William Morris
(Kelmscott Press)
The Rape of Lucrece from *The Poems of William Shakespeare,* 1893, woodcut, Biblioteca de Catalunya, Barcelona

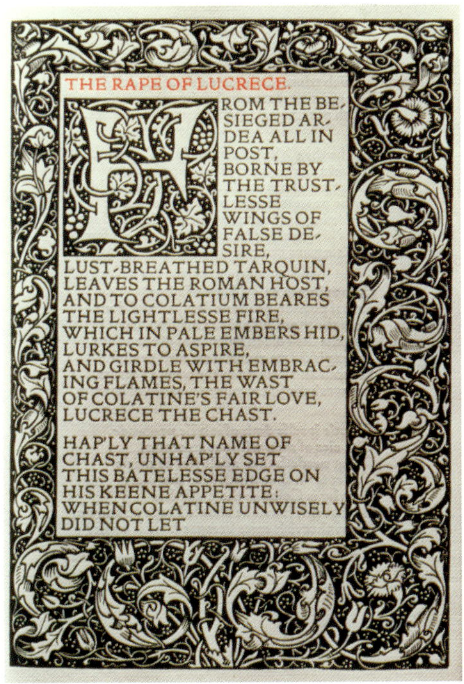
THE RAPE OF LUCRECE.
FROM THE BESIEGED ARDEA ALL IN POST, BORNE BY THE TRUSTLESSE WINGS OF FALSE DESIRE, LUST-BREATHED TARQUIN, LEAVES THE ROMAN HOST, AND TO COLATIUM BEARES THE LIGHTLESSE FIRE, WHICH IN PALE EMBERS HID, LURKES TO ASPIRE, AND GIRDLE WITH EMBRACING FLAMES, THE WAST OF COLATINE'S FAIR LOVE, LUCRECE THE CHAST.

HAP'LY THAT NAME OF CHAST, UNHAP'LY SET THIS BATELESSE EDGE ON HIS KEENE APPETITE: WHEN COLATINE UNWISELY DID NOT LET

including his own works. He took great pains to find a paper mill that could produce unbleached paper, eventually settling on Batchelor and Son, who produced handmade paper using linen specially for him and adorned it with a variety of watermarks. Morris would not use just any printing ink, but had a special mixture supplied by Gebrüder Jaenecke from Hanover, who made the most saturated and intense colors available at the time. The vellum that Morris selected for the bindings was provided by a company in Middlesex.

Morris, who also took medieval crafts as his model in other fields, admired Nicolas Jenson, a punch cutter, printer

William Morris
(Kelmscott Press)
Kelmscott Chaucer with
woodcuts by E. Burne-Jones
1896
Private collection

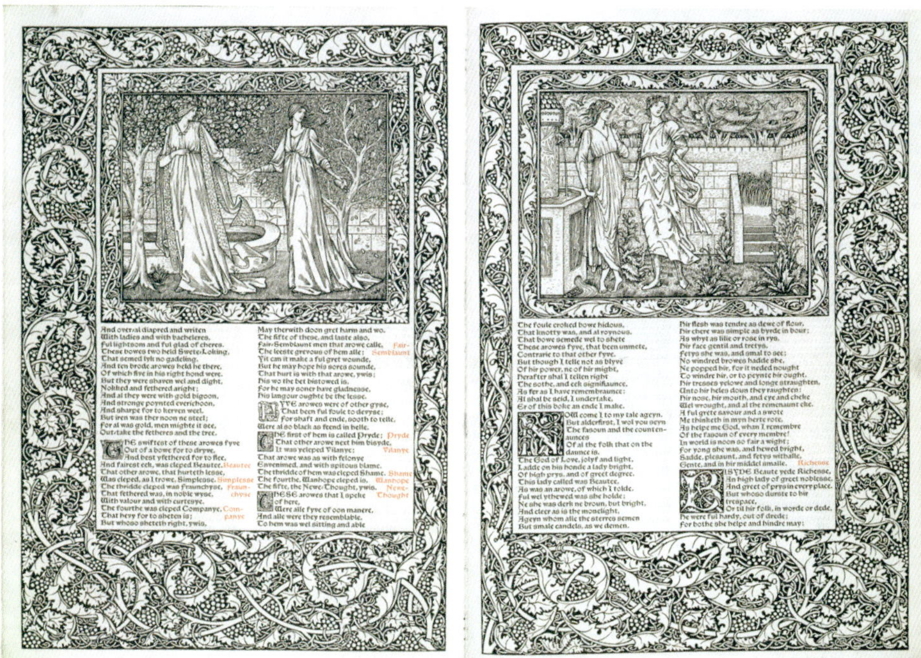
And over-al diapred and writen
With ladies and with bacheleres,
Ful lightsom and ful glad of cheres.
These bowes two held Swete-Loking,
That semed lyk no gadeling.
And ten brode arowes held he there,
Of which five in his right hond were.
But they were shaven wel and dight,
Nokked and fethered aright;
And al they were with gold bigoon,
And stronge poynted everichoon,
And sharpe for to kerven weel.
But iren was ther noon ne steel;
For al was gold, men mighte it see,
Out-take the fetheres and the tree.
THE swiftest of these arowes fyve
Out of a bowe for to dryve,
And best yfethered for to flee,
And fairest eek, was cleped Beautee. Beautee
That other arowe, that hurteth lesse,
Was cleped, as I trowe, Simplesse. Simplesse
The thridde cleped was Fraunchyse, Fraun-
That fethered was, in noble wyse, chyse
With valour and with curtesye.
The fourthe was cleped Companye, Com-
That hevy for to sheten is; panye
But whoso sheteth right, ywis,
May therwith doon gret harm and wo.
The fifte of these, and laste also,
Fair-Semblaunt men that arowe calle, Fair-
The leeste grevous of hem alle; Semblaunt
Yit can it make a ful gret wounde,
But he may hope his sores sounde,
That hurt is with that arowe, ywis;
His wo the bet bistowed is.
For he may soner have gladnesse,
His langour oughte be the lesse.
FYVE arowes were of other gyse,
That been ful foule to devyse;
For shaft and ende, sooth to telle,
Were al so black as feend in helle.
THE first of hem is called Pryde; Pryde
That other arowe next him bisyde,
It was yeleped Vilanye; Vilanye
That arowe was as with felonye
Envenimed, and with spitous blame.
The thridde of hem was cleped Shame. Shame
The fourthe, Wanhope cleped is. Wanhope
The fifte, the Newe-Thought, ywis. Newe-
THESE arowes that I speke Thought
of here,
Were alle fyve of oon manere,
And alle were they resemblable.
To hem was wel sitting and able

The foule croked bowe hidous,
That knotty was, and al roynous.
That bowe semede wel to shete
These arowes fyve, that been unmete,
Contrarie to that other fyve.
But though I telle not as blyve
Of hir power, ne of hir might,
Herafter shal I tellen right
The sothe, and eek signifiaunce,
As fer as I have remembraunce:
Al shal be seid, I undertake,
Er of this boke an ende I make.
NOW come I to my tale ageyn.
But alderfirst, I wol you seyn
The fasoun and the counten-
aunces
Of al the folk that on the
daunce is.
The God of Love, jolyf and light,
Ladde on his honde a lady bright,
Of high prys, and of greet degree.
This lady called was Beautee,
As was an arowe, of which I tolde.
Ful wel ythewed was she holde;
Ne she was derk ne broun, but bright,
And cleer as is the monelight,
Ageyn whom alle the sterres semen
But smale candels, as we demen.
Hir flesh was tendre as dewe of flour,
Hir chere was simple as byrde in bour;
As whyt as lilie or rose in rys,
Hir face gentil and tretys.
Fetys she was, and smal to see;
No windred browes hadde she,
Ne popped hir, for it neded nought
To windre hir, or to peynte hir ought.
Hir tresses yelowe and longe straughten,
Unto hir heles doun they raughten;
Hir nose, hir mouth, and eye and cheke
Wel wrought, and al the remenaunt eke.
A ful grete savour and a swote
Me thinketh in myn herte rote,
As helpe me God, whan I remembre
Of the fasoun of every membre!
In world is noon so fair a wight;
For yong she was, and hewed bright,
Sadde, plesaunt, and fetys withalle,
Gente, and in hir middel smalle. Richesse
BISYDE Beaute yede Richesse,
An high lady of greet noblesse,
And greet of prys in every place.
But whoso durste to hir
trespace,
Or til hir folk, in worde or dede,
He were ful hardy, out of drede;
For bothe she helpe and hindre may;

and calligrapher who was active in the mid-15th century. Jenson was born in France, learned the art of printing from Gutenberg in Mainz and worked in Venice in his later years. He developed Jenson antiqua, a type from which all later antiqua types were derived and which was famous for its clarity. Jenson used it to print the writings of the ancient author Pliny, and Morris owned a copy of this edition. This was Morris's starting point in developing his own typefaces, which were adapted to the contents of the books. In order to publish an edition of the *Legenda Aurea,* a collection of saints' legends from the early Middle Ages, Morris created his "Golden" type. "Troy" type was produced for an edition of the medieval poem *The Recuyell of the Historyes of Troy* by Raoul Le Fèvre.

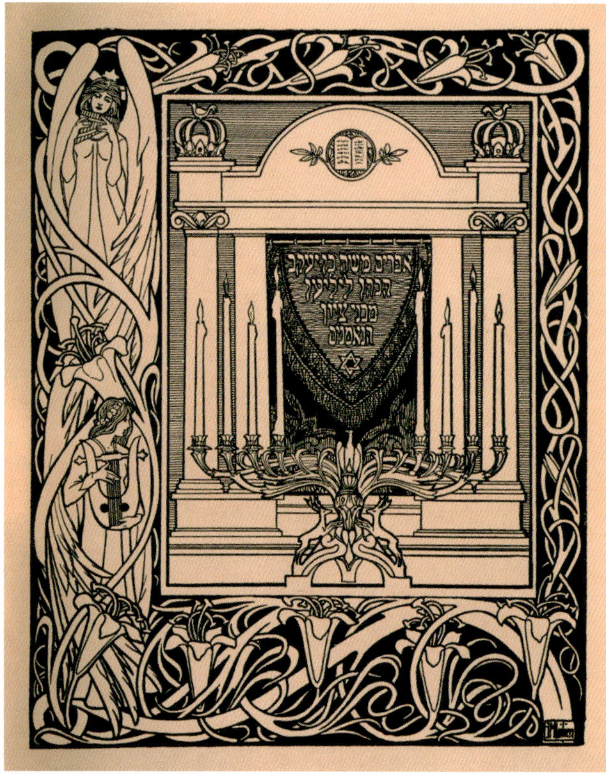

Heinrich Vogeler
Book page

The masterpiece of the Kelmscott Press, however, was an edition of Geoffrey Chaucer's *Canterbury Tales.* Here Morris perfected his vision of the ideal book, which consisted in dividing the page into a clearly readable field for text and an ornamental or pictorial framework. His friend Edward Burne-Jones contributed a series of 87 woodcuts to

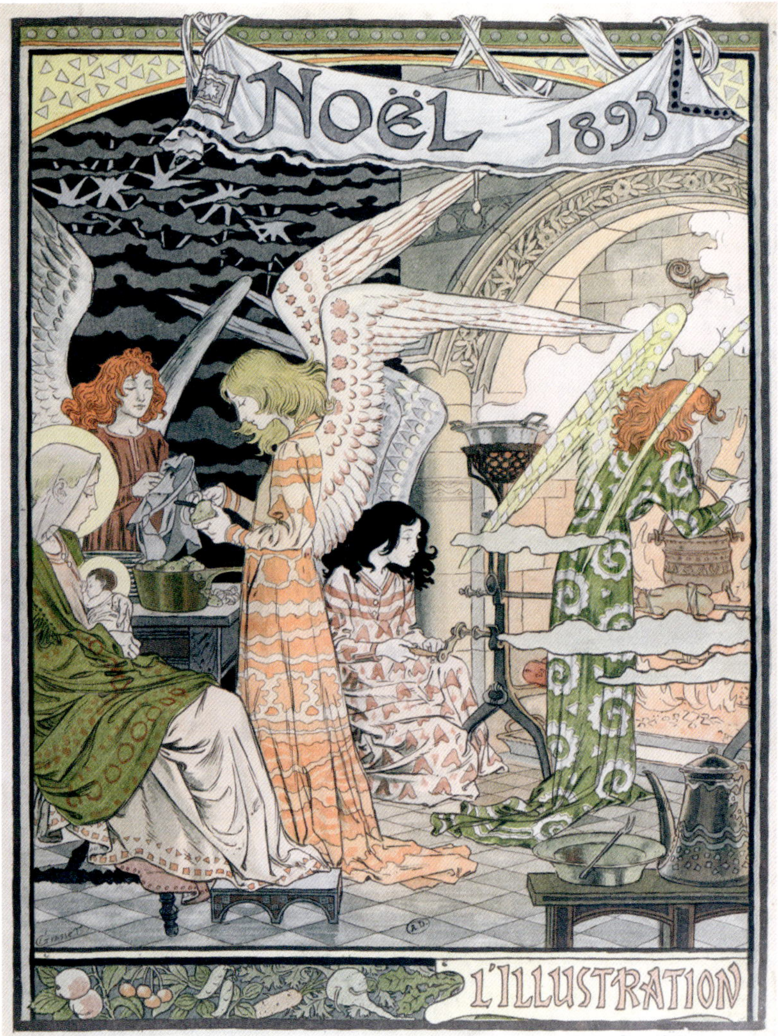
NOËL 1893
L'ILLUSTRATION

illustrate the medieval text. For this edition, too, Morris developed a new typeface: the "Chaucer" type. The aesthetic scheme for the book envisaged a special binding, which was done by Thomas James Cobden-Sanderson. Three months before his death in October 1896 Morris received a finished copy of the book, which Burne-Jones described as "a pocket-sized cathedral." Cobden, who had trained as a lawyer, discovered his passion for the art of the book in 1873 and gained a reputation as a bookbinder. In 1900 he founded his Doves Press directly opposite Kelmscott House, having established his Doves Bindery a few years earlier. In contrast to Morris he succeeded in persuading Emery Walker to join him as a partner in the firm. Under Walker's influence the Doves Press produced pages with a conspicuously restrained design. The emphasis lay on the typeface, without any ornamental framework or illustrations. In 1901 Cobden published an essay entitled *The Ideal Book or Book Beautiful,* in which he pointed out the essential aspects of an ideal book: "A harmony of content and form, to design the book creatively and make it a whole, drawing on the same sources of experience as the author." He chose the texts for his editions with great care, and published Goethe's *Faust,* among other works. The main work of the Doves Press was the *English Bible,* which was issued in five volumes between 1903 and 1905. The use of printing ink in contrasting colors was particularly impressive in this edition. The red lettering of the first line of the Book of Genesis had enormous aesthetic appeal. Nevertheless, a disagreement with Walker, who handed over the lead type used by Doves Press to Cobden when he left the company, ended in Cobden throwing the type into the river Thames.

The movement to produce artistic books that began in England had a major influence on German bibliophiles, poets and craftsmen. Within a few years private printing presses in Germany were making a highly successful con-

An extremely popular painting in the Louvre by the Spanish Baroque artist Bartolomé Estéban Murillo depicts the angels' kitchen as a vision of St Diego of Alcalá. The loving angels who care for Mary so touchingly after the birth of Jesus were much copied.

Eugène Grasset
Angels' Kitchen, Christmas 1893, color lithograph
Bibliothèque des Arts Décoratifs, Paris

tribution to the field of book design. Grand Duke Ernst Ludwig of Hesse founded the Ernst Ludwig Presse in Darmstadt, with Ernst Wilhelm Kleukens at the helm. With Fritz Helmut Ehmcke and Georg Belwe, Kleukens had already set up the Steglitzer Werkstatt in Berlin, one of the leading companies for bibliophiles, in 1907. Otto Eckmann created a typeface specially for the young owners of the workshop in order to design more eye-catching flyers for advertising the small company. This type looked as if it had been written with a Japanese calligraphic brush, and its rounded organic forms were well suited to contemporary taste. Production of the type at the Klingspor type foundry was relatively expensive, but the results were a success and are now regarded as the Art Nouveau typeface par excellence.

In 1911 Ludwig Wolde and Willi Wiegand established the Bremer Presse, modeling it on the example of the English Doves Press. In their own workshop they dedicated themselves to producing books with a beautiful appearance, and designed editions for bibliophiles that usually did not run to more than 250 copies. Their first publication, in 1913, was Hugo von Hofmannsthal's *Die Wege und die Begegnungen.* Hofmannsthal kept up his association with the Bremer Presse as an adviser and after the First World War assisted in founding of a publishing house that emerged from it.

Aubrey Beardsley
Cover for *The Savoy*
nos. 1 and 2
1896, lithograph
Private collection

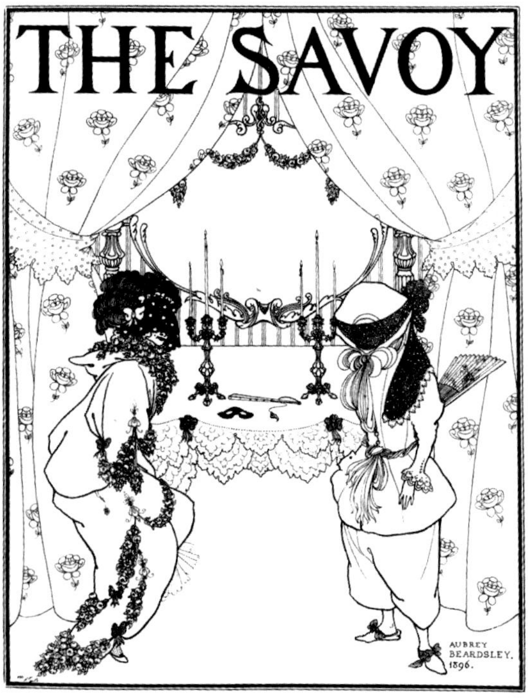

In 1913 Henry Graf Kessler founded the Cranach Presse in Weimar and, together with Henry van de Velde and Elisabeth Förster-Nietzsche, devoted himself to publishing the writings of Friedrich Nietzsche. A bibliophile edition of *Thus Spoke Zarathustra* was Kessler's greatest project, for which Georg Lemmen, a close friend of van de Velde, designed a new type. Kessler was personally involved in the production of this type. Although Kessler had considered using illustrations by Stuck in the early years – the idea for the project originated in 1897 – he later found van de Velde's style much better suited to the work of Nietzsche. Van de Velde had chosen an ornamental and abstract complement to the texts that was intended to reflect its claim to timelessness. The philosopher's sister, too, who had had a previous edition of Nietzsche by Heinrich Köselitz pulped, was extremely satisfied with the approach. However, it was not until 1908 that the edition of *Zarathustra* designed by van de Velde was finally published by Insel-Verlag. It was a resounding commercial success.

Heinrich Vogeler had enormous success as a book illustrator. Rilke thought he had a particular talent for adorning books, as "his calm and coherent but intrinsically opulent line is more suitable than any other to accompany like a song the procession of noble letters." This acknowledgment by the poet, lauding the sensitive interpretation of a text in pictorial form, shows the outstanding importance of literary illustration for the bibliophile movement at the turn of the century. Illustrations, originally decorative additions that

Cover for
The Yellow Book
1894, lithograph
Private collection

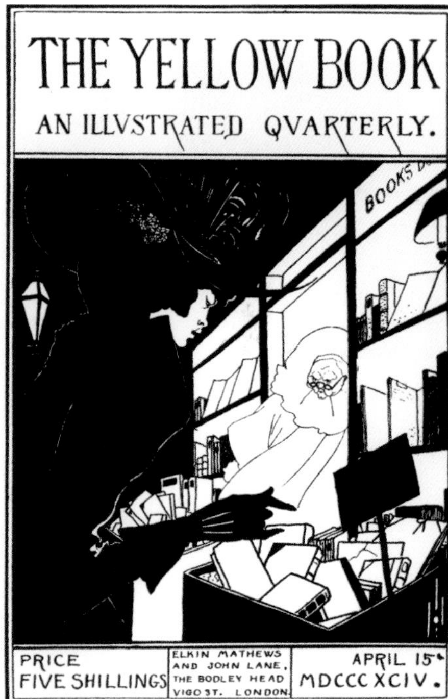

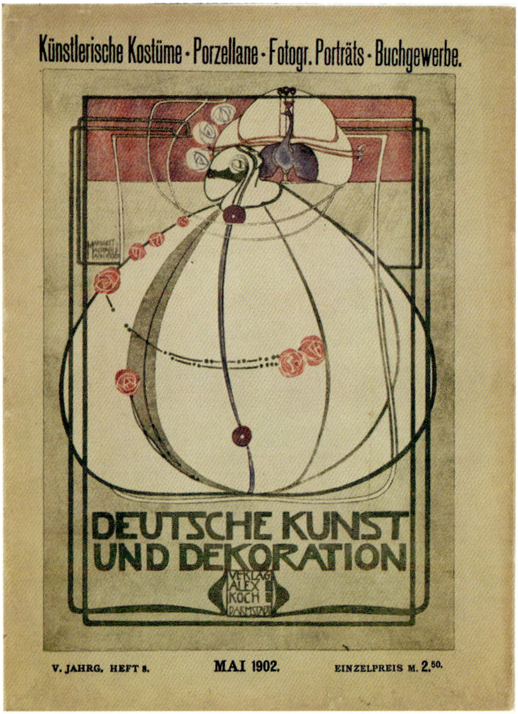

Margaret MacDonald Mackintosh
Deutsche Kunst und Dekoration
1902, magazine cover
Private collection

had a largely subordinate purpose, were now often imbued with a meaning that went beyond the text, as in Aubrey Beardsley's famous illustrations for Oscar Wilde's *Salome*. Beardsley was the "illustrator laureate" for the literary and art quarterly *The Yellow Book*, in which he made a name for himself with bold graphic work in black and white. The name of the periodical derived from the yellow book that Wilde's figure Dorian Gray always carried with him, whose decadent contents appeared to bring about his ruin. Wilde preferred not to elaborate on whether Huysmans' *Against Nature* had been the inspiration for the idea of the yellow book. Beardsley, who had made a close study of the Japanese stencil technique, produced eccentric illustrations for *The Yellow Book*. However, he later quarreled with the publishers because, as a consequence of Oscar Wilde's trial, an angry mob appeared in the magazine offices demanding the dismissal of Beardsley. Beardsley then founded the magazine *The Savoy* in 1896 with Leonard Smithers, for whose writings, which were partly pornographic, he produced the appropriate illustrations. This was without doubt work of a type that was sold under the counter – in contrast to a great deal of graphic work that was published as a supplement to art magazines. This led to lively collecting activity and the foundation of specialized galleries. Nouveau Salon des Cent was one such gallery, attracting collectors of work by the leading lights of graphic art such as Toulouse-Lautrec, Steinlen, Mucha and Grasset. The newly developed technique of lithography made possible a painterly implementation of motifs that was hitherto unknown in the field of graphics, so that the motifs could now be designed according to prevailing fashion. Calendar designs, in which various seasonal themes stimulated the urge to collect, were popular. Enthusiasm for the new poster art led to a genuine craze which contemporaries named "affichomania." Illustrations for the magazine *Jugend* were much in demand and quickly became cult objects. This led to rivalry to get hold of a copy when a new issue appeared. The rejection of mass production, which elsewhere met with resistance from the reformers, here favored the spread of the formal vocabulary of Art Nouveau. Book art and printed graphics became an essential part of the renewal of aesthetics, and the latter, in particular, provided even those of limited means with access to art.

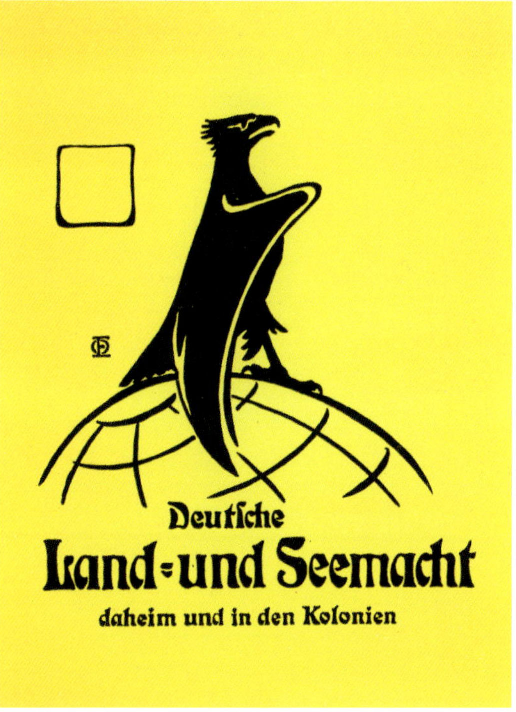

Otto Eckmann
Book cover for *Deutsche Land- und Seemacht*
1905

Literature of the Decadent Era

Aubrey Beardsley
The Black Cape
Illustration for Oscar Wilde's *Salome*
1893, ink on paper
22.4 × 15.9 cm
University Library, Princeton, New Jersey

"I love jewels and all those unnecessary and beautiful things whose uselessness increases their price." The sight of the shop windows of the Paris jewelers gave Oscar Wilde the idea of writing the story of Salome, whom he saw before him sparkling with jewelry. *Salome* was a masterpiece of decadent literature, full of obsessions and too extreme even for the *fin de siècle* in the wild lust of its dangerous female protagonist.

SALOME: I am amorous of thy body, Iokanaan! [...] Suffer me to touch thy body.
IOKANAAN: Back! daughter of Babylon! By woman came evil into the world. Speak not to me. I will not listen to thee. I listen but to the voice of the Lord God.
SALOME: [...] There is nothing in the world that is so black as thy hair....Suffer me to touch thy hair.
IOKANAAN: Back, daughter of Sodom! Touch me not. Profane not the temple of the Lord God.
SALOME: There is nothing in the world so red as thy mouth.... Suffer me to kiss thy mouth.
IOKANAAN: Never! daughter of Babylon! Daughter of Sodom! Never!
SALOME: I will kiss thy mouth, Iokanaan. I will kiss thy mouth.

Wilde wrote the play in French in 1891 during a stay in Paris. When it premiered in 1894 with Sarah Bernhardt in the leading role, the author was in prison after being sentenced for gross indecency. The father of his long-standing friend Lord Alfred Douglas prosecuted Wilde, unable to accept the openly homosexual relationship between the married writer and his son Alfred. Lord Alfred Douglas had Salome translated into English and brought about its publication in England.

This private catastrophe meant the end of the promising career of Oscar Wilde, a dandy and aesthete who had been a remarkable figure in the European scene for decadent literature. Wilde was born in Dublin in 1854. His father was a doctor, his mother an ambitious amateur writer. The young Irishman was a gifted scholar who studied Classics at Trinity College, Dublin and Oxford, where he was awarded the Newdigate Prize for his poem *Ravenna.* His dandyish behavior attracted much attention, as well as criticism from the censorious society of the Victorian era. Wrapped in a velvet cloak and deploying extravagant gestures and sparkling wit, Wilde knew how to fascinate and provoke his contemporaries. Although he was openly homosexual, in 1884 he married Constance Lloyd, who had been a successful author of children's books before the marriage, and was to bear him two sons. However, she was not the love of his life. Wilde's dramatic relationship with Alfred "Bosie" Douglas, who was notorious in London for his noisy quarrels and unrestrained reconciliations, was more important to him. In 1891, when Douglas appeared in his life,

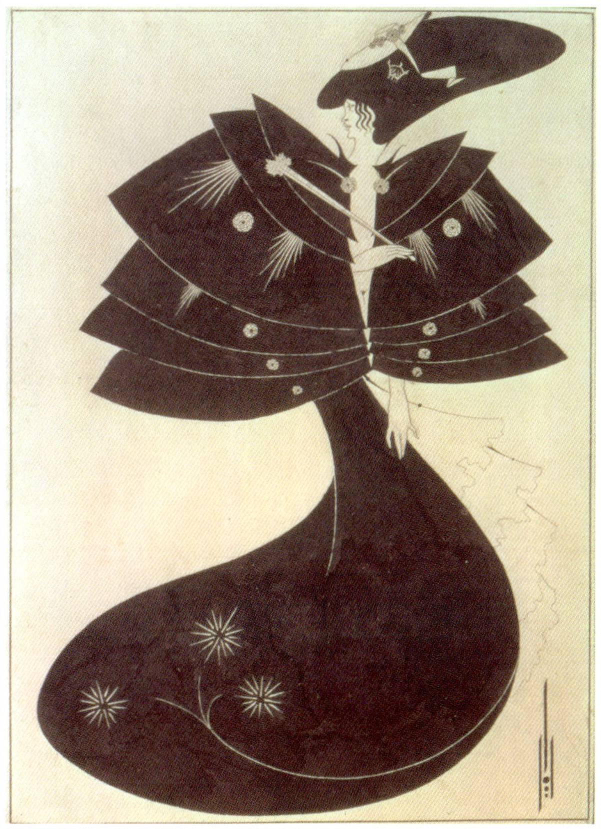

Wilde completed his novel *The Picture of Dorian Gray.* He had worked for several years as the editor of the magazine *Woman's World,* but henceforth writing took center stage, and he

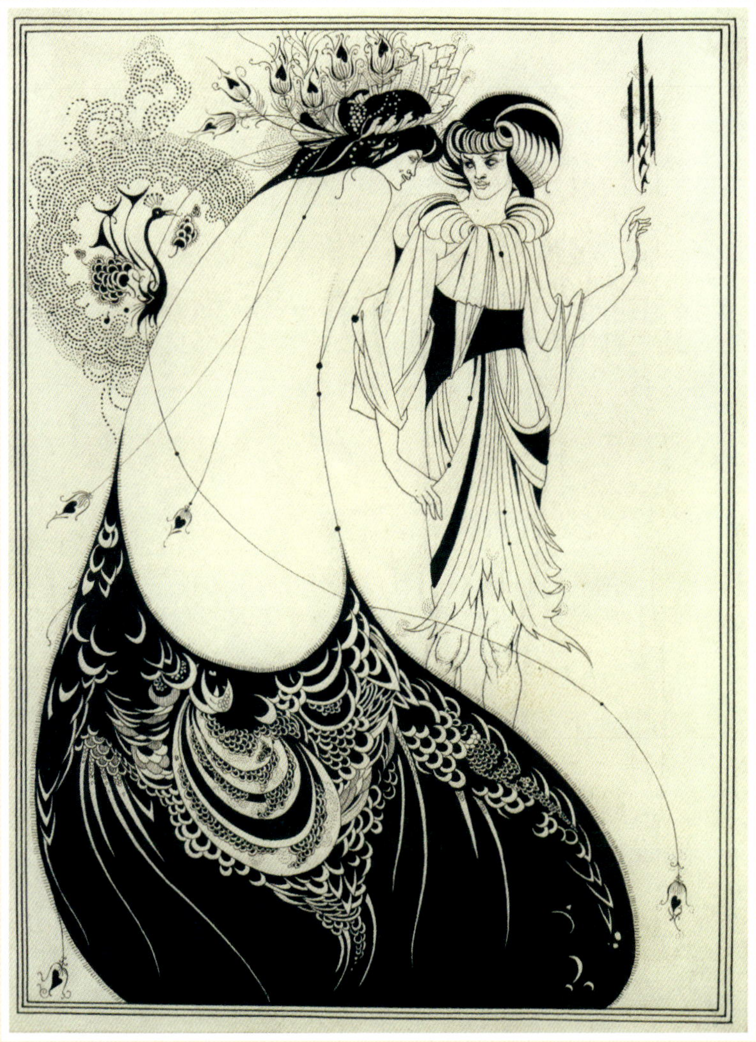

achieved huge success with comedies of manners such as *The Importance of Being Earnest* (1895). However, he did not take the lawsuit for libel that he was pursuing at this time against his lover's father very seriously. With his barbed wit and scintillating rhetoric, he expected to win the case. However he had failed to take account of the humorless stubbornness of the exponents of Victorian morality, who cited works including *The Picture of Dorian Gray* as evidence of Wilde's indecent behavior. On 25 May 1895 he was sentenced to two years' imprisonment with hard labor. It is not difficult to imagine how this turned the dandy and poet into a broken man. After his release he hoped to regain a place in society in *fin de siècle* Paris, but died there in a hotel, impoverished and lonely, on 30 November 1900.

The reception of *Salome* in the following years was greatly influenced by its adaptation as an opera by Richard Strauss, who had already caught the attention of the public by interpreting *Thus Spoke Zarathustra* in music. Wilde's one-act play had its premiere as an opera in 1905, and for a long time this version overshadowed Wilde's original drama.

Aubrey Beardsley's eye-catching black-and-white illustrations also played an important part in shaping the perception of Wilde's play. Beardsley's work, which was influenced by Japanese prints, was a sensation. Wilde reacted enthusiastically to a drawing that Beardsley showed him. Their later collaboration was less harmonious, as Wilde was not willing to accept the associative style of the illustrations, which were often far removed from the text and seemed to him in parts "not oriental enough" and too superficially erotic.

A small book that the eponymous hero of *The Picture of Dorian Gray* always carries with him may be a reference by the author to Joris-Karl Huysmans, whose book *À rebours* (Against Nature), published in 1884, was a kind of Bible for aesthetes and dandies.

Napoleon Sarony
Portrait of Oscar Wilde
1882, photograph
Stapleton Collection, England

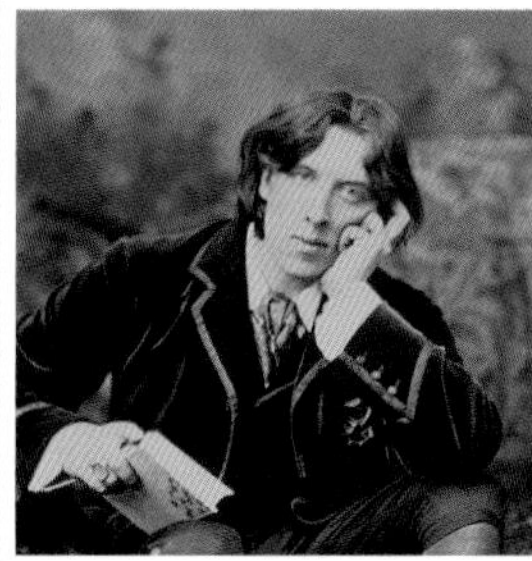

Aubrey Beardsley
The Peacock Dress, illustration for Oscar Wilde's *Salome*
1893, black ink and pencil on paper
22.7 × 16 cm
Fogg Art Museum, Harvard University Art Museums

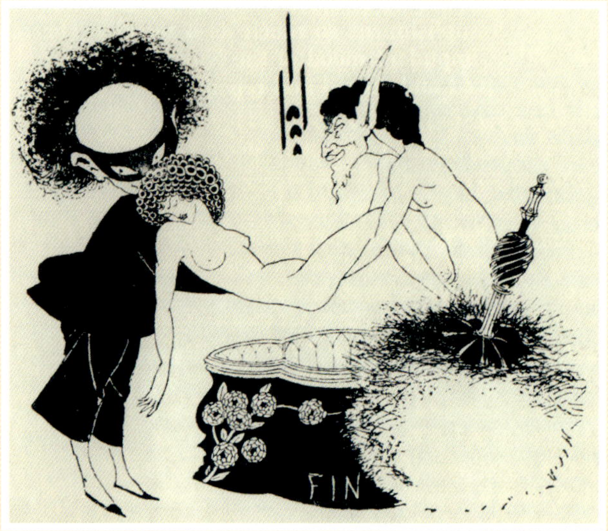

Aubrey Beardsley
Final illustration for Oscar Wilde's *Salome*
After 1893, lithograph
Private collection

Wiener Verlag
Cover of *The Confusions of Young Törless*
1906, color lithograph
Private collection

"It was a book full of poison," wrote Wilde. "The heavy odor of incense seemed to cling about its pages and to trouble the brain." The protagonist of *Against Nature* is Jean Floressas Des Esseintes, a Parisian aristocrat of nervous disposition who makes his country retreat into a kind of ivory tower in which he can devote himself to the life of an aesthete as if in an artificial world. He celebrates colors and perfumes, surrounds himself with exotic plants and covers the shell of his tortoise with gold and gems. He trains his sense of taste by means of a liqueur organ invented by himself. His contemplation of paintings by Gustave Moreau and Odile Redons and his reading of the works of Baudelaire, Poe and Mallarmé brings on heady visions until, exhausted by overstimulation of the senses, he is forced to abandon his retreat.

The subjective and aesthetic view of the world presented in this book permeates the literature of the period. In Proust's mammoth work *In Search of Lost Time,* too, the reader encounters a sensitive, aesthetic dandy who philosophizes about the nature of art and even regards it as the aim of his life, for which he strives but at which he repeatedly fails. Authors such as Robert Musil in *Törless* and *The Man without Qualities* described the inner structure of their characters and searched for a new type of literature that could react to the inward disintegration of outward forms. "Who am I? How did I become what I am? What else am I? Do I not seem to be merely decorative?" – these are the words that Thomas Mann gives to Thomas Buddenbrook in his novel of 1901, *Buddenbrooks: The Decline of a Family,* which provided an interpretation of the mood of society.

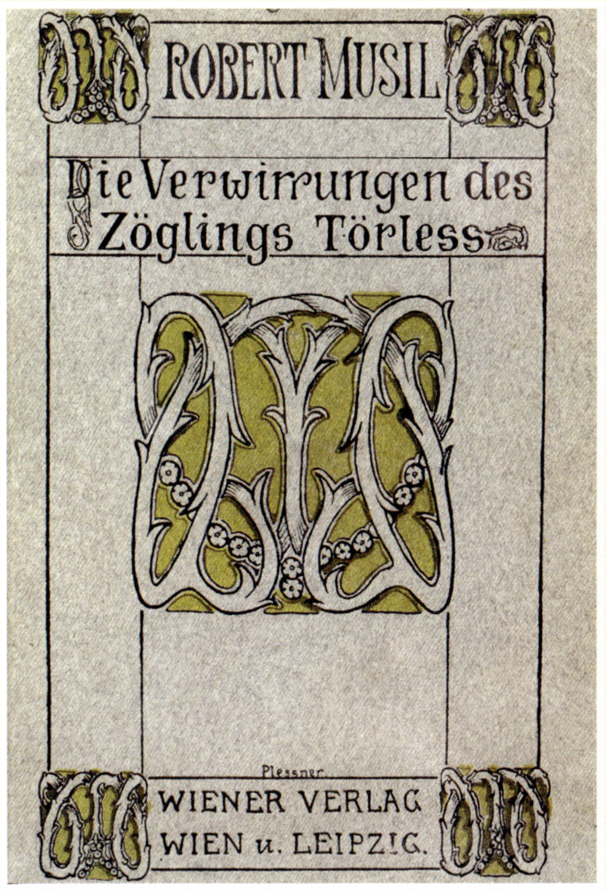

The literary answer to the mood of the *fin de siècle* appeared like a thunderbolt in the shape of *Zarathustra,* which the poet-philosopher Friedrich Nietzsche presented in four parts. It appeared between 1883 and 1885 under the full title *Thus Spoke Zarathustra: A Book for All and None.* It is the story of a man of action and an artist who aims to create a new human being, the übermensch. Starting from

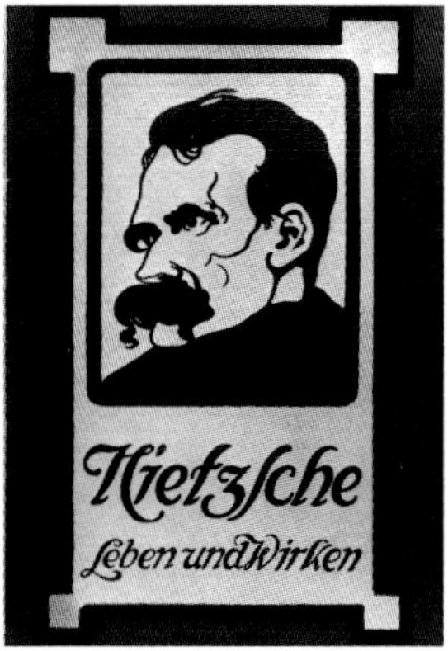

Adapted from Hans Olde's *Nietzsche on his Sickbed*
Title page of J. Reiner's *Friedrich Nietzsche,* 1909
1899, etching in the manner of a woodcut

the premise that God is dead, Zarathustra wishes to establish a new religion. The nihilism of this work struck a chord with the zeitgeist of the last years of the century and was enthusiastically received by artists and writers of those years.

"Here is the hell for hermits' thoughts: here are great thoughts seethed alive and boiled small.
Here do all great sentiments decay: here may only rattle-boned sensations rattle!
Smell you not already the shambles and cookshops of the spirit? Steams not this city with the fumes of slaughtered spirit?"
Nietzsche, Thus Spoke Zarathustra, part three, *Passing By*

Nietzsche, who had campaigned for a thoroughgoing spiritual and cultural renewal of society since he was a young professor in Basel in the 1870s, increasingly became a cult figure in his later years. The ambitious projects of his sister, who looked after him after mental illness took hold, undoubtedly contributed to this. In Weimar, where Nietzsche died on 25 August 1900, she saw to the founding of a Nietzsche archive, worked with Count Henry Kessler on publication of his writings and supported the erection of a massive Nietzsche Monument, of which Henry van de Velde was to be artistic director. The powerful language of Nietzsche's works had an especially great influence on the "George Circle," a group of young writers around the poet Stefan George. They rejected a decadent civilization and saw themselves as a community of the elect, performing cult rituals and asserting their aesthetic superiority. Stefan George himself was influenced by the Symbolist literature of Mallarmé, whom he met while staying in Paris. In the magazine *Blätter für die Kunst* (Pages for Art) George pursued the principle of art for art's sake: "Every true artist has been visited at some time by a longing to express himself in a language of which the unholy masses would never make use, or to choose his words in such a manner that only initiates recognize their noble meaning." George often took part in the "Mardis" (Tuesday meetings) that were held in Mallarmé's Paris apartment from 1877. It was a rendezvous for all the authors who had a significant part in shaping artistic trends in the late 19th century: Émile Verhaeren, Maurice Maeterlinck, Oscar Wilde, Joris-Karl Huysmans, Paul Valéry, André Gide, Rainer Maria Rilke.

Unknown artist
Übermensch decoration
for Friedrich Nietzsche's
Thus Spoke Zarathustra
Berliner Illustrierte Zeitung
1903

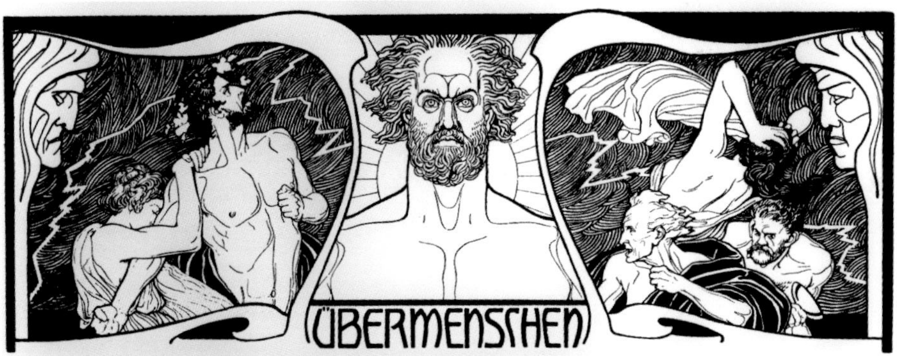

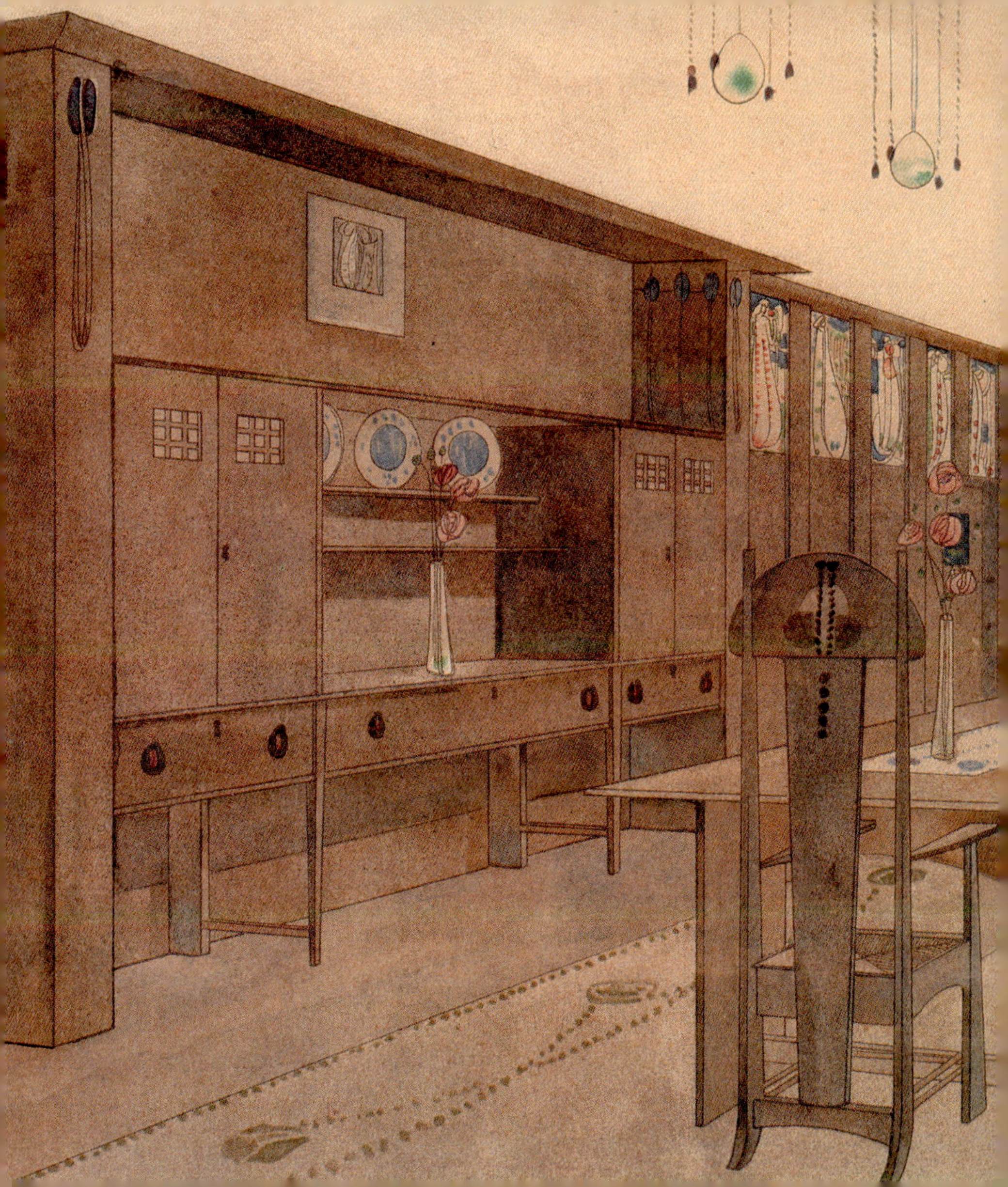

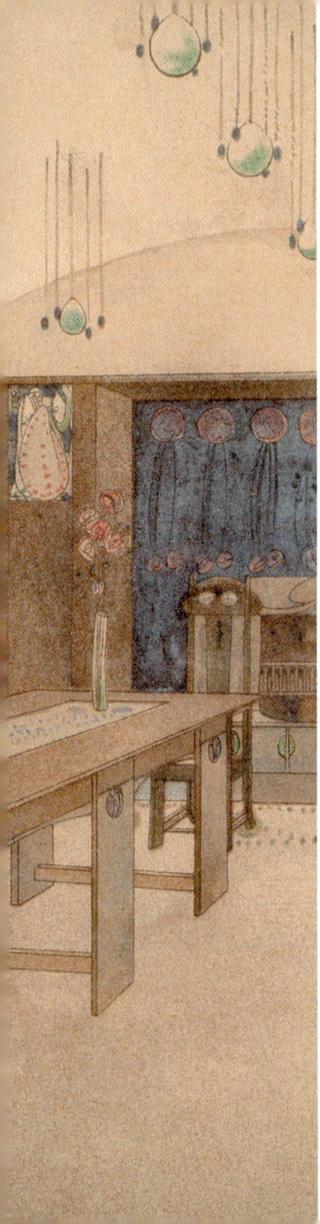

Total Works of Art

The unity of art and life, which was of central importance in the philosophy of Art Nouveau, inevitably led to the idea of the gesamtkunstwerk: the total work of art. The basis for this had already been established in the Romantic period with the idea that all the arts should be combined to a single great whole. In his religious and mystic view of the world, Philipp Otto Runge converted this idea to an experience of space in which he aimed to unite all the arts. Richard Wagner coined the phrase "work of art of the future," in which the artist would become the creator of his own cosmos. Synesthetic experience also became a major theme for Symbolist painting.

Charles Rennie Mackintosh
House of an Art Lover: The Dining Room
Sheet 14 of the portfolio *Masters of Interior Design*
Darmstadt 1902, watercolor

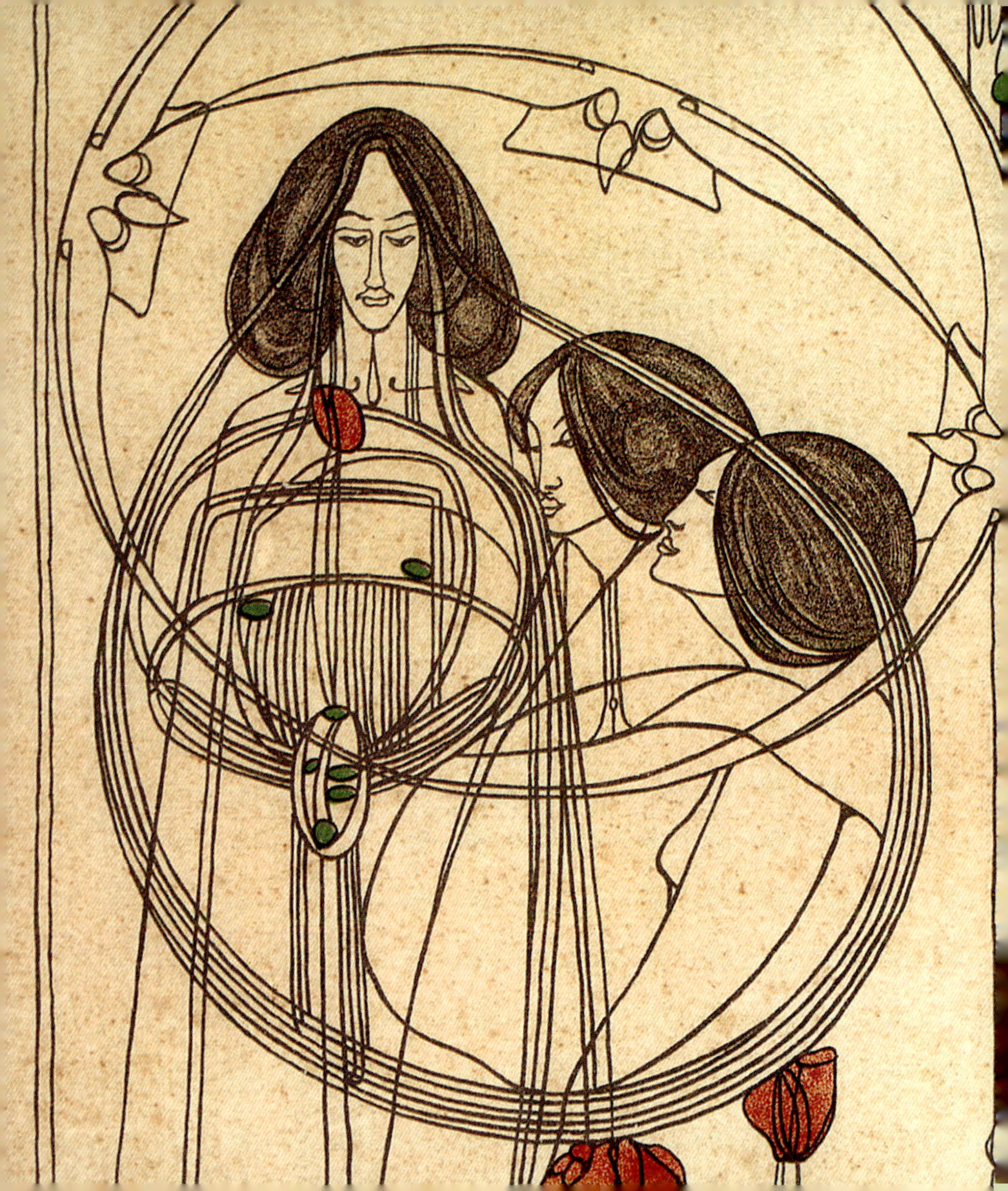

A Design for Modern Life

The publisher Alexander Koch had a large part in the establishment of the artists' colony on Mathildenhöhe in the German city of Darmstadt. His support for new forms of crafts, which he advocated from 1890 in his art magazine *Innendekoration* (Interior Decoration) and later in *Kunst und Dekoration* (Art and Decoration), had a significant influence on the grand duke of Hesse, who had several rooms of his palace decorated in the "new" style in 1897. To this end he invited the English artists Mackay Hugh Scott Baillie and Charles Robert Ashbee to Darmstadt. They enthusiastically set to work to redesign a drawing-room. When Alexander Koch held a competition in *Kunst und Dekoration* in 1901, Scott Baillie entered and carried off the first prize. However, the true winner of the competition, which set the task of designing "a spacious house of an art lover in the modern style" was the Scottish artist Charles Rennie Mackintosh. Unfortunately Mackintosh sent in his entry, which he had produced in collaboration with his wife Margaret Macdonald, after the closing date, and it could not be considered for the prize. Nevertheless, this design attracted so much attention that it was awarded a special prize.

The principle of designing a house that no-one had actually commissioned had the advantage that the designs could be produced with great creative freedom. The

Charles Rennie Mackintosh
Cover of portfolio:
Masters of Interior Design
(left: detail)
Darmstadt 1902, watercolor

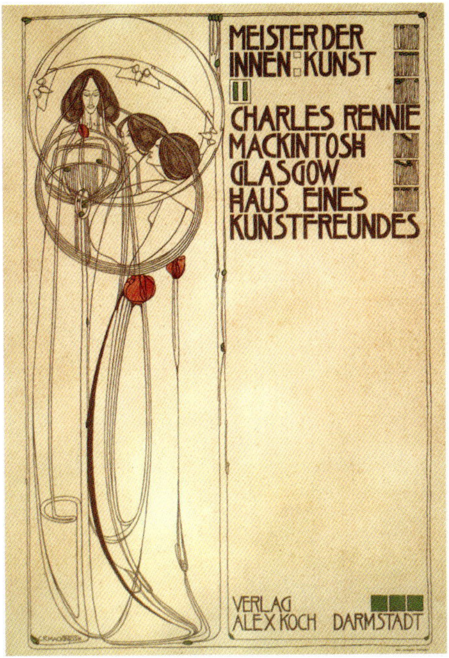

idea that this was being done for an art lover naturally entailed a high aesthetic standard in every detail. Mackintosh, who had already exhibited at the Vienna Secession, impressed the jury with a consistently austere style which seemed unbelievably modern in comparison to the Art Nouveau interiors, of which people had seen enough by that time. Mackintosh entirely adapted the appearance of the rooms to their individual functions. In the music room he fully integrated the obligatory piano into the whole decorative concept. In Mackintosh's design the harmonious unity of every single detail of the interior was implemented in a near-perfect manner.

The home as a total work of art is a logical continuation of the artist's residence, for which Morris pointed the way with his Red House. Van de Velde, too, developed this approach, initially in his own houses, and later perfected it in, for example, Villa Esche, where he subordinated everything, right down to the owner's pipe, to an overall aesthetic scheme. Mackintosh also implemented this aim of creating a total work of art at the Hill House. Here the furnishings are perfectly attuned to the surroundings of each room, an idea that Mackintosh had put into practice in his famous furnishings for a chain of tea rooms in Glasgow. The fact that his furniture designs are today viewed without any relation to the idea of a gesamtkunstwerk is a trend of which he would certainly not have approved. The actual

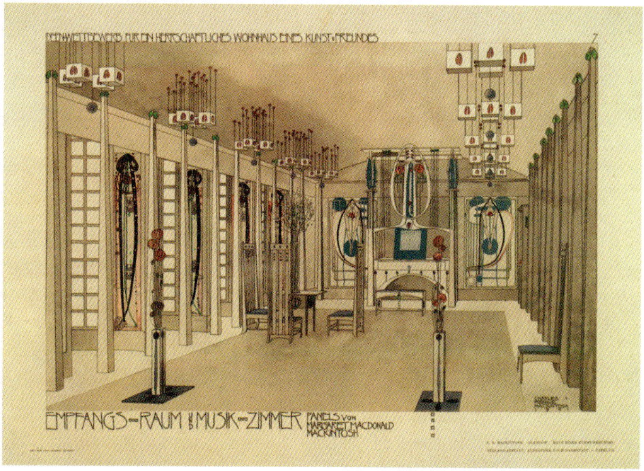

Charles Rennie Mackintosh
House of an Art Lover: Drawing Room and Music Room
Sheet 7 of portfolio:
Masters of Interior Design
Darmstadt 1902, watercolor

construction of the House of an Art Lover in 1989, 100 years after it was planned, can be seen in a sense almost as making amends. However, this initiative by fans of Mackintosh in Glasgow faced the difficulty that the house existed only in the form of watercolors and pen-and-ink drawings: there were no architectural plans that could be used.

Kabarett Fledermaus

The theatre was the main field in which the idea of a total work of art came to fruition. It was no coincidence that many modern artists gave thought to the reform of the theatre or took part in schemes of decoration and scenery in the theatre. In the Vienna Secession circles, above all, many artists took part in gesamtkunstwerk projects related to the theatre. One particular enterprise that gained fame far beyond the city of Vienna interwove painting, graphic art, sculpture and literature. The theatre and cabaret Fledermaus opened on 19 October 1907 with a sumptuous program for 300 guests. Marc Henry, who had founded the cabaret Elf Scharfrichter (Eleven Executioners) in Munich, acted as compère for the evening, and the aesthetic program for the new project had been made known in advance. It was announced that: “All the senses should be at least stimulated, if not satisfied, and none of the arts is excluded from making a contribution with its own means to the intended overall effect. [...] without employment of external instru-

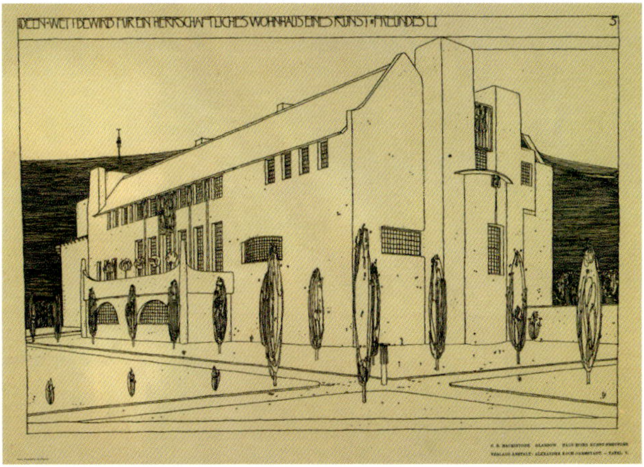

Charles Rennie Mackintosh
House of an Art Lover: Perspective View of Exterior
Sheet 5 of portfolio:
Masters of Interior Design
Darmstadt 1902, watercolor

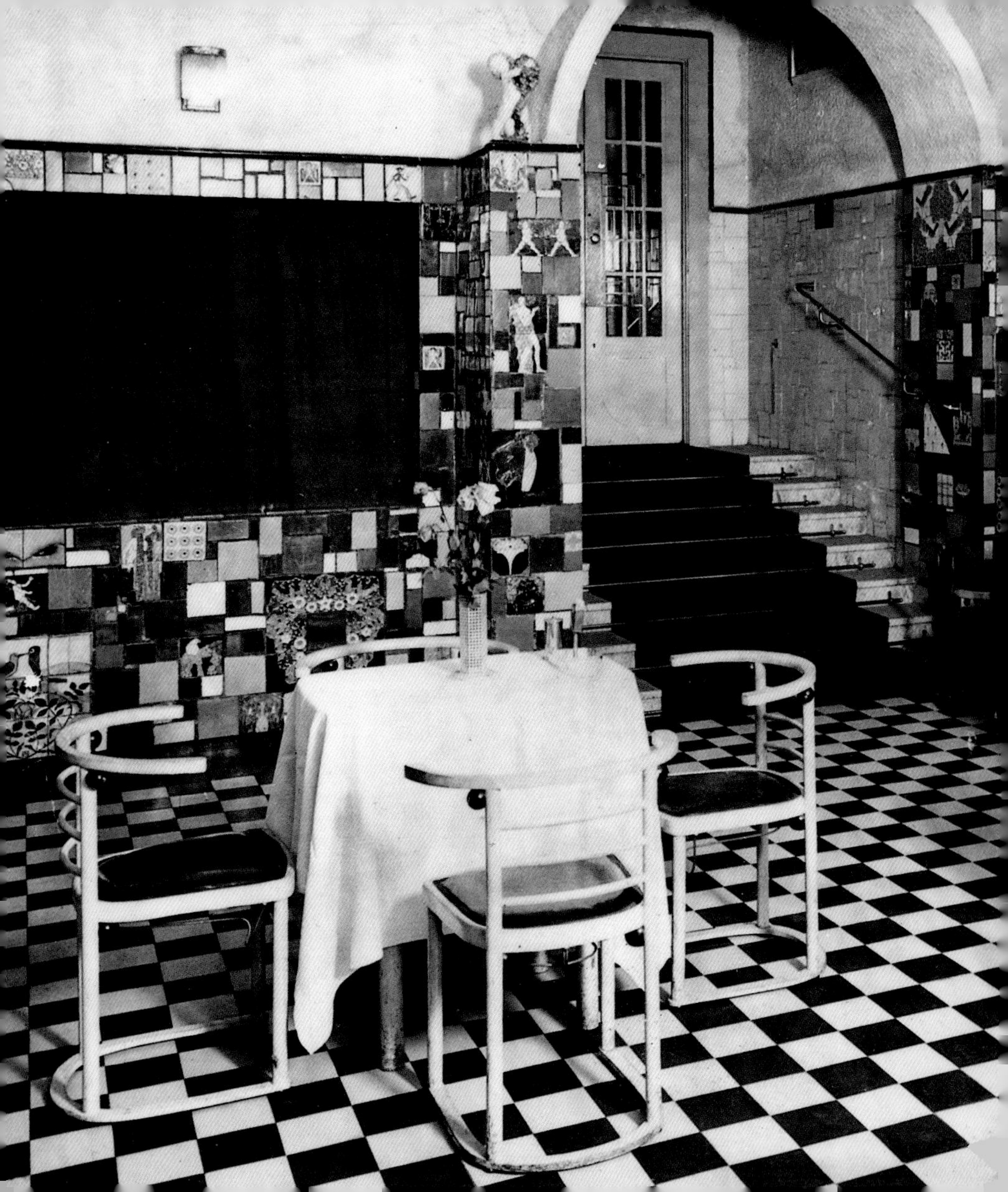

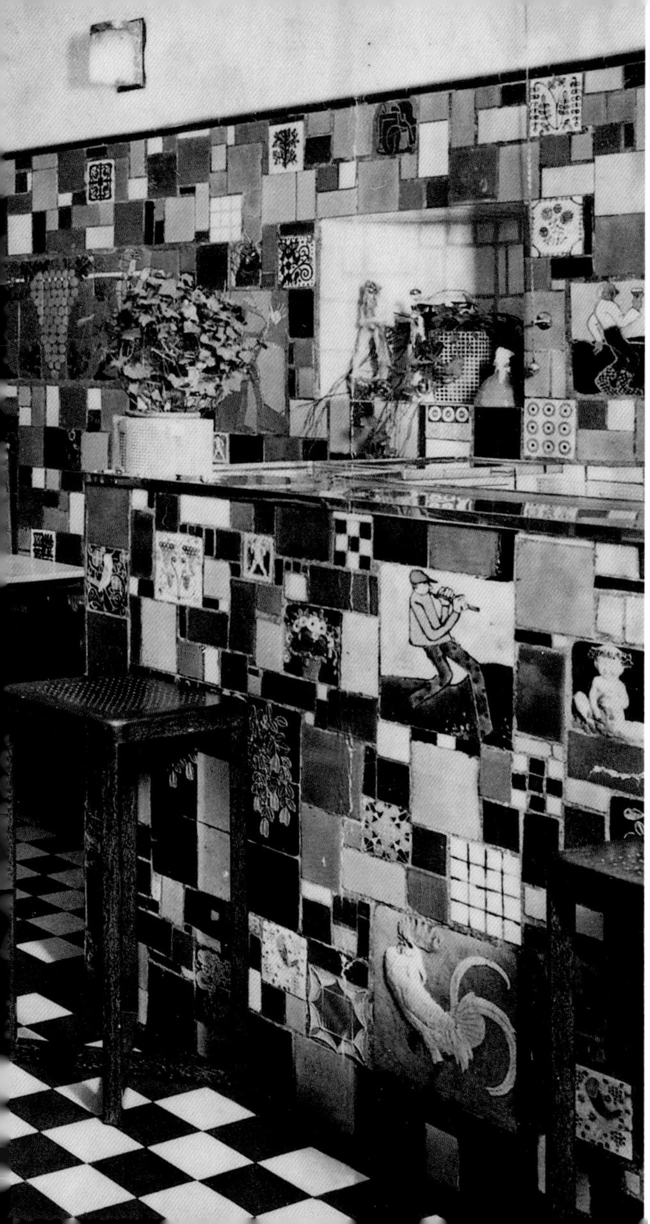

The architecture of the bar is by Joseph Hoffmann, whose signature is unmistakable in the floor tiles. The colorful collage of lively ceramics on the wall tiles, however, is by Bernhard Löffler, head of the ceramics department of the Wiener Werkstätte.

Kabarett Fledermaus
View of the bar
Photo in: *Kunst und Dekoration* XXIII, October 1908 – March 1909
Österreichisches Theatermuseum, Vienna

Gustav Klimt
Stoclet Frieze, Expectation, 1909
Preliminary design for the *Stoclet Frieze*
Mixed media on paper
193.5 × 115 cm
Österreichisches Museum für Angewandte Kunst

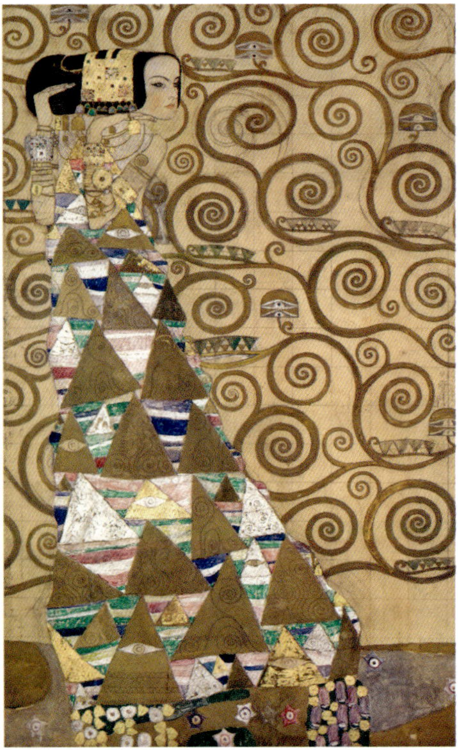

ments the so-called 'ideal distance' from the stage will be suspended, and in the perception of the audience the stage will be appear to have been placed in the middle of the auditorium, at the heart of events."

The publisher's information of the slim brochure revealed all the names behind this ambitious undertaking. The theatre was built by Josef Hoffmann, who was assisted in decorating it by such artists as Gustav Klimt, Oskar Kokoschka, Berthold Löffler and Emil Orlik. The literary participants included Peter Altenberg and Hermann Bahr, the musicians Leonhard Bulmans and Karl Scherber. As the Wiener Werkstätte was the guiding spirit that breathed life into the project, the theatre director was its manager Fritz Waerndorfer. The entire fittings and furnishings, which were designed by the Wiener Werkstätte down to the very last detail, including the badges worn by the staff, were subject to the aim proclaimed by the authors of the project: "It has been important to us to design every detail of our small theatre meticulously and thoroughly as an honest exercise in art along organic lines, and as artists to devote the same loving attention to the most inconspicuous aspects as to the important ones. [...] Through the combined effect of all of this, we hope to have achieved what was mentioned at the beginning: a place to serve the culture of entertainment."

Until April 1913 Kabarett Fledermaus played a leading role in the cultural life of Vienna. A great deal of turbulence in the management of the company prevented it from running on an even keel in commercial terms. In consequence the cabaret, which had less and less success, was turned into a musical theatre and the auditorium was much altered, ruining the original scheme of decoration.

Josef Hoffmann
Palais Stoclet, view of exterior
Brussels, 1905–11

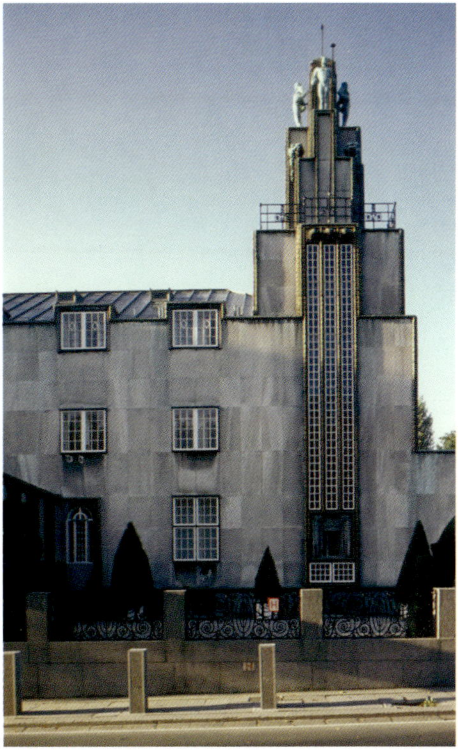

Palais Stoclet

Work on plans that united architecture and interior design to a single aesthetic whole was a central theme of many Art Nouveau architects. Famous examples can be noted from Brussels to Barcelona. However, the Wiener Werkstätte not only imposed its aesthetic on the outer shell. In collaboration with other art forms, it also brought about the intellectual permeation of new spatial concepts. One house that represented the aesthetic design of the private sphere in exemplary fashion was Palais Stoclet in Brussels.

The Belgian manufacturer Adolphe Stoclet commissioned Joseph Hoffmann in his capacity as a member of the Wiener Werkstätte to build this fine town house between 1905 and 1911. In accordance with the social standing of his art-loving patron, Hoffmann not only integrated every detail of the interior into an overall scheme, but also created prestigious spaces for social communication. Gustav Klimt completed the interior design with an aesthetic program which must have met the aspirations of Stoclet and his wife to the full. As if it were a stage set, Klimt made the dining room, which Hoffmann had designed as a double cube of six by twelve

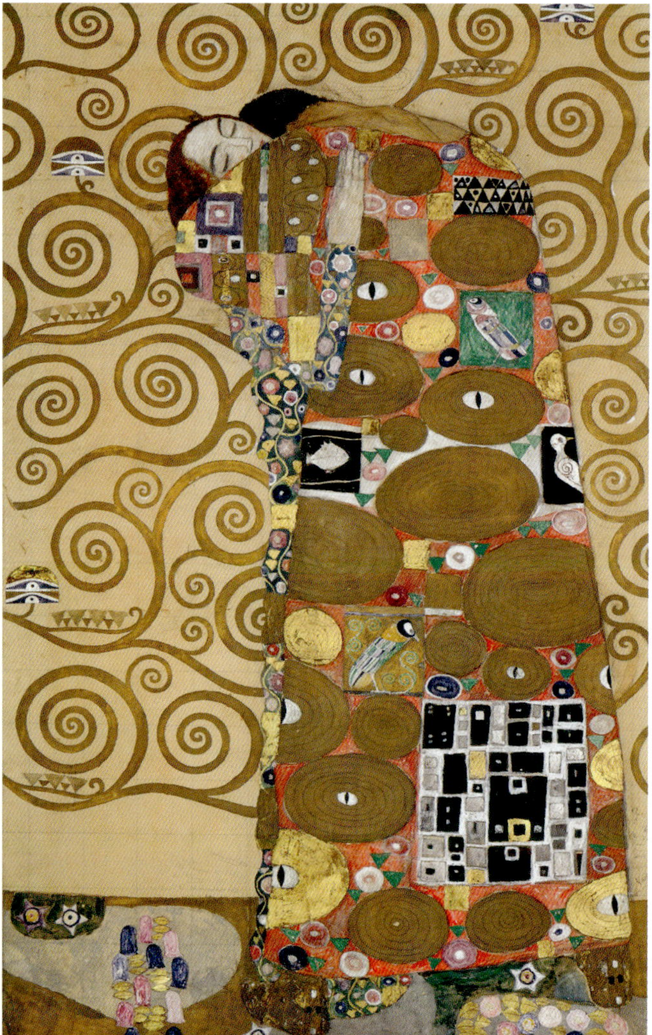

meters, the highlight of the house. He planned a frieze which would leave everyone who entered the room spellbound through its unusual fusion of ornament and figures on two mosaics, each seven by two meters in size, which faced one another. Many subjects with which Klimt had been occupied in the preceding years reappeared in the *Stoclet Frieze*. The embrace motif is the kiss which stands at the forefront of his oeuvre and which he had already included in the *Beethoven Frieze.* The extraordinary feature of the ornamentation is, above all, its abstraction. This is apparent in the "knight," a wholly non-representational figure that is positioned in the line of sight when entering the room. The knight is the guardian of art, the supreme ideal, and is a further impressive symbol of the whole theme of the dining room.

In contrast to the couple whom Klimt joined together in *The Kiss,* in *Fulfillment* the man and the woman are a single motif that hardly shows two individuals. Instead the idea of one merging into the other is reproduced as a paradigm in a block of ornament.

The Beethoven Exhibition

From the beginning the Secessionists had made it clear that spreading the new art was a matter close to their hearts. They therefore not only extended invitations to artists from abroad, but also put on exhibitions that were thematically arranged and didactically presented. In the series of exhibitions that were held each year in the Secession Building, which was specifically built for this purpose, one stands out: the Beethoven Exhibition of 1902. It was a much-anticipated event, which opened on 15 April and revolved around the theme of Ludwig van Beethoven's famous Ninth Symphony. A sculpture of the great composer by Max Klinger stood at the center of the exhibition. Josef Hoffmann had the overall direction of the project, in which 21 artists were involved.

The declared aim of the exhibition was to create a unity of space, murals and sculpture. An expensive bibliophile exhibition catalogue complemented this, and of course the concept included a performance of the Ninth Symphony

Gustav Klimt
Stoclet Frieze,
Fulfillment, 1909
Preliminary design for the *Stoclet Frieze*
Mixed media with gold leaf on paper
194 × 121 cm
Österreichisches Museum für angewandte Kunst, Vienna

conducted by no less a person than Gustav Mahler, who thus made his contribution to this total work of art.

The walls of the Secession Building were part of a program of frescoes in which Alfred Roller and Ferdinand Andri participated. As the aim was to create an incomparable gesamtkunstwerk, the commission was not allocated to the members of the Secession on egalitarian principles, and thus Gustav Klimt received the task of designing no less than three large wall surfaces. He decorated them with a frieze that surpassed all previous work. He created a series of images, an interpretation of the music of the Ninth Symphony, to be read from left to right in rhythmic succession and divided by means of unpainted areas: yearning for happiness; suffering humanity entreats the knight in shining armor; hostile forces (the giant Typhoeus and the three gorgons); sickness, madness, death, lasciviousness, wantonness, intemperance and gnawing grief. Through a gap in the right wall it was possible to take a look at the "inner sanctuary," Klinger's sculpture. The frieze continues with the choir of angels and redemption: the kiss for all the world. Once again art is the supreme ideal image of reconciliation.

Klinger depicted Beethoven as a classical deity – an idea that occurred to him while playing the piano and which he reinforced with allegorical scenes on the plinth. The coloring of the figure, an unusual feature, was initially greeted with a total lack of comprehension by the public.

Max Klinger
Ludwig van Beethoven
1897–1902, marble, bronze, ivory and mosaic
Height 150 cm (total 310 cm)
Museum der Bildenden Künste, Leipzig

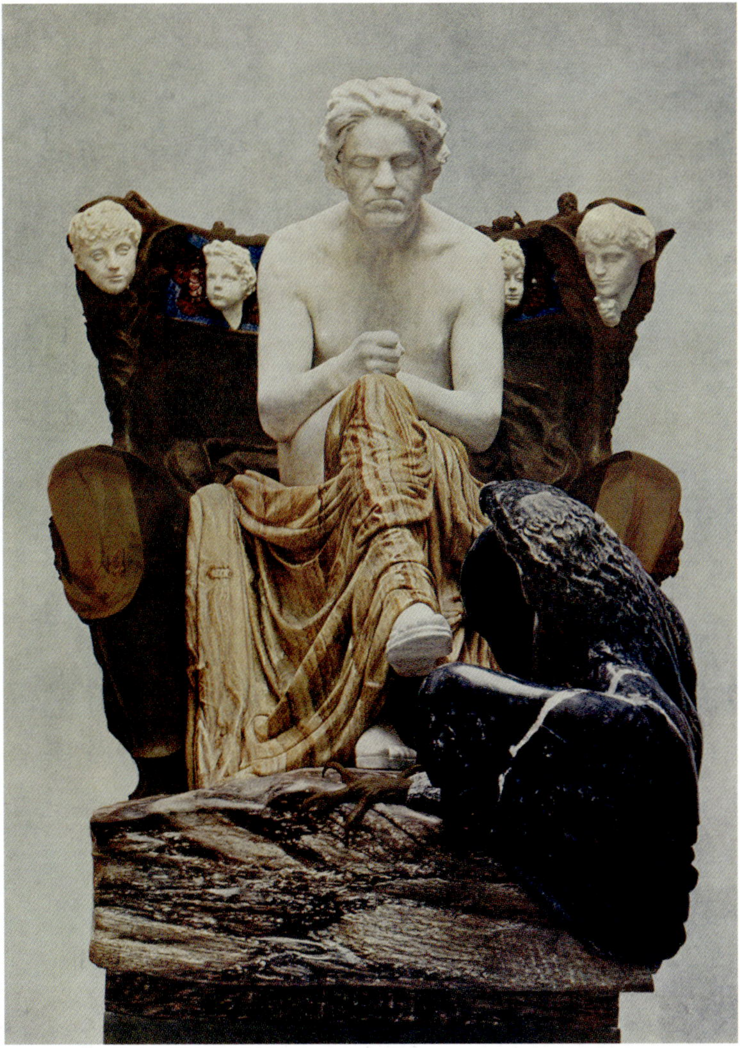

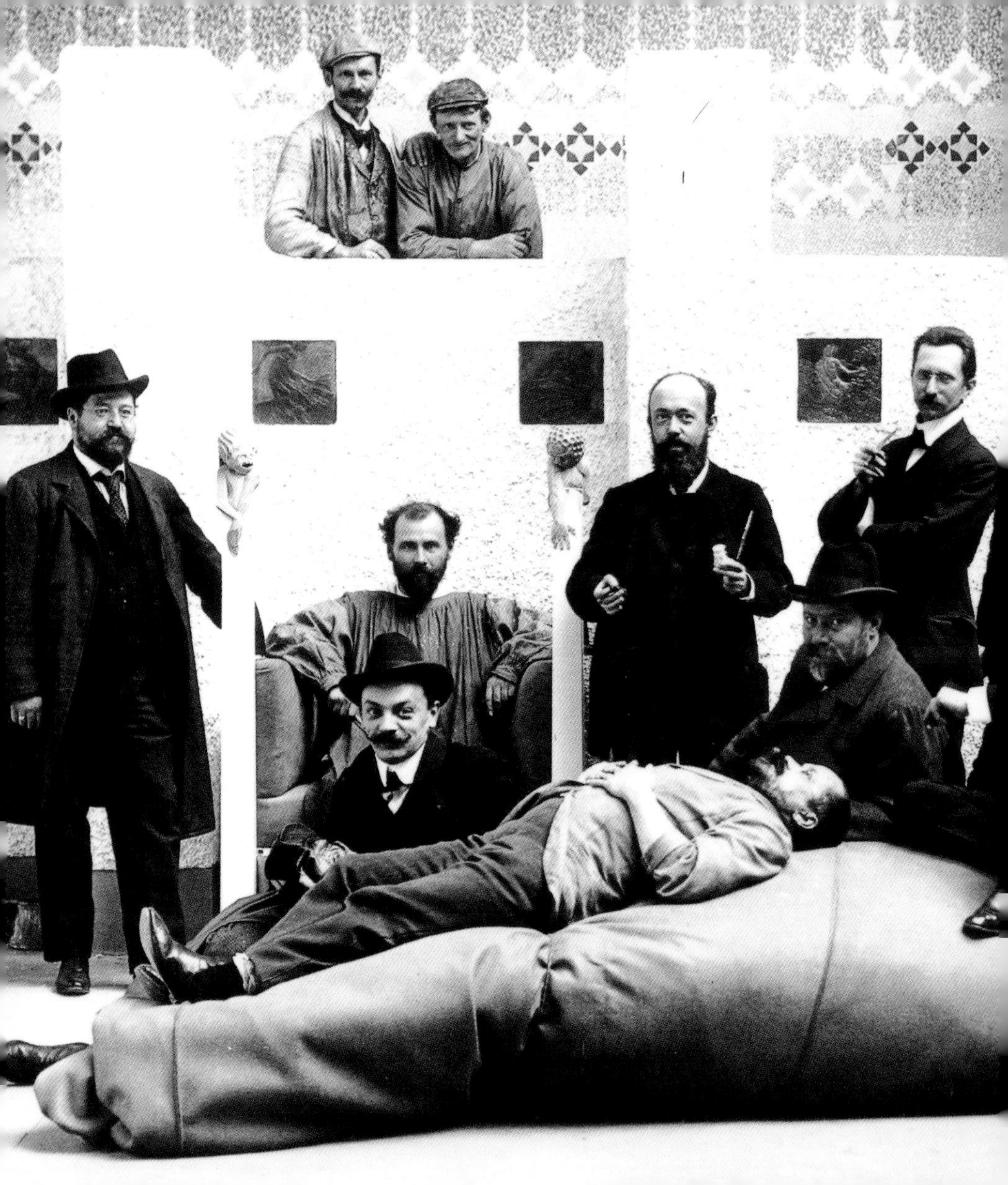

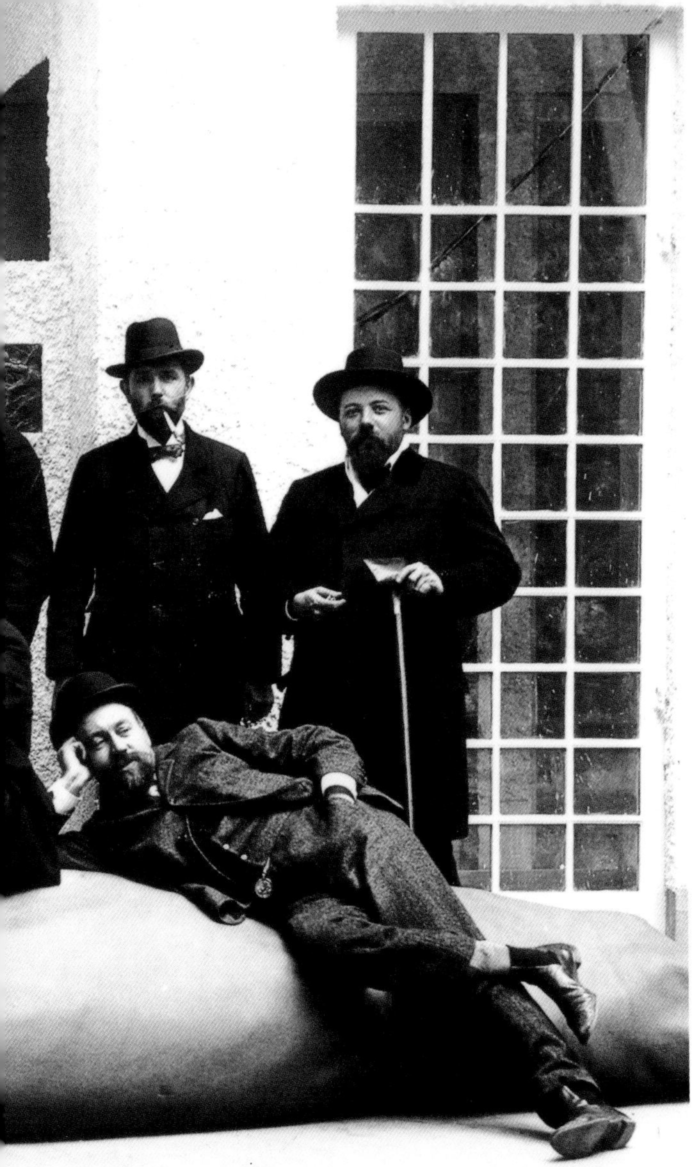

Gustav Klimt and the Vienna Secession on the occasion of the exhibition for Max Klinger's sculpture of Beethoven in the Secession Building.
Left to right: Anton Stark, Gustav Klimt, Kolo Moser, Adolf Böhm, Maximilian Lenz, Ernst Stöhr, Wilhelm List, Emil Orlik, Maximilian Kurzweil, Leopold Stolba, Carl Moll, Rudolf Bacher

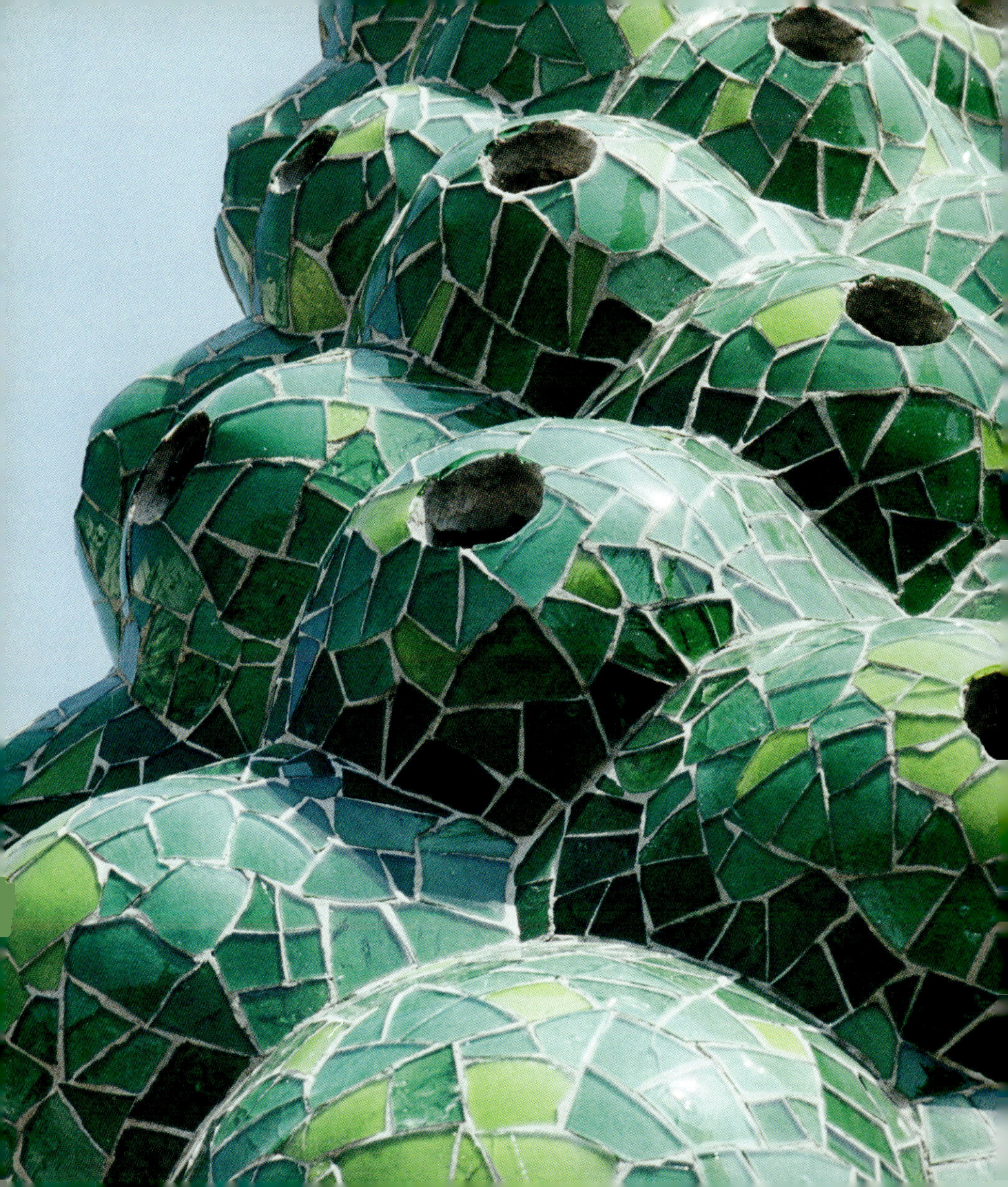

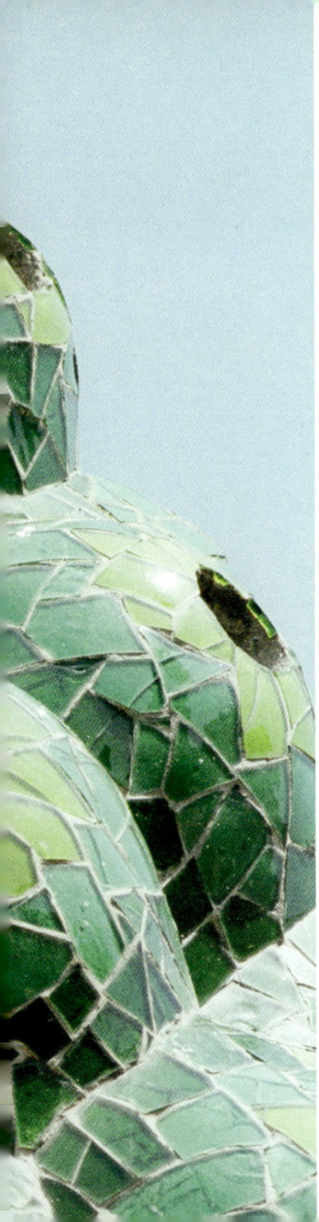

Antoni Gaudí

No-one could have suspected that the old man in a worn suit who was admitted to the hospital for the poor on the morning of 7 June 1926 was the famous architect Gaudí. He had been hit by a tram on the way from Mass to his place of work at Barcelona's most famous building site. After his death three days later, his final resting place was in the crypt of his most important work: the Temple Expiatori de la Sagrada Família. Gaudí was known beyond the borders of Spain as an architect of genius. As a representative of Modernisme Català, the Catalan version of Art Nouveau, he put his stamp on the city of Barcelona. His buildings are surprising and novel architectural works on the road to the modern age.

Antoni Gaudí
Palau Güell
Decorative elements on the roof
(detail)
Barcelona, 1886–89

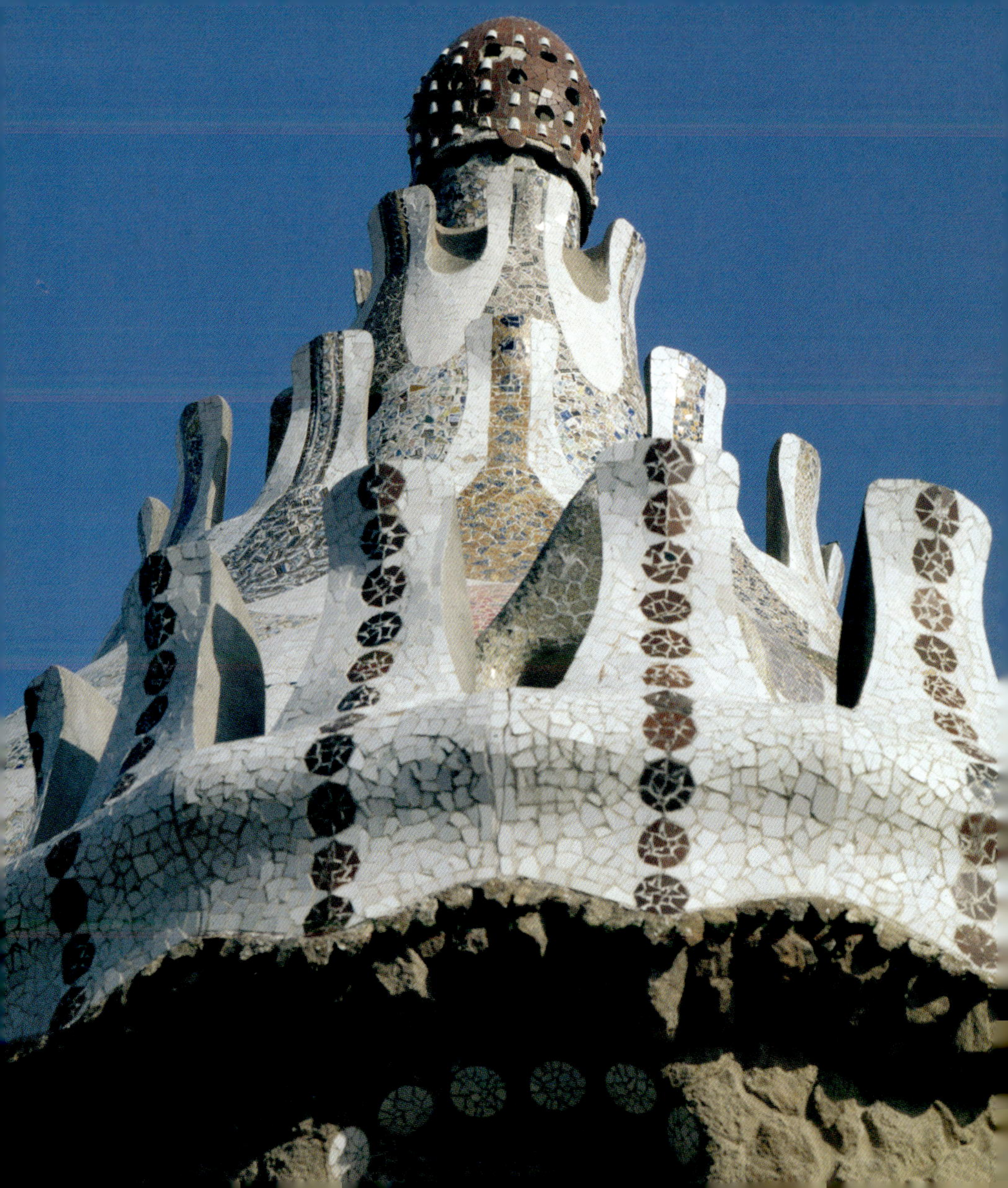

Boldness and Poetry

Antoni Gaudí i Cornet, born in 1852, was a shy boy who suffered from rheumatism and therefore had very little contact to children of his own age. He preferred to stay on the sidelines and watch. This developed into an exceptional gift for observation which enabled him to experience the beauty of nature. When not quite twenty years of age he was allowed to leave his home village for Barcelona, about 100 kilometers away, in order to study architecture. He graduated in 1878 only with difficulty – not because he lacked talent, but because he was different. The ideas of the young Gaudí often made his teachers despair. When the students were given the task of designing the entrance to a cemetery, Gaudí did not rest until he had produced exact sketches of the street and the surroundings of the cemetery, including a funeral procession making its way there. In his very first designs, his holistic view of architecture, which later resulted in brilliant innovations, was already evident. Through a friend Gaudí received his first major commission immediately after completing his studies. His task was to build club premises, workshops and houses for a workers' cooperative in the suburb of Mataró. He set to work with enthusiasm and designed many buildings, of which only the assembly hall and a porter's lodge were completed. The young architect even designed a flag for the Sociedad Cooperativa La Obrera Mataronense, and

Antoni Gaudí
Parc Güell
View of part of the right-hand porter's lodge
Barcelona, 1900–14

Antoni Gaudí
Palacio Episcopal (bishop's palace)
Today: Museo de los Caminos
Astorga, Léon province, Spain, 1889–93

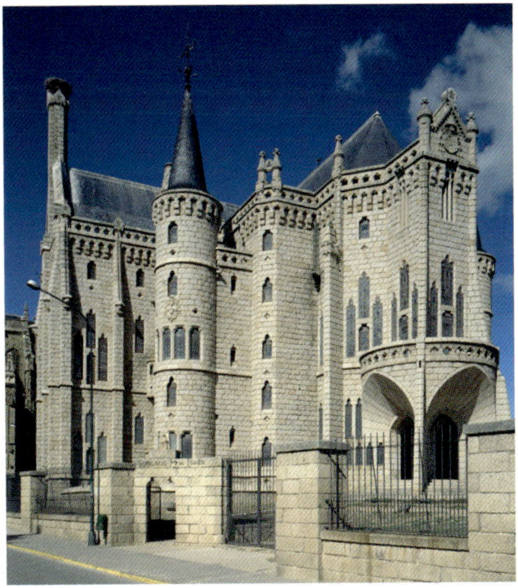

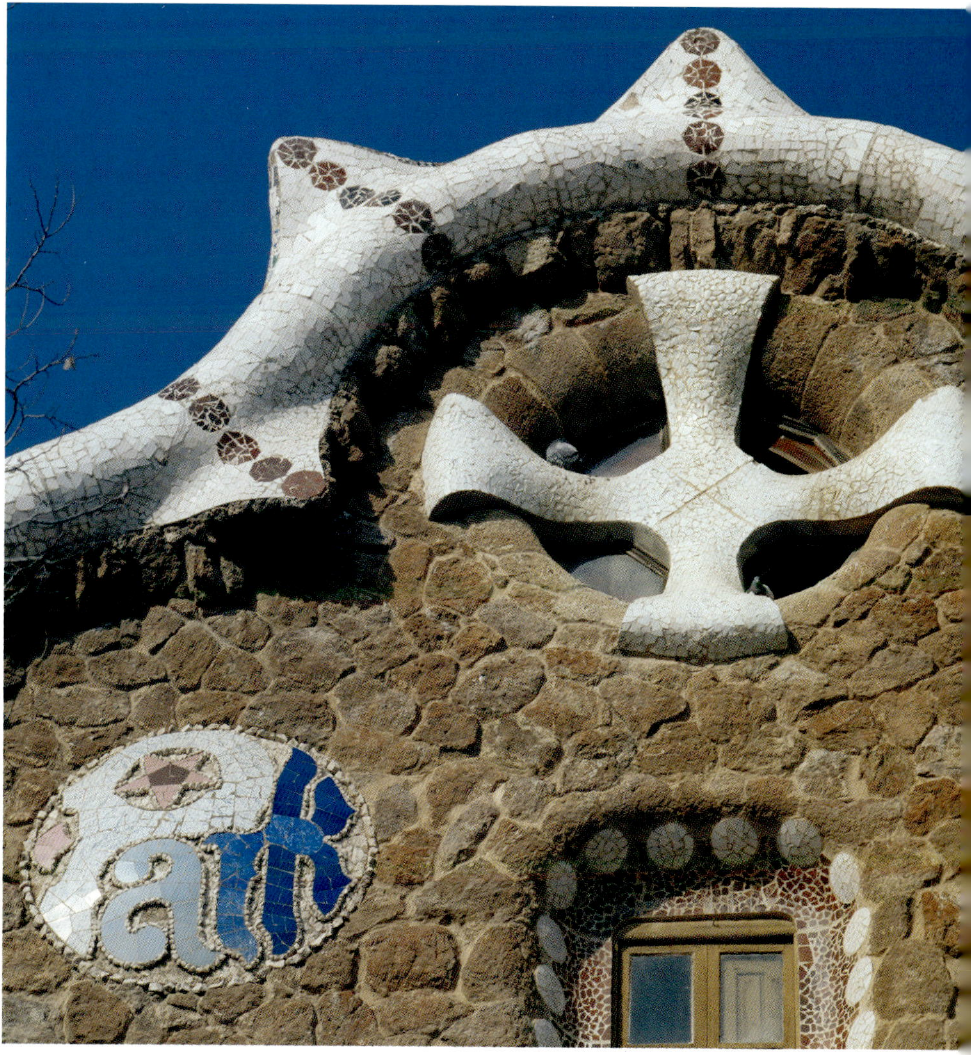

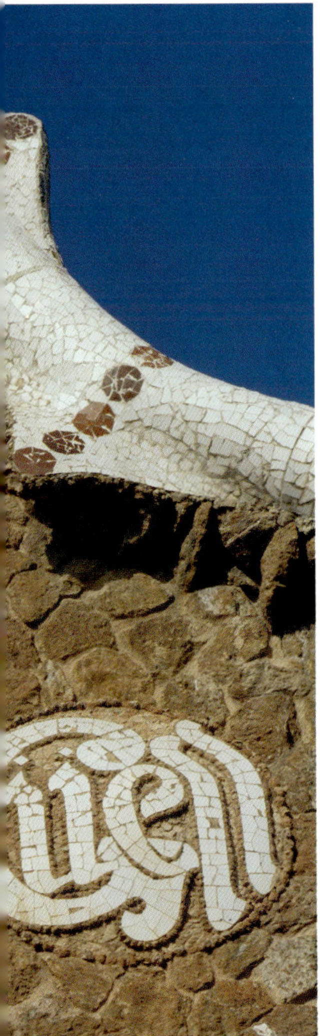

the plans were shown at the world exhibition of 1878 as an example of modern social facilities for workers. The rich industrialist Eusebi Güell saw them, and what followed was one of the most productive friendships in the history of art. The wealthy aristocrat Güell, who felt an obligation to the English ideal of social welfare, gave Gaudí a whole series of important architectural commissions in the following years. The design of Parc Güell is a model project and the greatest achievement of their collaboration.

Parc Güell

The park was intended to fulfill several purposes. Firstly it was meant to act as an example of a place of recreation at the edge of the city, on the model of the garden city movement, and to be a residential estate for a total of 60 families. In addition the wealthy patron wished to demonstrate the harmony of architecture and nature, and finally to use the project as a reference for the concrete produced in his own plant. Gaudí planned the park on hilly terrain, incorporating its natural features into the design. For example, he decided that the roads leading to the park would wind up the hill in serpentine bends, and in some places built around existing trees.

Antoni Gaudí
Parc Güell
View of part of the right-hand porter's lodge
Barcelona, 1900–14

However, as in the project for the workers' cooperative in Mataró, the complex did not proceed beyond its beginnings. Only the administration building and porter's lodge today convey an impression of the ambitious architecture with which Gaudí aimed to satisfy the demands of his friend and patron. It is not unlikely that Gaudí, who worked as a designer of stage sets from time to time, was influenced by the backdrops for the opera *Hansel and Gretel,* which he was building at the time. The imaginative, fairy-tale quality of the designs suggests this. The special feature of a "fifth" façade resulted from the original plans, which would have given the residents of the houses lying higher up a view of the buildings at the entrance. The left-hand building, described as a house for children, is adorned by a tower that is not merely disproportionately high – it rises ten meters above the small and relatively low structure – but also a pioneering example of a framework of iron supports, employed here for the first time by Gaudí. The use of ceramic tiles throughout the park is a specialty of Gaudí that he had already resorted to with success elsewhere. Apart from its decorative effect, which is especially marked in sunlight, this technique known as *trencadis* had the practical advantage that the tiles

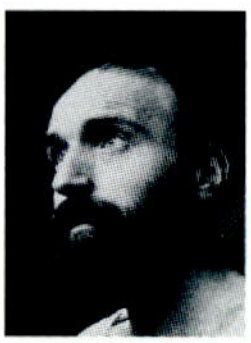

Antoni Gaudí
Self-portrait
Photograph
Private collection

Antoni Gaudí i Cornet

1852 – 1926

25 June 1852 Born in rural Catalonia, the son of a coppersmith

1873–78 Studied architecture in Barcelona

1878 Builds hall of a factory for a workers' cooperative in Mataró; start of his friendship with Eusebi Güell i Bacigalupi, Count of Güell

1871–89 Works on Parc de la Ciutadella; designs a cascade while a student

1883–1926 Sagrada Família

1883–88 Casa Vicens, summer house for the ceramics manufacturer Vicens

1888 Street lamps for the Plaza Réal

1888/89 School for the Order of St Theresa

1889–93 Bishop's palace in Astorga

1898–1900 Casa Calvet

1900–14 Parc Güell

1900–09 Torre Bellesguard, part of a villa at the foot of the Serra de Collserola

1903–13 Alterations to the Cathedral of Majorca

1904–06 Casa Batlló

1906–10 Casa Milà

1908–16 Crypt for a planned church in Colonia Güell

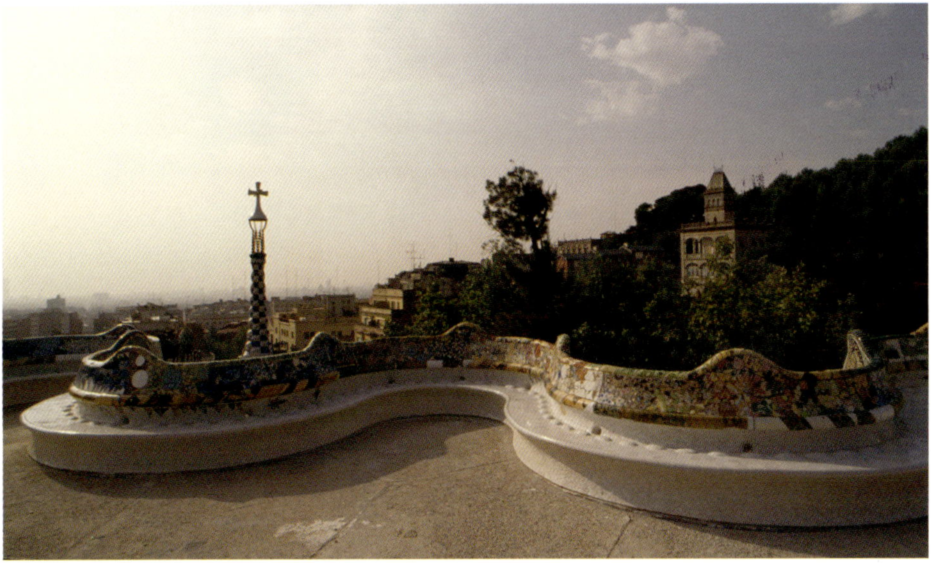

Antoni Gaudí
Parc Güell
Endless bench (partial view)
Barcelona, 1907–12

were waterproof. On the one hand, this kept the concrete base layer dry and gave it a longer lifetime. On the other hand, Gaudí used the run-off in an ingenious system for collecting rainwater. The famous salamander-like dragon in the middle of the steps at the entrance, along with the snake's head above it, is the overflow for this system, which stores water in a subterranean cistern and thus relieves the dryness of the terrain.

The columned space, which was originally intended as a covered marketplace, and the extensive square above it are survivals from the initial idea of creating a garden city. They were to be on-site meeting places for the residents. The benches, a feature to facilitate communication which Gaudí made between 1907 and 1912, are the best-known motif from Parc Güell. It is a further impressive demonstra-

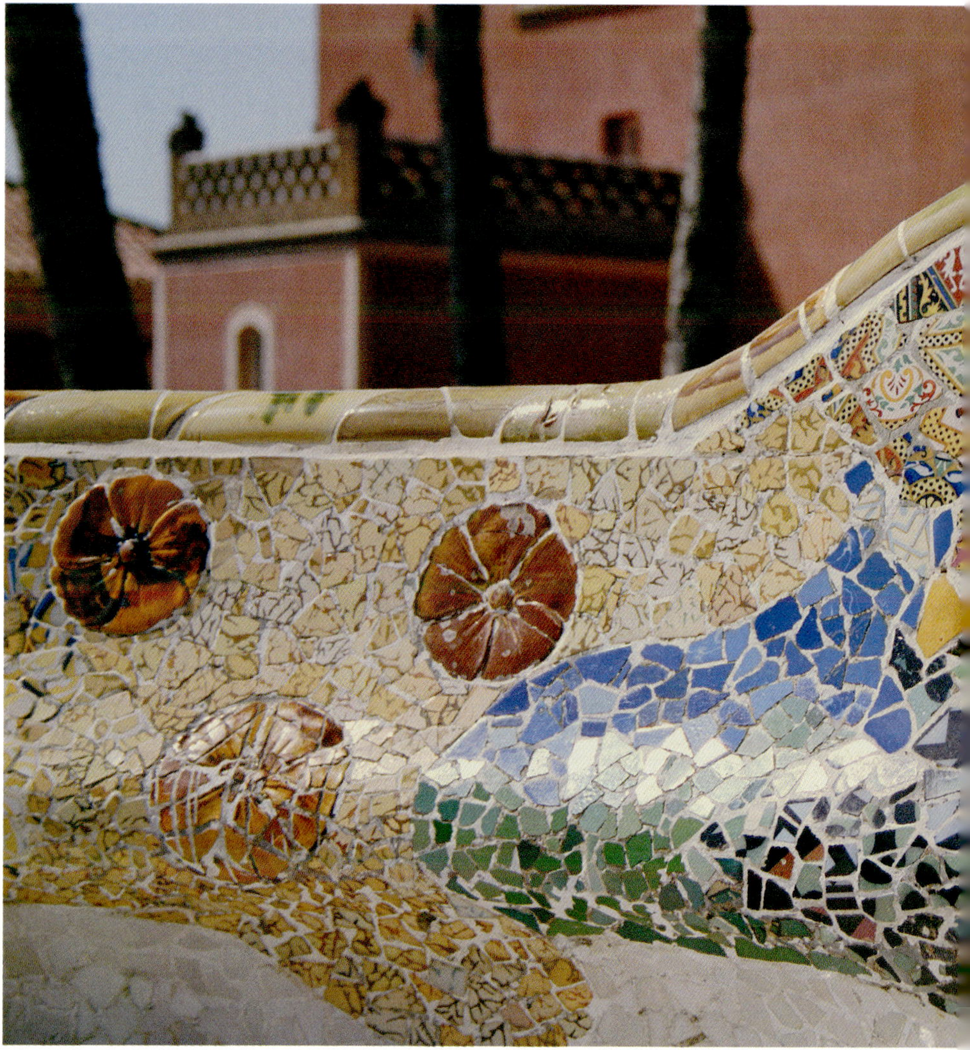

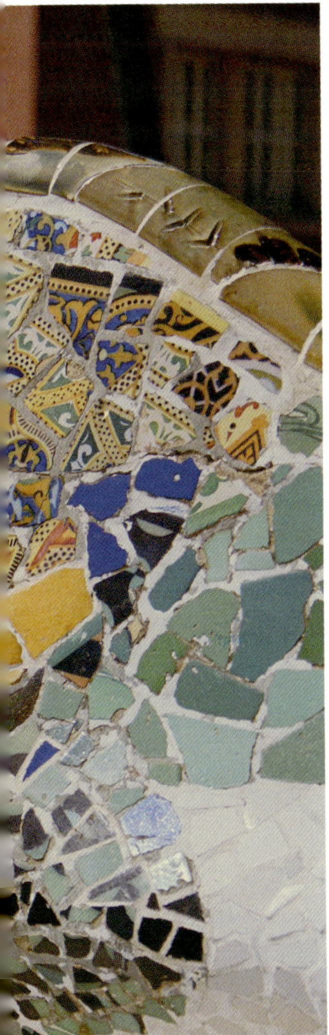

tion of the way in which the architect subordinated everything to nature, with its serpentine shape and even the curve of the seat, formed according to the outline of a worker who was asked to sit on the wet plaster.

Parc Güell is an urban project in the tradition of the reform movement at the turn of the century, which in this instance produced a truly radical modern approach. Despite, or perhaps because of, its lofty aim of providing a new model for living and working in a large city, it was not possible to complete the project. Later Gaudí lived with his aged father in one of the two finished houses – the architect, however, was Francisco Berenguer.

For God by the People

The building project to which Gaudí dedicated his life and which has become the emblem of Barcelona, unfinished to this day, lies in the center of the Catalan capital. José Maria Bocabella, the proprietor of a religious bookshop, wished to build a church in honor of the Holy Family, without support from the diocese and financed solely by donations from the congregation. Bocabella was the inspiration and the driving force behind the project. It was at first entrusted to the diocesan architect Francisco del Villar, who started to build a neo-Gothic church in 1882 but soon quarreled with his patrons. A new architect was therefore needed. Initially Juan Martorell, who had already been involved as the superintendent of construction work, was considered, but

Antoni Gaudí
Parc Güell
Endless bench (detail)
Barcelona, 1907–12

Martorell declined graciously and suggested his young assistant, Antoni Gaudí. Thus one of the greatest building projects of the age was handed to Gaudí, then only 31 years old. On 3 November 1883 he took on the task and made it his life's work. It was to occupy him for the following 43 years, until his death.

Although Gaudí was not opposed in principle to the neo-Gothic style, as his episcopal palace in Astorga shows, for Sagrada Família he envisaged a completely different type of design. He wished the architecture to fulfill an educational function. This approach was without doubt entirely in accordance with the philosophy of the Josephinists (disciples of St Joseph), who gave the commission to build the church. In the course of the city's expansion from the mid-19th century, the area around Sagrada Família was built up, with blocks of houses laid out in a grid. Del Villar had aligned the church to the norms specified by this layout. Gaudí had to fit in with these conditions when planning the continued construction of the church. He revised his plans several times in search of a way of optimizing the given situation. First he completed the crypt, where Mass was held for the first time in 1891. Here he retained the existing neo-Gothic style of his predecessor. Then he turned his attention to the east end, using a system of overlapping triangles to design a new type of façade, which was dedicated to the Nativity. The framework within which the program of sculptures was placed consisted of columns in the form of palms and other floral ornamentation placed on the back of tortoises. The doors with the themes of faith, love and hope have an impressive sculptural quality. Originally Gaudí foresaw a color scheme for this façade, as in his opinion color had an important role in architectural planning: "In architecture the form takes fourth place. Position comes first, dimensions second, material and color third, and form fourth."

After the death of his sister Gaudí looked after not only his aging father but also his young niece. He lived with them in this house in Parc Güell and left it only after the death of his father. Following a crushing disappointment in his youth, there was never again a woman in Gaudí's life.

Francesc Berenguer
House Parc Güell
Gaudí lived here from 1906

Gaudí did not complete his plan for the west façade until 1917. Here he designed a less prominent program of figures, and subordinated everything to the image of Christ's Passion. The realization of these plans began only after his death. With the Christmas Façade and the Passion Façade, the programmatic emphasis on the life of Christ had been established, and the third façade, on the south side, was originally intended to depict the Last Judgement. However, the four towers that rise above the east façade are the last phase of construction that Gaudí himself succeeded in completing. The initial plan envisaged 18 towers for Sagrada Família, and Gaudí intended to illuminate the church so that it would shine far and wide as a religious beacon. He regarded light as the mother of the sculptural arts. "The vertical and parabolic form of the towers is the union of gravity with light. A lamp

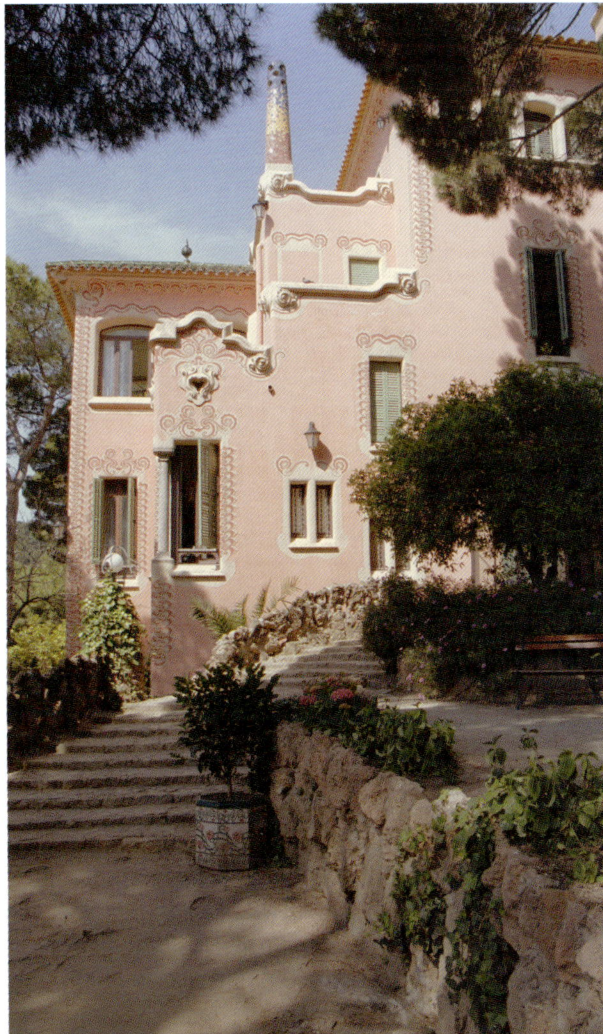

will be attached to the very top of the cathedral; like natural light, which also shines down from heaven. This illumination will lend color and glory to the building on religious holidays and at the same time will be the most beautiful adornment of the city."

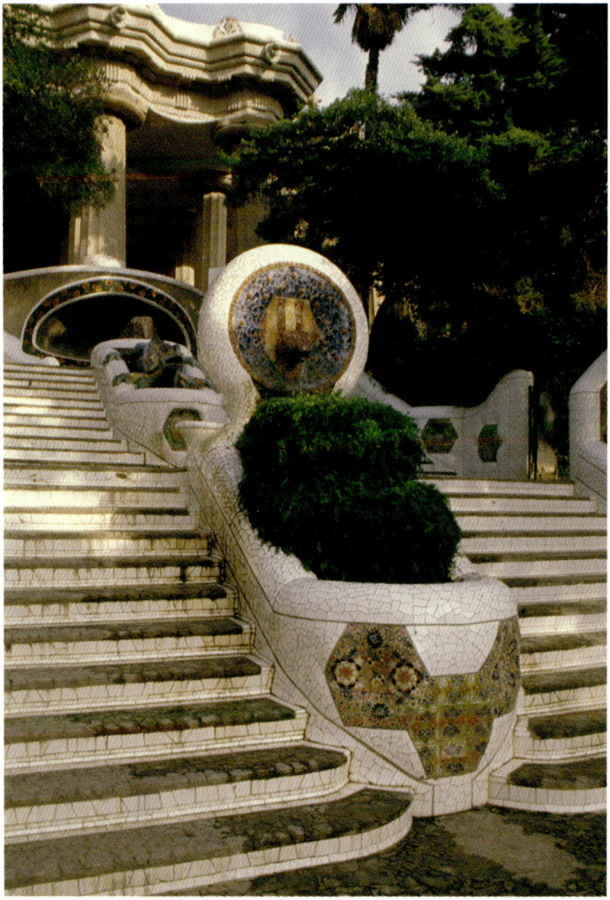

The diagonal, tree-like supports are a special characteristic of the church. They carry the weight of the vaults and make flying buttresses in the medieval manner obsolete. For Gaudí this aspect of Gothic architecture was nothing more than a "crutch," and he carried out experiments of his own that revolutionized the construction of weight-bearing and supporting structural elements. He had long been working with a so-called "hanging model" which enabled him to calculate precisely how the forces in a building should be distributed. To do this he made a system of cords from which little leather bags filled with balls of lead were suspended. By photographing this and reversing the image to an upright position, he had the perfect model for his structure. Many experts were and are opposed to the continuation of the work after Gaudí's death, wishing to keep the building as it was in 1926. In 1936 a group of fanatics burst into the workshops at Sagrada Família and destroyed many drawings. The confusion resulting from the Spanish Civil War stopped construction, which only went ahead again in the 1950s. The church is now growing steadily, although, astonishingly, it has no planning permission. Gaudí regarded the completion of the church as a matter of fate. "The people are building the cathedral of La Sagrada Família and it reflects their nature. This work is in the hands of God and dependent on the will of the people. The architect who lives among the people and turns to God fulfills his work. Providence with its untiring plans will complete the task."

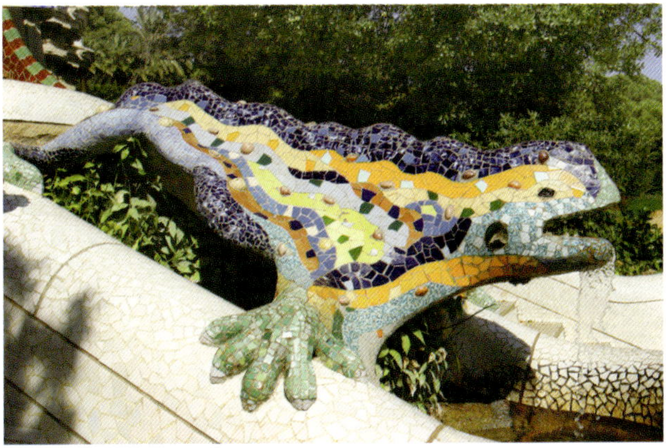

Antoni Gaudí
Iguana at the entrance to Parc Güell

Modernisme Català

What is probably Gaudí's most exciting project stands on Passeig de Gracìa at the heart of the new district of Eixample: a town house that he built for the textile manufacturer Josep Battló between 1905 and 1907. To be precise, it is the renovation of an existing building. In this work Gaudí exploited the potential of *Modernisme Català,* which was a banner of Catalan identity in modern architecture. The opulent design of the façade relates the story of Sant Jordi, the patron saint of the Catalans. The fearsome dragon appears on the roof of the house above the bones and skeletons of its victims, which were depicted as façade decora-

Antoni Gaudí
Entrance to Parc Güell with fountain; beyond it the *Hall of 100 Columns*

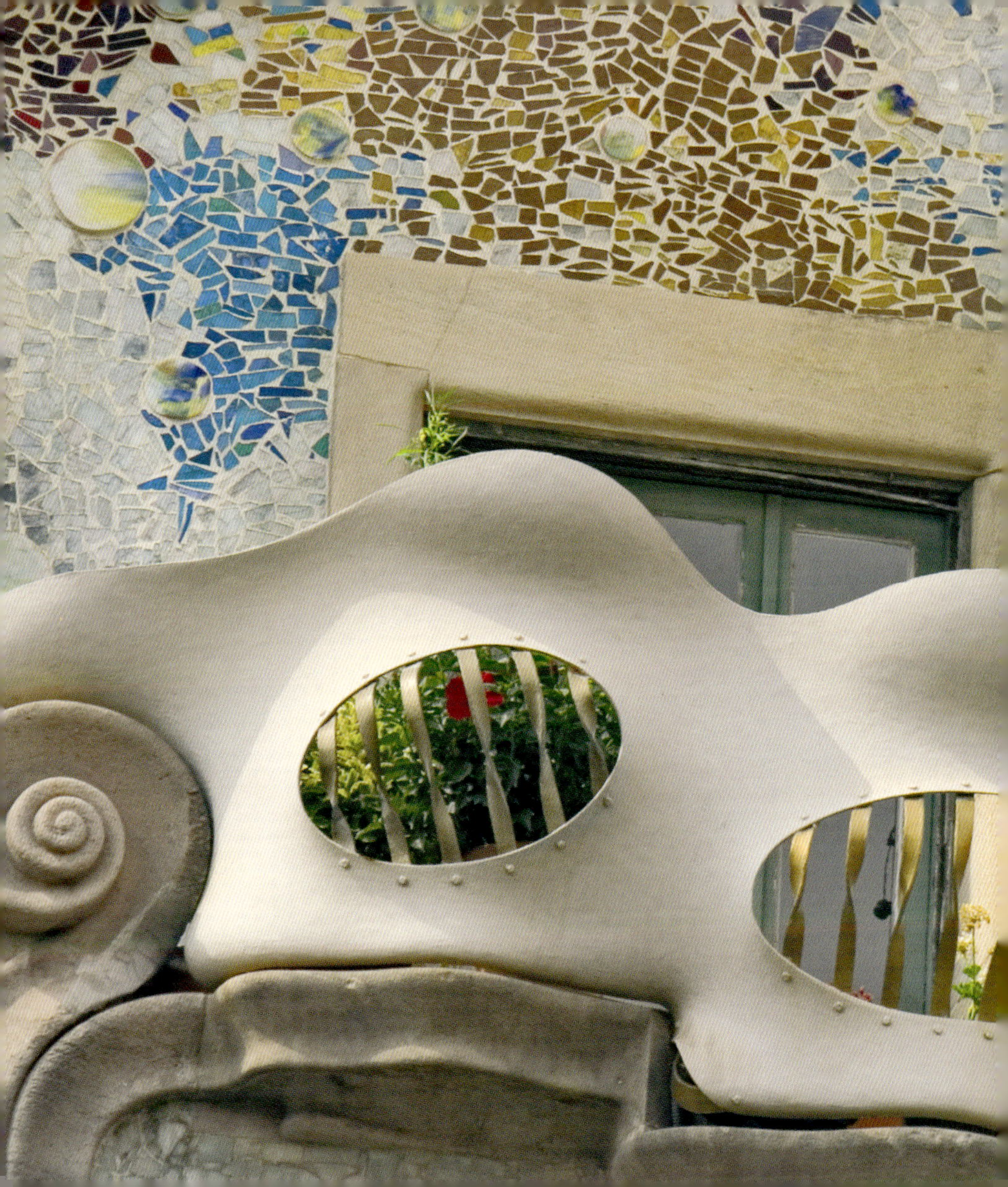

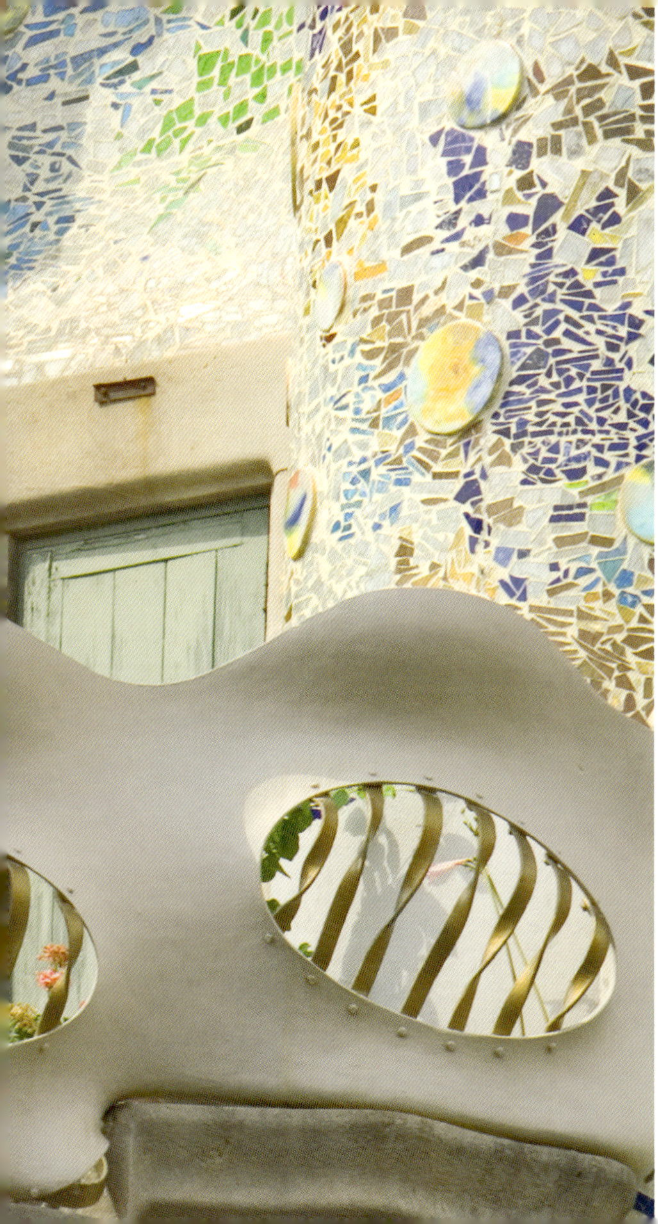

Gaudí's long-standing assistant Josep Maria Jujol was involved in this façade. The remarkable shapes of the balconies of Casa Batlló, which have their full effect when illuminated in the evening, look like gruesome, decadent skulls.

Antoni Gaudí
Casa Batlló
Detail of balcony railing
Barcelona, 1905–07

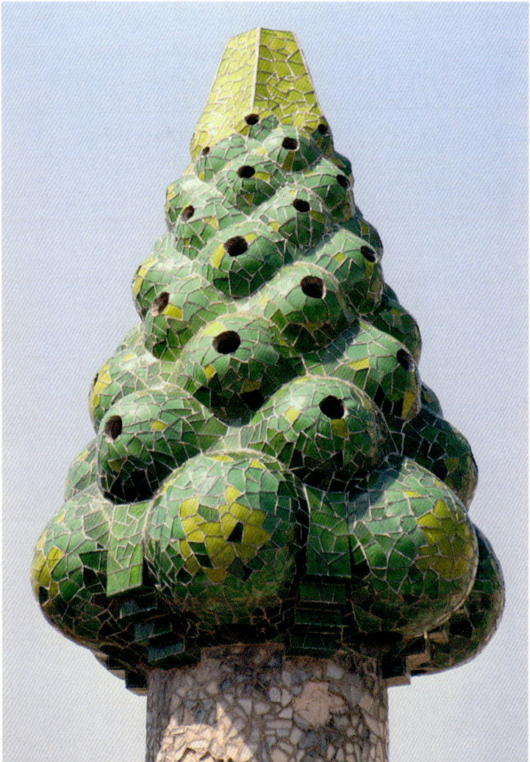

Antoni Gaudí
Palau Güell
Decoration of the roof (detail)
Barcelona, 1886–89

tion with the assistance of several local sculptors. In this building, too, Gaudí attached importance to the details, especially in the interiors. In the attic the typical form of the "Catalan vault" can be recognized. Gaudí had used this for years, taking advantage of ancient, traditional building methods. The arches, which are borne entirely by the strength of the individual bricks, had a remarkable load-bearing capacity that amazed even experienced workers. Here too, in technical matters, the strength of Gaudí's identification with the history of Catalonia is evident. He spoke only Catalan on principle and looked for associations with patrons who shared his sentiments. In this way many of his buildings amount to a political statement. In another project, Casa Calvet, Gaudí went so far as to adopt the forms of Catalan Baroque architecture in order to point out that it was rooted in history. On the façade of Sagrada Família, too, there are many references to Catalonia. "All species of bird native to Catalonia appear on this façade."

At Casa Milà, where work began at approximately the same time as at Casa Batlló, Gaudí for the first time took astonishing liberties in designing the interior, which makes do without any load-bearing walls. He imagined that Casa Milà might one day serve as a hotel, and in this radical rejection of traditional forms of building showed how modern he was in terms of the functionality of his works. They were flexible and variable, but never lacked a characteristic façade, which in the case of this town house is an unusually coherent and flowing surface. The truly sensational feature is again the design of the roof, which is an almost surreal landscape. Eccentrically twisted chimneys and heaped-up terraces are an invitation to explore its surface. In addition to a thoroughly thought-out system of ventilation, Gaudí also planned an underground car park and lifts, which were not installed until a later date. These practical considerations resulted from the idea of a total work of art that adapts all aspects of the architecture and its surroundings to the people who live there. Antoni Gaudí was in many ways a precursor of modern architecture, and young architects made the pilgrimage to Barcelona – Gaudí himself never traveled – to exchange ideas with him. After meeting him in 1907, Walter Gropius wrote: "His intensity captivated me and seemed to me a highly desirable characteristic of human activity, but I lacked the maturity to understand his unique boldness and inventive talent as a designer of buildings."

Antoni Gaudí
Sagrada Família
Detail of top of tower
Barcelona, 1883–1926
(still unfinished)

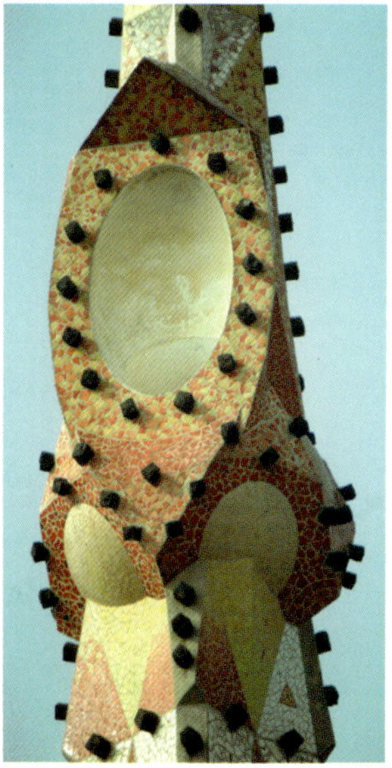

Following double page:
Antoni Gaudí
Sagrada Família
Detail of interior, vault
Barcelona, 1883–1926 (still unfinished)

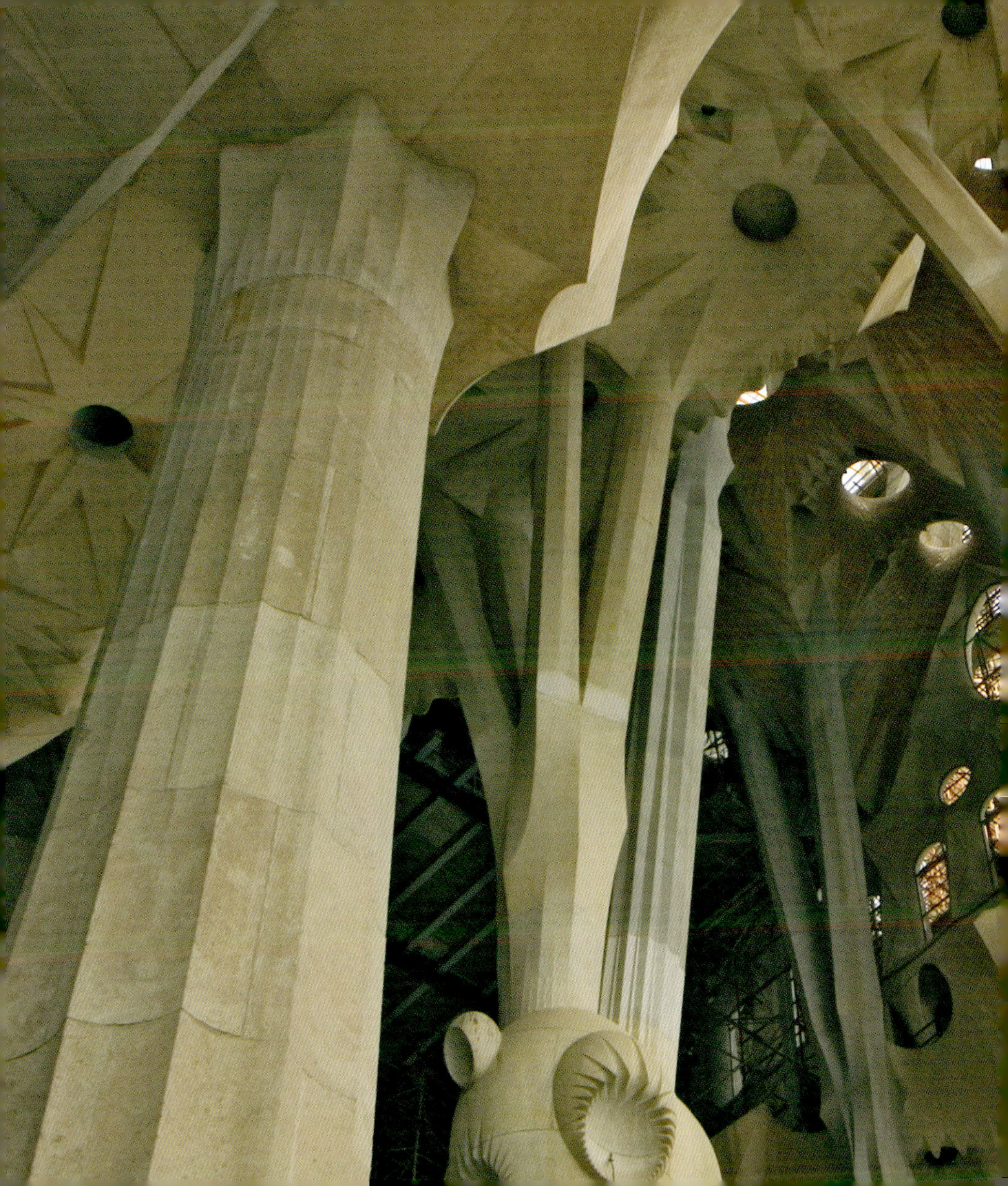

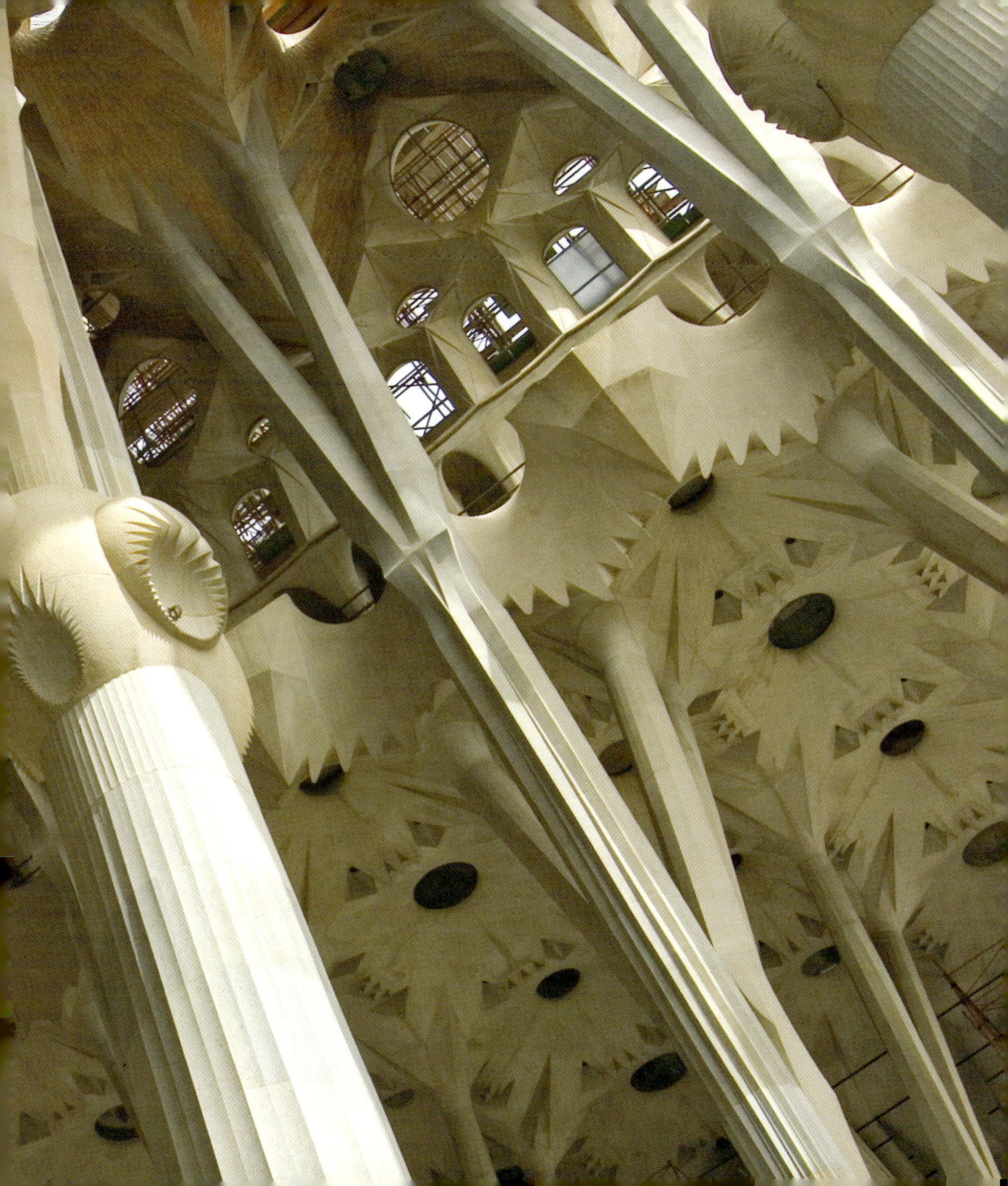

The Threshold of a New Era – World Exhibitions and Other Dreams

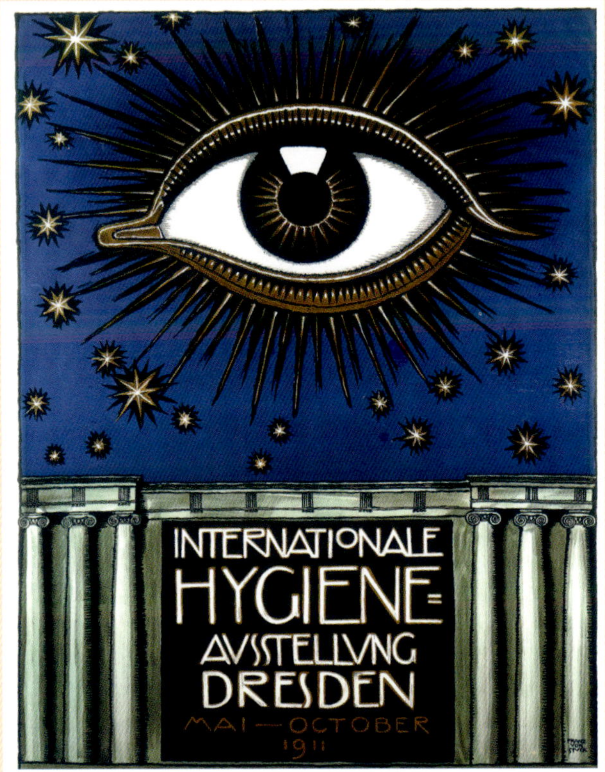

It was drawn on blotting paper and designed by a builder of greenhouses: the Crystal Palace, home of the first world exhibition, the Great Exhibition of 1851, was a new wonder of the age, built of iron and glass. Its length was an unbelievable 563 meters, its width 124 meters. Like a man-made sky, its roof covered several exotic trees and a crystal fountain. The largest mirror in the world stood in its long central space. This glass palace, which extended across Hyde Park like a colossus, held a great fair of inventions and paid tribute to progress. It was a panopticon of technology, including of course the steam engine. The exhibition became a demonstration of the might of Great Britain as a world power, and was also a magnet for mass tourism. It was the symbol of a new age, and a presentation of the future.

The exhibition realized a vision of Prince Albert. Its aim was to be "a true witness to and a lively picture of the state of development which the whole of humanity has attained in this great work." This was the birth of a series of world exhibitions that paralleled the evolution of society towards the modern period. They reflected the capabilities of their time and provided examples of how contemporaries intended to arrange their world. The world exhibition in Paris at the end of the century became a kind of super-show, of course. Its purpose, as the French minister of trade announced, was to be "a summary of the 19th century" and to put a spotlight on the "philosophy" of the century. The main attraction was the Palace of Electricity, which drew visitors in their thousands. The entire exhibition grounds were like a colorful sea of illuminations. This showed how the future was then envisaged: as bright as day even at night, with everything functioning automatically.

Tellingly, this vision of the future world had already played its part in the science fiction novels of Jules Verne. His descriptions of an ideal city with an ingenious system of lighting appeared in 1895 in *Propeller Island,* and the equipment of the legendary *Nautilus,* Captain Nemo's submarine, included technical gadgets that even worked 20,000 leagues beneath the sea. The opulence of the fittings cited in Verne's novels was also evident in the elaborate furnishings of Art Nouveau interiors, which gave rise to the term "Style Jules Verne."

"Belief in uninterrupted, irresistible 'progress' truly had the power of a religion in that age: belief in this progress was even stronger than belief in the Bible, and its gospel seemed to gain unshakable proof every day from new marvels of science and technology. [...] In the streets electric lights burned at night in place of dim gas lamps, the shops extended their seductive glow from the high streets out into the suburbs, thanks to the telephone people could speak to other people far away, they flew along at unprecedented speeds in horseless carriages, they fulfilled the dream of Icarus by ascending into the skies." (Stefan Zweig)

Joseph Paxton
Crystal Palace for the Great Exhibition of 1851
Photograph, 1900
Sammlung Archiv für Kunst und Geschichte, Berlin

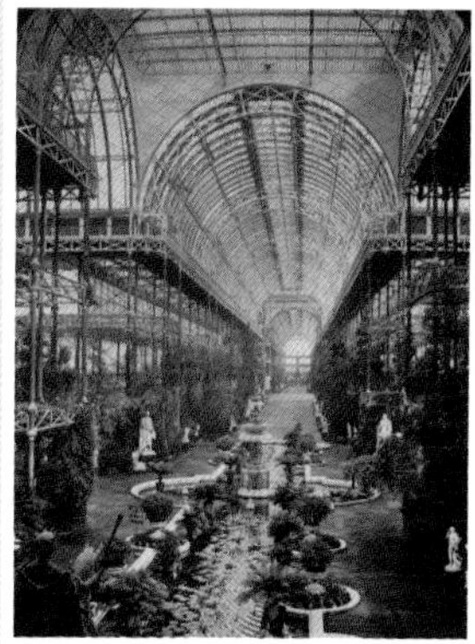

Franz von Stuck
Poster for the International Hygiene Exhibition in Dresden
1911, color lithograph
Staatliches Kupferstichkabinett, Dresden

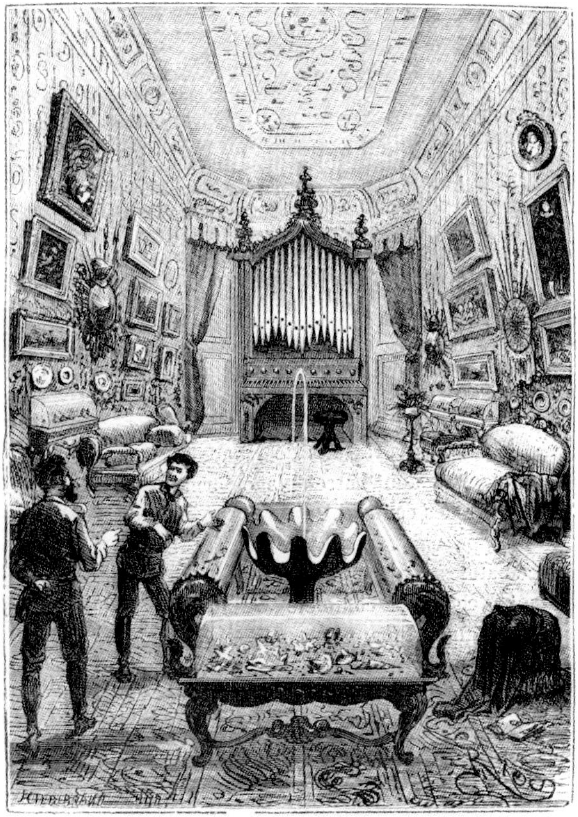

Henri Théophile Hildibrand
The interior of *Nautilus,* illustration of Jules Verne's novel
20,000 Leagues under the Sea
1877, etching
Bibliothèque Nationale, Paris

While, on the one hand, the numerous world exhibitions were wholly devoted to the technical achievements of the years around 1900, on the other hand the reform movement manifested a divergent view of the age to come. It was characterized by a marked retreat towards nature and a natural life. Here the focus was on human beings, their bodies and their needs. One of the highlights of this movement was the German Hygiene Exhibition of 1911 in Dresden, for which Franz von Stuck designed a poster. The mystic eye – like the eye of a seer in the midst of an ocean of stars – unmistakably showed that the reformers had a sense of mission. In artistic circles, especially, these new themes stimulated discussion about concepts for future life and led to the founding of artists' colonies at a distance from the urban centers.

One example of the many "drop-outs" who emerged from the reform circles was the group that settled on Monte Verità near Ascona in 1900. A community of idealists formed under the leadership of Henri Oedenkoven, the son of a manufacturer, and the pianist Ida Hofmann. They had vegetarian tendencies and a marked abhorrence of a society dominated by militarism. It was the pacifist philosophy of the reformers, above all, which attracted artists and writers such as Hans Arp and Hermann Hesse before and after the First World War. Isadora Duncan, too, belonged to the group, and developed her expressive style of dance in these circles. The principal idea of the group was to establish a sanatorium for natural healing, where they could try out progressive methods such as "air baths," in which patients would sojourn naked in the open air. If clothes were worn, then this was the "reform clothing" that appeared in this period, which did not confine the body and represented a healthy alternative to the corset.

It was not only the supporters of nudism who held heated debates about the need for fashion to be better suited to the natural characteristics of the human body. Campaigners for women's rights who were active at this time also saw liberation from the corset as liberation from the social restrictions on women. Many artists, too, gave thought to the topic, and the "reform dress" became an item of craftwork. In 1904 the artist Alfred Mohrbutter wrote as follows about women's dresses: "And then, surrounded here by these new, simple furnishings

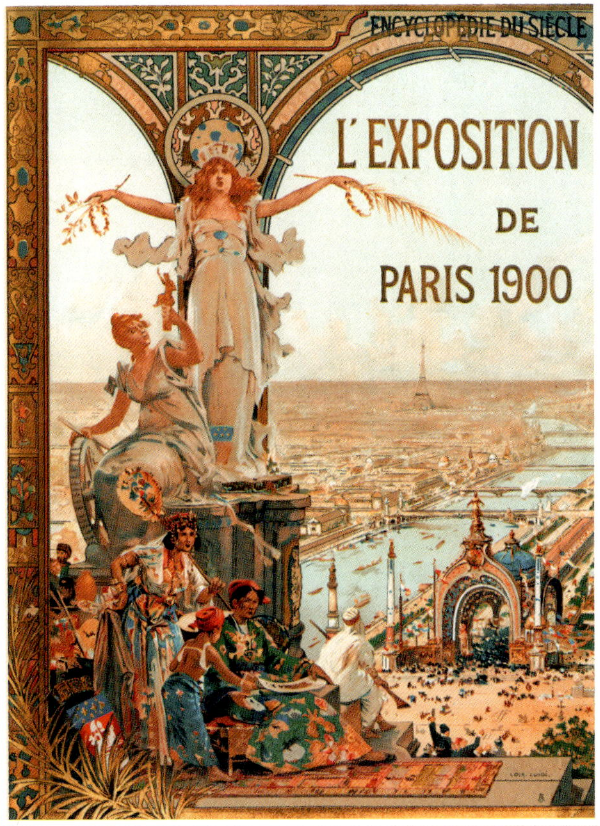

Louis Loir
Poster: *L'Exposition de Paris 1900*
1900, color lithograph

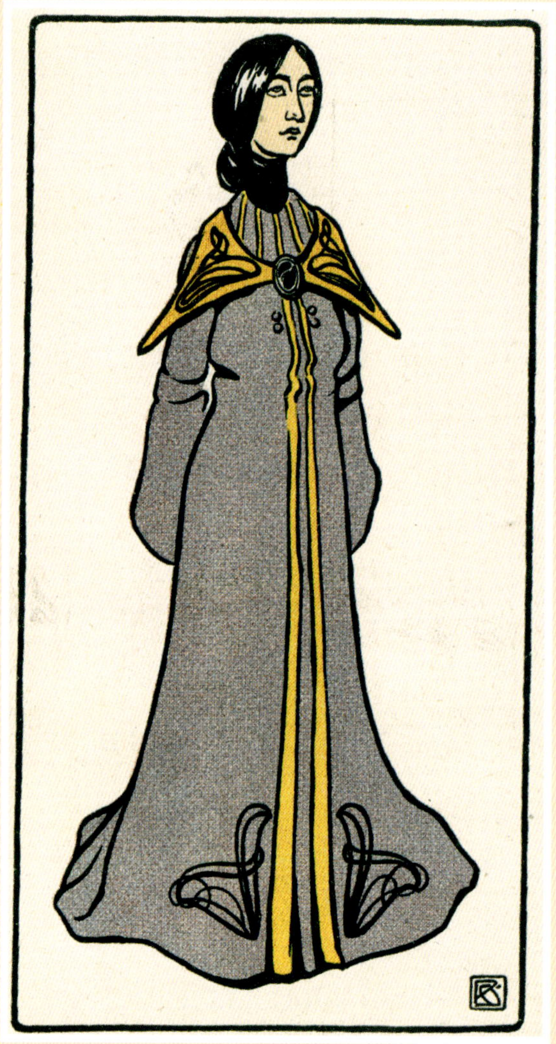

and carpets, it suddenly became clear how meaningless the dresses of our women have become (...) We were amazed at ourselves for being able to bear such things for decades when we finally discovered that a woman's dress, too, can and must be meaningful and consistent, like an item of furniture or a carpet, that it has an idea, a decorative idea, that awaits realization. And all at once this discovery elevated the dress to the status of a work of art."

Henry van de Velde is regarded as the pioneer of these artistic dresses. The director of the textile museum in Krefeld had asked him to provide designs. In his program of furnishings for his own house, Bloemenwerf, Van de Velde had already included clothing for his wife in the overall plan, and he continued to pursue this course in later projects, for example Villa Esche in Chemnitz. The typical feature of his women's dresses is their organic line, which van de Velde fully adapts to the gently falling curve of the clothing. The ornamental scheme is the same as that of his crockery, cutlery and upholstery.

Gustav Klimt, too, took to the loose reform clothing with enthusiasm and often wore a long caftan. The women in some of his portraits wear reform clothing, some of which was made in the Wiener Werkstätte. The most frequent orders for these modern clothes came from Emilie Flöge, who ran a fashion store with her sisters and may have been responsible for making Klimt receptive to new ideas in fashion. However, it must be concluded that the dissemination of reform dress was confined to artistic and intellectual circles: the rest of society was unwilling to dispense with clothes that drew attention to the female form.

The mood in the years at the turn of the century was ambivalent. On the one hand there were fears that the world was going under, a feeling of gloomy decadence that resulted from weariness with the old ways. On the other hand, many looked forward to a new age that would be better, healthier and happier. Society at the turn of the century was seized by a mood of elation, which was later even to extend to the First World War as a means of creating a tabula rasa. The task of designing this new world was handed to artists, who enthusiastically accepted the commission.

On 19 October 1901 Albertos Santos-Dumont, coming from St. Cloud, flies around the Eiffel Tower in his airship no. 6, photograph

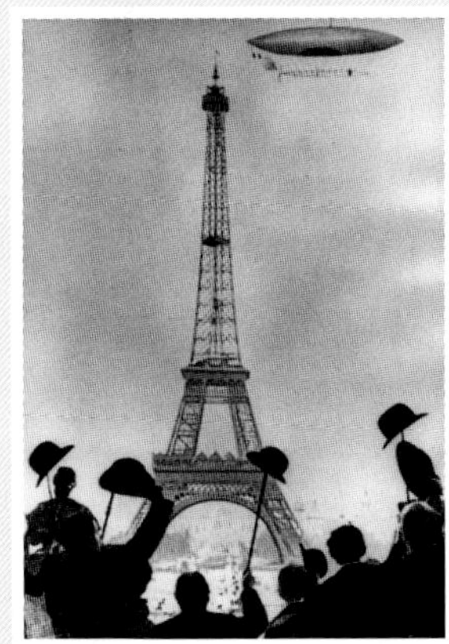

Meggendorfer Blätter
Our Contemporaries – The Reform Lady
1904, color lithograph
Sammlung Archiv für Kunst und Geschichte, Berlin

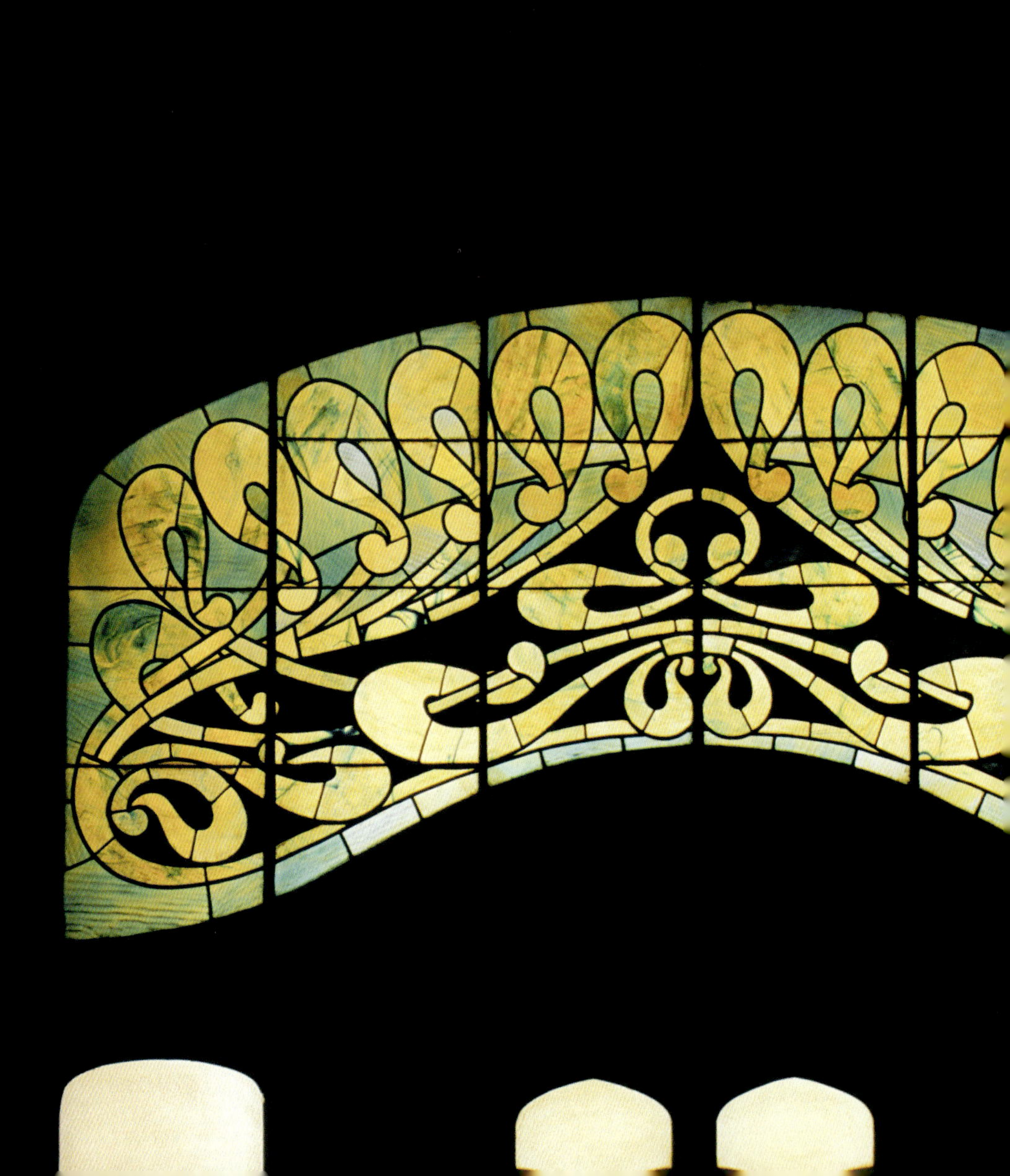

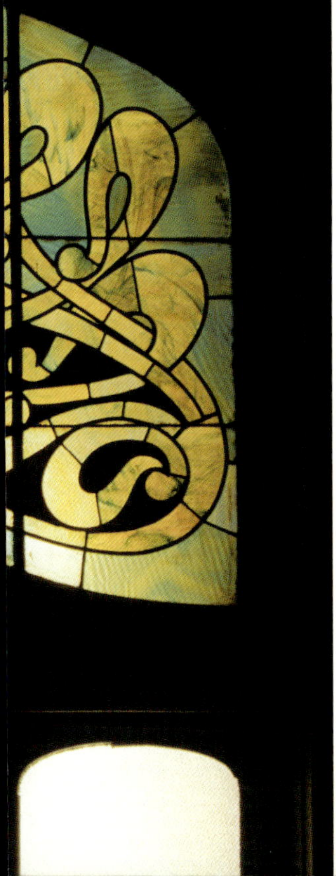

Henry van de Velde

A movement spread across Europe, maintained by a network of creative artists. One artist, who stood in the vanguard, was passed on from Brussels via Berlin to Paris, and then on to Weimar. After an intermezzo in Holland and a return to provincial life, he ended up in Switzerland. These were the principal staging posts in the life of Henry van de Velde; he made his distinctive mark in every one of them. He took on the role of a pioneer in the evolution of Art Nouveau to modern art. Struggling against difficult circumstances, fighting for recognition and against depression, van de Velde was the catalyst of a new course in architecture and crafts, a man who set benchmarks in the 20th century.

Henry van de Velde
Stained glass on the staircase of
Hôtel Otlet, Brussels
1894–1900, architect Octave
van Rysselberghe

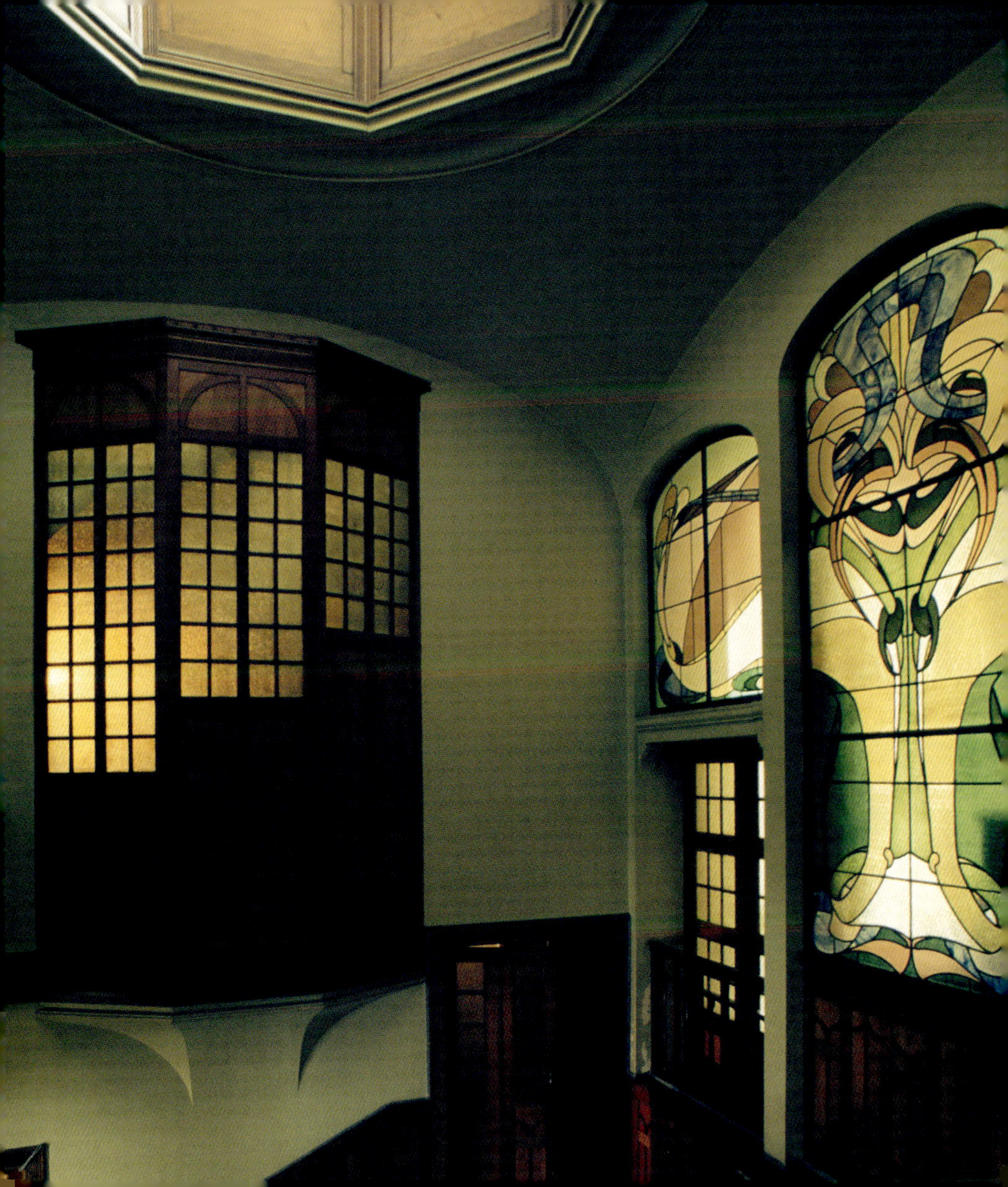

A Painter Converted

Henry van de Velde began his artistic career as a painter, attending the Academy of Fine Arts at Antwerp against the will of his parents. He was born in that city in 1863, son of a well-established family of pharmacists. Now, in 1880, he set out to be a painter in the post-Impressionist style. After a period in Paris, in 1887 he founded the *Association pour l'Art Indépendant* in Antwerp and one year later joined a group called "Les XX". This community, which had formed in Brussels in 1887, organized many exhibitions which documented the current work of avant-garde artists. However, as early as 1889 van de Velde commented that he saw "few prospects" in entering his work for the exhibitions, as the only possible result was rejection by "an ironic, mocking or angry public."

This assessment led to a fundamental change in his artistic career, which – partly under the influence of the works of Morris and Ruskin – he increasingly envisaged in the context of a "new social order." He lost interest in trends in painting. In 1893 he took over responsibility for the graphic design of the magazine *Van Nu En Straks* and started to design a carpet that his aunt made in appliqué work. In the same year he made the acquaintance of Maria Sèthe, a pupil of the painter Théo van Rysselberghe, and married her in 1894. She shared and actively supported his interest in the renewal of arts and crafts.

Henry van de Velde
Interior design of the staircase of Hôtel Otlet, Brussels
1894–1900, architect Octave van Rysselberghe

Henry van de Velde
Villa Esche
1902–11, Chemnitz

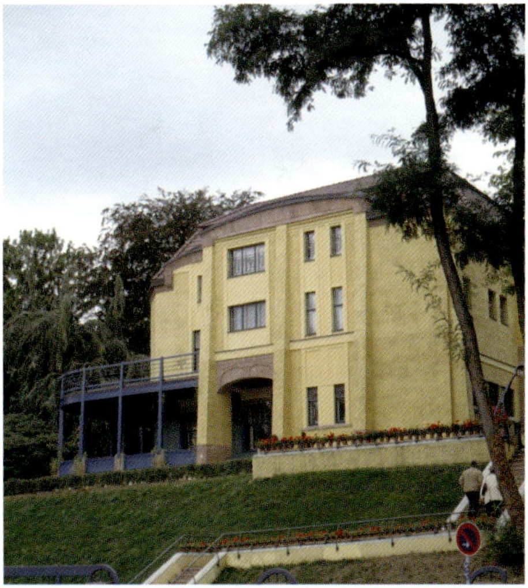

A New Start at Bloemenwerf

In 1895, when Henry van de Velde moved into his house, Bloemenwerf, in the high-class Brussels suburb of Uccle, his transformation into a designer on the English model appeared to be complete. Thanks to the support of his wealthy mother-in-law he was able to realize his ideal of a modern house, which he designed in a unified style from the first drawings down to the smallest detail of the interior.

It was a bold and new type of dwelling that corresponded to his ideas of simple forms. Van de Velde, who had no training as an architect, went to work almost naively, and the success of his design confirmed his belief that he had taken the right course. In the following years the artist's home became an important meeting place for all who were interested in a renewal of art and especially of crafts. Even Toulouse-Lautrec visited van de Velde at Bloemenwerf. However, two guests who came to the house independently of each other in July 1895 were to be much more significant: Samuel Bing and Julius Meier-Graefe. "Père Bing" immediately recognized the quality and individuality of the interior design and made sure to recruit the artist for his own purposes. The four interiors that van de Velde created for Bing's

Henry van de Velde
Photograph, 1950

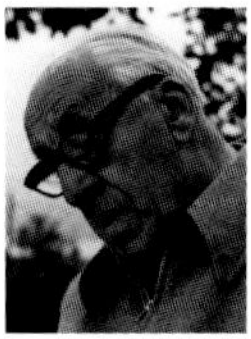

Henry van de Velde

1863 – 1957

Henry van de Velde saw himself as the father of the idea of the Werkbund, an association of German architects, designers and industrialists which organized an exhibition, the Deutsche Werkbund-Ausstellung, in Cologne in 1914: "The event in Cologne confirms my role as head of the movement in Germany." However, promoting commercial work did not for him mean the same thing as mass production, which was to play an important part in later design ideas. He never ceased to be an artistic designer who maintained his individual characteristics.

"It is my opinion that many industrialists think at times of the assured [...] clientele for whom their grandfathers worked [...]. What do they know of their customers today, who are the masses, and of the masses who are their customers, of the enormous masses in neighboring countries, on the five continents; the masses who are lost in the very moment you have won them; [...]"?

gallery in Paris were his stepping-stone to European artistic circles. The rooms, which had been criticized as *Yachting style* by the French art dealer Edmond de Goncourt at the opening of Maison Bing, were greeted enthusiastically at the Dresden art exhibition of 1897. In the following years van de Velde gained many commissions in Germany.

The art historian Meier-Graefe, who made his way to Bloemenwerf in summer 1895, reacted as keenly as Bing. In 1899 he opened La Maison Moderne in Paris and, parallel to Bing's activities, also achieved considerable success by placing the design of the façade and the interior decoration of the store in the hands of van de Velde.

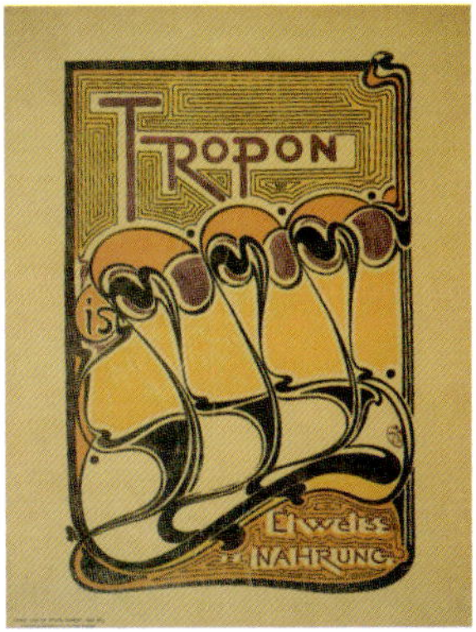

Henry van de Velde
Advertisement for Tropon
1898, color lithograph
36.8 × 27.8 cm
Supplement for *Pan* magazine
Private collection

Tropon and Afterwards

Meier-Graefe's main role, however, was to put the Belgian designer into contact with other patrons. The most important encounter for Henry van de Velde's future development was his meeting with Eberhard von Bodenhausen, who worked for the Tropon-Werke. The food supplements produced by this company, which belonged to the British earls of Douglas, were to be promoted in Germany. Bodenhausen, full of enthusiasm, proposed to recruit Henry van de Velde for Tropon. In 1897 the artist began to work for the company, which was based in a northeastern suburb of Cologne. He designed everything that is now known as the corporate identity of a company, from the letterhead to advertising posters and a variety of packaging – a consistent appearance for external presentation. This close collaboration between art and industry was a milestone in the development of modern design.

At the same time Meier-Graefe provided the contacts for many commissions in Berlin. Here van de Velde met Count Harry Kessler, who was to be an important mentor. Meier-Graefe asked van de Velde to furnish his Paris apartment, work that brought forth the legendary bean-shaped

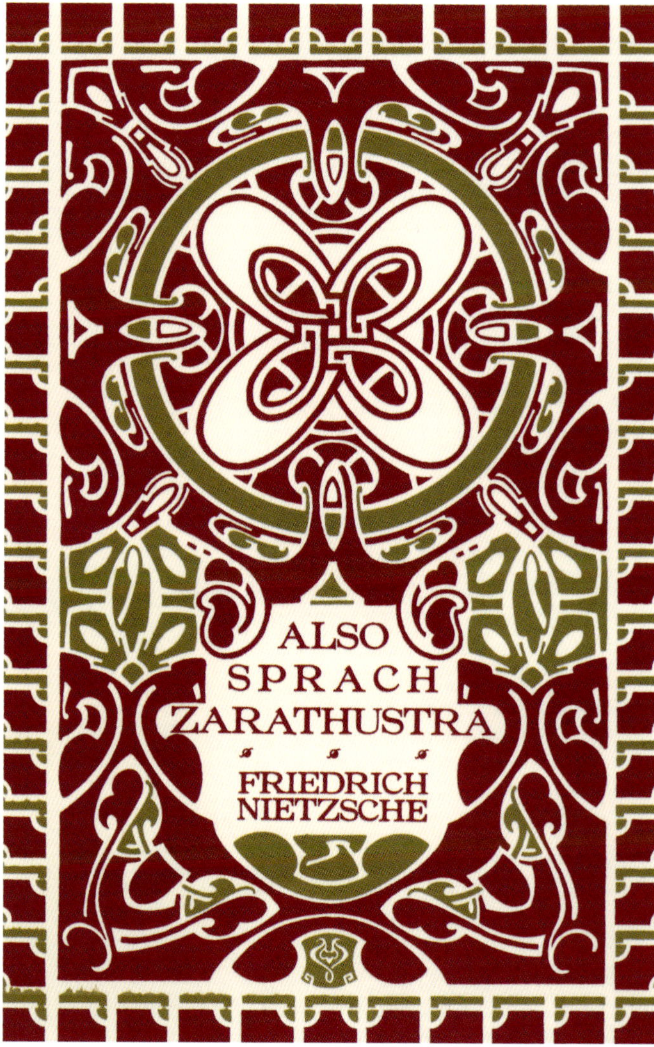

Henry van de Velde
Title page of *Thus Spoke Zarathustra* by F. Nietzsche
1908, color lithograph

desk, an item unrivalled in its logical, close-to-the-body form. Bodenhausen and Douglas also ordered such desks, and there was a waiting list of other potential purchasers.

Henry van de Velde Inc. Art Workshops

With so many orders, often to be carried out simultaneously, it was only a matter of time before founding a workshop became a business necessity. It was well known that van de Velde, an artistic genius through and through, was hopeless with money. He regarded the handling of orders, including dealing with suppliers, as an unreasonable imposition on him. Therefore Eberhard von Bodenhausen and Earl Douglas, in alliance with Curt Hermann and van de Velde's mother-in-law, who was once again willing to provide money, decided to found a company. In 1899 van de Velde opened his own workshop in Ixelles. He now seemed to have achieved his goal of living a life that was unified with his work. Everything seemed wonderful!

Unfortunately the situation did not remain as rosy as this. For one thing, van de Velde was not used to working on a commercial basis, and for another his investors expected a quick return on their money. Van de Velde broke down under the weight of these expectations and had to be admitted to a sanatorium to recover. But salvation was at hand: the bankrupt company was taken over by the Berlin art dealer Hermann Hirschwald, who offered to merge van de Velde's workshop with his own company, Hohenzollern-Kunstgewerbe. In October 1900, with a heavy heart, van de Velde moved to Berlin with his family. He had already carried out a number of commissions there for interiors, and Hirschwald's connections ensured further recommendations. A special issue of the magazine *Dekorative Kunst* that was devoted to van de Velde brought him to the attention of Karl Ernst Osthaus, a patron of the arts from Hagen. This resulted in a commission to design a new building for

Like many of his contemporaries, van de Velde was a fan of Nietzsche from an early age and waited impatiently for translations of his works to be published in French. Later he regarded his commissions to work on magnificent editions of *Thus Spoke Zarathustra* and *Ecce Homo* almost as an honored award.

the Folkwang-Museum, which was completed in 1902. The house built for Osthaus in 1907/08, with its radical unity of architecture and modern interiors, became a rendezvous for the avant-garde artists who were the source of the so-called Hagen impulse. During work on the museum there were differences between Osthaus and Hirschwald about allegedly wrong deliveries of material. To what extent anti-Semitic views on the part of Osthaus played a role here can no longer be determined with any certainty. Renewed conflicts in the company resulted in van de Velde's second nervous breakdown. In 1901 the company was dissolved,

Henry van de Velde
Desk for Julius
Meier-Graefe, 1898

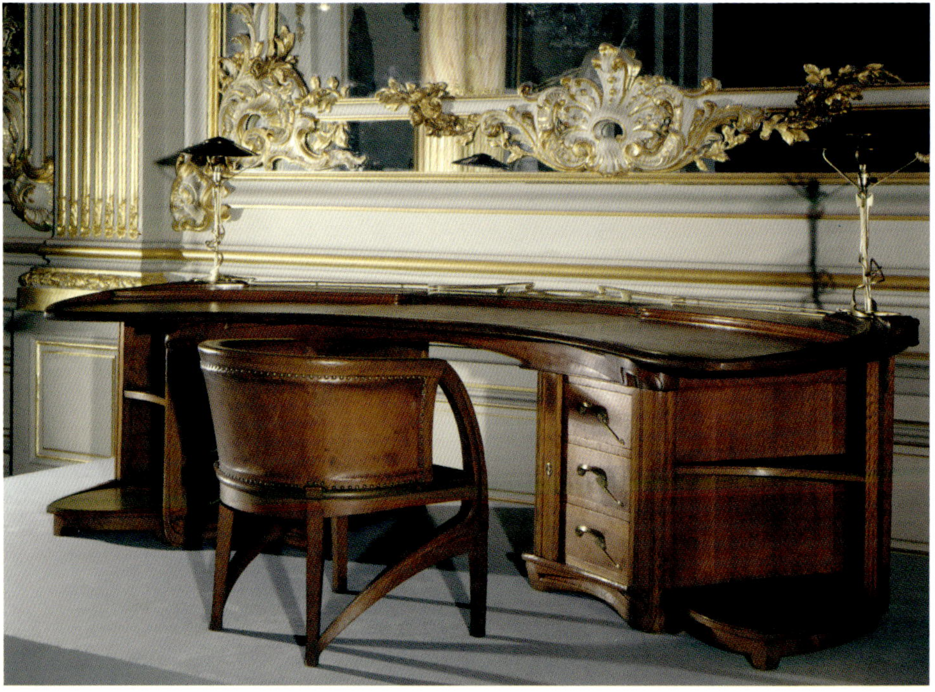

although Hirschfeld retained the rights to all designs produced by van de Velde up to the end of 1906.

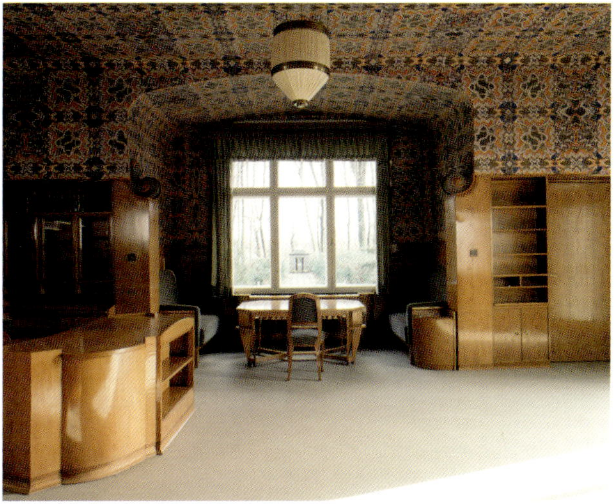

Henry van de Velde
Study in Haus Hohenhof in Hagen
Built in 1908 for Karl Ernst Osthaus

Salvation in Weimar

In this desperate situation van de Velde was helped by the close ties that he had formed to Count Harry Kessler in Berlin. For some time Kessler had been a friend of Elisabeth Förster-Nietzsche, and the two planned to attract the stricken van de Velde to Weimar.

On 15 January 1902 van de Velde was taken into the employment of Grand Duke Wilhelm Ernst of Weimar, with the job of advising the craftsmen of the region on questions of product design and advertising. For these tasks he thought it useful to establish premises, from which a seminar on crafts and later the Kunstgewerbeschule (School of Crafts) and the Bauhaus were to emerge. To this end Van de Velde designed a building, which was opened in 1907. With Kessler's guidance he was now associated with elite intellectual circles that intended to turn Goethe's Weimar into a modern center of the arts. However, these visionary plans did not come to fruition, and van de Velde fell from the grand duke's favor. After years of pressure Henry van de Velde tendered his resignation in July 1914. With the outbreak of war his situation became more and more intolerable and, plagued by depression, he hardly seemed capable of work.

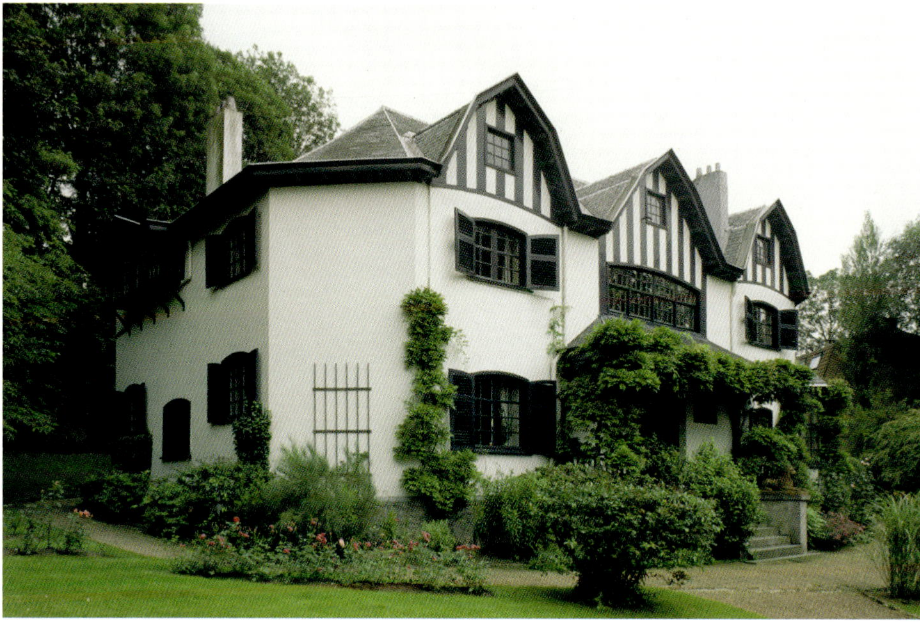

Henry van de Velde
Exterior of Haus Hohenhof in Hagen
Built in 1908 for Karl Ernst Osthaus

Holland and Later Years

"The commission from the Dutch patrons seemed to me [...] the only salvation." It came in the form of the Kröller-Müllers, a Dutch couple whose business interests had made them wealthy. Helene Kröller-Müller had leanings to the fine arts, employed an art teacher to initiate her into the mysteries of modern art and was in the process of building up a major collection. One of her favorite artists was Vincent van Gogh. From 1920 Henry van de Velde worked as the personal architect of the Kröller-Müllers. His principal task was to design a museum for the new collection. The foundation stone was laid on 21 June 1921 in the nature park De Hoge Veluwe, but implementation of van de

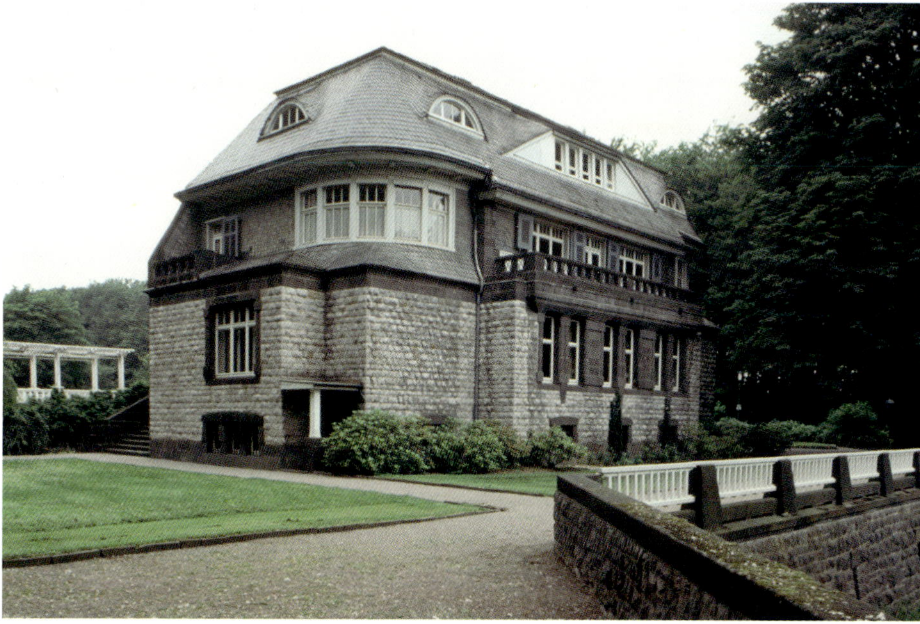

Velde's plans did not begin, in greatly reduced form, until 1936. For the world exhibition in New York in 1939 van de Velde, who had now taken on a professorship at the University of Geneva, was involved in the planning of the Belgian pavilion and became artistic adviser to the government of Belgium. The man who was so afraid of returning to his native country now seemed to be acknowledged as an expert there. After the death of his wife in 1943 he moved to Switzerland in 1947 and began to write his memoirs. Ten years later he died in Zurich at the ripe old age of 94.

Henry van de Velde
Exterior of Villa Bloemenwerf
Built 1894/95 for himself

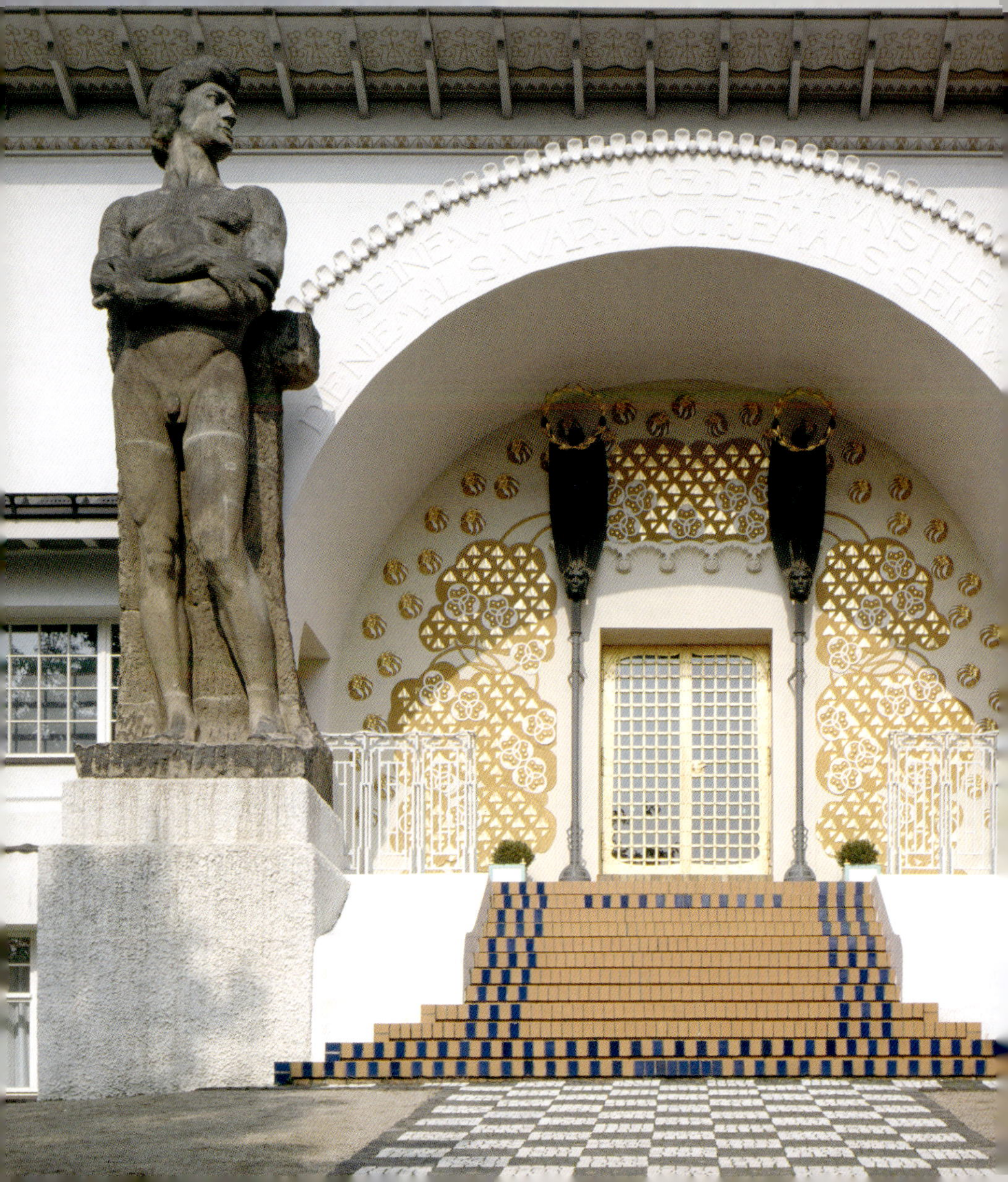
SEINE WELT ZEIGE DER KÜNSTLER
DIE NIEMALS WAR NOCH JEMALS

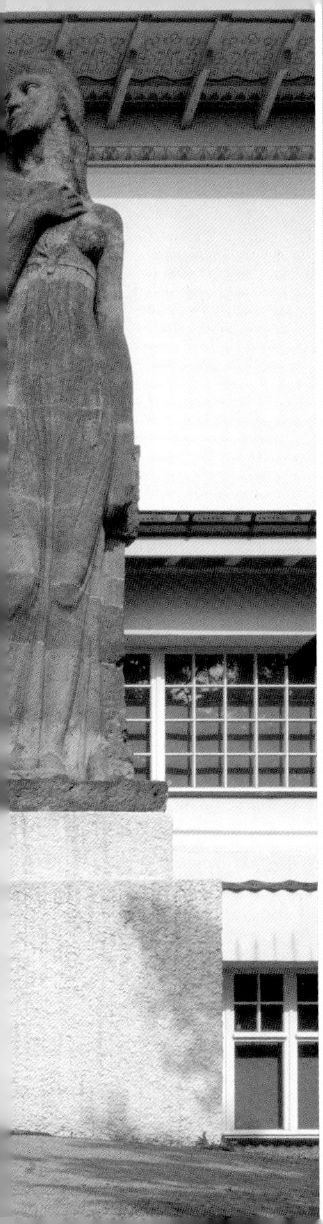

The Artists' Colony of Mathildenhöhe

"And where the eternal glow of the stars shines to us through the blue aether, where we are suffused with crystalline brightness, the clear spirit of the great design manifests itself to us in a diamond, there we perceive in heartfelt joy the right to a new life." The vision that was sketched in the opening ceremony of the most important exhibition of the Mathildenhöhe artists' colony in Darmstadt on 15 May 1901 makes it clear that this community was different from the other colonies and Secessions. A utopia was revealed here. The impulse for it came from a man who mobilized all the potential of the arts in order to give form to the new idea. That man was Ernst Ludwig, Grand Duke of Hesse bei Rhein, a grandson of Queen Victoria of England.

Joseph Maria Olbrich
Atelier building for the Mathildenhöhe artists' colony (Ernst-Ludwig-Haus)
1901, with colossal figures by Ludwig Habich

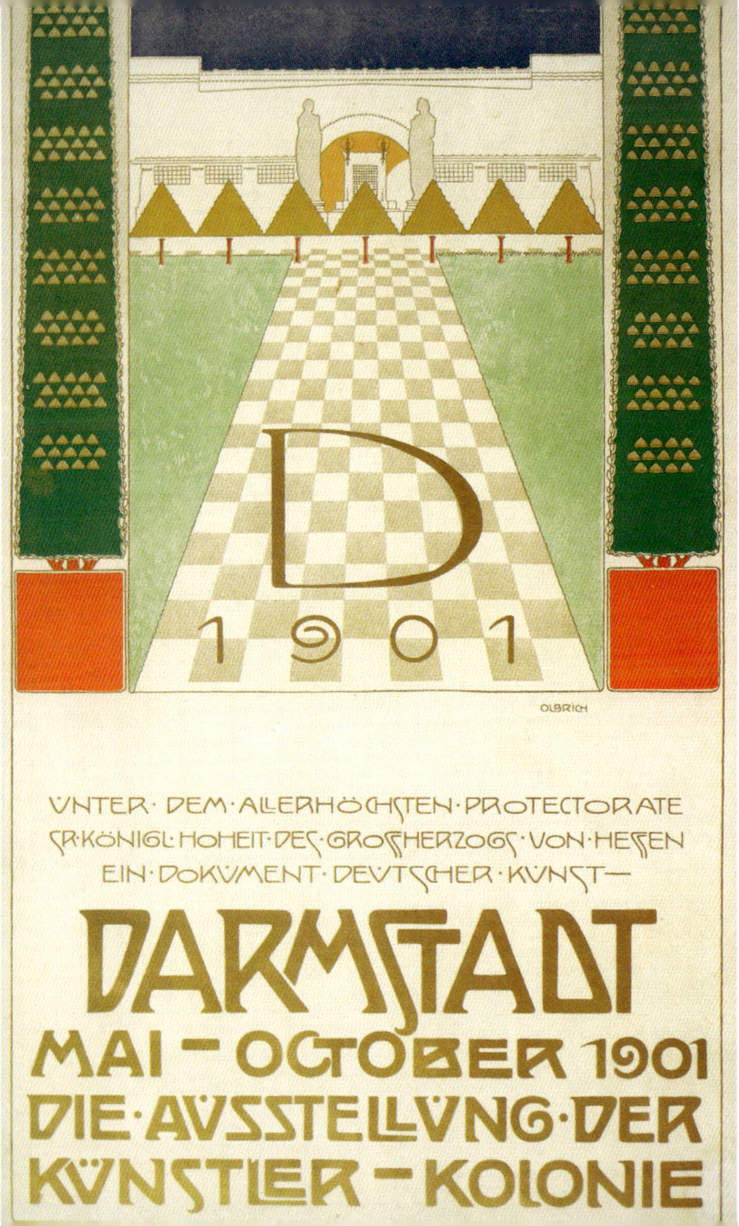
D
1901
OLBRICH
UNTER·DEM·ALLERHÖCHSTEN·PROTECTORATE
SR·KÖNIGL·HOHEIT·DES·GROSSHERZOGS·VON·HESSEN
EIN·DOKUMENT·DEUTSCHER·KUNST—
DARMSTADT
MAI - OCTOBER 1901
DIE·AUSSTELLUNG·DER
KÜNSTLER - KOLONIE

"May my land of Hesse flower, and with it the arts"

The grand duke and the publisher Alexander Koch recognized the need for new ideas to create a lasting connection between art and industry. Through his relations in England Ernst Ludwig had learned about the Arts and Crafts movement in early years and found there the potential to develop his provincial little state, which he hoped to transform into a flourishing region. He thought Wilhelmine Germany narrow and stuffy. His approach was that the freedom to think new thoughts required the freedom of a new environment. He promoted the rediscovery of old German materials and espoused the concept of medieval masons' lodges. Ernst Ludwig invited to Darmstadt one of the young talents of the new style of architecture, Joseph Maria Olbrich from Vienna, and commissioned him to design buildings on the hill named Mathildenhöhe for a new colony, where he hoped the spirit of the new age would prevail. The overarching philosophy of this enterprise was the unity of art and life. One by one he attracted the protagonists of a new era: Peter Behrens, Hans Christiansen, Patriz Huber, Ludwig Habich, Rudolf Bosselt and Paul Bürck. They formed the nucleus of the artists' colony. On 15 May 1901 an exhibition that caused a stir far and wide was inaugurated with a glittering ceremony. During the opening, which was

Joseph Maria Olbrich
Poster for the first exhibition of the artists' colony
1901, color lithograph
Private collection

Joseph Maria Olbrich
Study for the Olbrich Haus
1901, color lithograph
Private collection

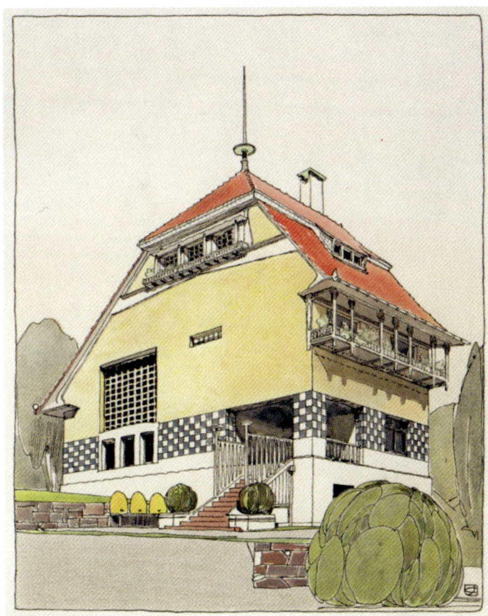

staged as a drama, a huge figure shrouded in a purple cloak strode down the steps of Olbrich's atelier building and declaimed to the theatrical sound of a tuba: "A new life is beginning for you. Grasp it and you will know happiness." The title of the exhibition could hardly have been more programmatic: *A Document of German Art.*

Franz von Stuck
Ernst Ludwig, Grand Duke of Hesse and bei Rhein
1907, oil on wood
Schlossmuseum, Darmstadt

New Architecture

The building was designed to impress and was christened Ernst Ludwig Haus after its patron. It provided space not only for exhibitions but also for the common life and work of a community of artists. In addition to the central atelier building, which was adorned by sculptor Habich's figures of *Man and Woman,* Olbrich designed further artists' houses, which were loosely grouped around the center of the Mathildenhöhe. The independent-minded Behrens, the only artist capable of challenging Olbrich's dominant position, supplied a highly symbolic and consistently thought-out style of architecture for the Darmstadt Art Nouveau circle with the plan of his own house. Everything in the house seemed to recall Behrens' idol Nietzsche: there were stylized eagles, a hidden reference to Zarathustra, on all sides.

The staged architecture on Mathildenhöhe was accompanied by technical

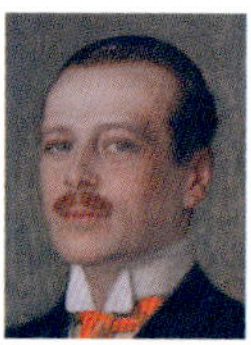

Grand Duke Ernst Ludwig

1868 – 1937

Ernst Ludwig was born in 1868, a scion of the cadet branch of the house of Hesse. When his father died unexpectedly young in 1892, Ernst Ludwig was abruptly thrust into the role of prince of his state. In 1894 he married his cousin Victoria Melita. In the same year his sister Alix married Tsar Nicholas II, whom she had met at Ernst Ludwig's wedding. In 1899 the grand duke traveled to England several times and established close links to the artists of the Arts and Crafts movement. In 1901 he divorced Victoria Melita and in 1905 married Eleonore zu Solms-Hohensolms-Lich, with whom he had two sons. In 1907 he founded the Ernst-Ludwig-Presse to promote publishing. In 1918 he was forced to abdicate, and Hesse-Darmstadt became a People's State. Ernst Ludwig died in 1937 in Schloss Wolfsgarten near Frankfurt.

innovations which made it possible to illuminate the group of houses in the evening in changing light according to an ingenious color scheme devised by Hans Christiansen. The terraced gardens around some of the buildings reflected the reforming ideals of the garden city movement, and the spirit of the modern age was also evident in progressive details such as faucets to mix hot and cold water, and central heating in Behrens' house.

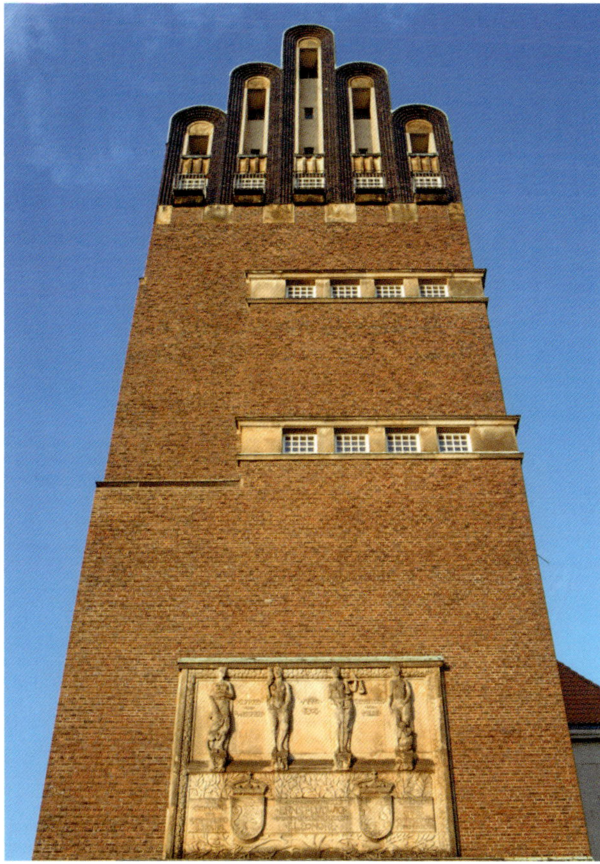

In 1905 the group celebrated its visionary patron Ernst Ludwig, who was marrying for the second time. Olbrich built the Hochzeitsturm (Wedding Tower), the proudest feature of the colony. This building, a combination of observation tower and monument, was a symbol of the community in stone: as if rising to take an oath, it seemed to express the hope of a community of artists for the future. However, this hope was not to be fulfilled. The different personalities among the artists held too stubbornly to their own characteristic ideas, the first seven left too quickly for other fields of activity, and new, less gifted artists arrived.

Joseph Maria Olbrich
Hochzeitsturm (Wedding Tower) in Darmstadt, Mathildenhöhe
Built 1907/08

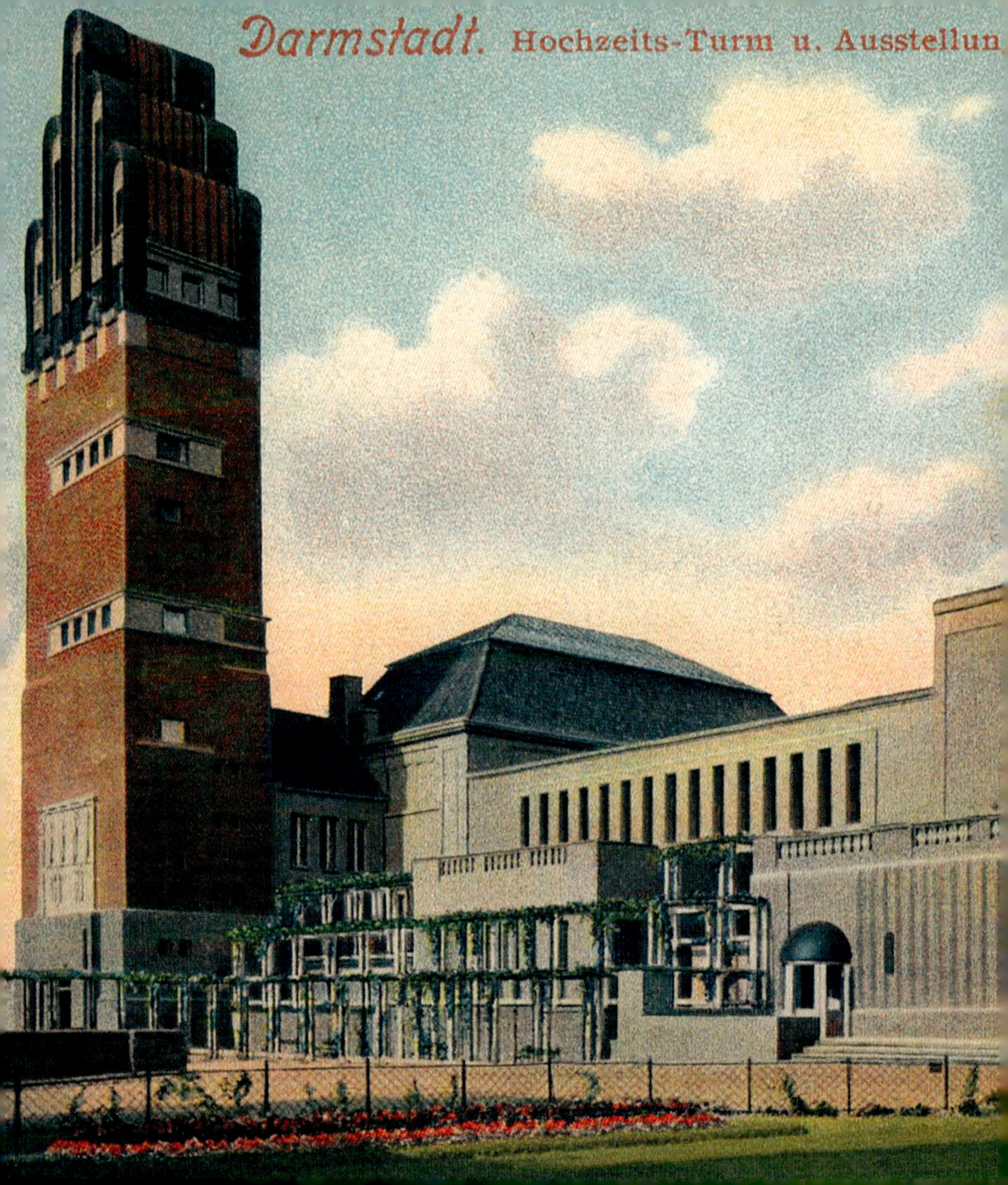
Darmstadt. Hochzeits-Turm u. Ausstellun

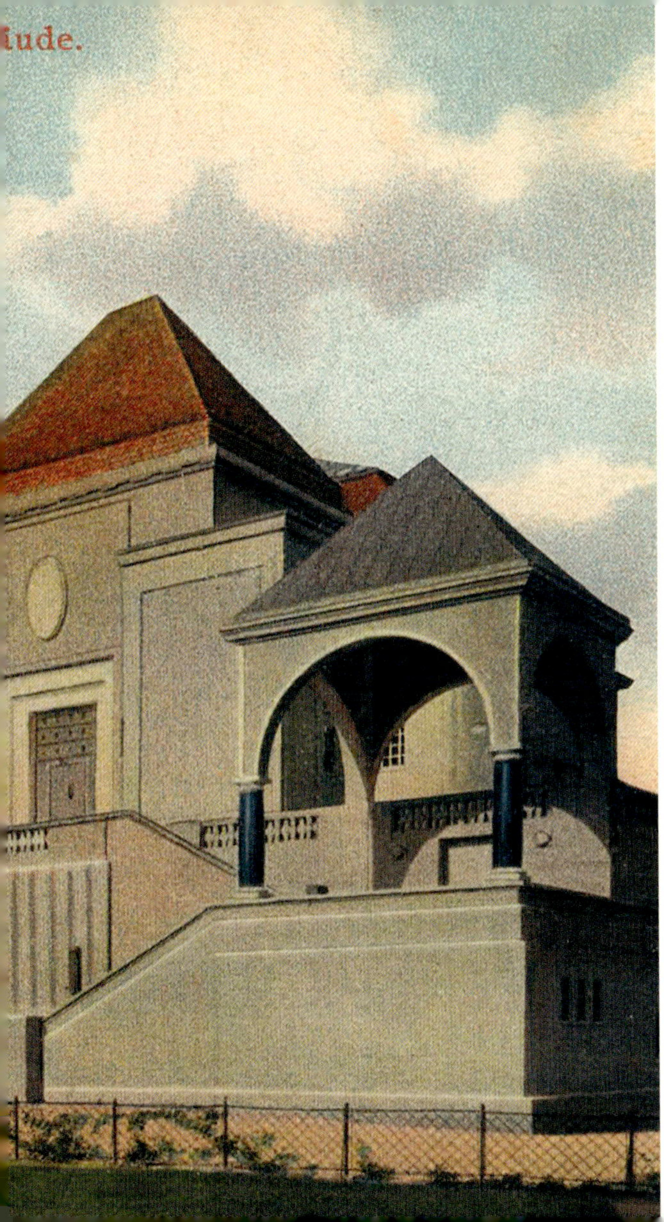

The exhibition building of the artists' colony in Darmstadt, also known as the Ernst Ludwig Haus, was completed in 1908. It was bright and spacious, and encouraged the collaboration that all artists' colonies preached by concentrating the studios in one place.

Mathildenhöhe artists' colony
Exhibition building with Hochzeitsturm
c. 1910, picture postcard based on colored photograph

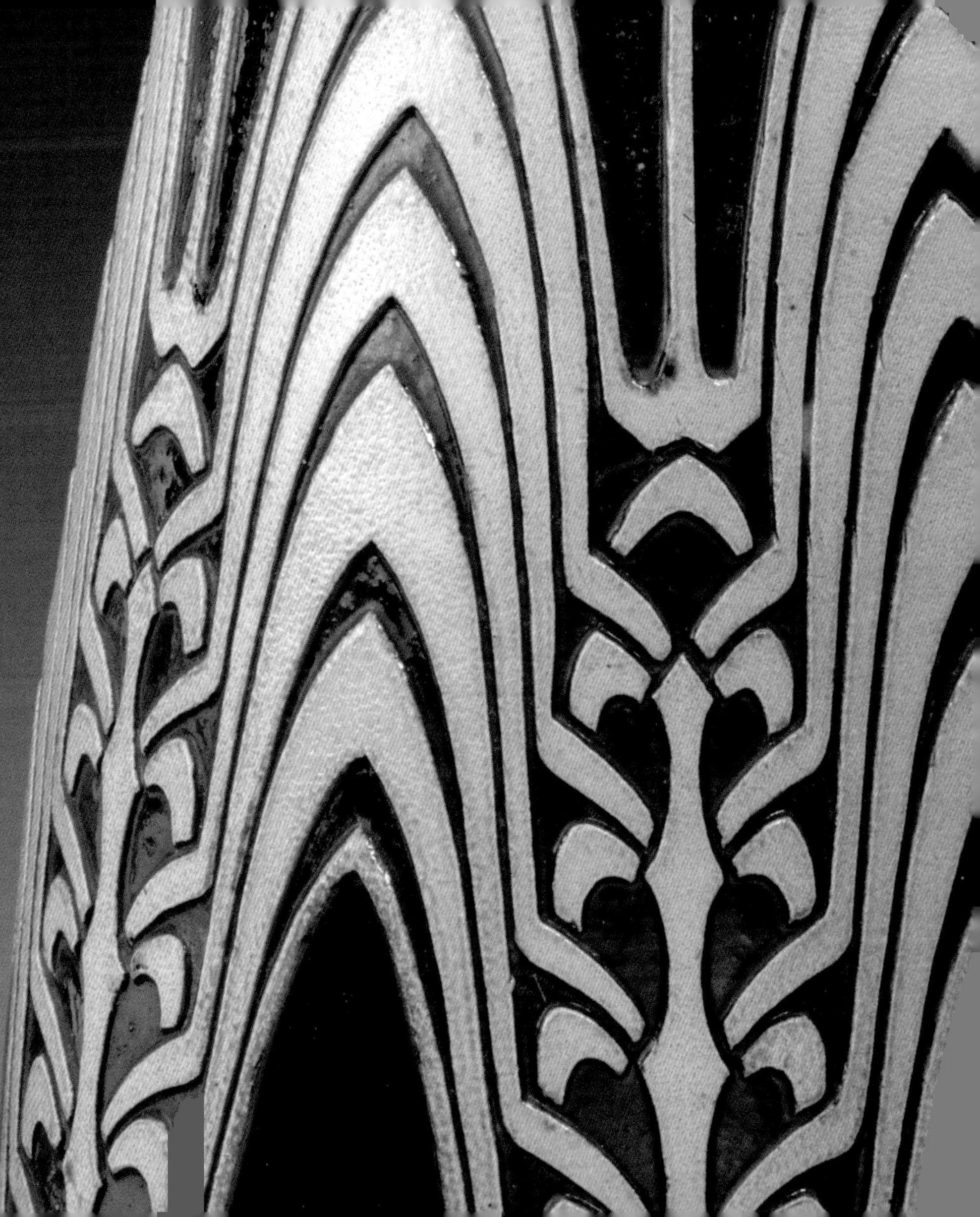

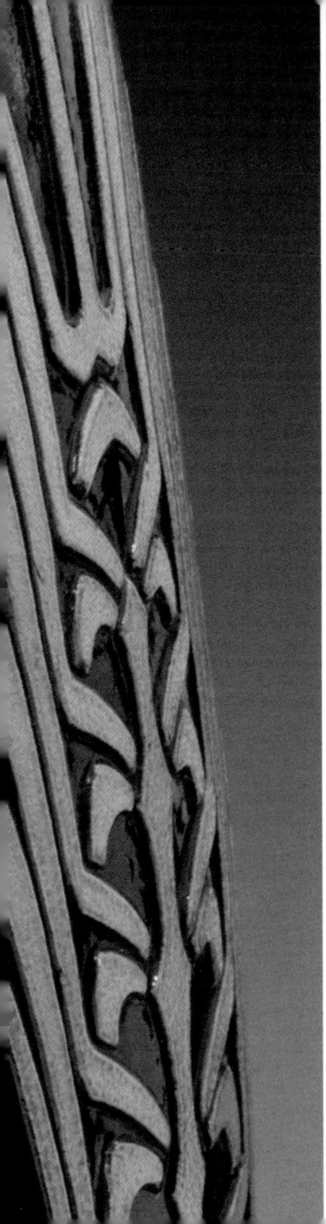

Peter Behrens

Peter Behrens is regarded as the first industrial designer. He went beyond the ideas of Henry van de Velde, who was the same age, and provided the decisive impulses for the emerging aesthetics of the modern age. Like his Belgian colleague he was a self-taught designer who gained widespread renown as an architect. From the very beginning, friends and allies had high expectations of the designer Behrens, believing that he was the man who could bring about the desired synthesis of all the arts in a unified style. His designs were part of a thoroughgoing transformation of taste in Germany that began with the emergence of Art Nouveau at the turn of the 19th century.

Peter Behrens
Jug
1907, stoneware with blue cobalt decoration
Indianapolis Museum of Art

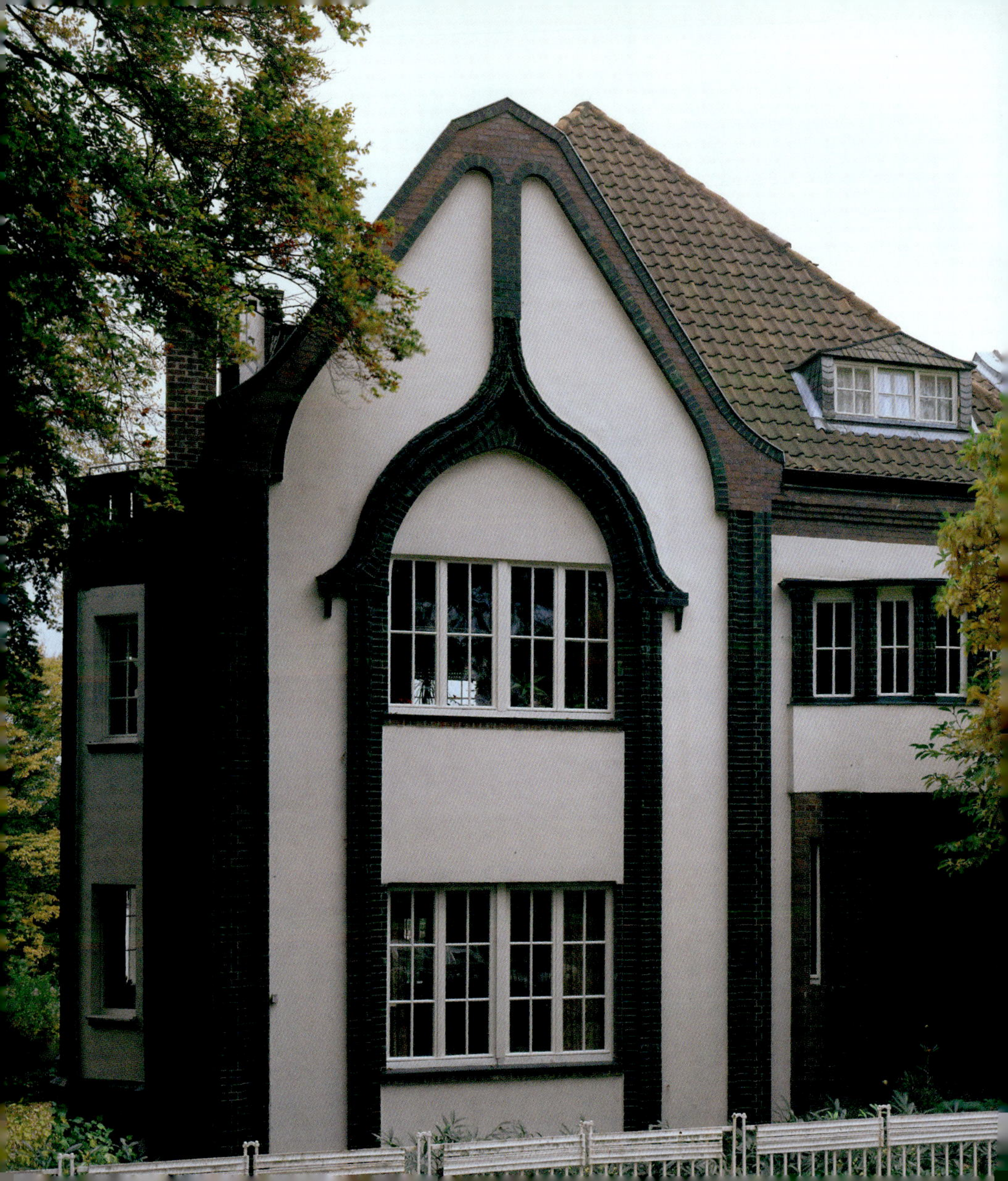

The Father of Modern Design

Having inherited a considerable fortune, the young Behrens began to study painting at the School of Applied Arts in Hamburg and the Academy of Arts in Düsseldorf, and then made his way to Munich, the center of the Art Nouveau movement in Germany, where he established contact in 1890 to August Endell, Bruno Paul and Richard Riemerschmid. Together they founded the Vereinigte Werkstätten für Kunst und Handwerk (United Arts and Crafts Workshops) in 1897. Four years previously Behrens had been a founder member of the Munich Secession. After working with modest success as a painter in his early years, he now produced several fine woodcuts and ornaments which drew attention, especially in *Pan* magazine. However, his work with other craftsmen in the Werkstätten was the decisive factor in his change of direction towards crafts. From this time he was occupied with designs for furniture, crockery, glass, carpets and fabrics.

In 1898 and 1899 Friedrich Carstanjen in *Pan* and Julius Meier-Graefe in *Dekorative Kunst* published important essays about Behrens, each accompanied by a version of his print entitled *Kuss* (Kiss). In this work Behrens revealed his gift for graphic work. His graphic designs are characterized by clear composition of surfaces. *Kuss,* with its emphasis on curving, snake-like hair presents the idea of Art Nouveau in its purest form.

**"Everything here is bright (...) this white is wonderfully complemented by the silver of the plaster ceiling, of the lamp, of the metal fittings and finally of the crockery, as well as the beautiful porcelain service decorated in silver on white."
J. Meier-Graefe**

A Great Opportunity in Darmstadt

The year 1899 was a decisive turning point for Behrens' later career as an architect. The grand duke of Hesse invited

Peter Behrens
Haus Behrens on Mathildenhöhe
Built 1900/01

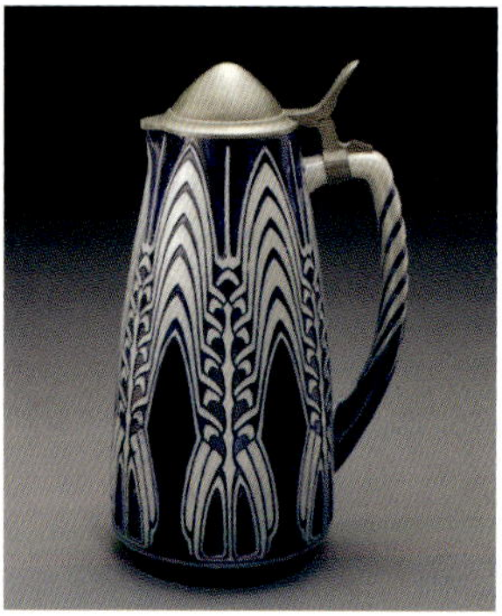

Peter Behrens
Jug
1907, stoneware with blue cobalt decoration
Indianapolis Museum of Art

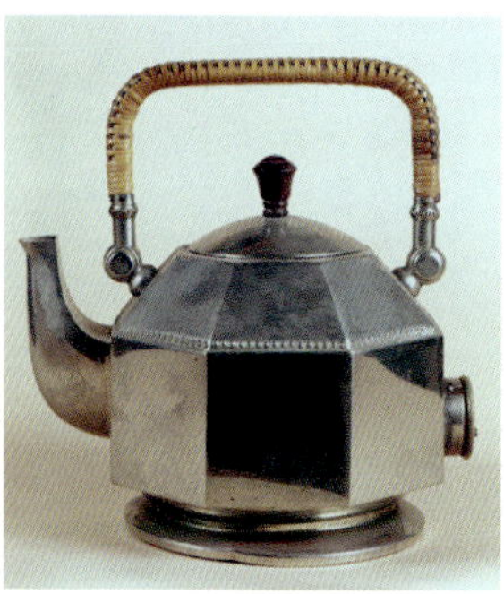

Peter Behrens
Kettle
Designed in 1908 for AEG
Haslam & Whiteway Ltd., London

him to Darmstadt to take part in the ambitious project of forming a colony of artists. According to the concept of the colony's first exhibition, all participating artists were to introduce themselves by designing their own house. Untrained in architecture but full of enthusiasm, Behrens set to work on a house that would represent something completely new.

Haus Behrens, which was built on Mathildenhöhe in 1901, is an expression of the artist's great admiration for Nietzsche, and is characterized by quotes from the philosopher's works, especially *Thus Spoke Zarathustra.* Behrens presented his house as the mirror of a great soul on the model of Zarathustra, who spoke through color and symbols in Nietzsche's work. Behrens' yellow floor and glowing red upholstery accurately reproduced descriptions in *Thus Spoke Zarathustra,* and the symbols of the eagle and the diamond, present in many places in the house, are direct references to the text. The diamond, which as a precious stone shines on everything with the "virtues of a world that still exists," is recognizable in many ornamental details of the house. The bright plastered façade reflects the generous allocation of space within and is structured with brickwork that reinforces the conspicuous vertical lines. The idea of a total work of art was applied consistently to all details of the interiors. In his plans for a new theatre, Behrens pursued the harmony of all the arts with even greater clarity. He wanted "space … music and verse, color and form" to work together and designed a circular theatre in which the audience would experience a completely new world.

In 1900 he explained his theories in a publication entitled *Feste des Leben und der Kunst* (Celebrations of Life and Art). He undertook "an examination of the theatre as the highest cultural symbol" in the context of a new aesthetic. When he was not able to achieve his plans in Darmstadt, he looked for new tasks. He increasingly found the artists' colony too restrictive. He believed that "Berlin is the only viable place for the fulfillment of the aesthetic culture that I dream of." In autumn 1902 he took part in a competition held by the Wertheim department store to furnish rooms for modern living. Small commissions and a teaching post at the School of Applied Arts in Nuremberg ensued.

The Düsseldorf Years

In 1904 Behrens became director of the Kunstgewerbeschule (School of Applied Arts) in Düsseldorf, where he set new standards. Within a few years he gave the school an excellent reputation. A single commission from the city of Düsseldorf, to design a reading room for the world exhibition in St. Louis, resulted in numerous contracts for special exhibitions. The outstanding project of these years was to plan an "alcohol-free restaurant," named Jungbrunnen, for the Düsseldorf Art and Garden Exhibition in 1904. The restaurant was strongly influenced by the Wiener Werkstätte, to which Behrens maintained links – he invited Josef Bruckmüller among others to teach in Düsseldorf. Behrens was impressed by the clear lines of the works that emanated from the circle around Koloman Moser and Josef Hoffmann. His style increasingly bore the traits of an approach to design that reduced crafts and architecture to individual geometric forms.

Success at AEG

In 1907 Behrens resigned from his position in Düsseldorf in order to take up a new challenge as artistic adviser to the Allgemeine Elektricitäts-Gesellschaft (General Electricity Company, AEG) in Berlin. In 1909 he designed a hall for the large turbines that AEG had been producing since 1902. For most historians of architecture this Turbinenhalle at AEG represents a milestone in modern architecture: a hall for the source of modern energy. With its striking

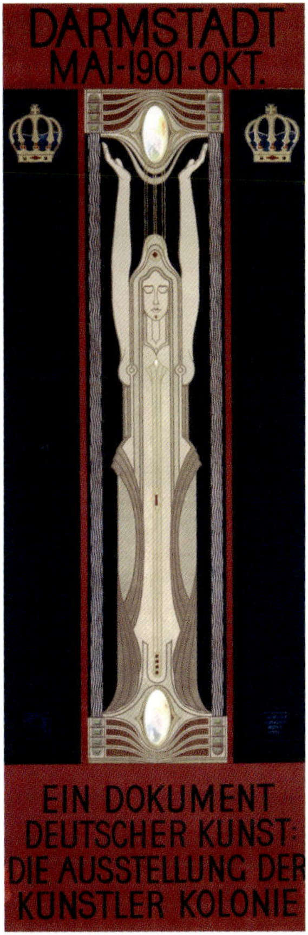

Peter Behrens
Poster for the exhibition
A Document of German Art
1901, color lithograph
(algraphy)

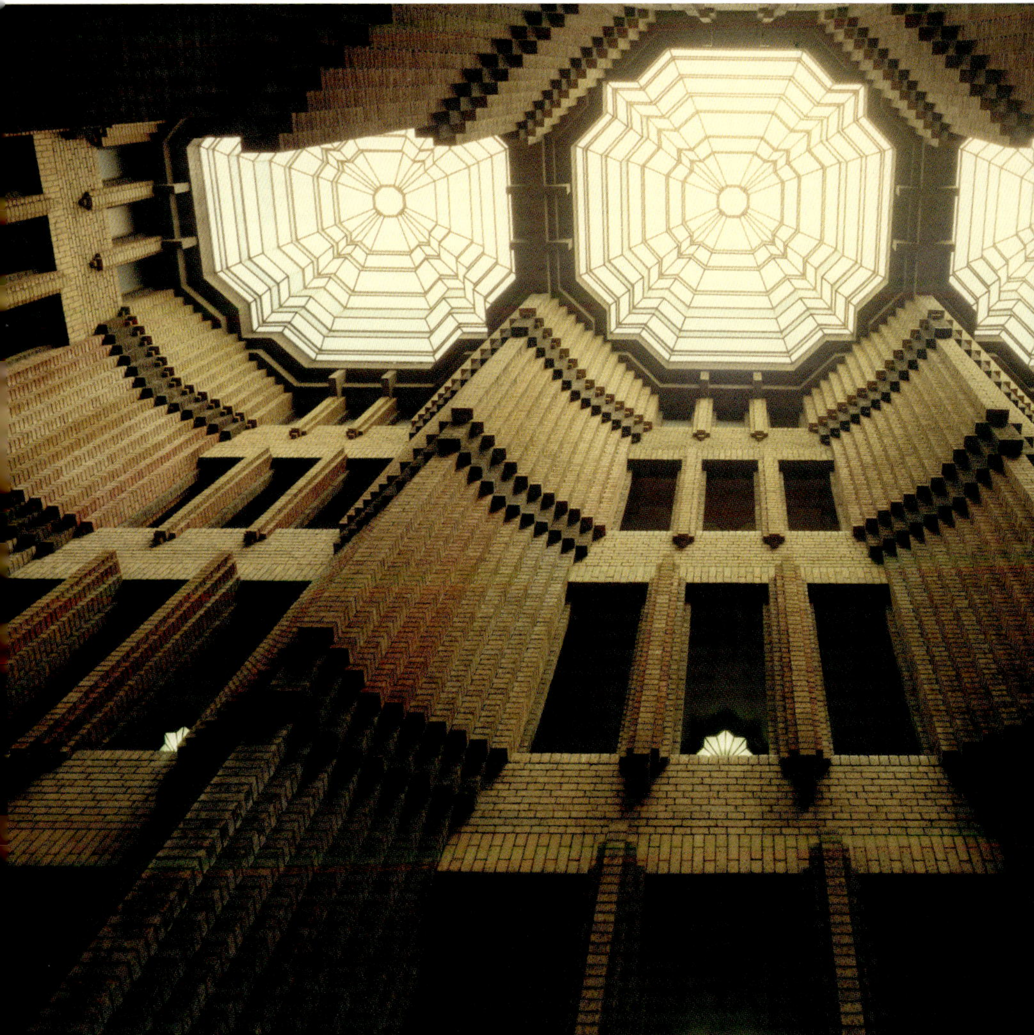

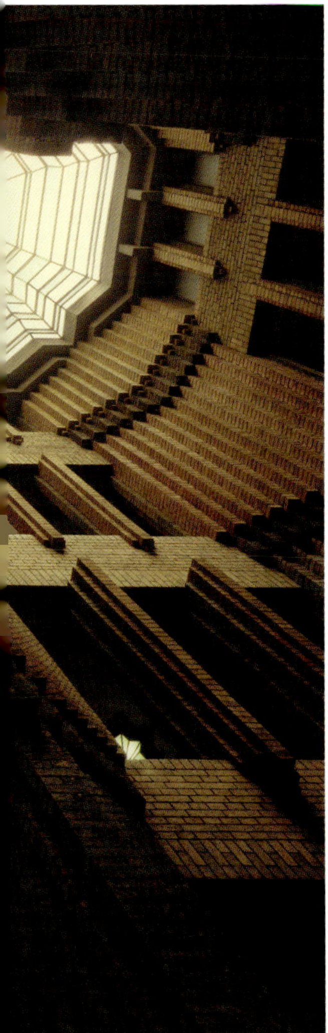

façade this building became the face of AEG and the expression of a new industrial culture. In the following years Behrens produced many designs for the company's letterheads and above all for its wide product range. The legendary kettle is an outstanding example of how modern industrial design should function: in a series of three basic forms Behrens introduced three different materials (pure brass, and brass coated with nickel or copper) and three different surface textures (smooth, hammered and flamed), which could be combined in three different sizes. This resulted in a total of 27 different versions of the product.

This successful cooperation with a company was to determine Behrens' design work in the years to come. In 1920 he once again set a benchmark for architecture with the headquarters of IG Hoechst in Frankfurt. His congenial interpretation of the company products by means of an avant-garde color scheme and the cathedral-like design of the entrance lobby made this building a highlight of modern architecture.

Peter Behrens
Headquarters of Hoechst AG
Interior of entrance lobby
Built 1920–24,
Frankfurt/Hoechst

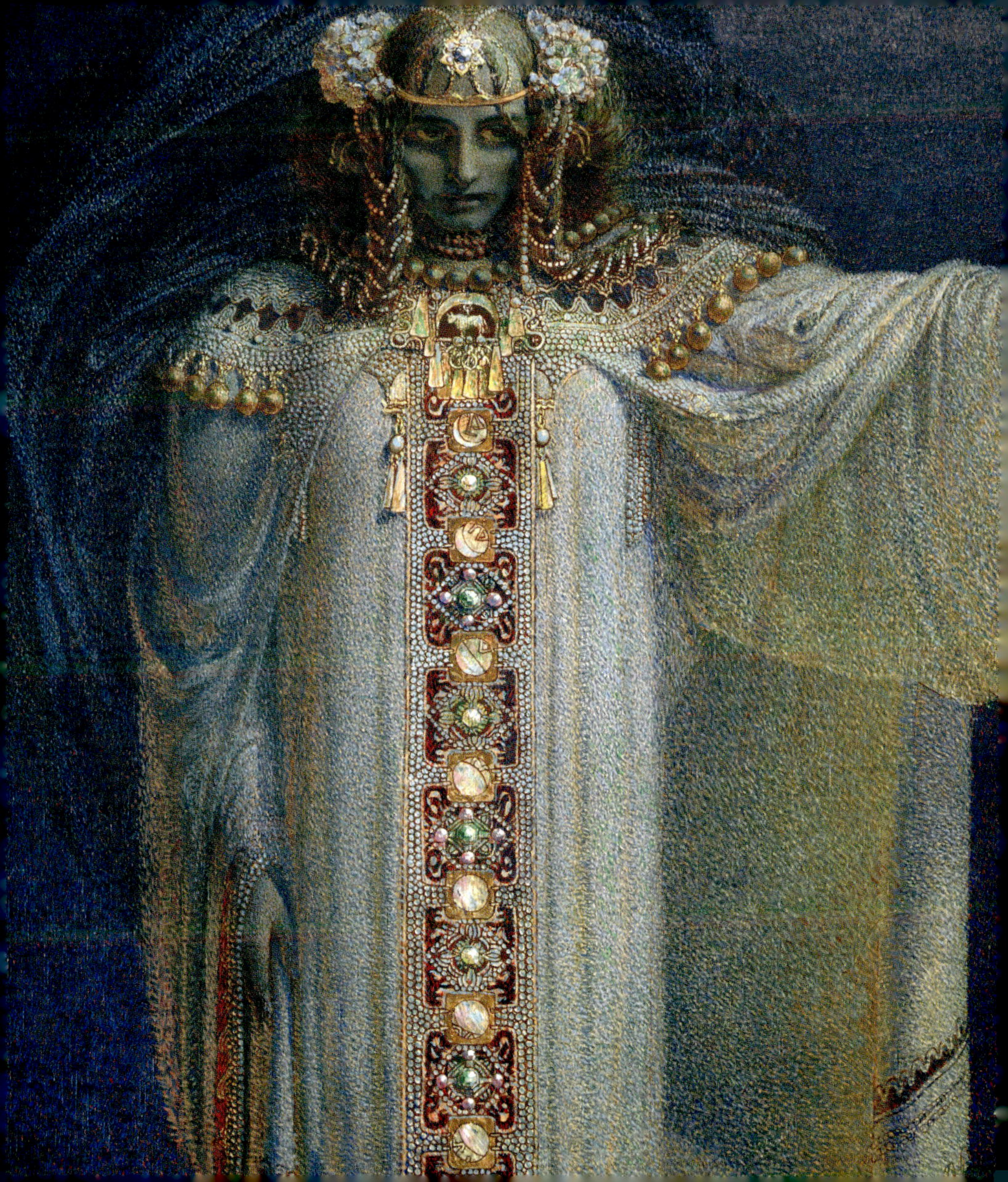

Dream versus Reality

Fin de siècle – have we reached the end of the century? Is the end of the world at hand, or at least does it seem to be time we became aware of what it is to be human and to take issue with the urgent questions of existence? In "traces perceptible to a fine sensibility" a pervading spirit of the times that contains dark premonitions can be registered. André Gide characterized this by calling for "chimeras rather than realities." The Symbolist painters were united in their rejection of the naturalist style. Their pictures represent not reality but states of mind. Symbols with a wealth of meanings and ancient myths gave a deep insight into the realm of the soul.

Vitezlav Karel Masek
The Prophetess Libuse
(detail of p. 250)
1893, oil on canvas
193 × 193 cm
Musée d'Orsay, Paris

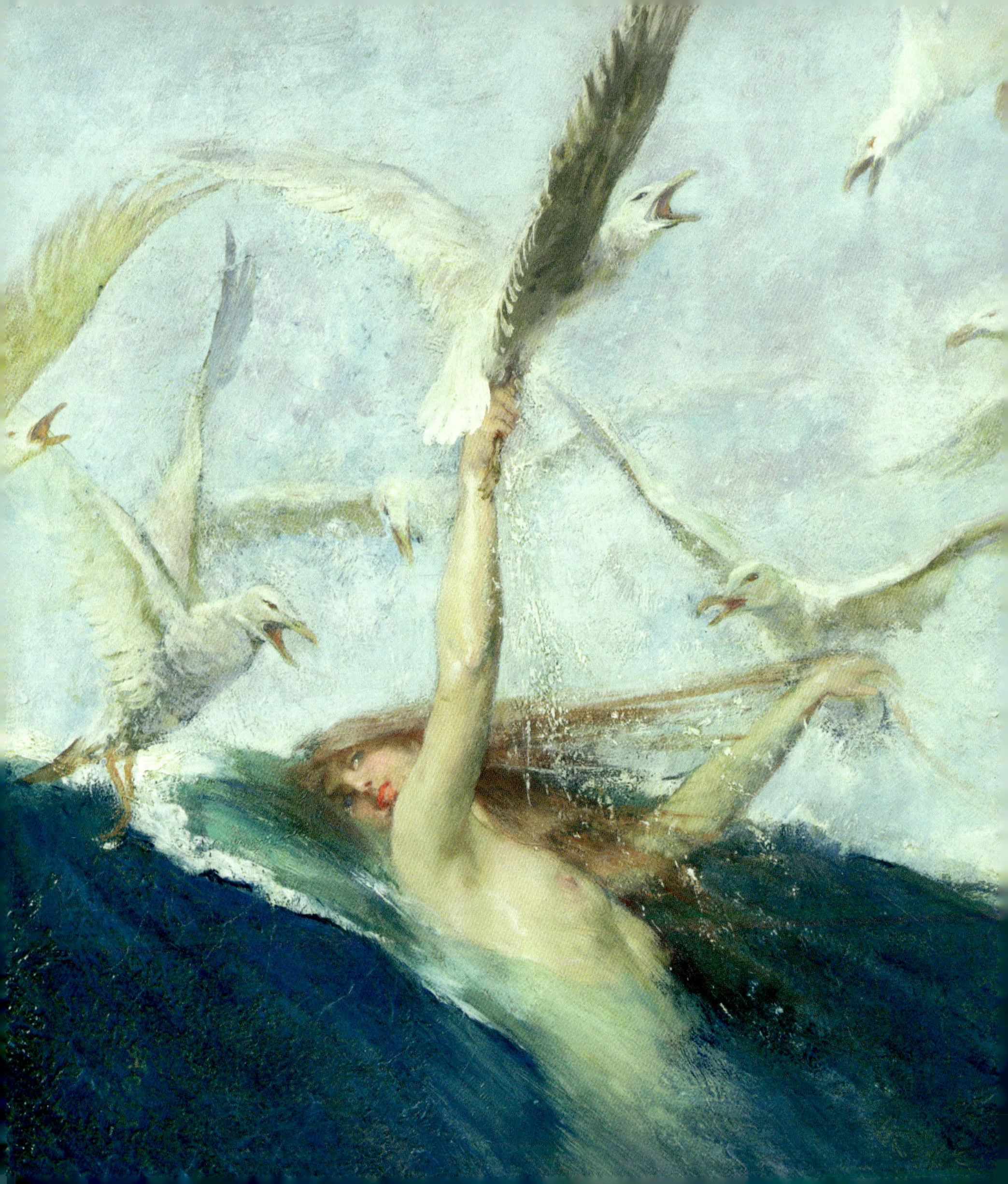

Between Decadence and Occultism

Several pages in the "bible of decadence," Joris-Karl Huysmans' *Against Nature,* are devoted to a description of paintings by Gustave Moreau. Works by this artist are also discussed in Proust's *In Search of Lost Time,* and Oscar Wilde is said to have written *Salome* after a picture of a princess drawn by Moreau made a deep impression on him. No clearer evidence could be furnished of the extent to which Symbolist literature was influenced by Symbolist art. This is, of course, also true in reverse: the writings of Mallarmé, Verlaine, Baudelaire and other poets appeared many times in Symbolist visual imagery.

Giovanni Segantini
Mermaid Tormented by Gulls
(detail)
Private collection

Gustave Moreau
Dead Poet and Centaur
1890, watercolor
Musée Gustave Moreau, Paris

Is it therefore any wonder that Orpheus, the symbolic figure of poetry, has a central role in the work of Gustave Moreau? When he presented a picture of Orpheus in the Paris Salon of 1865, he had to add a few lines of explanation – so far removed was this work from the conventional tradition of painting. He depicted an Orpheus whose severed head lay on a lyre – an aspect of the story from mythology that had never before been painted in this way, a reference to the dismemberment of the hero by the jealous maenads. In another painting Moreau portrayed the dead poet as an androgynous creature that is being pulled out of the sea by a centaur. In Symbolist painting the androgynous figure plays an important role. For one thing, many artists regarded it as an ideal that corresponded to the ancient myth of the former

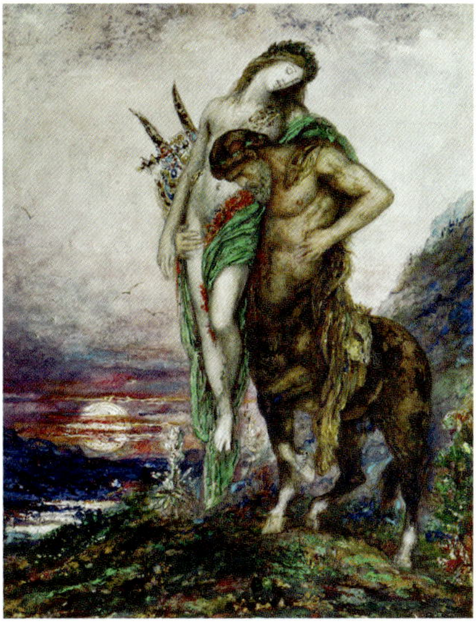

unity of man and woman. For another, the figure of an androgynous poet appeared to be the consummation of the ideal of creative mankind.

Gustave Moreau was a disciple of the Rosicrucian Josephín Pelladan, who held salons in Paris in 1892. Here the artist was seen as the priest of a great mystery. Moreau, who only believed in "what I cannot see and only in what I feel," adopted this mystic view of life. His works were visions of another world of demonic creatures, strange landscapes and disquieting feelings. They amounted to the antithesis of the prevailing materialism of the Third Republic and referred to models from the Renaissance more than they reflected contemporary naturalistic trends. Death, all the more when portrayed as here in androgynous beauty, was one of the themes of Symbolist painting, which was concerned with the subconscious and the secret fears hidden there. Long before Freud, psychologically inspired paintings made their appearance. The duality of Death and Eros, which had already played a part in the Romantic movement, was a central motif of Symbolism.

"As the purpose of poetry is to arouse thoughts in us, and that of music to express or evoke feelings, thus painting is meant to uplift"! The principal motif of the picture is not grief but the sublime – a feeling of something great and beyond time that lies in the tranquility.

The Symbolist Manifesto

"The essential characteristic of Symbolist art consists in never conceptualizing an idea or expressing it directly. And therefore images of nature, the deeds of men and all tangible phenomena may never themselves be visible in this art, but are symbolized by traces that are perceptible to a fine sensibility, by secret affinities to the original ideas." These were the words that Jean Moréas, a poet of Greek origin, used in 1886 to describe the manifesto of Symbolism in the magazine *Figaro Litteraire*. The essential contribution of Symbolism to modern art was to turn away from naturalism and towards an art that incorporated the unconscious and the invisible world. The enthusiasm of the Surrealists for Symbolism underlines the importance of this

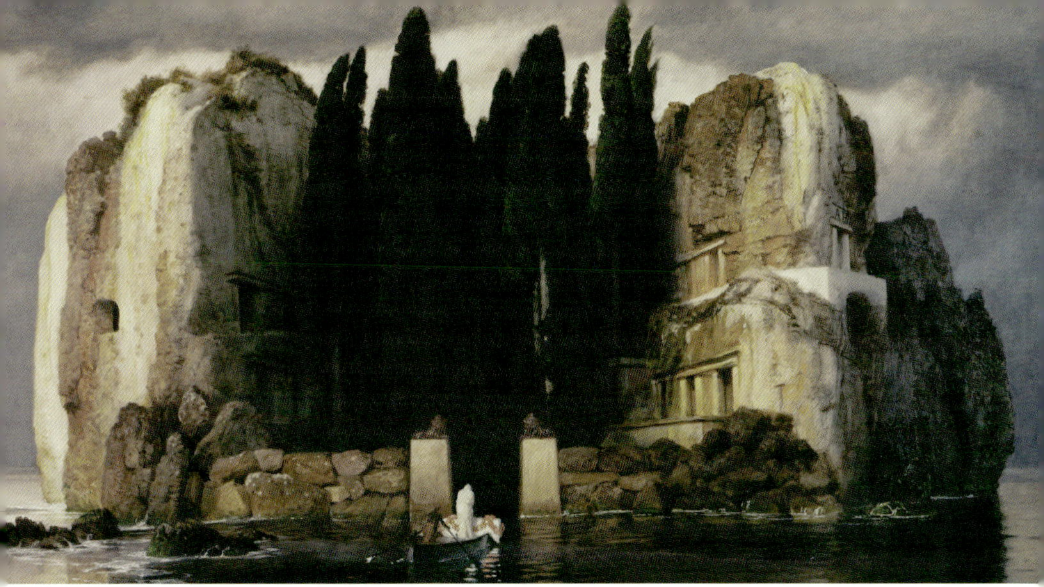

movement in art, which began in France under the influence of literary trends but soon spread to all of Europe. The artists of the late 19th century were unanimous in hoping for the advent of a "spiritual epoch," which seemed to them appropriate to the particular situation of the *fin de siècle.* They felt alienated from the existing bourgeois world; the worlds that they created to counter it were often shaped by religious ideas.

Arnold Böcklin
The Isle of the Dead, 1886
Varnish colors on mahogany
80.7 × 150 cm
Museum der Bildenden Künste, Leipzig

Arnold Böcklin

"You will be able to enter in your dreams the dark world of shadows, until you believe that you can feel the gentle breath of wind that ruffles the surface of the sea. Until you hesitate to make any sound that disturbs the solemn stillness."

Thus Böcklin wrote to his client, a rich widow for whom he had painted the second version of *The Isle of the Dead.* The painting, which he had first begun in 1880 after

Following double page:
Paul Gauguin
Where do we come from? What are we? Where are we going?
1897, oil on canvas
139.1 × 374.6 cm
Museum of Fine Arts, Boston

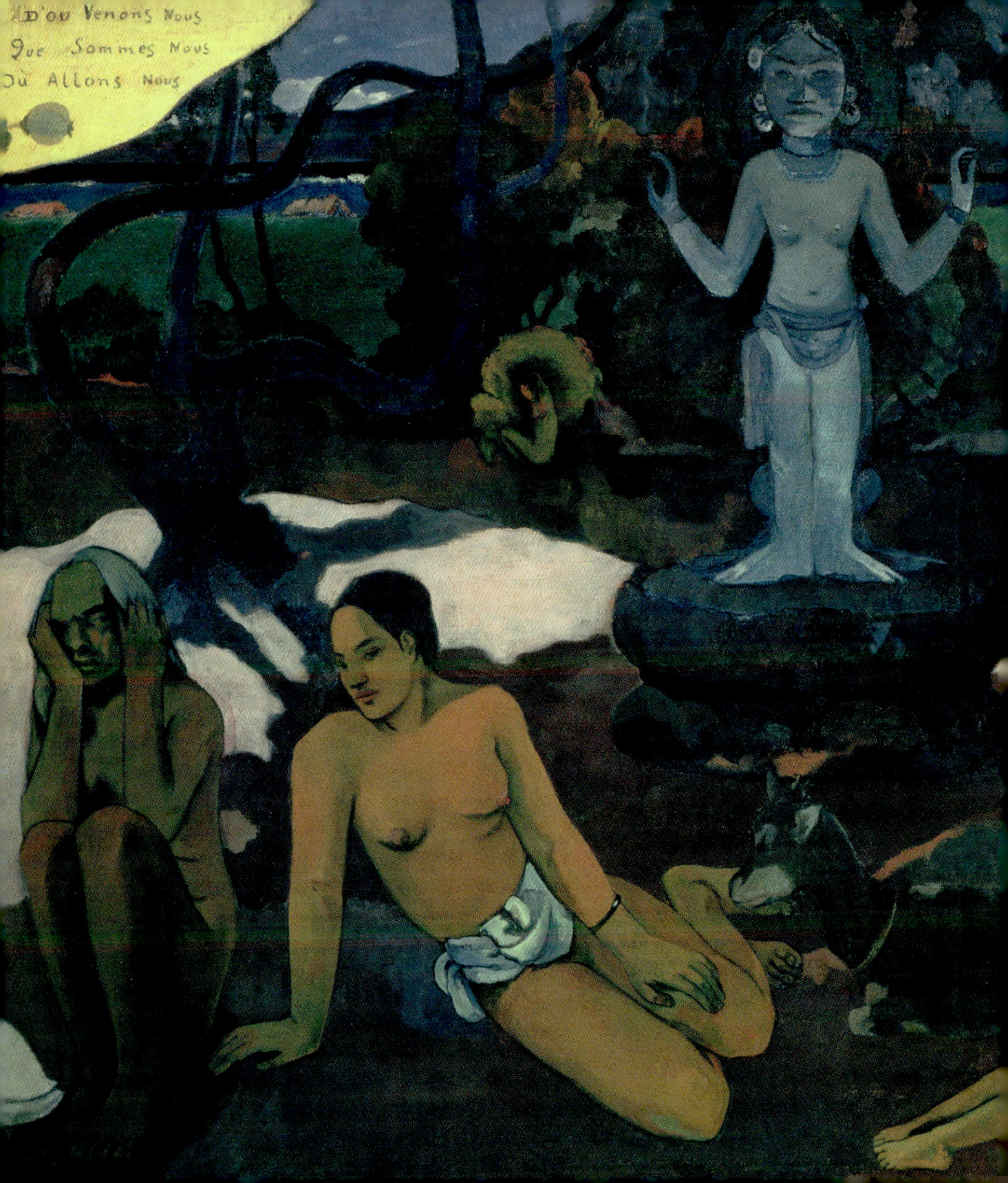
D'ou Venons Nous
Que Sommes Nous
Où Allons Nous

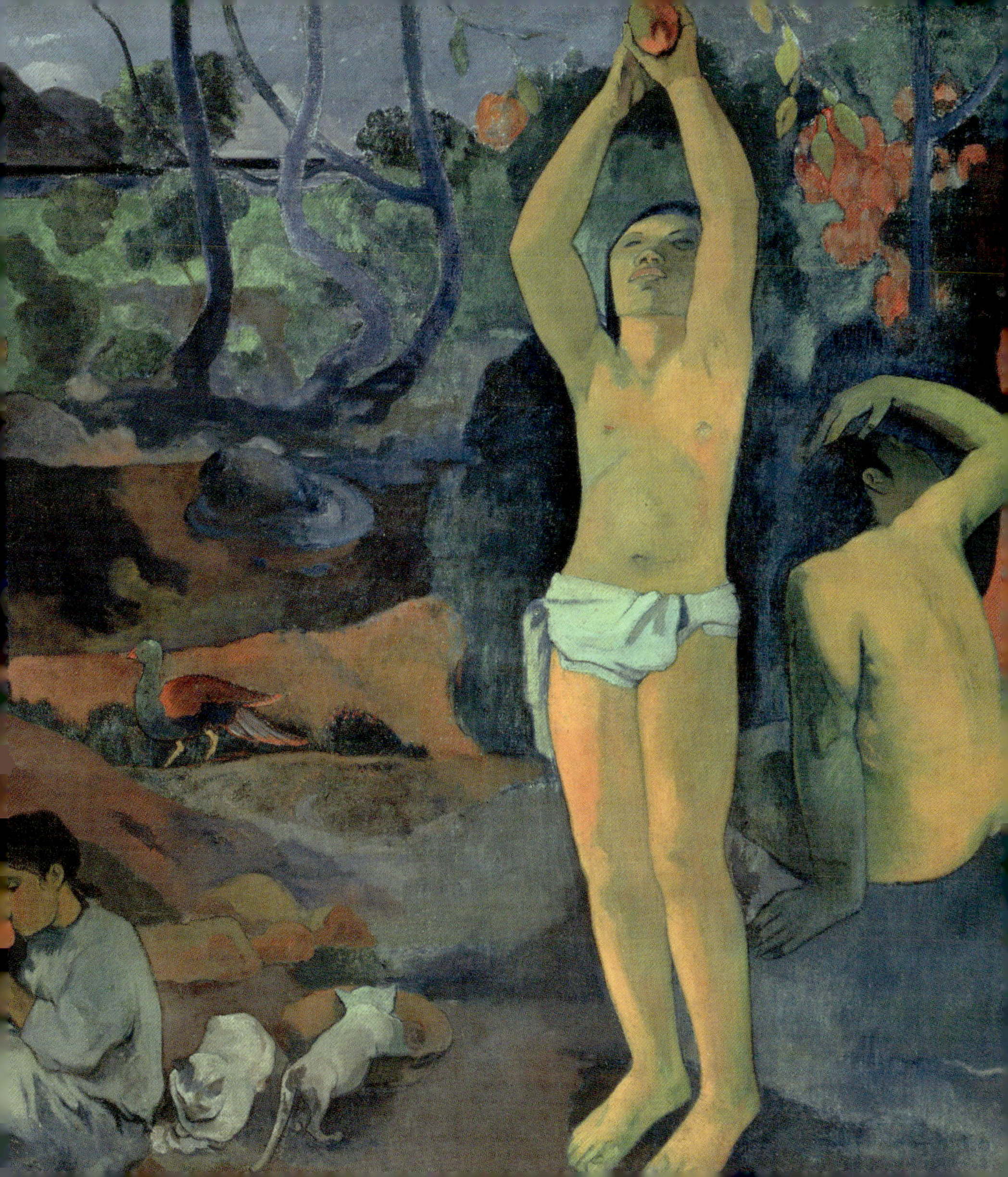

Fernand Khnopff
Sleeping Medusa
1896, pastel on paper
72 × 29 cm
Felix Labisse Collection, Neuilly

Fernand Khnopff
I lock my door upon myself
1891, oil on canvas
72 × 140 cm
Neue Pinakothek, Munich

a commission from his patron Günther Alexander, is regarded as the finest example of those landscapes of the soul which are a common motif in the melancholy art of Symbolism. Böcklin, who lived in Florence at that time, produced five versions of the picture, for which he probably took the romantic island of Capri as his model. Originally he painted it without the white figure that was later to escort the coffin across the water to the island in a boat and anchor the scene in ancient mythology. From the third version, which Böcklin made for the gallery owner Fritz Gurlitt, he added his initials to the door lintel of the mausoleum-like building: an unambiguous interpretation of the picture as a memento mori. The popularity of the motif in the following years is shown by the fact that the art museum in Leipzig ordered a version of its own in 1886. Beyond the symbolic character of the motif, the painting takes on the role of a synesthetic experience, in which the focus is on the perception of tranquility. The musical inter-

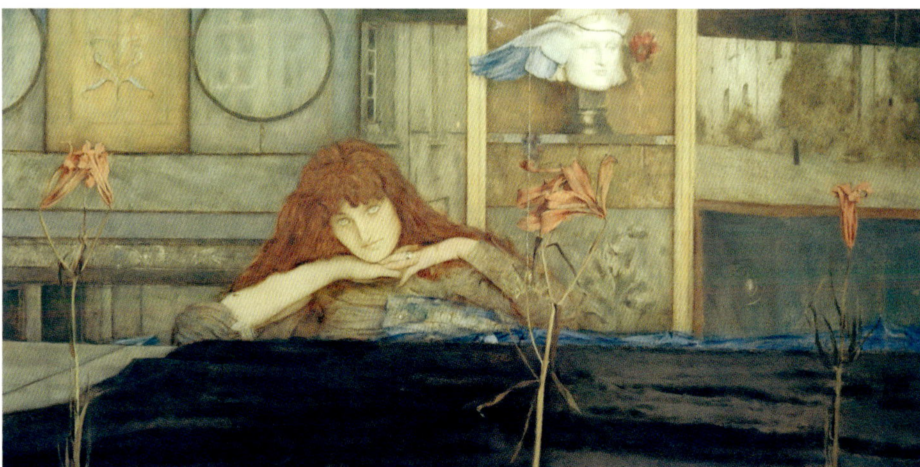

pretation of the picture by composers such as Max Reger also makes this clear. Symbolist art paid special attention to synesthesia as a correspondence between the inner and outer worlds.

The particular mood of the painting, which Böcklin was also able to evoke in other, mostly gloomy landscapes, gives the viewer the opportunity for sympathetic observation and is thus a kind of yardstick by which the meaning of nature is emphasized. Its divine power is reflected in a pantheistic manner, an approach that is also evident in the case of Caspar David Friedrich and shows how closely were the links between the Symbolists and the basic traits of the Romantic movement. When asked about the meaning of *The Isle of the Dead,* Böcklin once answered that he did not paint riddles, but that the picture is what the viewer sees. Two years after the last version, Böcklin painted *The Isle of Life* as a kind of opposite to it, but this work did not have a comparable effect as a landscape of the soul: the darkness of melancholy seems to have been an essential characteristic of Symbolist painting.

Fernand Khnopff

The motif of the melancholy, the introverted and the secretive can also often be found in the paintings of the Belgian Symbolist Fernand Khnopff. A line from a poem by Christina Rossetti, the sister of the Pre-Raphaelite painter, made a lasting impression on Khnopff: "I lock my door upon myself" became the title of a painting of 1891 that combines a number of puzzling references into a visual collage. Khnopff,

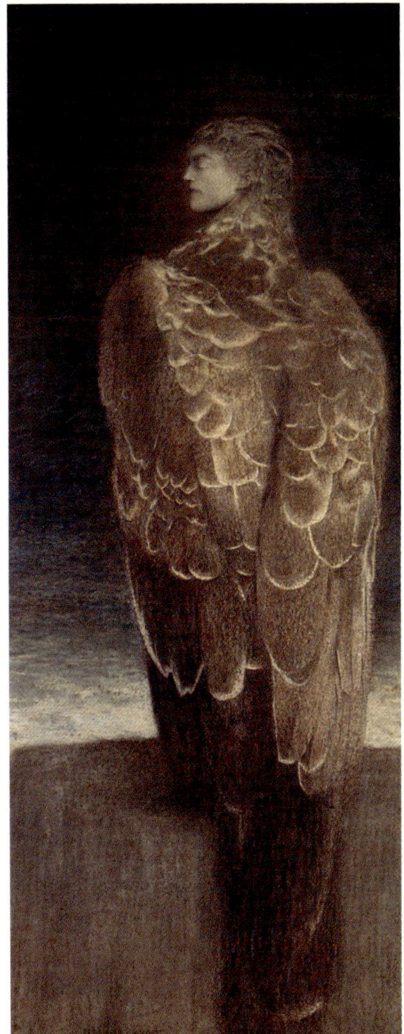

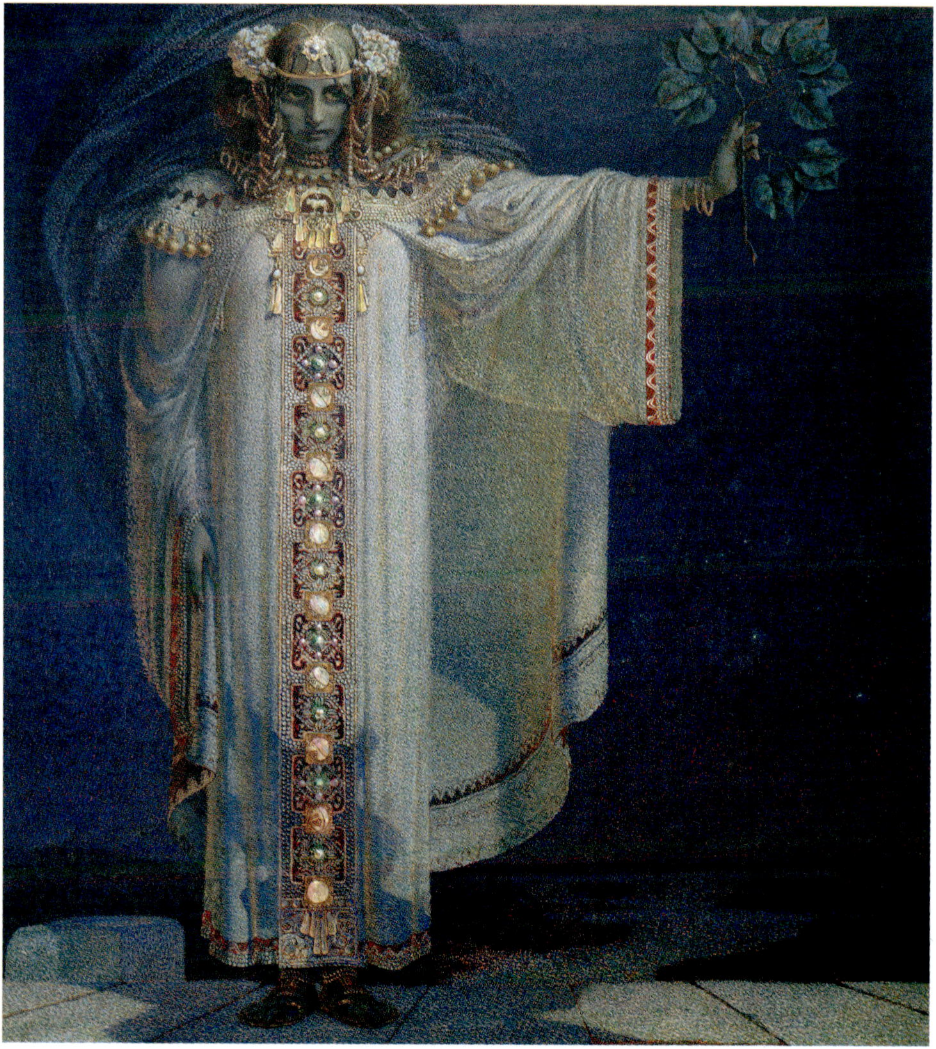

whose front door was adorned with the words "On n'a que soi" (one has only oneself), lived as an introverted dandy in the Brussels art scene. He had a golden circle on the floor of his studio for the purpose of meditating and was said often to take part in spiritualist séances. The mask of Hypnos, the god of sleep, can be seen in the background of the painting *I Lock My Door Upon Myself.* The brother of Hypnos is Thanatos, or Death. Sleep, dream, trance: these motifs recur in many paintings by the Belgian Symbolist. However, the depiction of sleeping figures was popular among artists other than Khnopff. Ferdinand Hodler succeeded in translating the aura of the world of dreams into the nervous outlines of his individual style. Poppy flowers give the dream an intoxicating quality. In the shape of Leighton's *Flaming June,* a peculiarly sunken figure, the exploration of the subconscious, which C. G. Jung saw as the task of sleep, plays a part. The extremely long hair, on which the beautiful *femme fragile* rests, creates a strange effect.

The symbol as a representation of something that has no tangible form is a formula particularly noticeable in the paintings of Fernand Khnopff. "Is it possible, as skeptics maintain, that a work of art contains only what we ourselves find in it; that we admire it not for its innate values, but because it touches some of our own feelings and we only look for a mirror of our own soul in it"? By making his pictures obscure and puzzling, Khnopff moved to a different level of representation. In some of his paintings his sister Marguerite appears in translucent, immaterial robes, almost as if she were a medium from another world. The androgynous type of woman exemplified by his sister, which is also already present in paintings by the Pre-Raphaelites, became Khnopff's trademark. His famous work *Caresses* was a success in 1898 at the exhibition of the Vienna Secessionists, where artists such as Gustav Klimt were deeply impressed. Khnopff's influence on Klimt's work is obvious.

According to a legend the prophetess Libuse founded the city of Prague. She was famed and notorious for her power of seeing the future. The decorative band of her robe depicts the phases of the moon as a sign of her supernatural gift.

Vitezlav Karel Masek
The Prophetess Libuse
1893, oil on canvas
193 × 193 cm
Musée d'Orsay, Paris

Although Khnopff often worked on the basis of photographs, nothing could have been further from his intentions than a naturalistic view of the world. Even views of his home town of Bruges turned into Symbolist ciphers, in which the viewer imagines terrible secrets behind the church towers and canals. His painting of *Sleeping Medusa* of 1896 left Khnopff's studio only after his death in 1921. It is an unusual work, which embodies nothing of the deadly danger of Medusa. On the contrary, the main motif is the quietness and stillness of the sleeping figure with an idealized "eternal" horizon in the background. Spiritual retreat into a state of active silence, just as meditation requires, is enhanced in the context of the strange iconography of this depiction of Medusa.

Lord Frederic Leighton
Flaming June
c. 1895, oil on canvas
120.6 x. 120.6 cm
Museo d'Arte de Ponce, Ponce, Puerto Rico

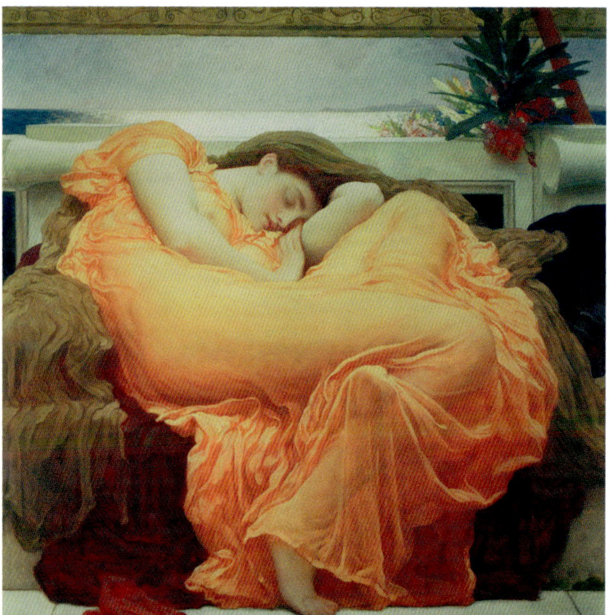

"No sooner are the lips still than the soul awakes and sets forth on its labors, for silence is an element that is full of surprise, danger and happiness, and in these the soul possesses itself in freedom." Maurice Maeterlinck, *The Treasure of the Humble,* 1892

The Search for a Lost Paradise

The group known as *Les Nabis,* from the Hebrew word for prophet, came together in 1888 in order to introduce the principles of theosophy into art. The artists Maurice Denis and

Paul Sérusier pursued the ideal of an all-embracing brotherhood of humankind, an idea that had a lasting influence on artists such as Paul Gauguin. Gauguin, who had long wished to live in the tropics, set off in 1891 to find his dream of the South Seas. In 1888 he had turned to painting themes with a clear religious background, for example *Jacob's Fight with the Angel,* and from the South Seas now produced works which showed his perception of painting as a continuation of the idea of creation. The most powerful example of his new-found religious feeling, and at the same time a trailblazing Symbolist painting, is his monumental *Where do we come from? What are we? Where are we going?,* which he painted within the space of just a few weeks in 1898, shortly after a serious heart attack and just before attempting to commit suicide. He published his memoirs at the same time, which suggests that the almost four-meter-long painting was in a sense the artist's legacy. The picture, which is read from right to left, represents a visionary mix of transience and hope which seems to be founded on the Christian story of Creation, on the one hand, while also falling back on Tahitian myths on the other.

Whereas Gauguin's quest took him to the exotic world of the South Seas, the Italian painter Giovanni Segantini went to the solitude of the Swiss mountains for the same reason: the search for renewal, inspiration and stimulus. His last words, as he was dying of peritonitis on the Schafberg in 1899, are said to have been "I want to see my mountains." This happened while he was in the midst of work on what was a genuinely programmatic

Ferdinand Hodler
The Dream
1897, watercolor on board
95 × 65 cm
Kunsthaus Zürich

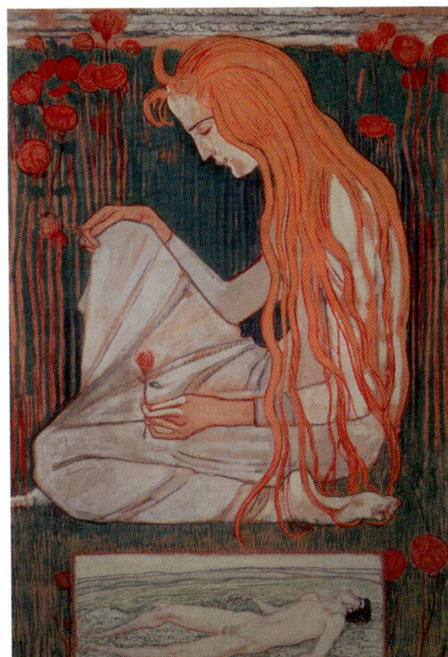

All cultures have their protective beings – in Buddhism they are the Bodhisattvas, and Shamanism has guardian spirits. The mood of the years around 1900 was conducive to the idea of enlightened beings that would guide humans safely through the turbulence of the *fin de siècle*.

painting of the 19th century, planned to be completed for the world exhibition of 1900. Nature, the cycle of the seasons, captured in the form of a triptych, amounted to a pantheistic vision of life. He aimed to depict the grandeur of nature and of life itself simply, without pathos. *Life – Nature – Death,* the title of a work that later became known as the *Alpine Triptych,* shows the importance of landscape as a symbol of life. Segantini, who also painted dark themes such as *Unnatural Mothers,* was a painter of light, which in his Symbolist phase he used not in the manner of the Divisionists, but which appeared to him to be the promise of salvation through the divine light. In an era when the Enlightenment had transformed religion into a feeling, which could take on individual traits, art supplied new "altarpieces" for pantheistic or theosophical beliefs. These were expressed primarily in images of paradisiacal innocence and visions of a golden age that was to come.

The Dutch artist Jan Toorop painted Symbolist works that were characterized by a new religious sentiment. He was born in Java, the son of Dutch Protestants, and converted to Catholicism in 1905. His guardian angel differs from the angel of love which Segantini placed in the vastness of the mountains. Toorop's is a majestic angel, with the symbol of freemasonry perceptible on its breast, spreading its broad outstretched wings to protect the figures of mothers beside it.

On one side, dark powers and disturbing feelings; on the other fables of light and the mythology of religious awakening. The multiplicity of themes in Symbolist art is as wide as its variations of style. Just as Art Nouveau was a phenomenon rooted in its time, here too there are connections to the spiritual and intellectual movements of the period, whether in literature, philosophy or religion. The final chord of the century, accompanied by a decadent yearning for death, is conversely also a call for renewal in

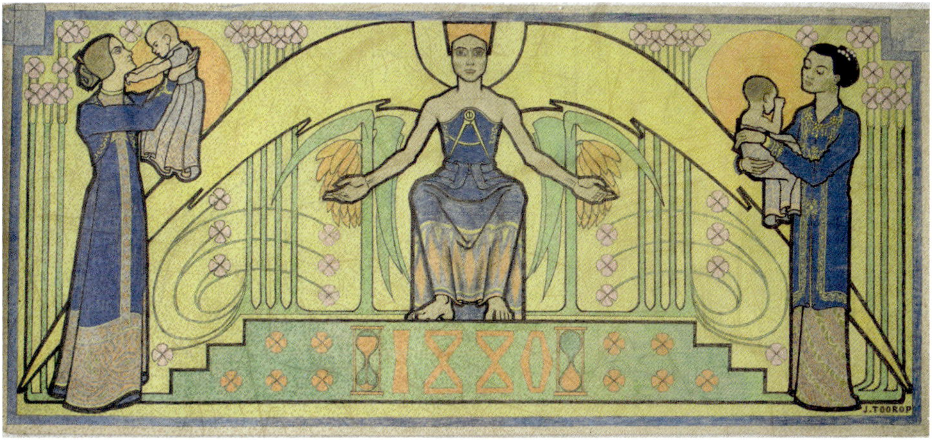

the modern age. The realm of the indeterminable, the human feelings, the visionary character of these years are all characteristics of avant-garde movements in art such as Expressionism and Surrealism which a short time later rang in the start of a new era.

Jan Theodore Toorop
Guardian Angel
Private collection

The "angel of life" is a motif that frequently recurs in the work of Segantini, who here once again depicts this being in an extremely clear relationship to his pantheistic landscape. The spring of life bubbles with his favorite mountain panorama as a backdrop.

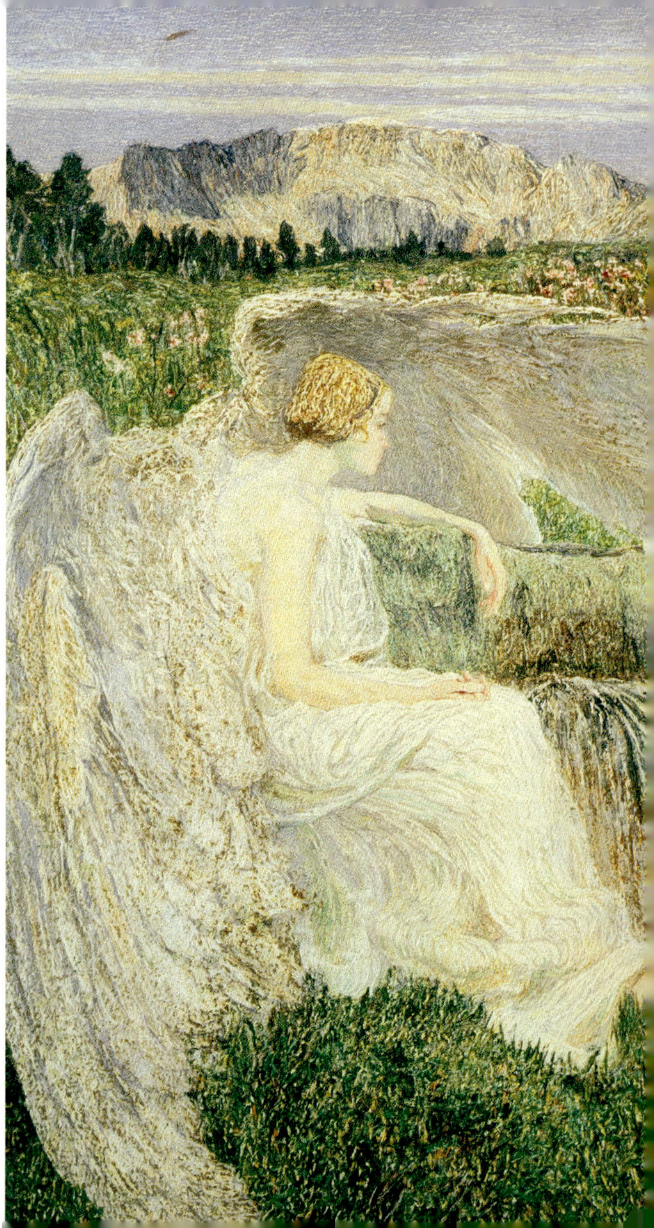

Giovanni Segantini
Love at the Spring of Life
1896, oil on canvas
70 × 98 cm
Galleria d'Arte Moderna, Rome

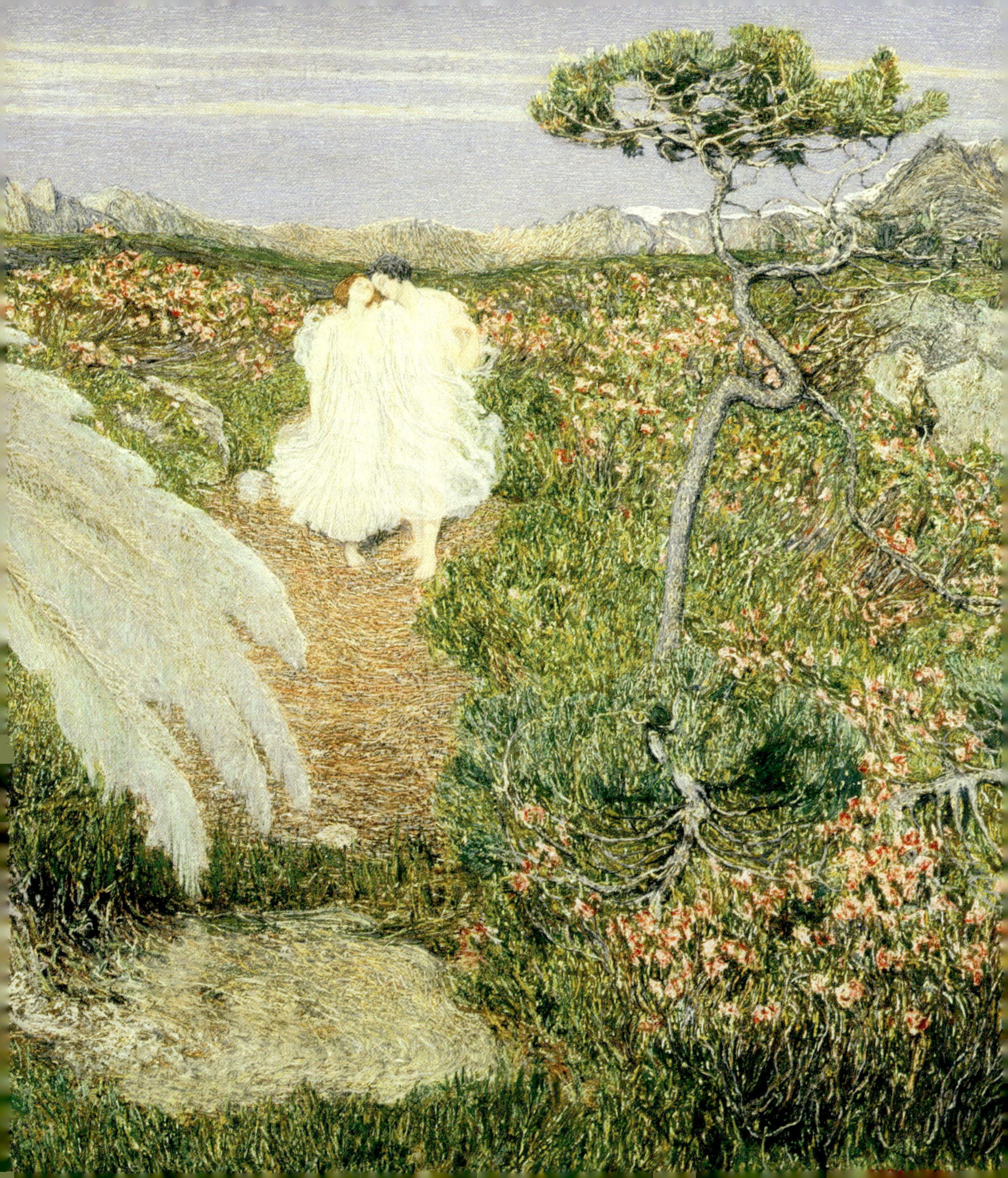

Gustav Mahler – An Artistic Figure of the *Fin de Siècle*

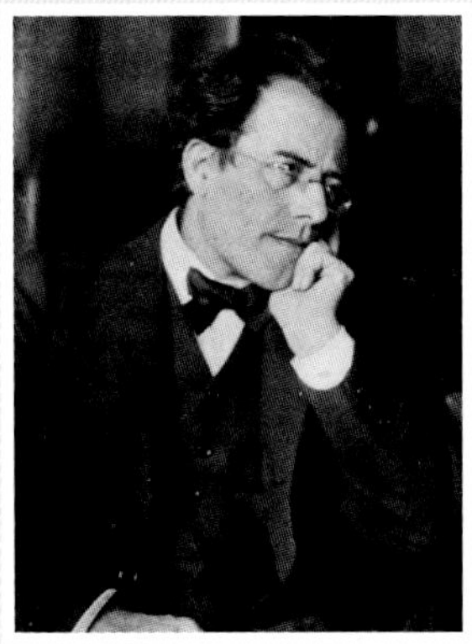

Gustav Mahler
Portrait photo *c.* 1905

Theodor Zasche
Caricature, *Mahler the Opera Conductor*
Below is Wilhelm Jahn, director of the Hofoperntheater, whom Mahler succeeded
1897, drawing

Gustav Mahler, who was born in Bohemia in 1860, was already writing songs at the age of six – for a girl whom he adored from a distance. Yearning is a recurring pattern in Mahler's youth, which was marked by numerous dramatic romances. His marriage to Alma Schindler, who was greatly admired in avant-garde circles, was also to end unhappily due to an unfulfilled passion.

After successfully completing his studies at the Vienna Conservatory in piano, music theory and composition, Mahler began to travel through the provinces of the Austrian empire, where he earned a living as conductor in towns such as Bad Hall. From there his success at much more famous venues began. At the age of just 25 he became principal conductor in Prague. After periods in Leipzig, where unrequited love for the daughter of Carl Maria von Weber inspired his First Symphony, and Budapest, he was appointed conductor of the opera house in Hamburg. Here he established important contacts to the German music scene. Among other persons he visited Cosima Wagner in Bayreuth. She had a high opinion of the young and successful composer, but due to her anti-Semitism was never willing to invite him to conduct in Bayreuth. This experience was one of the factors that led Mahler to convert to Catholicism in 1892. In many applications that he made, he felt discriminated against as a Jew. Shortly after his conversion he successfully applied for a position in Vienna, and began his conquest of Viennese *fin de siècle* society as conductor of the Hofoper, the court opera house.

Fateful Encounter

In 1901 Mahler settled in Vienna with his sister Justine, who ran his household. Through an invitation to one of the literary salons held by the journalist

Berta Zuckerkandl he made the acquaintance of leading representatives of the Vienna Secession. Among them was its chairman Carl Moll, who came accompanied by his stepdaughter Alma Schindler, a great beauty. Mahler immediately fell in love with the young woman. Despite the difference in their ages Alma was not to be dissuaded from marriage, seemingly not even by Mahler's strict demand that as his wife she would have to subordinate her wishes unconditionally to his. On 9 March 1902 the composer and the artist's daughter were married. At the wish of her husband, Alma stopped composing, an activity which had hitherto given her great pleasure. The couple had two daughters, born in 1902 and 1904.

Conductor and Composer

Recognition of Mahler's qualities as a composer came in phases, which were repeatedly interrupted by his work as a conductor. When he conducted a performance of his Third Symphony in Amsterdam in late 1903, the applause lasted several minutes and from that time he was seen as one of the most significant modern composers. He used elements of folk music, for example by including a fire brigade band in the background of his First Symphony, and unusual instruments such as cow

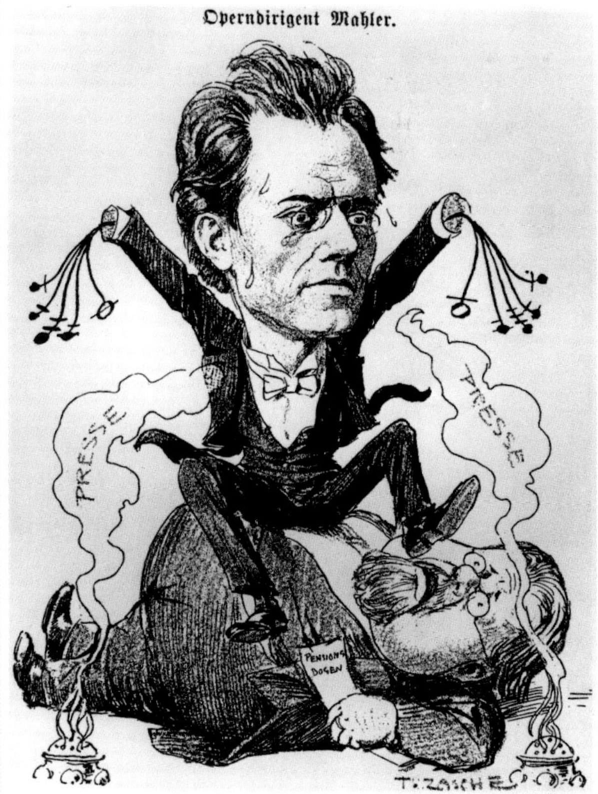

Caricature of the premiere of Mahler's First Symphony in Budapest
From: *Belond Istok,* 24.11.1889

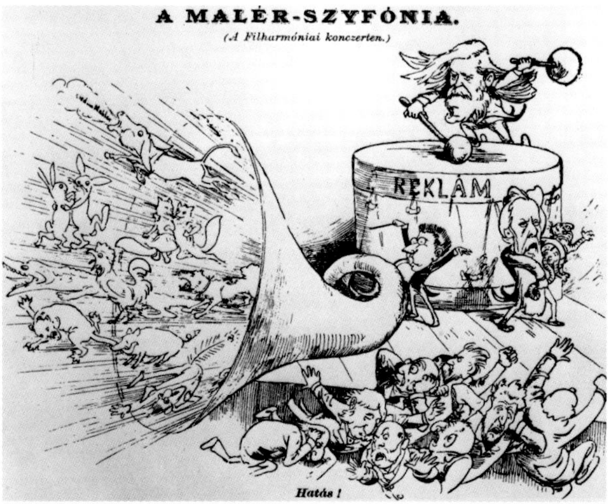

Gustav Klimt
The Knight
Detail of the *Beethoven Frieze,* supposedly a portrait of Mahler
1902, casein paint and gold on plaster
Österreichische Galerie Belvedere, Vienna

bells. In 1888 Mahler had already turned his attention to Romantic lieder, composing music for the texts collected by Clemens Brentano and Achim von Arnim entitled *Des Knaben Wunderhorn* (The Youth's Magic Horn). He continued in this Romantic vein in the famous *Kindertotenlieder* (Songs on the Death of Children), settings of texts by Friedrich Rückert – a sad theme that matched the melancholy taste of the time. Mahler now directed performances at the Hofoper in Vienna in a spectacular manner, having an epoch-making influence on the way opera was staged. For example, he insisted on darkness in the orchestra pit, a practice which involved him in repeated conflicts. His purpose was to evoke the magic of the music, and no distraction from its enjoyment was permitted.

The Year of Destiny

1907 was an especially difficult year for Gustav Mahler. His elder daughter died of diphtheria, and he was subject to persistent criticism in the press that originated in anti-Semitic sentiment. In very poor health himself, he began to occupy his mind with existential questions about life and began one of the major works of his later years: *Das Lied von der Erde* (The Song of the Earth). He took his inspiration from German verse adaptations of ancient Chinese poetry. The influence of exotic literature is reflected in the music, showing that in search of inspiration the composer was treading paths similar to those of the painters of the time. The individual titles of the movements, for example *Of Youth, Of*

Beauty and *The Farewell,* are a mirror of the issues of the age and at the same time a record of the atmosphere in Vienna in the early 20th century. Nevertheless, Mahler's personal problems grew, and after much hesitation he decided to bow to public pressure and resign from his position at the Hofoper. However, at this time he was already looking forward to an engagement at the famous Metropolitan Opera in New York, and his resignation was therefore not only caused by disappointment at lack of recognition. The artists of the Vienna Secession gave Mahler a truly royal send-off. A few years earlier Klimt had depicted him as one of the protagonists on the *Beethoven Frieze*. On 15 May 1902, on the occasion of the Beethoven Exhibition, Mahler, like a knight in golden armor, had conducted the fourth movement of the Ninth Symphony, and lent an extra dimension to the interpretation of the great work envisaged by the Secessionists. Klimt had indeed depicted him as a golden knight. It only remained for him to pass his pithy and fitting comment on Mahler's departure: "It is over"!

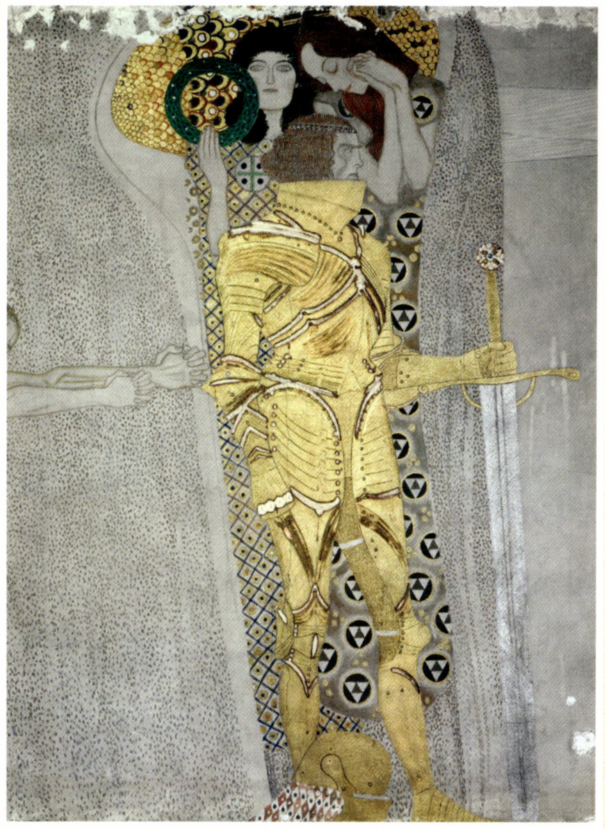

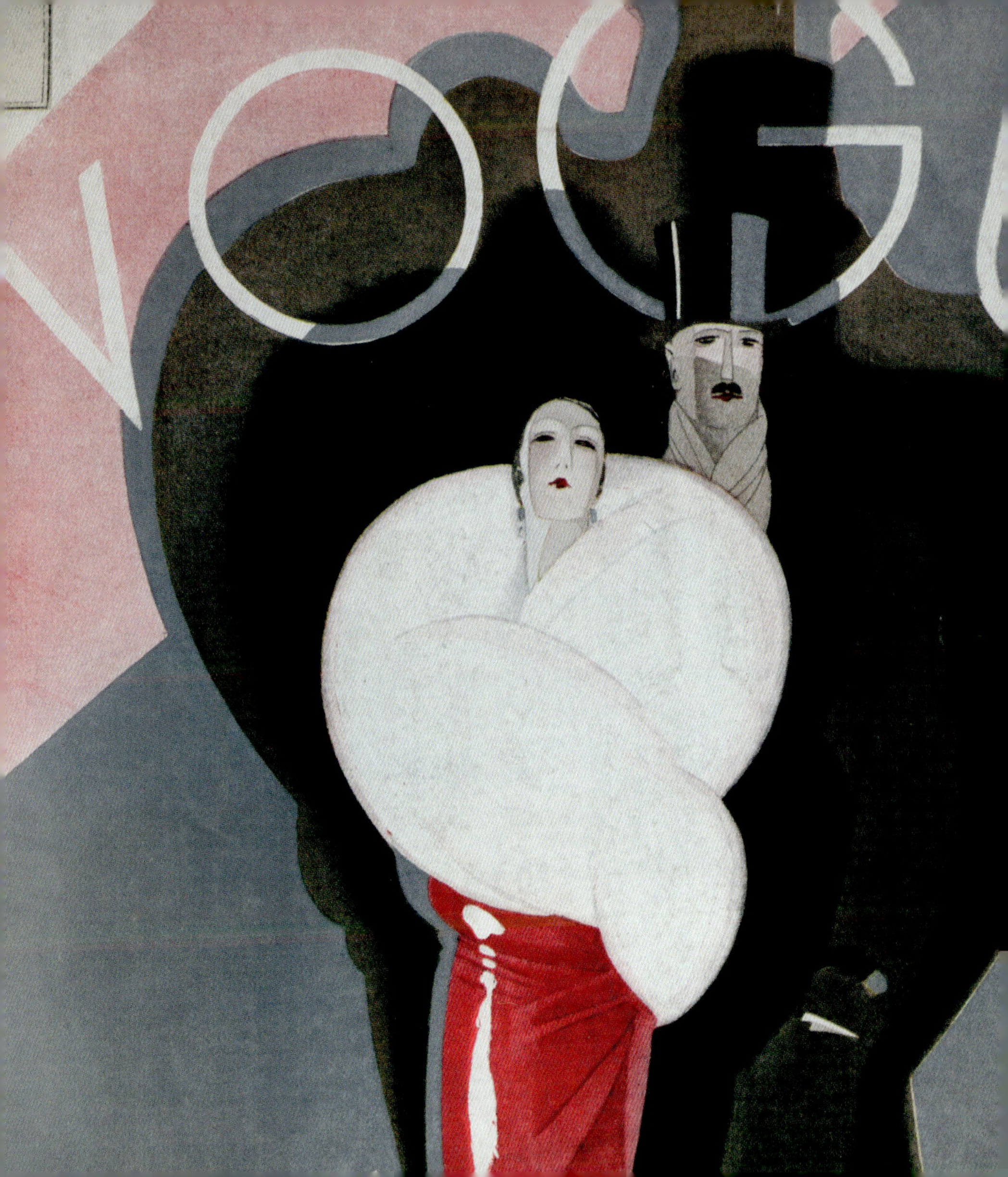
VOG

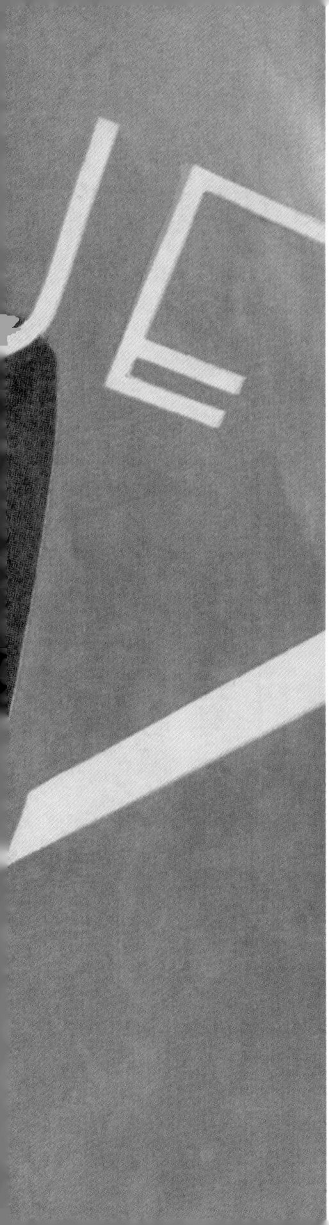

Luxurious and Exotic – Art Deco

The "Golden Twenties" are known as a synonym for luxury and joie de vivre. The contemporary emphasis on the beautiful things in life was an expression of this. High-class materials were used in extravagant fashions and sumptuous interior furnishings. Elegant forms and saturated colors enhanced the beauty of the decorative arts. The latest in design was presented at an international exhibition which the Société des Artistes Décorateurs held in Paris in 1925. This was the birth of the term "Art Deco". This new aesthetic was transported around the world in the opulently equipped Orient Express and the lavish interiors of gigantic steam liners.

Cover illustration for *Vogue*
(detail of p. 268)
November 1926, color lithograph
Bibliothèque des Arts Décoratifs

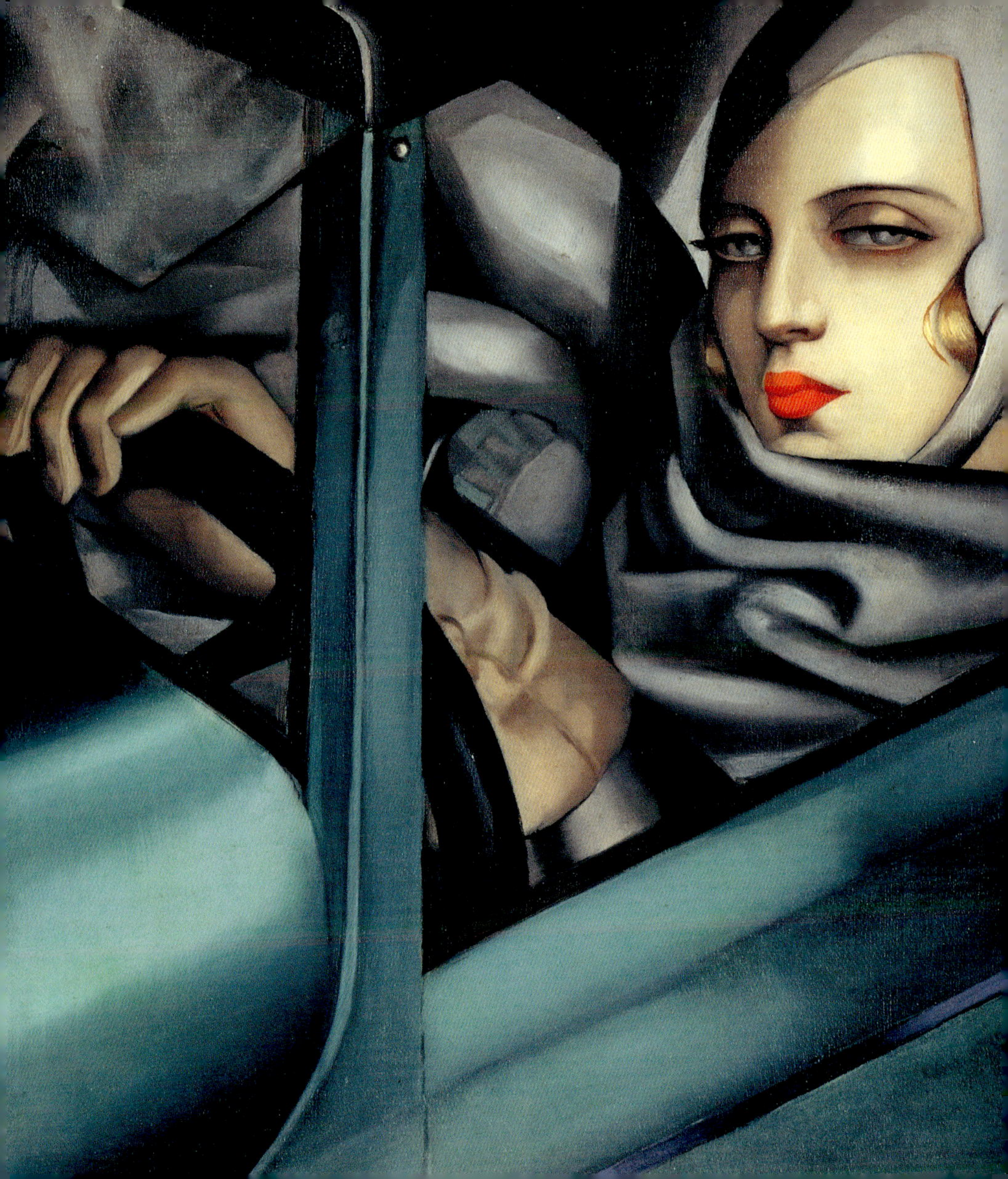

Brave New World

The quest for beauty, and the associated demand that art and life should be unified, accorded great importance to crafts in the period of Art Nouveau. After the shock of the First World War there was a pause to draw breath, but soon economic growth began and lasted for several years – years that were marked by a great desire for luxury and elegance. This, in combination with the avant-garde tendencies of modern art, led to a mood of light-heartedness that has been fittingly described as a "dance on the edge of the volcano." However, the glamorous years did not last long. In 1929 the stock exchange crash started a collapse that later led to Nazi rule and the Second World War.

Tamara de Lempicka
My Portrait (self-portrait)
1929, oil on wood
35 × 27 cm
Private collection

Dagobert Peche
Cachepot, Wiener Werkstätte
1922, pale base, white glaze, black paint

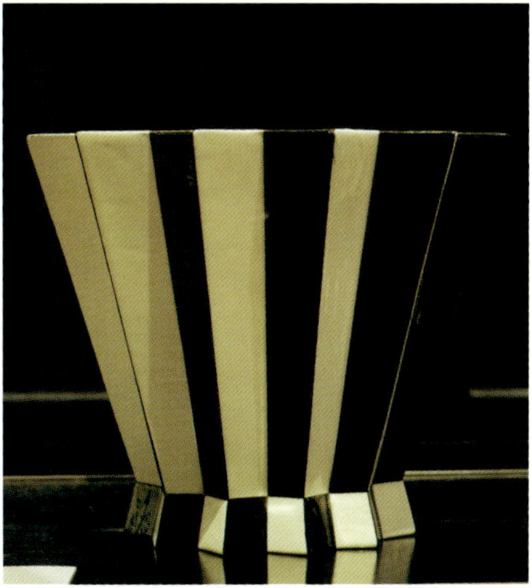

Tamara de Lempicka

One protagonist of the "golden years" was the painter Tamara de Lempicka. She embodied as no-one else the "new woman" who was self-confident and went her own way. She was born in 1898 to an upper middle-class Polish family. De Lempicka herself maintained a lifelong silence about her true place of birth. She was a *femme fatale* of painting, who cultivated her own image by means of inventions about her life story. In later years she was also reluctant to reveal the name of one of her most important teachers: Maurice Denis. After her first steps towards an artistic training while staying with relatives in St Petersburg, Lempicka took lessons in painting from Denis while, filled with zest

Tamara de Lempicka
Photograph, 1928

for life, she was living in exile in Paris from 1919. However, Tamara de Lempicka quickly progressed beyond the mystic themes and rounded forms of her Fauvist teacher. She preferred to spend hours in the Louvre, examining the masterpieces of the Italian Renaissance. A trip to Italy that she undertook in 1922 with her first female lover confirmed her intention to follow the smooth style of painting of Italian masters like Botticelli and Bronzino. The prevailing mood of hedonism that developed in the interwar period favored the painting of nudes, which was highly fashionable at this time. Even provocative depictions such as *Two Girlfriends,* in which Lempicka openly showed her lesbian leanings, hardly brought her moral censure. Her second teacher, André Lhote, ensured in his role as jury member of the Salon des Indépendants that this painting was presented to a wider audience in Paris.

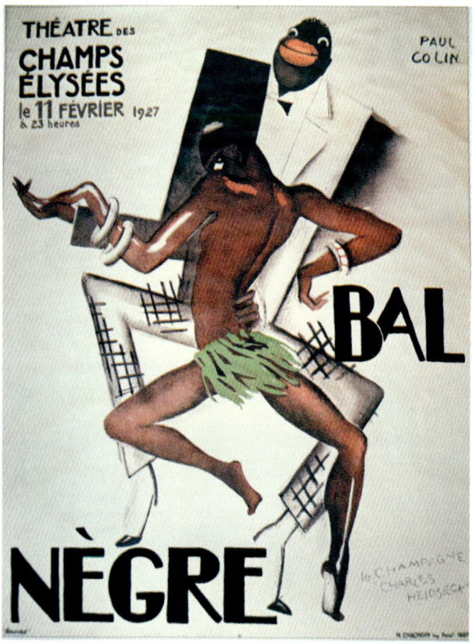

Paul Colin
Poster for Bal Negre with Josephine Baker
1927, color lithograph
Private collection

In 1925 Tamara de Lempicka's work was shown at the Art Deco exhibition in Paris, and to this day her powerful style of painting is associated with the Art Deco movement. Her luxurious way of life and cultivation of an image as a *femme fatale* on the lookout for sexual adventure undoubtedly contributed to this link. In her self-portrait at the wheel of a speeding open-top Bugatti she displayed fearless vigor and presented a myth of adventure and freedom, with herself in the role of the dashing "flapper." This female image, to which her friend Coco Chanel also made a decisive contribution, was a recurrent theme in advertising in the 1920s, and also appeared in the cinema and magazines. The "new women," sporting cigarette holders and hair cut short, haunted night clubs, where they took whatever they fancied. One of these spirited women performed in the Revue Nègre, grinning shamelessly, and electrified night-owls with her dancing. Her name was Josephine Baker. In 1925 her revue was imported from America for its premiere in the stylish Comédie des Champs-Élysées. The exotic "African" feeling had been a fashion in the New World, and now it came across the ocean to Europe. Josephine Baker, almost naked, performed crazy contortions while twirling a skirt of papier-mâché bananas. She was the superstar of the Roaring Twenties. Ernest Hemingway called her "the most sensational woman anyone ever saw." She was the emblem of a society which loved everything that was exotic, exquisite and luxurious. That she was made into a diva of Art Deco was mainly the work of her costumers and her

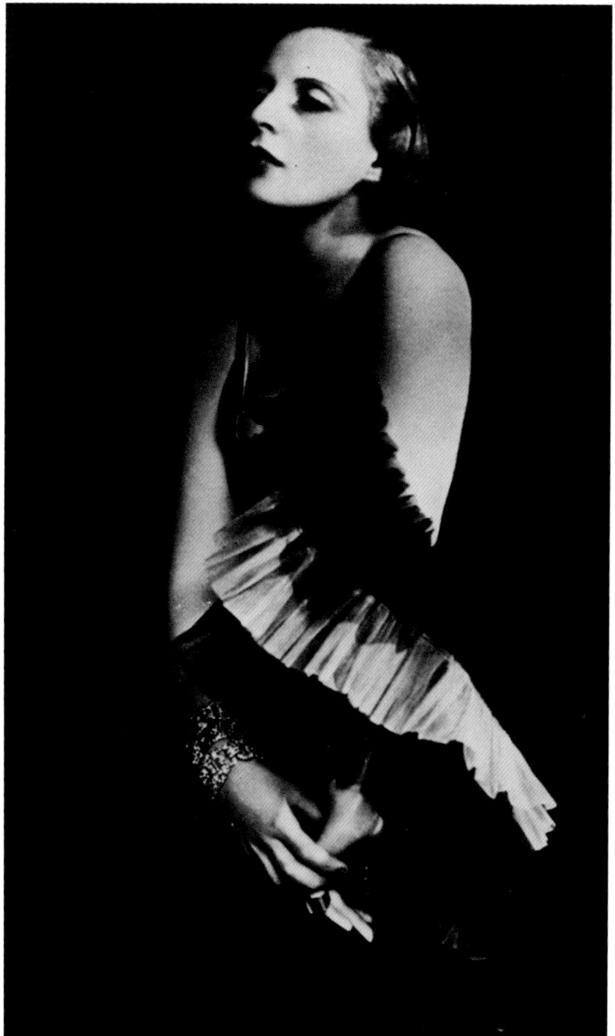

manager, who gave her a leopard with the intention of emphasizing her exotic cat-like nature even further for the public. The success of the revue relied on lots of show with glittering costumes; Baker's costumes were small, but nonetheless stage-managed with precision.

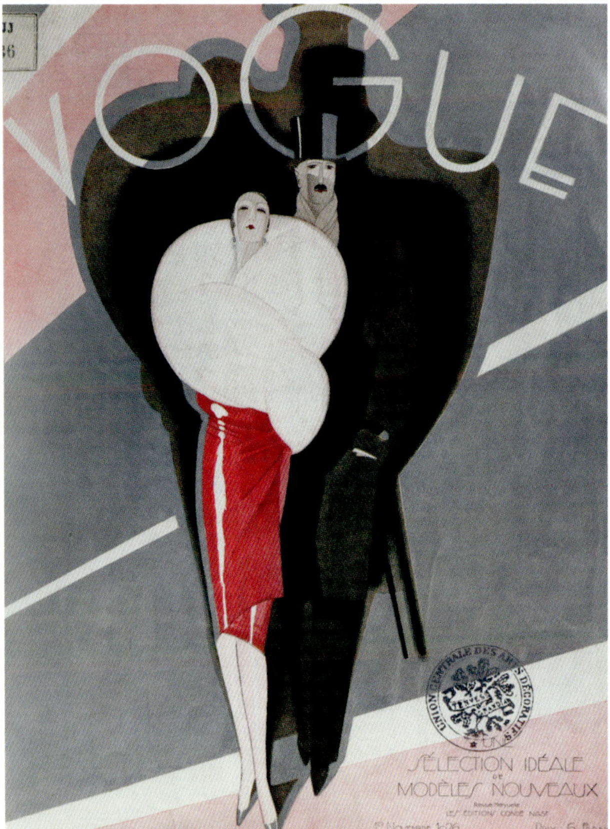

Cover illustration for *Vogue,* November 1926, color lithograph
Bibliothèque des Arts Décoratifs

A Life Devoted to Fashion and Elegance

The world of costumes and stage sets was also the world of the fashion designer Erté, who was born in St Petersburg under the name Romain de Tirtoff and is said to have designed his first costume at the age of just five years. As a 19-year-old he came to Paris, worked for the leading fashion houses and took his place in the pantheon of couturiers through an exclusive contract with the fashion magazine *Harper's Bazaar.* He went on to a career in the USA, where he helped to shape the appearance of shows and Hollywood films as a designer of stage sets and costumes. Erté, who liked to work at night with a blue lamp that bathed his designs in cool light, put his stamp on the elegant fashion of Art Deco by blending abstraction with a romantic, exotic style to create an unmistakable look. The names alone of the various series of drawings which he produced right up to the late 1980s show the range of his thematic references: *Zeus & Hera, Scheherazade, The Metropolis, Paris Days and Nights, The Divas!* His worldly style made women into goddesses whose stages were the jazz clubs and intellectual salons, and set the scene for their theatrical entrances.

Albert Levy
Interior with furniture by Émile Jacques Ruhlmann
1924, stencil print
Private collection

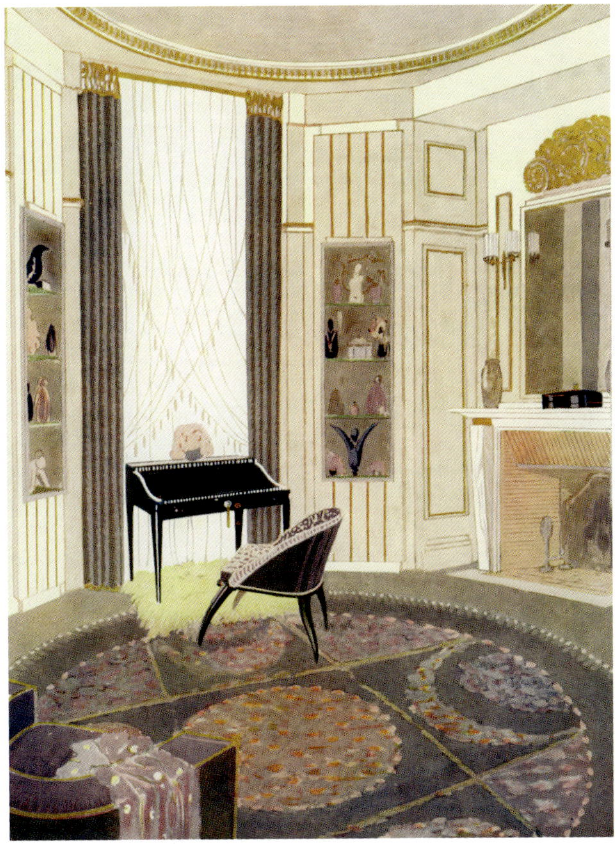

One of the leading couturiers of the Golden Twenties was Paul Poiret, who made costumes for Josephine Baker, among others. On the basis of the reform dress he created a novel, elegant outfit for the "new woman," clothing her in flowing robes, adorning her with oriental turbans or presenting her in a trouser skirt. His ideas came from Sergei Diaghilev's *Ballets Russes,* the sumptuous colors from artists such as Henri Matisse. His fashion was modern and mondaine, sometimes with bold abstract patterns. He commissioned contemporary artists, Raoul Dufy for example, to design his fabrics and employed renowned photographers to show his creations to best advantage. However, Poiret also belonged to a new generation of fashion designers who influenced the development of crafts by commissioning up-to-date interiors. He is reported to have himself designed furniture that drew on the austere style of the Wiener Werkstätte. Geometric and black-and-white decorative elements were especially popular.

Precious Items

Macassar ebony and ivory intarsia: there are hardly more precious materials. It was the declared aim of furniture designer Émile Jacques Ruhlmann to create items of timeless elegance by means of simple forms but extremely precious materials and painstaking manual work. He was aware that these extraordinary one-of-a-kind pieces of furniture would be restricted to a clientele that was accustomed to luxury. Moreover, the amount of labor and the expense of the materials meant that he made almost no profit. However, his view was that "fashion is not made among ordinary people," and so he produced his treasures for crown princes, maharajas and film stars. Here the ideals of Morris & Co. had been superseded once and for all, and the ability to lead an aesthetic life once again depended on the customer's bank balance. What remained was the importance of craftwork and appreciation of the material, which Ruhlmann took to extremes by often working on an item for months and continually urging on his master craftsmen to reexamine the piece one more time until his execution of it seemed perfect. Beauty as perfection, aesthetics as an attitude of demanding the ultimate: this was how Ruhlmann made his mark on the 1920s. He participated in the Art Deco exhibition of 1925 with a design for the "house of a collector," thus demonstrating once again the connection to the Art Nouveau idea of designing a total work of art.

Erté (Roman de Tirtoff)
Costume design: lady in black, with fur, hat and dog on a lead (detail)
c. 1980, serigraph

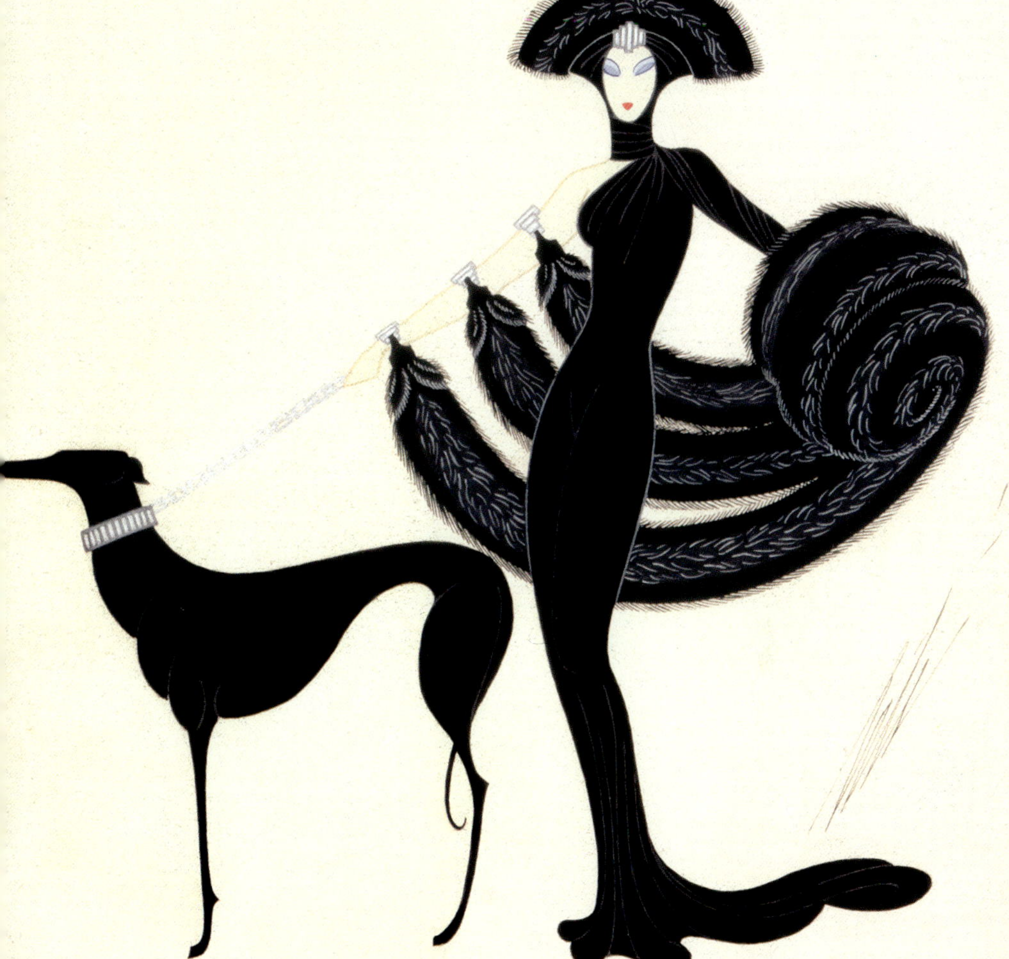

Glossary

Aesthetics
This concept is Greek in origin and means "sensory perception." The adjective "aesthetic" is sometimes used as a synonym for "beautiful." Since the 18th century aesthetics, the philosophy of beauty or art, has been one of the basic fields of philosophy.

Avant-garde
A military term for the vanguard which is applied to progressive elements in the fine arts, music and literature, as well as in politics. In all of these fields the word avant-garde implies a degree of radicalism.

Bauhaus
A school founded by Walter Gropius in Weimar in 1919 to train the "ideal" artist, i.e. an artist who is not narrowly specialized. As in a medieval cathedral workshop, all the arts were intended to work hand in hand at the Bauhaus.

Belle époque
The "beautiful period" enjoyed by the upper-middle classes around the year 1900, marked by a relatively high standard of living combined with a pronounced taste for pleasure and the beautiful things in life.

Bourgeoisie
This historical term originated in France to denote the class between the nobility and the peasants. In the context of social change in the late 19th century this class was of particular significance, as the bourgeoisie replaced the nobility as patrons of the arts.

Cancan
A dance from the French music halls that was performed in 2/4 time at a lively tempo. The dancers lifted their long skirts and petticoats and waved them to and fro. As the authorities feared a decline in moral standards, the dance was officially banned, which only made it even more attractive for the cabarets, revues and bars.

Dandy
A man who dresses in an ostentatious and exquisite style. According to Baudelaire, a dandy must live in front of a mirror night and day. A sarcastic sense of humor and aristocratic nonchalance are further hallmarks of a dandy, who would rarely soil his hands with hard work.

Decadence
The original meaning of this word relates to the decline of a culture, or decay. However, in the years around 1900 it also denoted a sublimation of the mood of decline into an enhanced sensory perception, combined with a certain morbidity. In literature one of the interesting phenomena of this period is the emergence of "black romantic" writing characterized by such themes as death, mourning, yearning, night and madness.

Deutscher Werkbund
Herrmann Muthesius is regarded as the pioneer of the Deutscher Werkbund, which was formed in 1907. It was founded in Munich, with particular support from van de Velde, in order to put into practice ideas of up-to-date, beautiful and useful everyday items. The relationship to industrial production played an important part.

Divisionism
Small areas of unmixed pigment are applied to the canvas, in order to produce a more brilliant color effect for a viewer standing a little distance away than by applying mixed pigments. The best-known use of this technique is the work of Pointillist painters, but it was practiced by other artists at much earlier periods.

Ébéniste
A term that gained currency during the Rococo period in France as a name for highly skilled cabinetmakers who worked with extremely precious materials such as ebony and were able to make magnificent works of art for their patrons at royal courts. Abraham Roentgen and his son David, for example, were famous ébénistes.

Eclecticism
The Greek word *eklektós* means "selected." The concept of eclecticism that derives from it was used initially without any value judgment to denote the combination of elements from differing styles to form a new stylistic unity.

Expressionism
This school developed on the basis of the emotionalization of art that was initiated in the years around 1900 by Symbolism. Typical features of Expressionist painting are tension and a high degree of individualization. Between 1905 and 1918 various groupings such as *Die Brücke* and *Der Blaue Reiter* represented the Expressionist style in Germany.

Fin de siècle
Émile Zola used this phrase in 1886 in his book *L'Œuvre.* It quickly became a fashionable expression that characterized the mood of the late 19th century. The tension in the air at this time derived from the simultaneous existence of doomsday pessimism and euphoria about the future.

Flappers
An American word for young women who liked to frequent jazz clubs, where they danced the Charleston, smoked and drank. They dispensed with the moral precepts that had previously been adhered to and lived an unconventional, uninhibited life.

Freemasons
The society of Freemasons was founded in the 18th century in the spirit of the Enlightenment. It aimed for the moral perfection of its members through freedom, brotherliness, tolerance and humanity. The Freemasons harked back to the virtues of the medieval guilds of masons, and thus took the compass and set square as their symbols.

Four Macs
The Four, for short, were Frances and Margaret MacDonald, Charles Rennie Mackintosh and James Herbert MacNair, the proponents of the so-called *Glasgow Style.* This variant of Art Nouveau developed in the 1890s under the influence of Mackintosh and other representatives of the Glasgow School. Archaic Celtic ornamentation and Japanese influences are hallmarks of their style.

Garden city movement
Ebenezer Howard's book *Tomorrow: a Peaceful Path to Real Reform* was published in 1898 as an answer to the spread of poor living conditions in industrial society. The work expounded his idea of green belts within cities. In the early 20th century this model was adopted elsewhere, for example in the garden city Hellerau near Dresden, which was built from 1909 by Richard Riemerschmid and others.

Gothic
The English Arts and Crafts movement regarded Gothic art as the last style that had produced its own canon of forms. The new designs of Arts and Crafts referred to the models of Gothic art and created a style that was not, like neo-Gothic, conceived as an imitation of medieval Gothic work but merely adopted individual elements of it. The theories of the architect Eugène-Emmanuel Viollet-le-Duc, who called for "a new Gothic style," were incorporated into buildings designed by architects from Hankar to Gaudi. His writings on Gothic flying buttresses in connection with construction in iron had a major influence on the new style.

Industrial society
Social change went ahead on the basis of increasing industrialization. Industrial society was marked by a pronounced individualism that was attributable to the new conditions of living and work. Division of labor, the demarcation of different areas of society and a higher standard of living were its hallmarks. The majority of

the population lived in towns and cities.

countries and to North America.

materials are inserted into a base layer.

Japonisme
The influence of Japanese art, first in France and later in all of Europe, enriched the work of contemporary artists. Van Gogh was one of the first artists who collected Japanese colored woodcuts and even copied them. The art of Japanese masters of *ukiyo-e* (the genre of colored woodcuts of the Edo period between 1603 and 1868) such as Katsushika Hokusai (1760–1849) was enthusiastically received and collected by connoisseurs.

Lebensreform
"Reform of life": a movement originating in Germany and Switzerland around 1900 advocating a return to nature and opposing the prevailing materialism and belief in technical progress. Many of its adherents promoted naturism and natural healing. These ideas spread to other European

Lithography
The process of printing from a stone originated in the discovery that certain types of stone are able to absorb colored ink. The motifs that are to be printed are drawn on sandstone using greasy inks and fixed in the stone by means of a caustic solution. Water is applied, and is repelled by the greasy drawing. After this, printing ink is applied, which in turn is repelled by the moisture and adheres only to the drawn areas.

Marquetry or *marqueterie*
The practice of covering a surface with thin pieces of veneer of different colors, usually wood, which are joined together like pieces of a jigsaw puzzle to produce a pattern picture. Marquetry should not be confused with intarsia, a similar procedure in which small pieces of wood or other

Naturalism
Literature of the school of Naturalism took on the task of portraying the social conditions of the late 19th century as they really were. Writers such as Émile Zola established a view of society that was unfalsified and in no way idealized. The visual arts, too, did not remain immune to this approach, but here the term Naturalism relates more to the representational function of painting than to critical commentary or interpretation. The latter is more apparent in the work of Realist painters such as Gustave Courbet.

Nietzsche cult
This term refers to the reception of the philosopher Nietzsche and the importance of his work for literature and the fine arts in the period around 1900, especially in Germany. Not just individual elements

such as the übermensch Zarathustra, but also Nietzsche's language and world view were taken up in artistic work at this time. The elevation of Nietzsche to a cult figure was due in no small measure to the archive founded in Weimar by his sister.

Pre-Raphaelite Brotherhood
In 1848 John Everett Millais founded the Pre-Raphaelite Brotherhood with like-minded artists such as Dante Gabriel Rossetti. Their aim was to portray nature as exactly as possible in their paintings. They looked back to the masters of the quattrocento, the period before Raphael was active.

Romantic movement
The Romantic period in fine art from the late 18th to the mid-19th century was characterized above all by firm rejection of the quotation of antiquity that was typical of neo-Classicism. The dominant themes of Romantic art were individual feelings and the storms of the soul. The principal motif was longing, which was symbolized by a blue flower.

Séance
A spiritualist session in which one person normally plays the role of medium in order to make contact with supernatural phenomena. The medium enters a trance and in this state is able to report on what he or she allegedly experiences on the other side.

Surrealism
This artistic current began with a literary movement which specialized in producing texts by excluding the conscious mind, for example using methods such as automatic writing. The young Surrealist artists and poets adopted from Symbolist painting and literature a preoccupation with the unconscious and dreams. The group that formed around André Breton in 1921 also took an interest in the new science of psychoanalysis.

Synesthesia
The original Greek term means simultaneity of feeling and denotes in physiological terms the perception of two different sensory stimuli at the same time. For example music can be seen if colors are perceived that have been allocated to different notes.

Sphinx
This creature from Greek mythology was the daughter of Typhon and Echidna. It lived outside Thebes and posed riddles for passers-by, who lost their lives if they could not answer correctly.

Theosophy
"Divine wisdom," the attempt to experience God by means of supernatural phenomena. As propagated by Helena Petro-

vna Blavatsky it acquired esoteric traits.

Urbanization
Migration into the cities created large conurbations with an environment that became increasingly confined, fast-moving and hectic. Technical innovations such as electric light and the temptations of fashion and advertising also swept through urban society. Pessimists attacked social injustice and prostitution, while optimists greeted the emergence of cosmopolitan intellectual circles.

Utopia
An ideal world; derived from Greek *u* (negation) and *topos* (place).

Victorian age
The period of the reign of Queen Victoria, from 1837 to 1901, was marked by continuing industrialization, the status of Britain as a great power and a tendency to puritanical moral values.

Further Reading

Anderson, Stanford-Owen: Peter Behrens and a new Architecture for the Twentieth Century. London 2000

Balk, Claudia: Theatergöttinnen. Inszenierte Weiblichkeit. Clara Ziegler, Sarah Bernhardt, Eleonora Duse. Basel Frankfurt 1994

Barnes, Rachel: The Pre-Raphaelites and their World. London 1998

Best, Bettina: Secession und Secessionen. Idee und Organisation einer Kunstbewegung um die Jahrhunderwende. Berlin 2000

Benton, Charlotte: Art Déco 1910–1939. London 2003

Bergos Masso, Joan: Antonio Gaudi. Der Mensch und das Werk. Ostfildern-Ruit 2000

Beyme, Klaus von: Das Zeitalter der Avantgarden. Kunst und Gesellschaft 1905–1955. Munich 2005

Birnie Danzker, Jo-Anne: Loie Fuller. Getanzter Jugendstil. Munich 1995

Bisanz-Prakken, Marian: Heiliger Frühling. Gustav Klimt und die Anfänge der Secession 1895–1905. Vienna/Munich 1998

Blakesley, Rosalind: The Arts and Crafts Movement. Phaidon 2006

Buchholz, Kai et al. (ed.): Die Lebensreform. Entwürfe zur Neugestaltung von Leben und Kunst um 1900. Darmstadt 2001

Buhrs, Michael et al. (ed.): Fledermaus Kabarett. 1907 bis 1913. Ein Gesamtkunstwerk der Wiener Werkstätte. Munich 2007

Calinescu, Matei: Five Faces of Modernity: Modernism, Avant-Garde, Decadence, Kitsch, Postmodernism. Durham: Duke University Press, 1987

Chodzinsky, Armin: Kunst und Wirtschaft. Peter Behrens, Emil Rathenau und der dm-Drogeriemarkt. Berlin 2007

Döring, Jürgen (ed.): Alfons Mucha. Triumph des Jugendstils. Heidelberg 1997

Draguet, Michel: Der Kuss der Sphinx. Symbolismus in Belgien. Ostfildern-Ruit 2007

Ehrhardt, Ingrid and Reynolds, Simon (Hrsg.): Seelenreich. Die Entwicklung des deutschen Symbolismus 1870–1920. Munich 2000

Eschmann, Karl: Jugendstil. Ursprünge, Parallelen, Folgen. Göttingen/Zurich 1990

Fahr-Becker, Gabriele: Jugendstil. Königswinter 2007

Falk, Fritz: Schmuckkunst im Jugendstil. Stuttgart 1999

Fiell, Charlotte and Peter: Charles Rennie Mackintosh. Cologne 1995

Franz, Erich: Freiheit der Linie. Von Obrist und dem Jugendstil zu Marc, Klee, Kirchner. Münster 2007

Frelinghuysen, Alicia Cooney: Louis Comfort Tiffany and Laurelton Hall. Yale University Press 2006

Gallé, Émile. Jugendstilmeister aus Nancy. Exhibition catalogue, Karlsruhe 2005
Greenhalgh, Paul: Art Nouveau, 1890–1914: Harry N. Abrams, 2000
Gross-Roath, Claudia: Das Frauenbild bei Franz von Stuck. Weimar 1999
Hardy, Alain-René: Art Déco Textiles. The French Designers. London 2006
Hofstätter, Hans: Symbolismus und Kunst der Jahrhundertwende. Cologne 1975
Hofstätter, Hans: Jugendstil. Graphik und Druckkunst. St. Gallen 2005
Husslein-Arco, Agnes et al. (ed.): Gustav Klimt und die Künstler-Compagnie. Vienna 2007
Kadatz, Hans Joachim: Peter Behrens. Leipzig 1977
Kirsch, Hans-Christian: William Morris – ein Mann gegen die Zeit. Munich 1996
Kretschmer, Winfried: Geschichte der Weltausstellungen. Frankfurt 1999
Marcilhac, Felix: René Lalique. 1860–1945. Maitre-Verrier. Paris 1989
Michailidis, Georgia: Der magische Kreis. Studien zum Thema "Magie" im Werk von Edward Burne-Jones und Fernand Khnopff. Frankfurt a. M., Berlin 1994
Natter, G. Tobias (ed.): Die nackte Wahrheit. Klimt, Schiele, Kokoschka und andere Skandale. Munich 2005
Pantus, Jan Willem: Jugendstil in Wort und Bild. Cologne 2001
Reynolds, Simon: William Blake. Norwich 1995
Roberts-Jones, Philippe (ed.): Brüssel, Fin de Siècle. Cologne 1999
Sawbridge, Peter: Tamara Lempicka, femme fatale des Art Déco. Ostfildern-Ruit 2004
Sembach, Klaus-Jürgen et al. (ed.): Henry van de Velde. Cologne 1992
Sembach, Klaus-Jürgen: Jugendstil. Cologne 1999
Sembach, Klaus-Jürgen and Schulte, Brigitte (ed.): Henry van de Velde. Cologne 1992
Stamm, Rainer and Schreiber, Daniel (ed.): Gaudi in Deutschland. Lyrik des Raums. Cologne 2004
Ulmer, Renate: Jugendstil in Darmstadt. Darmstadt 1997
Ulmer, Renate: Art Nouveau. Stuttgart 1999
von Hase-Schmundt, Ulrike: Jugendstilschmuck. Die europäischen Zentren. Munich 1998
van der Ree, Peter: Organische Architektur. Stuttgart 2001
Weisberg, Gabriel P. (ed.): La Maison Bing. Stuttgart 2004
Wolfschlag, Claus: Ludwig Fahrenkrog – Das goldene Tor. Ein deutscher Maler zwischen Jugendstil und Germanenglaube. Radeberg 2006

Index of Works

Picture credits

© akg-images, Berlin (7, 8, 9, 10, 11, 25, 26, 32, 38, 40, 42, 45, 49, 53, 54, 56, 62, 65, 66, 67, 68, 70, 78, 80, 83, 84, 85, 88, 90, 94, 103, 104, 113, 115, 125, 129, 140, 144, 146, 147, 161, 168, 169, 170, 172, 173, 174, 175, 183, 184, 186, 194, 197, 202, 206, 207, 209, 210, 211, 216, 218, 226, 229, 230, 237, 248, 256, 258, 259, 261, 265, 266; Archives CDA/Guill 220; Archives CDA/Guillemot 133; Archives CDA/St-Genès 75; Bildarchiv Monheim 155, 215, 221, 224; Bildarchiv Steffen 228; Electa 264; Hervé Champollion 110, 145; Hilbich 37, 41, 179, 193, 199, 203, 212, 214, 217, 222, 223; Andrea Jemolo 188, 189, 190; János Kalmár 6; Marion Kalter 61; A. F. Kersting 23, 27; Erich Lessing 28, 34, 44, 46, 64, 87, 89, 92, 93, 95, 96, 99, 102, 106, 107, 108, 136, 178, 180, 234, 243, 245; Robert O'Dea 30; Peter Seidel 238; Sotheby's 123, 126, 127, 138, 139), © ARTOTHEK/Blauel/Gnamm (2), © Bildarchiv Foto Marburg (33), © Bridgeman Art Library, Berlin (Biblioteca de Catalunya, Barcelona, Index, Barcelona 150, 153; Bibliothèque des Arts Décoratifs, Paris/ Archives Charmet 51, 118, 156, 158, 262, 268; Bibliothèque Nationale, Paris/Archives Charmet 208; Casa Batllo 200; Cheltenham Art Gallery & Museums, Gloucestershire 17, 18; Felix Labisse Collection, Neuilly 249; Fogg Museum 165; Haslam & Whiteway Ltd., London/DACS 236; Hermitage 69, 72; Indianapolis Museum of Art/DACS/Harold Victor Arts Fund 232, 236; Kunsthaus, Zürich, Lauros/Giraudon 253; Mazovian Museum, Plock 134; Mucha Trust 142; Musée de la Ville de Paris, Musée Carnavalet, Paris/Archives Charmet 148; Musée des Arts Décoratifs, Paris/Lauros 122; Musée d'Orsay, Paris 116, 137, 240, 250; Museo Calouste Gulbenkian, Lisbon 73; Museo de Arte, Ponce/The Maas Gallery, London 252; Museum of Fine Arts, Boston, Massachussetts, Tompkins Collection 246; Österreichische Galerie Belvedere, Vienna 260, 100; Parc Guell, Barcelona, Ken Welsh 198; Private Collection 20, 24, 76, 81, 130, 159, 160; Private Collection/The Fine Art Society, London 48, 242; Private Collection/Christie's Images 119, 120; Private Collection/DACS 271; Private Collection/DACS/Peter Newark American Pictures 267; Private Collection Joerg Hejkal 167; Private Collection, Ken Welsh 166; Private Collection, photo AISA 192; Private Collection, The Fine Art Society, London 14; Private Collection/The Stapleton Collection 15, 112, 152,154, 164, 227, 269; Private Collection/Whitford & Hughes 255; Rijksmuseum Kroller-Muller, Otterlo 60; Templo de la Sagrada Familia, Barcelona, Ken Welsh 204; University Library, Princeton/Peter Willi 163; Victoria & Albert Museum, London 12, 22, 52, 57), © IMAGNO/Austrian Archives (176), © Landesmuseum für Kunst und Kulturgeschichte, Münster (58)

Publisher's Information

Thanks to Felicitas Pohl and Anne Williams for their assistance in finding illustrations.

Original title: *Jugendstil*
ISBN 978-3-8331-4940-5
Project management: Lucas Lüdemann
Author: Anke von Heyl
Editors: Holger Möhlmann, Julian von Heyl
Picture editor: Holger Möhlmann
Graphics editor: Hubert Hepfinger
Layout: e.fritz, berlin06
Cover: Simone Sticker and rincón medien gmbh, köln
Cover illustration: Gustav Klimt, *Adele Bloch-Bauer I,* 1907 (cf. page 54)

Translated by John Sykes
Edited by ce redaktionsbüro für digitales publizieren
Typeset by ce redaktionsbüro für digitales publizieren
Project coordination for the English edition by Kristina Scherer

ISBN 978-3-8331-4941-2

Printed in China

10 9 8 7 6 5 4 3 2 1
X IX VIII VII VI V IV III II I

www.ullmann-publishing.com